# EDENSZERO

## 2 IRON TEARS

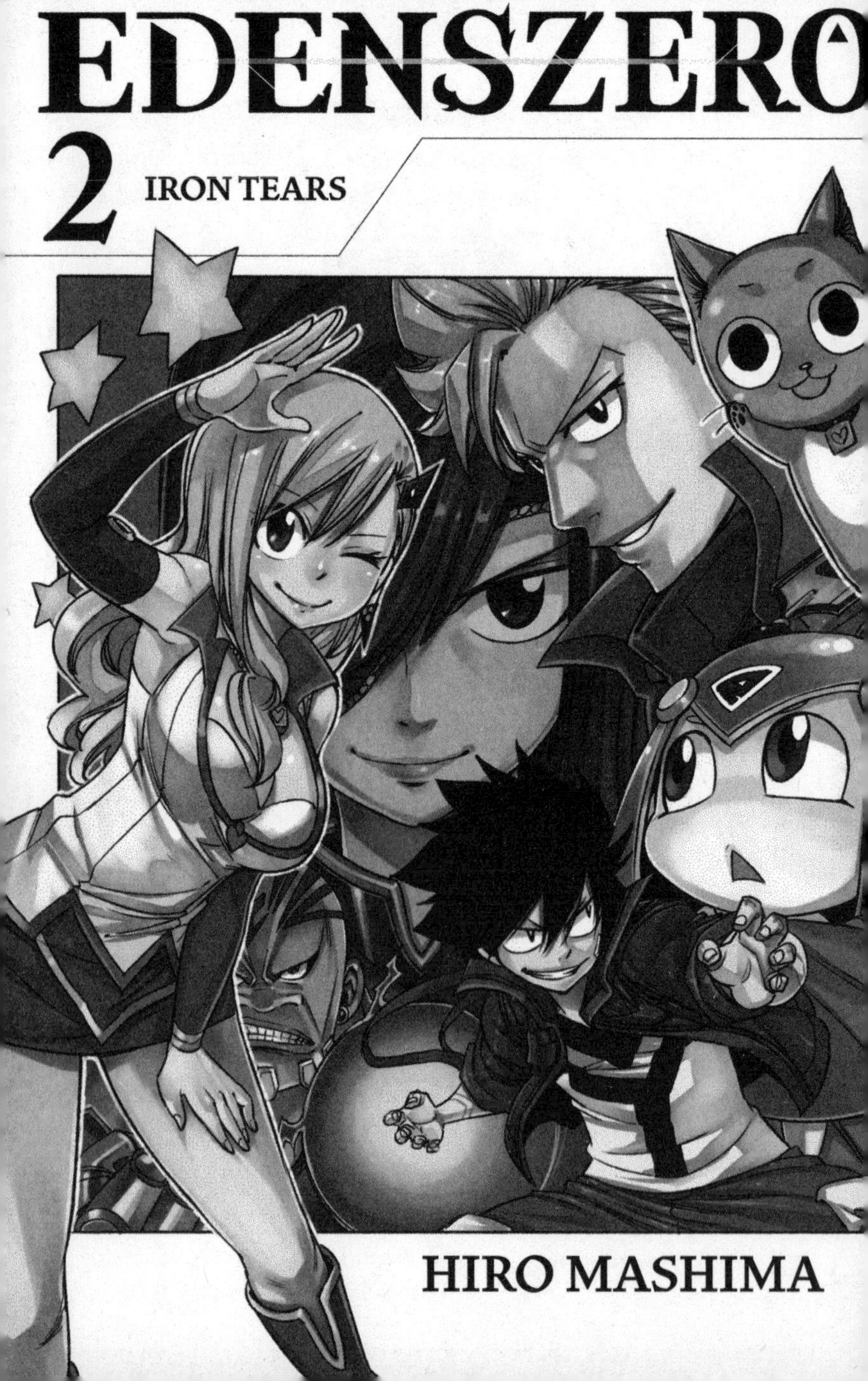

HIRO MASHIMA

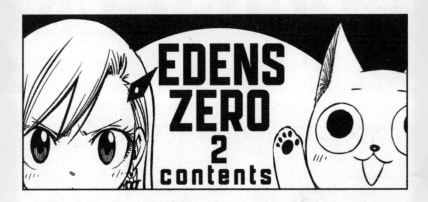

# EDENS ZERO 2 contents

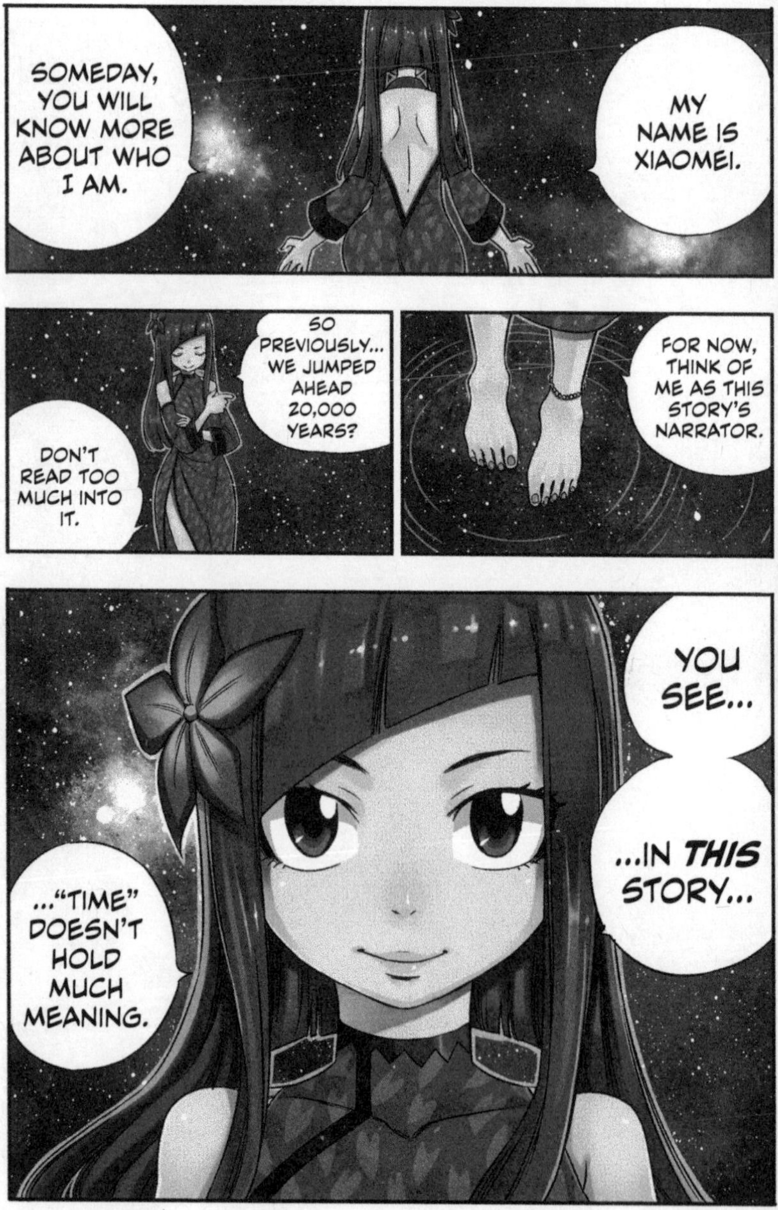
MY NAME IS XIAOMEI.
SOMEDAY, YOU WILL KNOW MORE ABOUT WHO I AM.
FOR NOW, THINK OF ME AS THIS STORY'S NARRATOR.
SO PREVIOUSLY... WE JUMPED AHEAD 20,000 YEARS?
DON'T READ TOO MUCH INTO IT.
YOU SEE...
...IN *THIS* STORY...
..."TIME" DOESN'T HOLD MUCH MEANING.

# CHAPTER 5: A MAN NAMED WEISZ

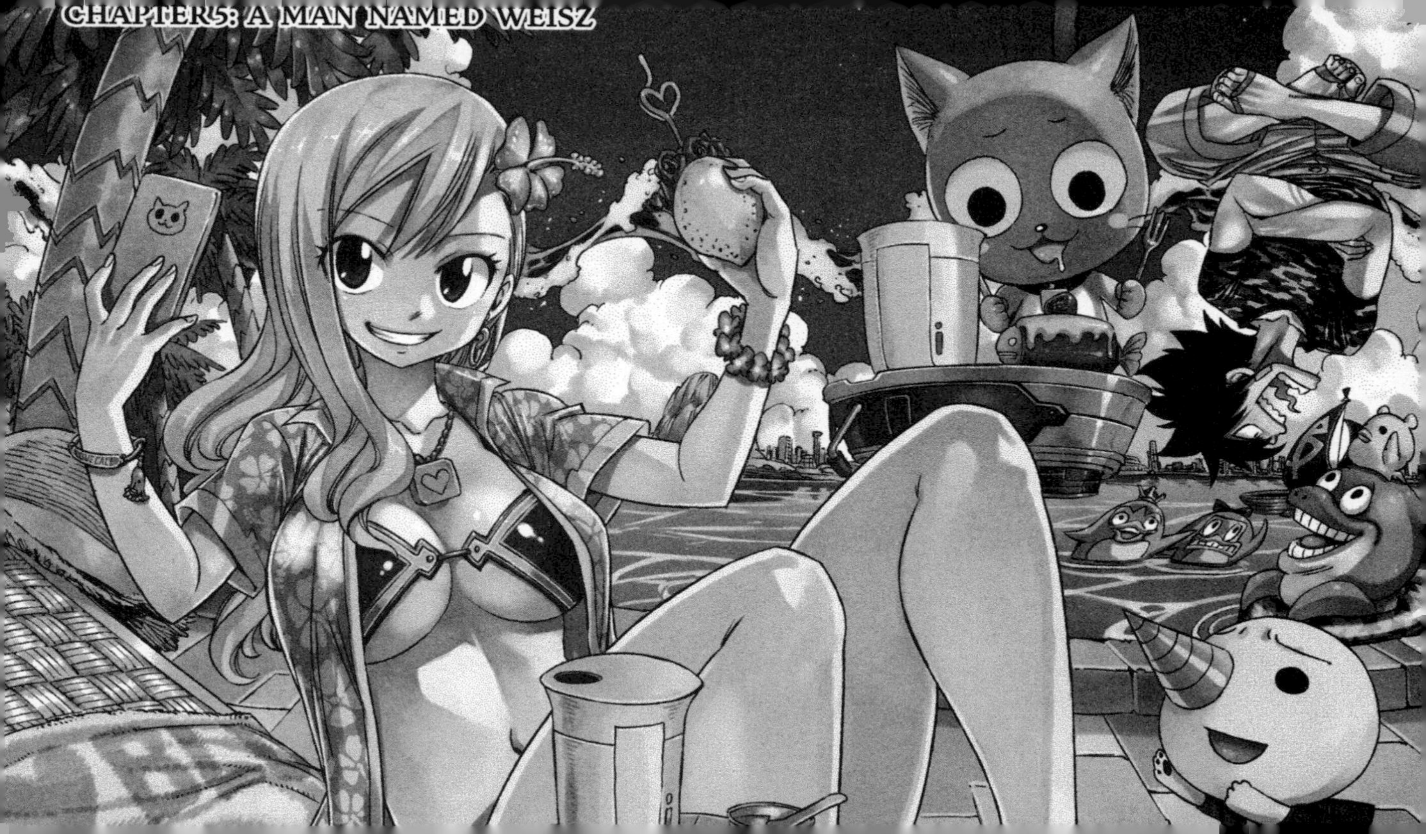

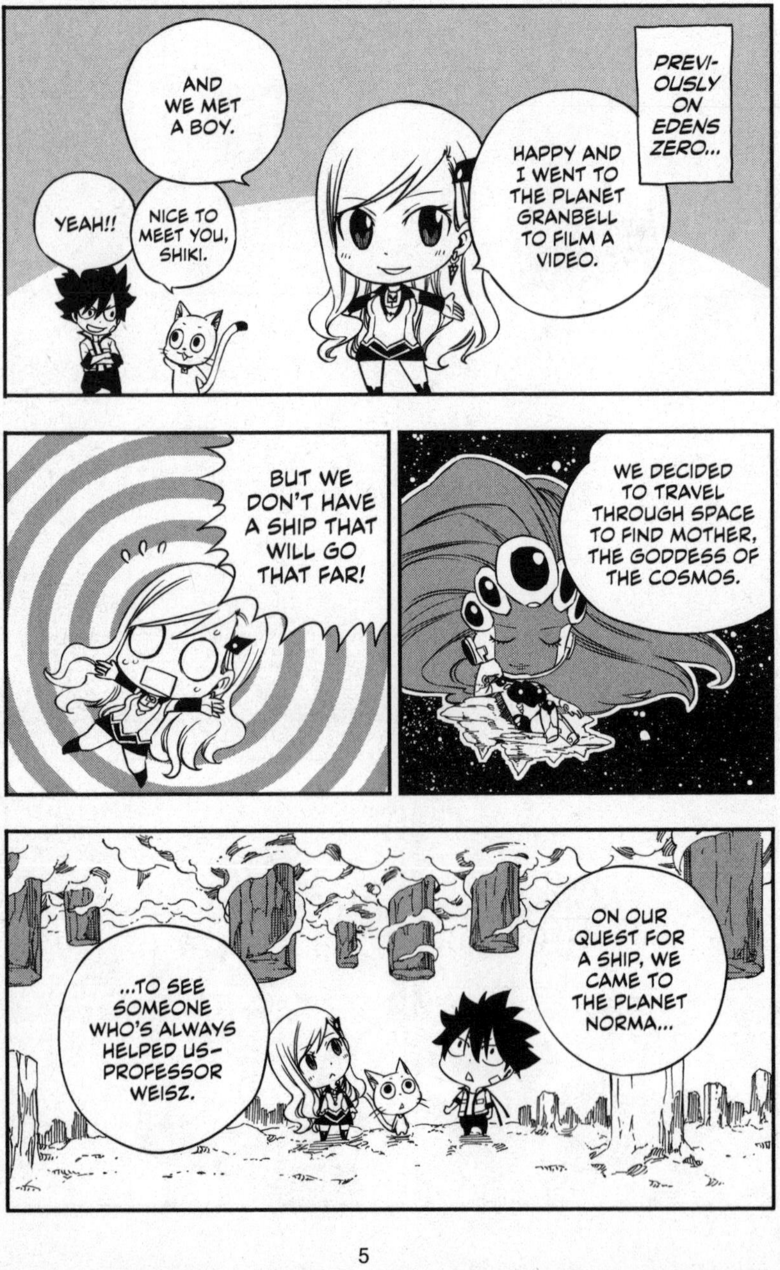
PREVIOUSLY ON EDENS ZERO...
HAPPY AND I WENT TO THE PLANET GRANBELL TO FILM A VIDEO.
AND WE MET A BOY.
NICE TO MEET YOU, SHIKI.
YEAH!!
WE DECIDED TO TRAVEL THROUGH SPACE TO FIND MOTHER, THE GODDESS OF THE COSMOS.
BUT WE DON'T HAVE A SHIP THAT WILL GO THAT FAR!
ON OUR QUEST FOR A SHIP, WE CAME TO THE PLANET NORMA...
...TO SEE SOMEONE WHO'S ALWAYS HELPED US- PROFESSOR WEISZ.

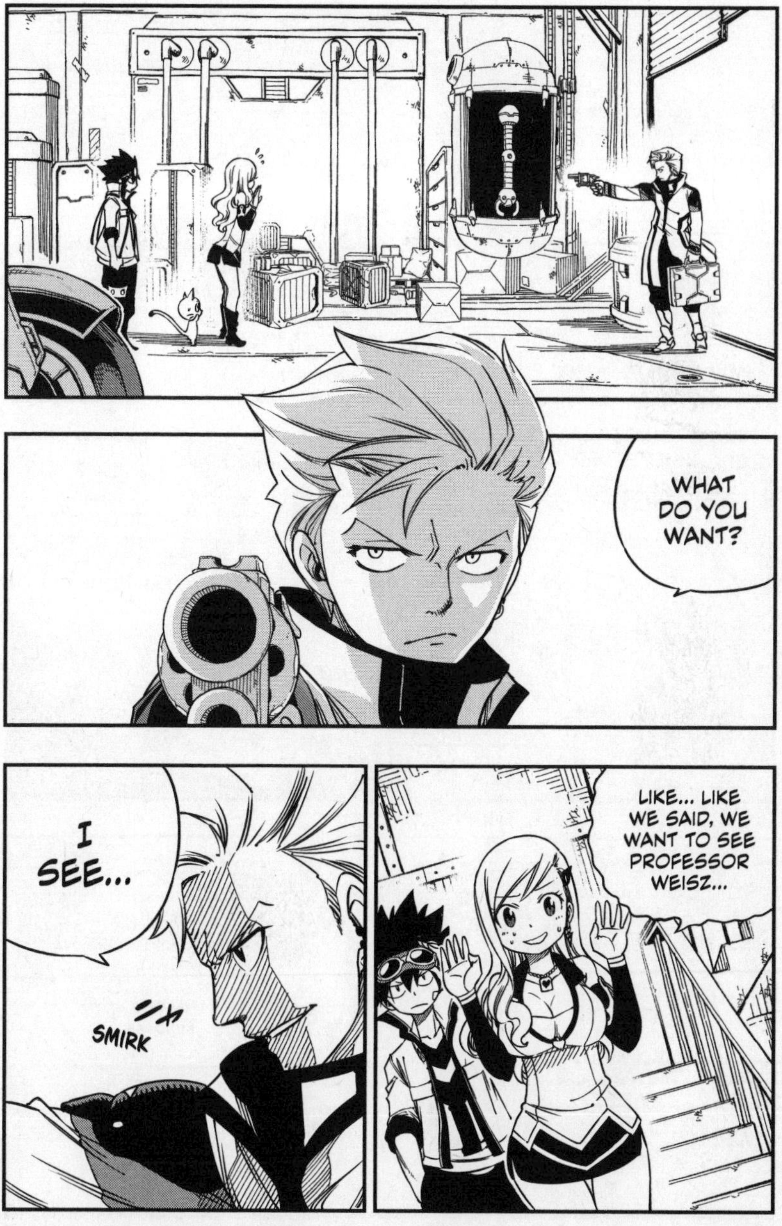
WHAT DO YOU WANT?
LIKE... LIKE WE SAID, WE WANT TO SEE PROFESSOR WEISZ...
I SEE...
SMIRK

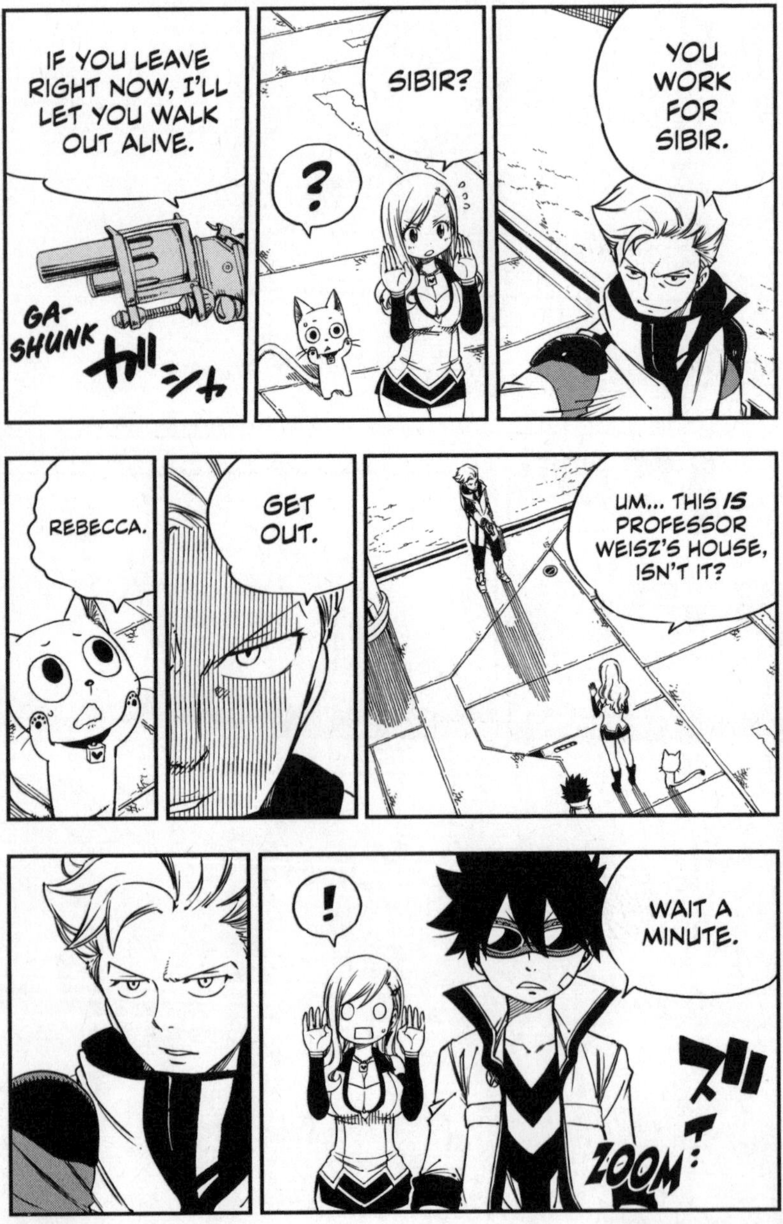
YOU WORK FOR SIBIR.
SIBIR?
?
IF YOU LEAVE RIGHT NOW, I'LL LET YOU WALK OUT ALIVE.
GA-SHUNK
UM... THIS *IS* PROFESSOR WEISZ'S HOUSE, ISN'T IT?
GET OUT.
REBECCA.
WAIT A MINUTE.
!
ZOOM

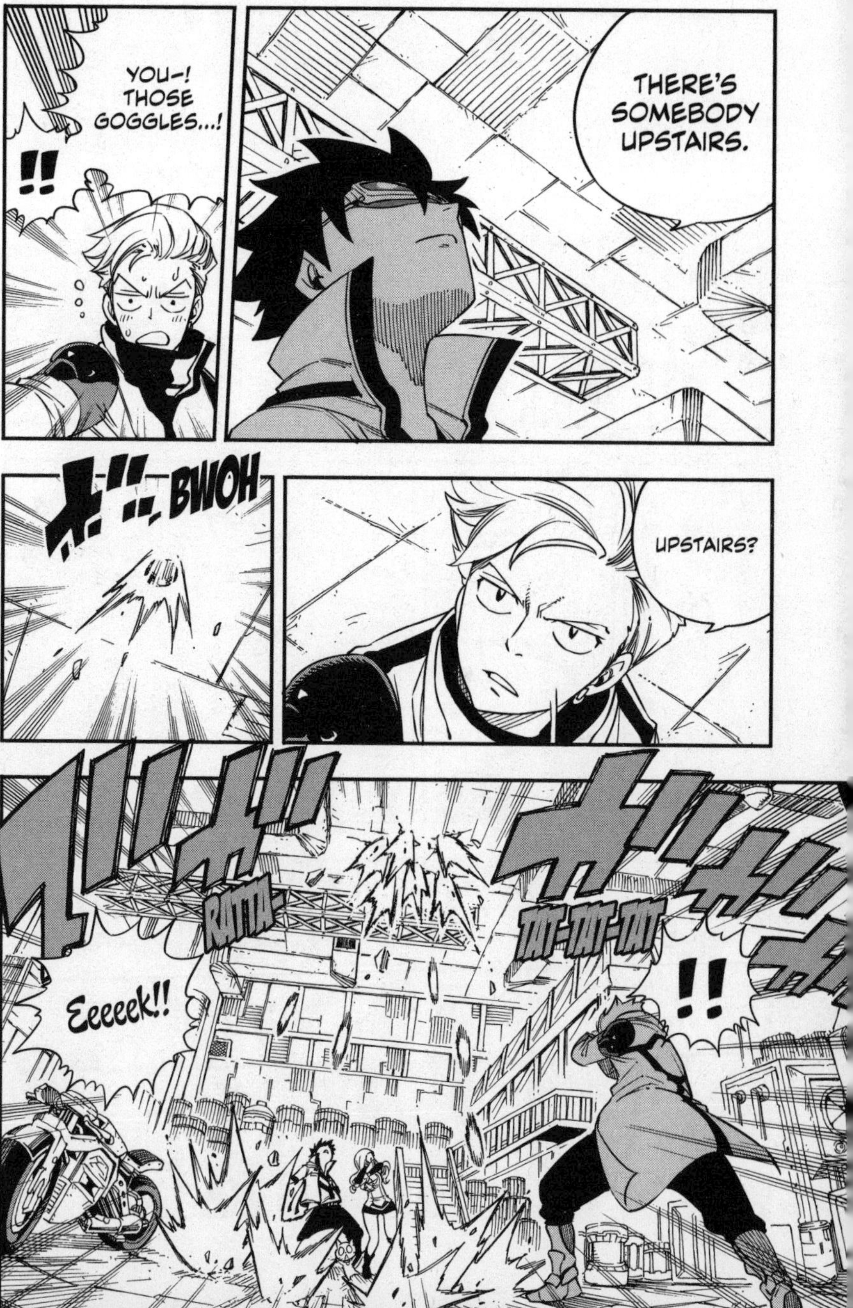
THERE'S SOMEBODY UPSTAIRS.
YOU-! THOSE GOGGLES...!
!!
UPSTAIRS?
BWOH
RATTA-
TAT-TAT-TAT
!!
Eeeeek!!

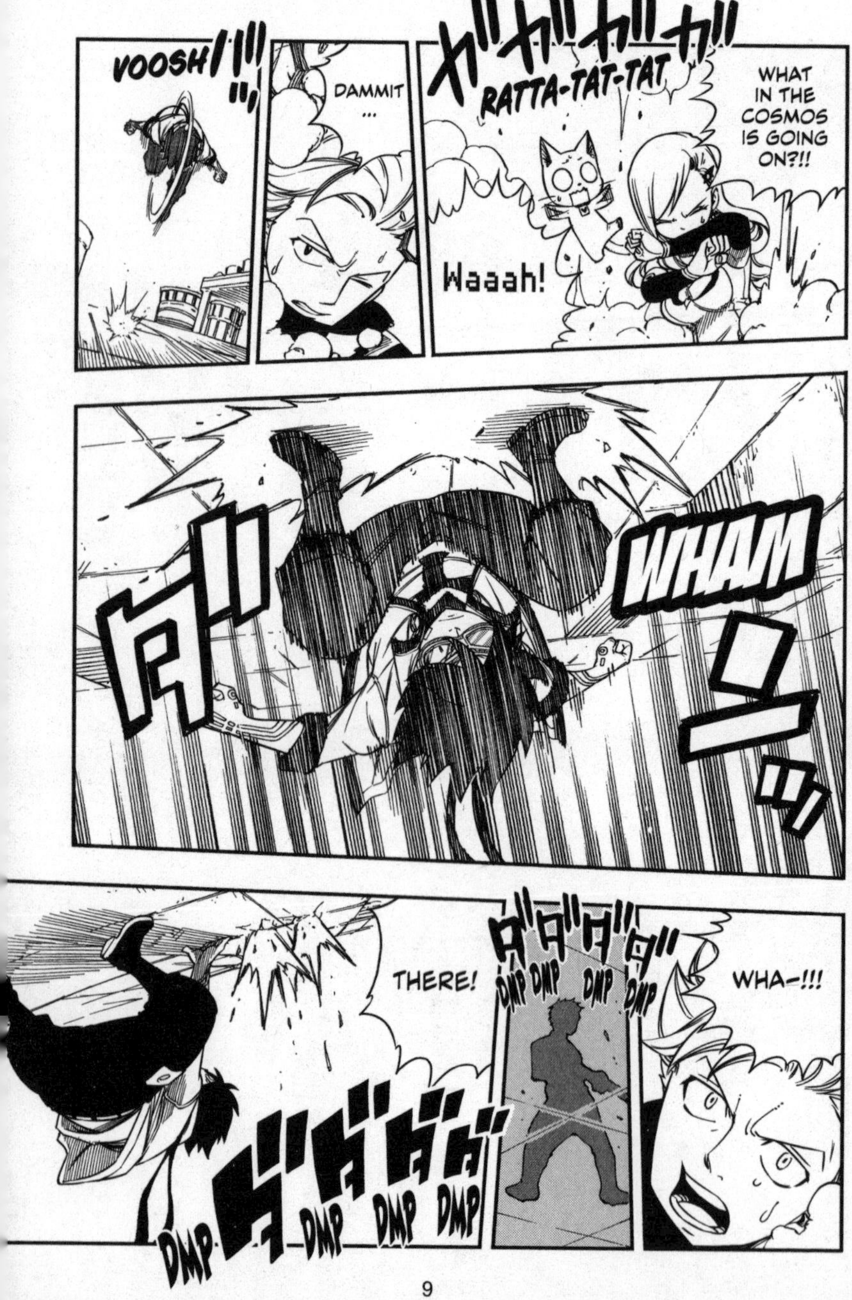
WHAT IN THE COSMOS IS GOING ON?!!
RATTA-TAT-TAT
Waaah!
DAMMIT ...
VOOSH!!!
WHAM
WHA-!!!
DMP DMP DMP DMP
THERE!
DMP DMP DMP DMP

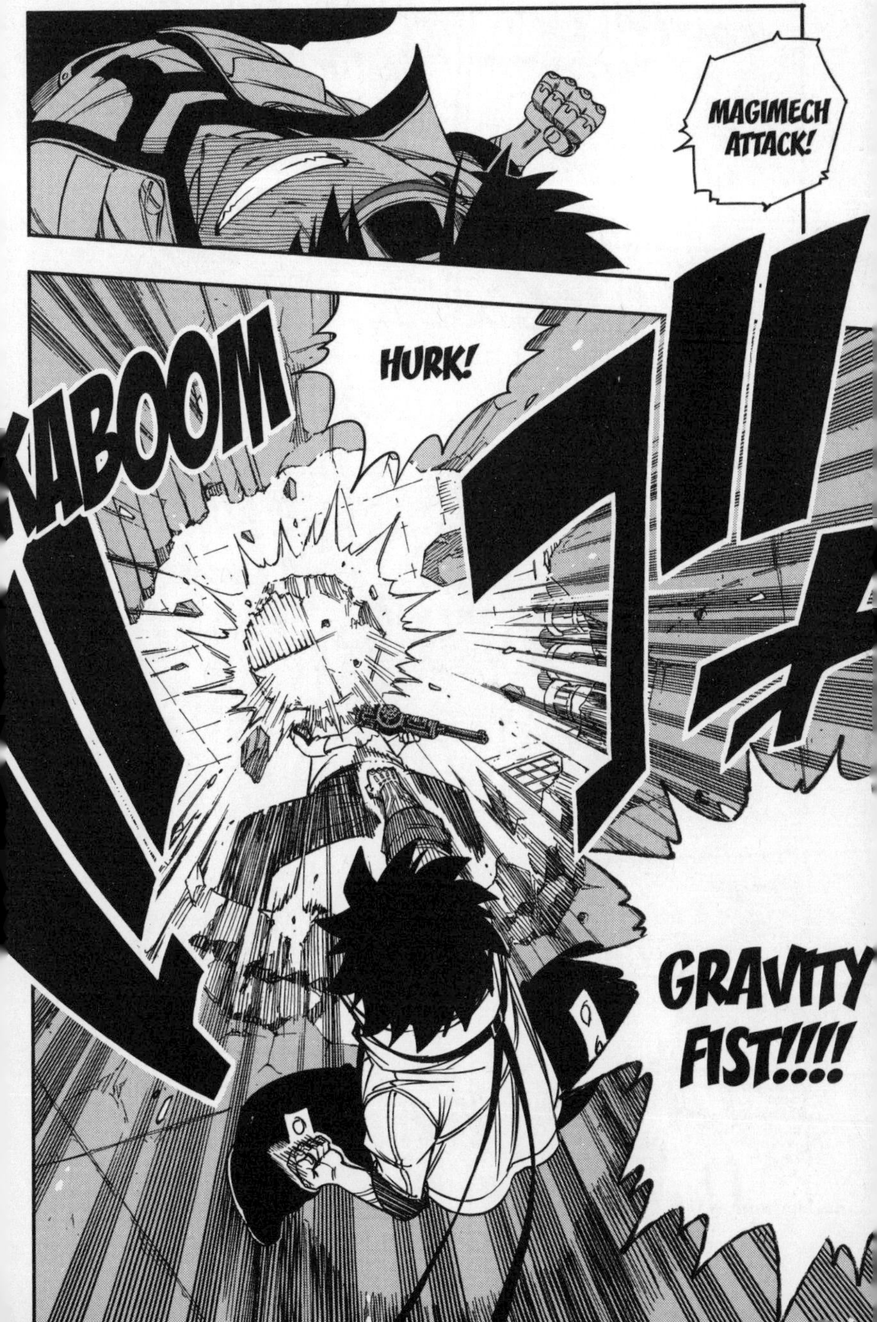
MAGIMECH ATTACK!
HURK!
KABOOM
GRAVITY FIST!!!!

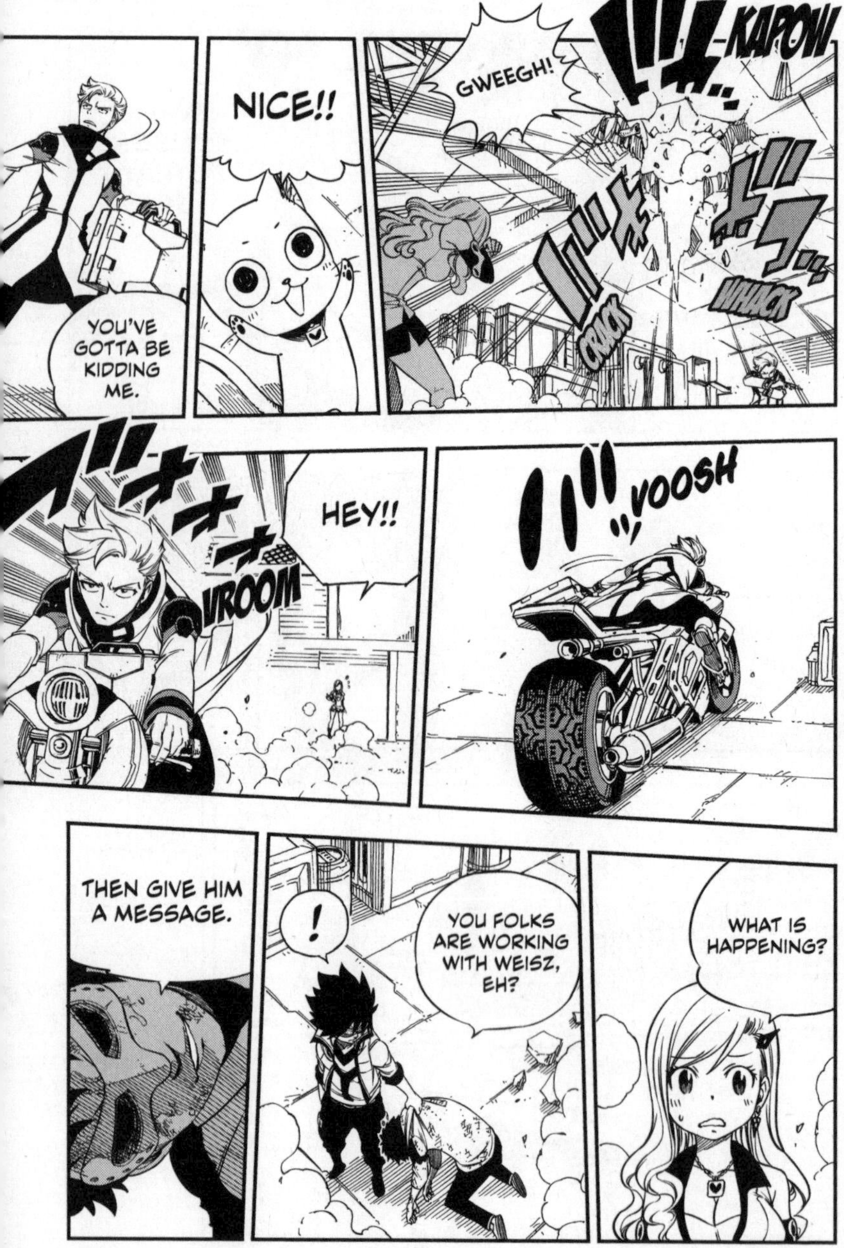

KAPOW
GWEEGH!
WHACK
CRACK
NICE!!
YOU'VE GOTTA BE KIDDING ME.
VOOSH
HEY!!
VROOM
WHAT IS HAPPENING?
YOU FOLKS ARE WORKING WITH WEISZ, EH?
!
THEN GIVE HIM A MESSAGE.

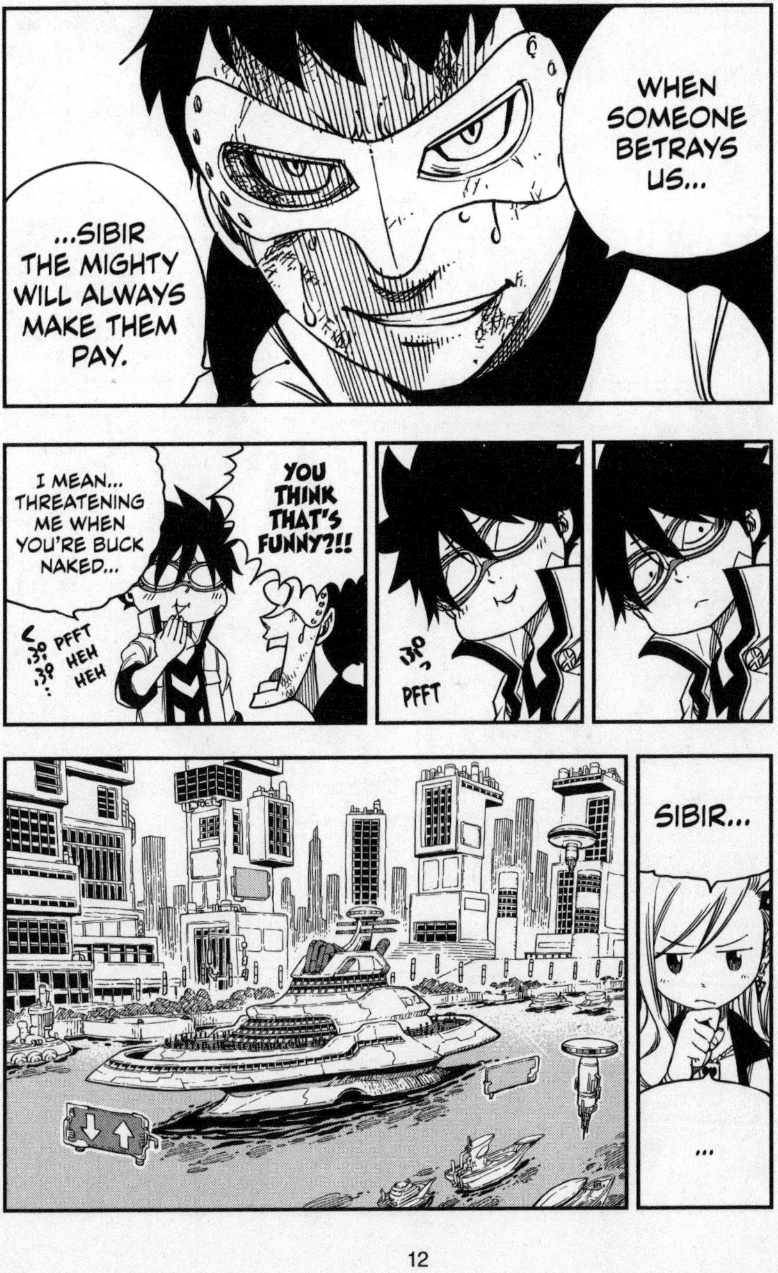
WHEN SOMEONE BETRAYS US...
...SIBIR THE MIGHTY WILL ALWAYS MAKE THEM PAY.
PFFT
YOU THINK THAT'S FUNNY?!!
I MEAN... THREATENING ME WHEN YOU'RE BUCK NAKED...
PFFT HEH HEH
SIBIR...
...

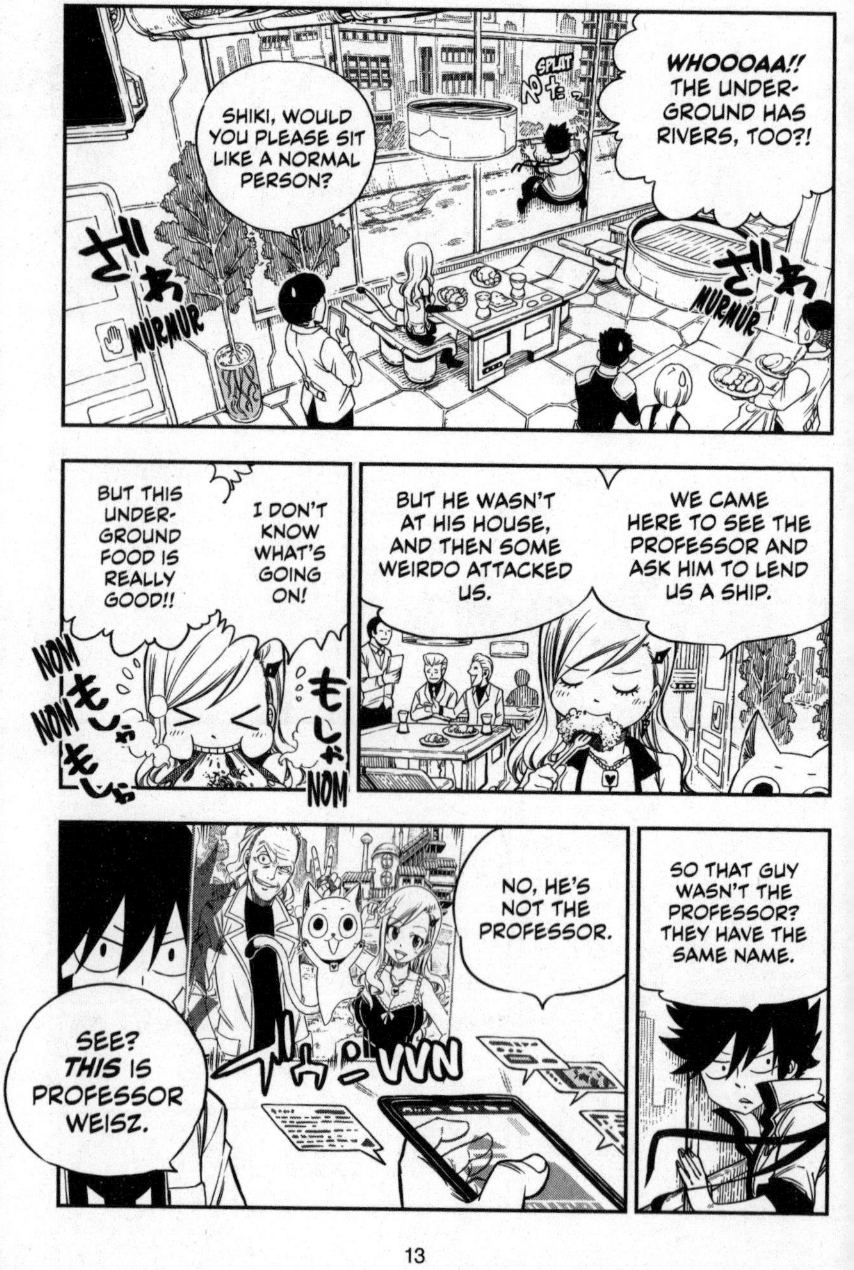
WHOOOAA!! THE UNDER-GROUND HAS RIVERS, TOO?!
SPLAT
SHIKI, WOULD YOU PLEASE SIT LIKE A NORMAL PERSON?
MURMUR
MURMUR
WE CAME HERE TO SEE THE PROFESSOR AND ASK HIM TO LEND US A SHIP.
BUT HE WASN'T AT HIS HOUSE, AND THEN SOME WEIRDO ATTACKED US.
I DON'T KNOW WHAT'S GOING ON!
BUT THIS UNDER-GROUND FOOD IS REALLY GOOD!!
NOM
NOM NOM
NOM
SO THAT GUY WASN'T THE PROFESSOR? THEY HAVE THE SAME NAME.
NO, HE'S NOT THE PROFESSOR.
VVN
SEE? *THIS* IS PROFESSOR WEISZ.

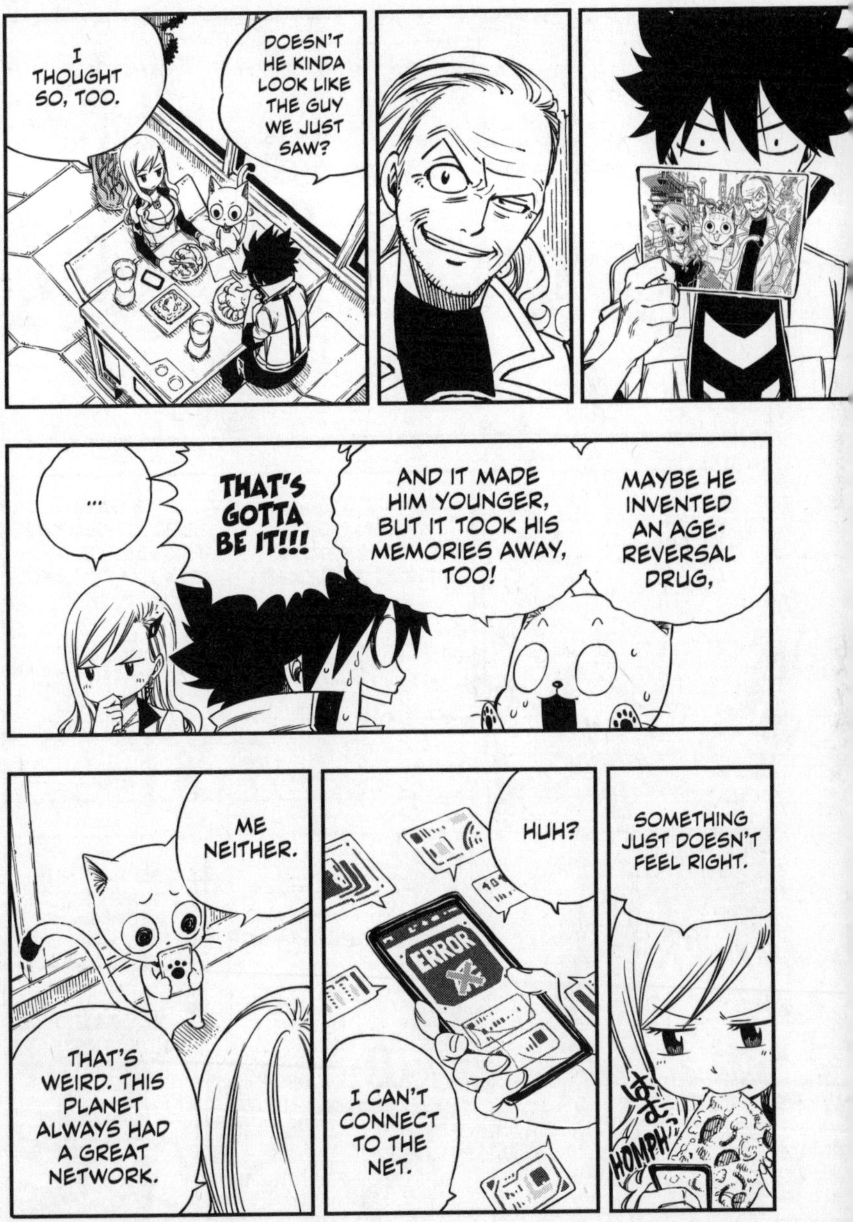
DOESN'T HE KINDA LOOK LIKE THE GUY WE JUST SAW?
I THOUGHT SO, TOO.
MAYBE HE INVENTED AN AGE-REVERSAL DRUG,
AND IT MADE HIM YOUNGER, BUT IT TOOK HIS MEMORIES AWAY, TOO!
THAT'S GOTTA BE IT!!!
...
SOMETHING JUST DOESN'T FEEL RIGHT.
HOMPH
HUH?
ERROR
I CAN'T CONNECT TO THE NET.
ME NEITHER.
THAT'S WEIRD. THIS PLANET ALWAYS HAD A GREAT NETWORK.

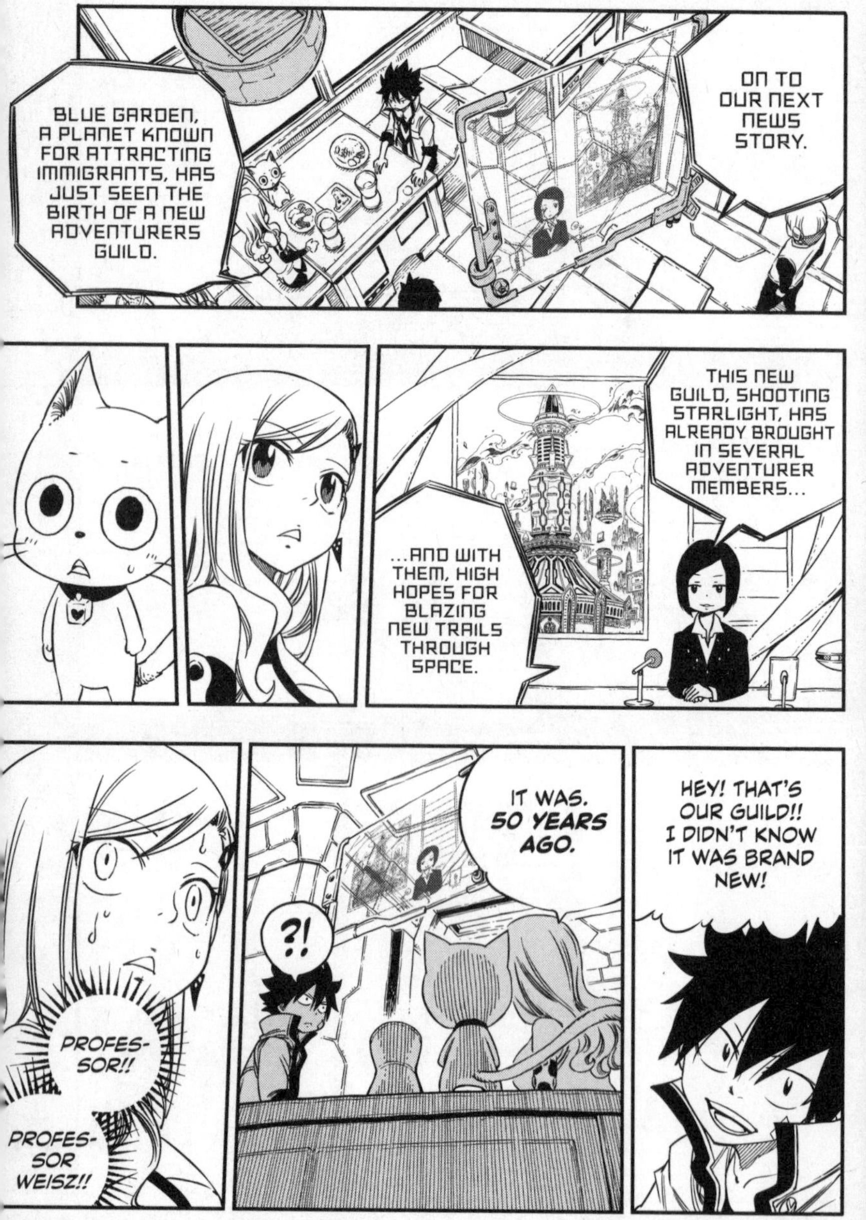
ON TO OUR NEXT NEWS STORY.
BLUE GARDEN, A PLANET KNOWN FOR ATTRACTING IMMIGRANTS, HAS JUST SEEN THE BIRTH OF A NEW ADVENTURERS GUILD.
THIS NEW GUILD, SHOOTING STARLIGHT, HAS ALREADY BROUGHT IN SEVERAL ADVENTURER MEMBERS...
...AND WITH THEM, HIGH HOPES FOR BLAZING NEW TRAILS THROUGH SPACE.
HEY! THAT'S OUR GUILD!! I DIDN'T KNOW IT WAS BRAND NEW!
IT WAS. 50 YEARS AGO.
?!
PROFES-SOR!!
PROFES-SOR WEISZ!!

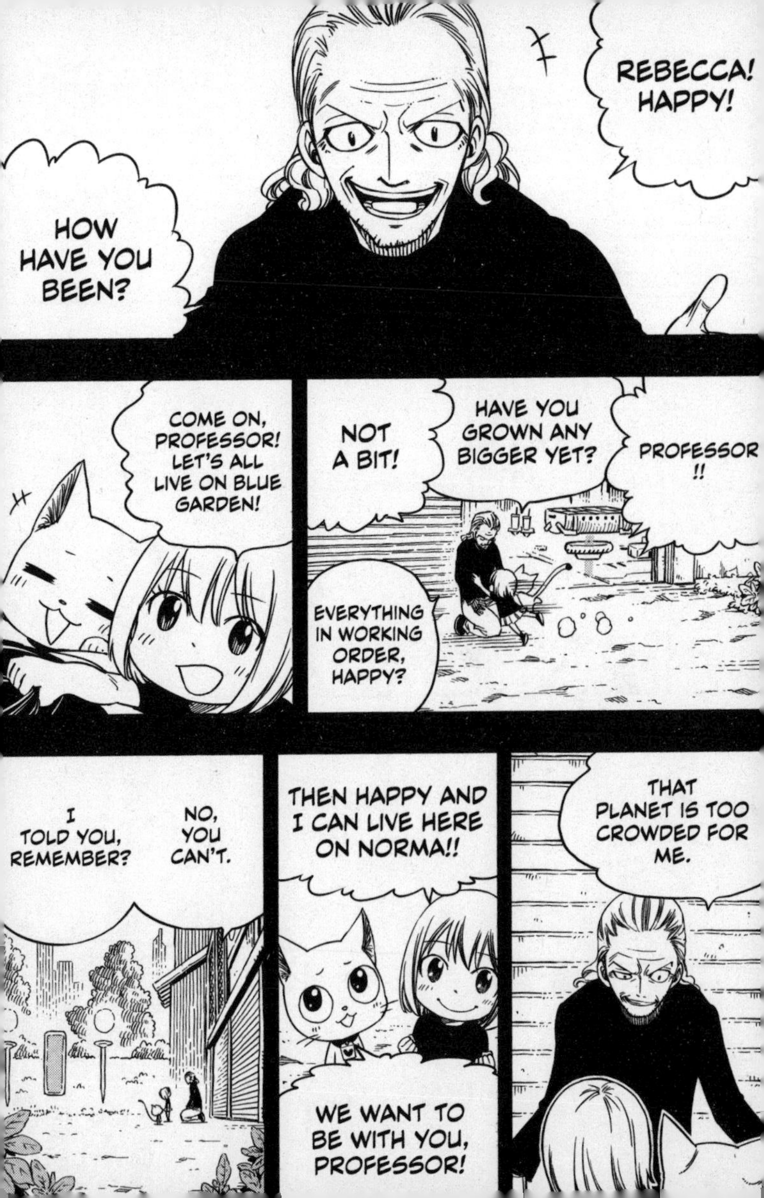
REBECCA! HAPPY!
HOW HAVE YOU BEEN?
PROFESSOR !!
HAVE YOU GROWN ANY BIGGER YET?
NOT A BIT!
EVERYTHING IN WORKING ORDER, HAPPY?
COME ON, PROFESSOR! LET'S ALL LIVE ON BLUE GARDEN!
THAT PLANET IS TOO CROWDED FOR ME.
THEN HAPPY AND I CAN LIVE HERE ON NORMA!!
WE WANT TO BE WITH YOU, PROFESSOR!
NO, YOU CAN'T.
I TOLD YOU, REMEMBER?

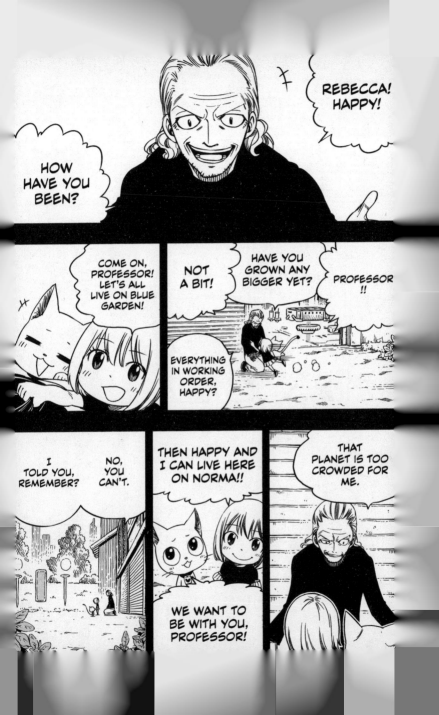

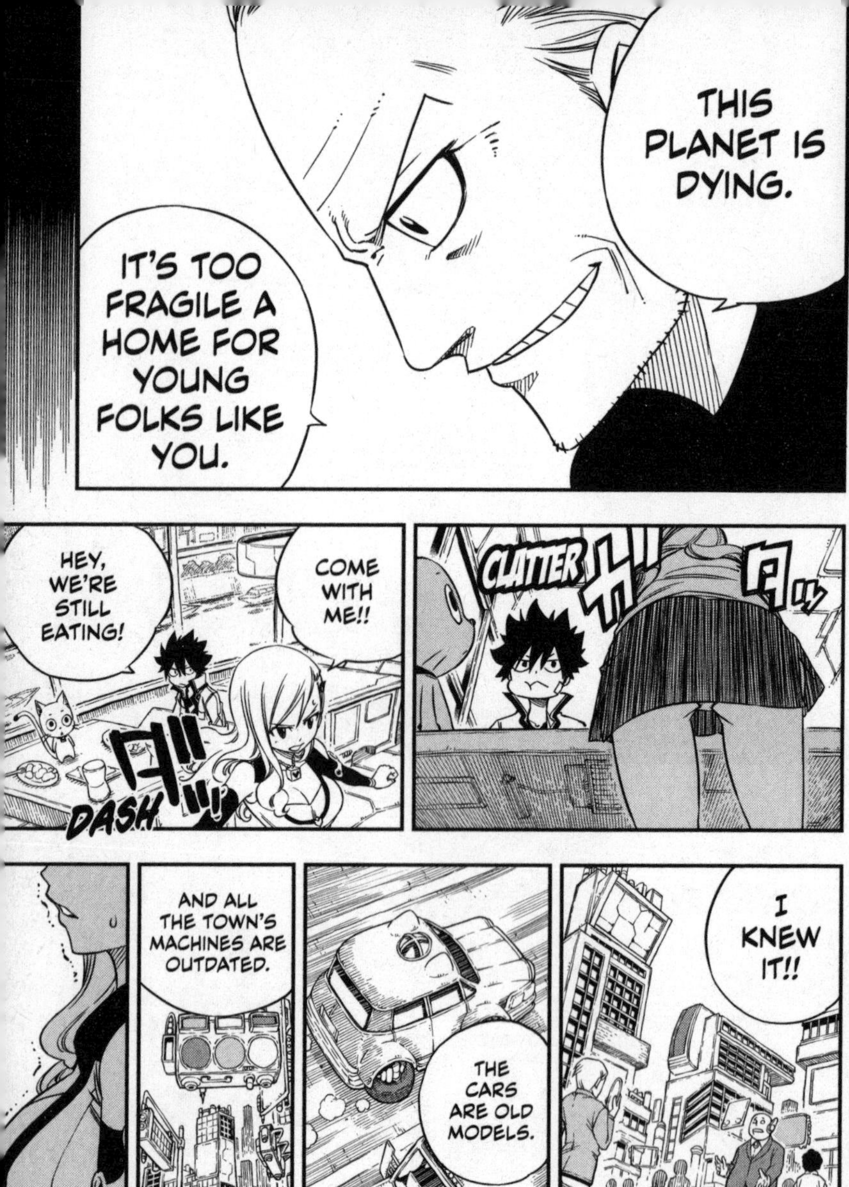
THIS PLANET IS DYING.
IT'S TOO FRAGILE A HOME FOR YOUNG FOLKS LIKE YOU.
CLATTER
COME WITH ME!!
HEY, WE'RE STILL EATING!
DASH
I KNEW IT!!
THE CARS ARE OLD MODELS.
AND ALL THE TOWN'S MACHINES ARE OUTDATED.

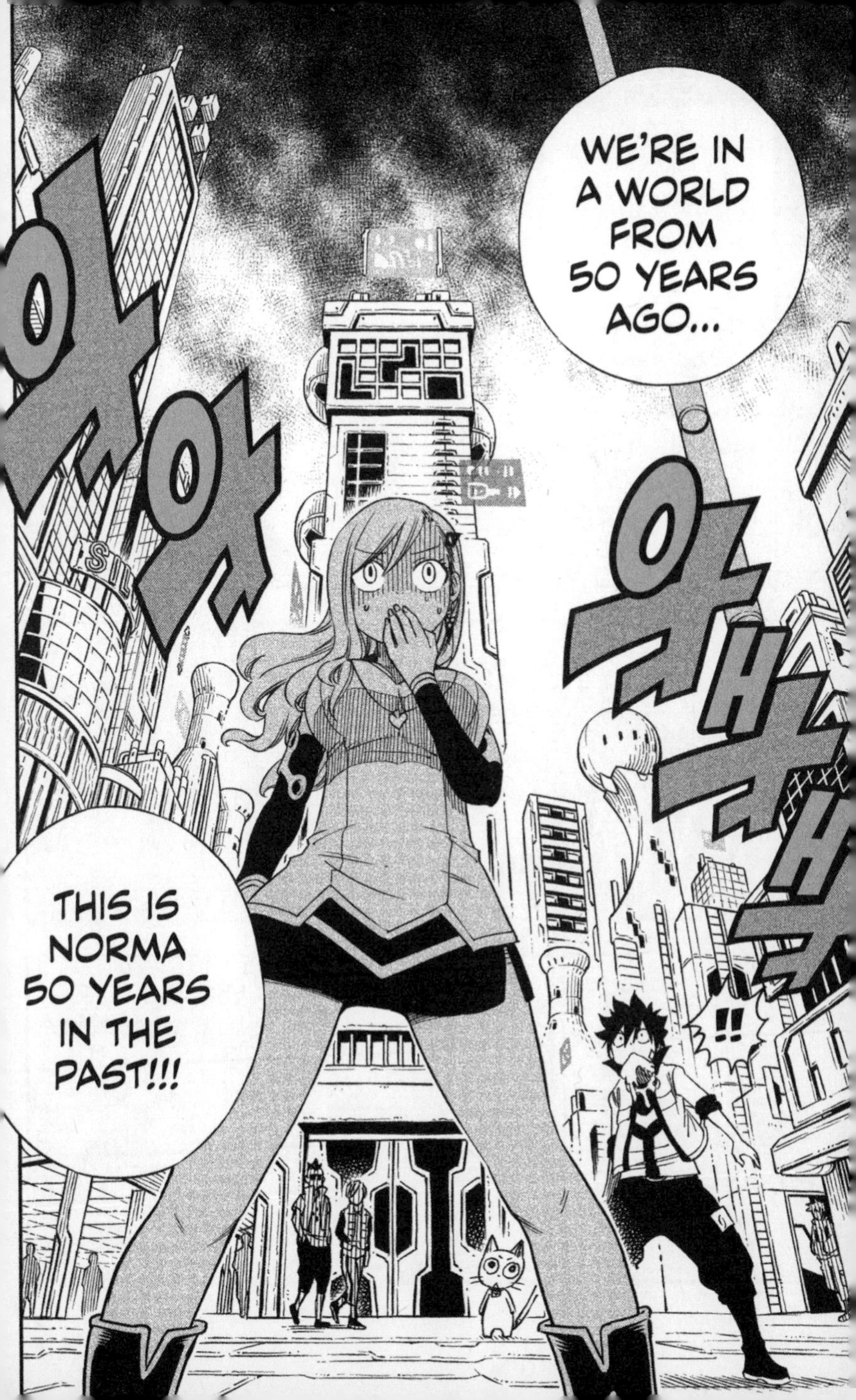
WE'RE IN A WORLD FROM 50 YEARS AGO...
THIS IS NORMA 50 YEARS IN THE PAST!!!
!!

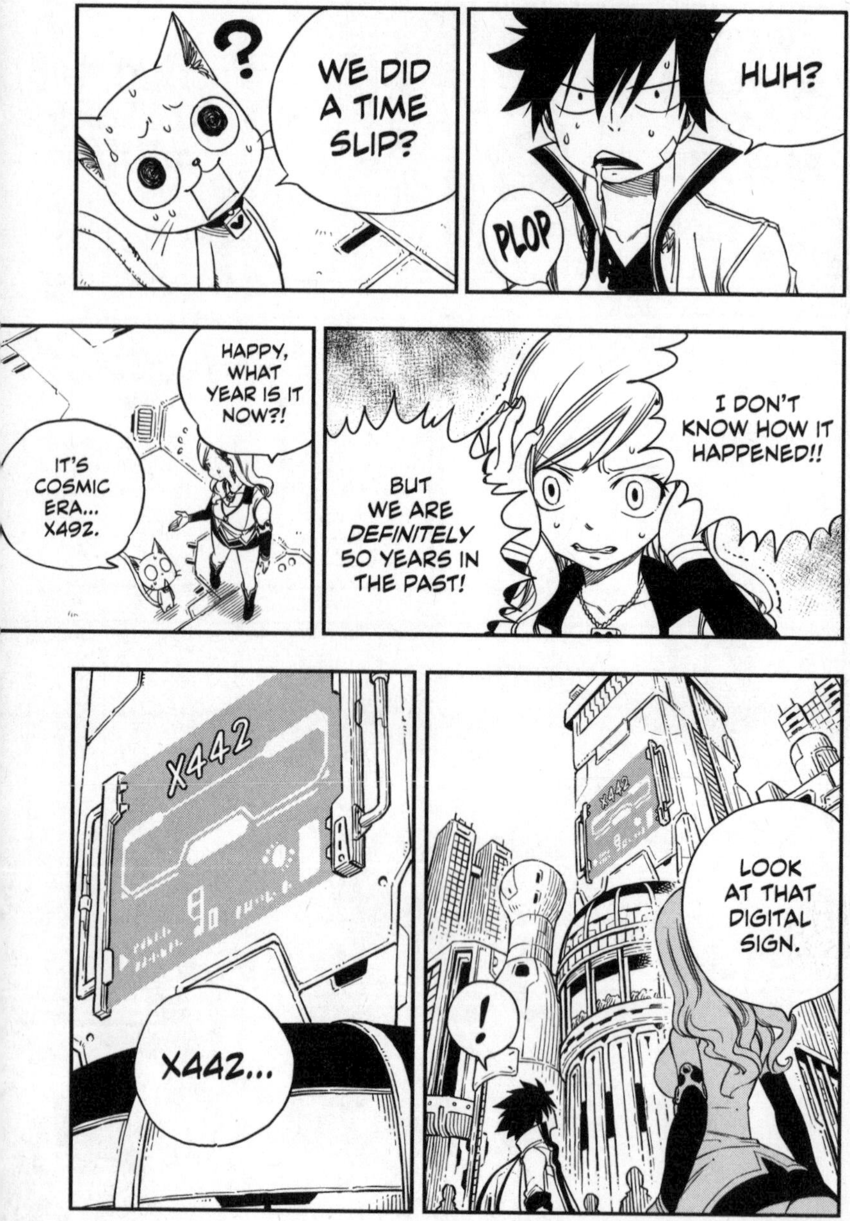
HUH?
PLOP
?
WE DID A TIME SLIP?
I DON'T KNOW HOW IT HAPPENED!!
BUT WE ARE *DEFINITELY* 50 YEARS IN THE PAST!
HAPPY, WHAT YEAR IS IT NOW?!
IT'S COSMIC ERA... X492.
LOOK AT THAT DIGITAL SIGN.
!
X442
X442
X442...

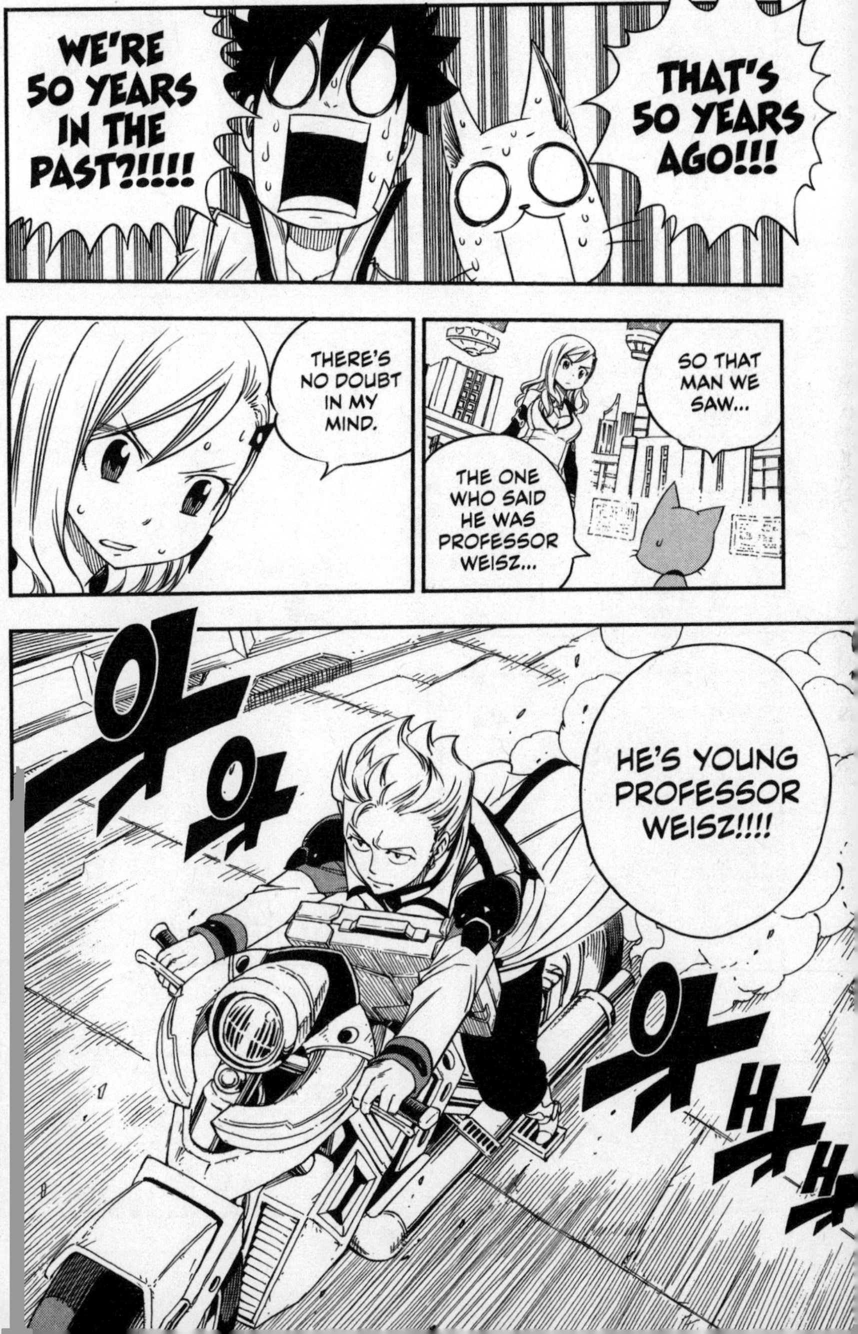
THAT'S 50 YEARS AGO!!!
WE'RE 50 YEARS IN THE PAST?!!!!!
SO THAT MAN WE SAW...
THE ONE WHO SAID HE WAS PROFESSOR WEISZ...
THERE'S NO DOUBT IN MY MIND.
HE'S YOUNG PROFESSOR WEISZ!!!!

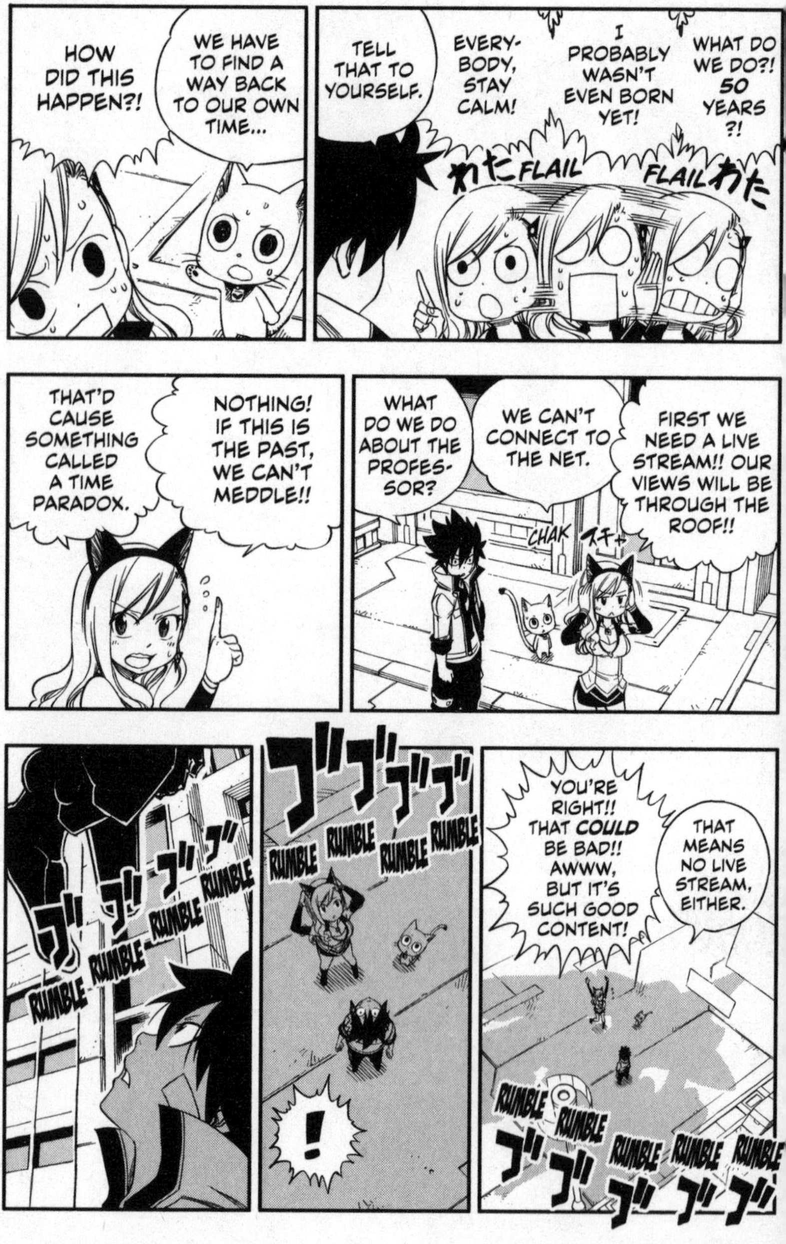
WHAT DO WE DO?! 50 YEARS ?!
I PROBABLY WASN'T EVEN BORN YET!
EVERY-BODY, STAY CALM!
TELL THAT TO YOURSELF.
わた FLAIL
FLAIL わた
WE HAVE TO FIND A WAY BACK TO OUR OWN TIME...
HOW DID THIS HAPPEN?!
FIRST WE NEED A LIVE STREAM!! OUR VIEWS WILL BE THROUGH THE ROOF!!
WE CAN'T CONNECT TO THE NET.
WHAT DO WE DO ABOUT THE PROFES-SOR?
CHAK スチャ
NOTHING! IF THIS IS THE PAST, WE CAN'T MEDDLE!!
THAT'D CAUSE SOMETHING CALLED A TIME PARADOX.
THAT MEANS NO LIVE STREAM, EITHER.
YOU'RE RIGHT!! THAT COULD BE BAD!! AWWW, BUT IT'S SUCH GOOD CONTENT!
RUMBLE RUMBLE RUMBLE RUMBLE RUMBLE
ゴゴゴゴゴ
ゴゴゴゴ
RUMBLE RUMBLE RUMBLE RUMBLE
!
ゴゴゴゴ
RUMBLE RUMBLE RUMBLE RUMBLE

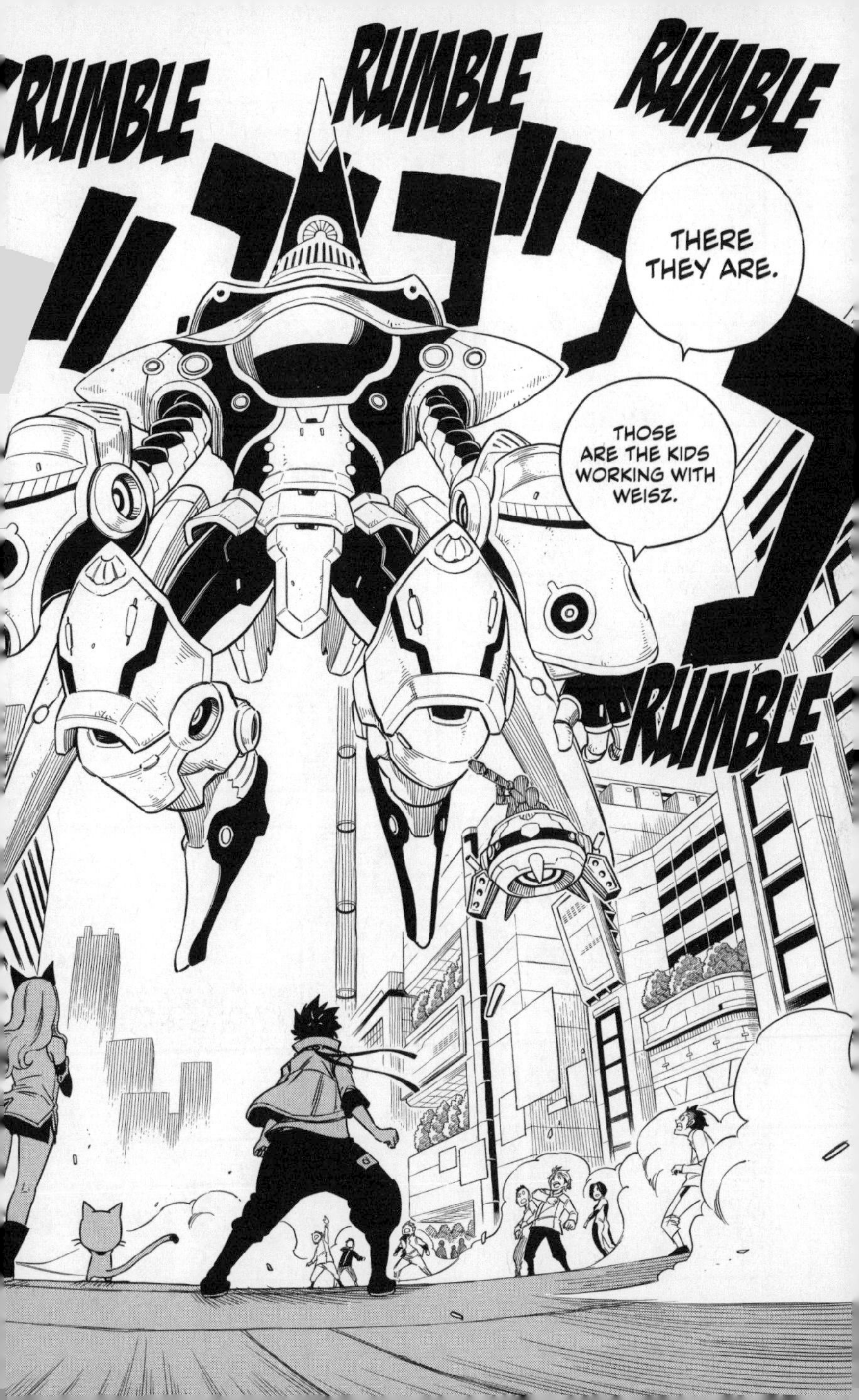
RUMBLE
RUMBLE
RUMBLE
THERE THEY ARE.
THOSE ARE THE KIDS WORKING WITH WEISZ.
RUMBLE

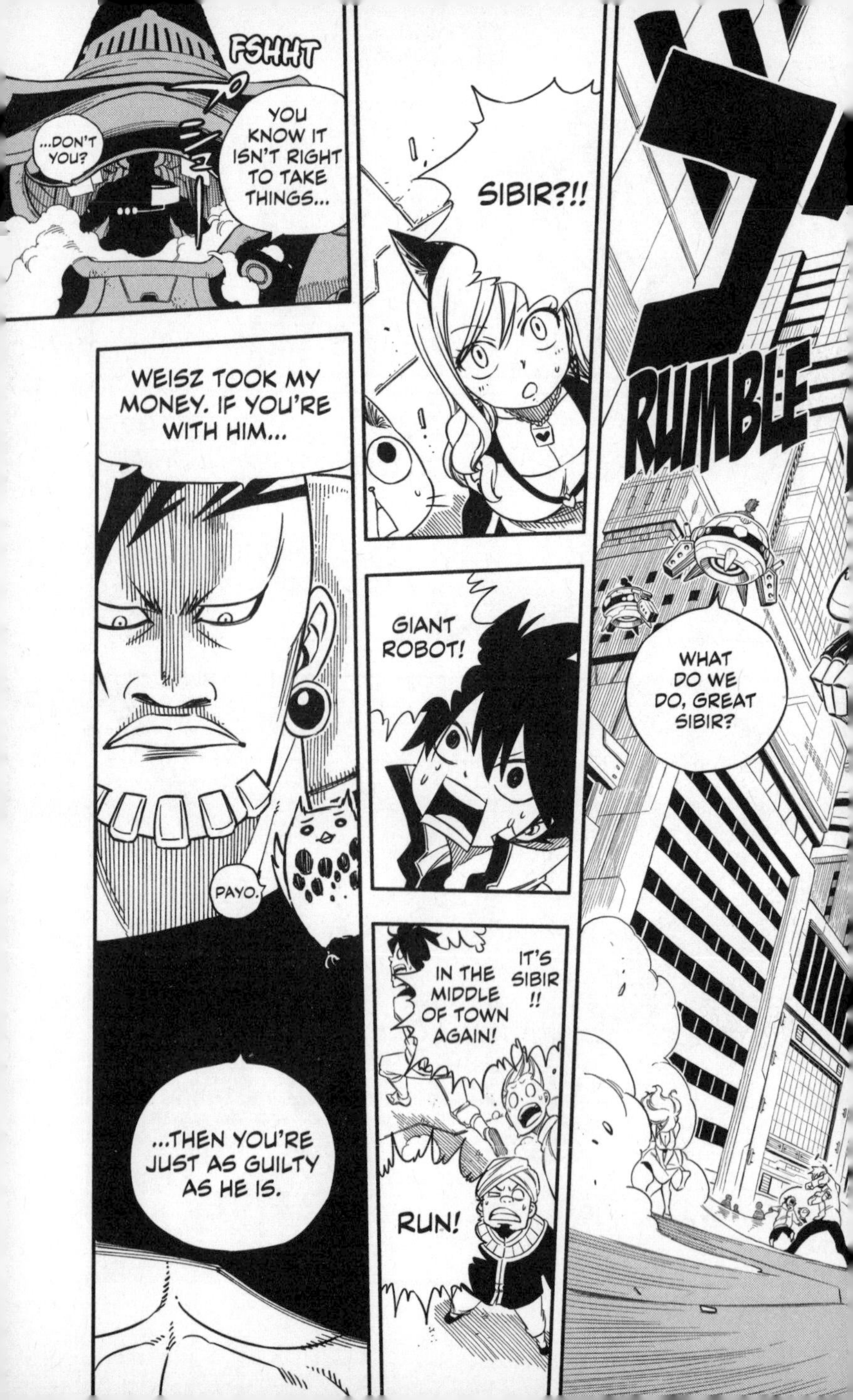
RUMBLE
WHAT DO WE DO, GREAT SIBIR?
SIBIR?!!
GIANT ROBOT!
IT'S SIBIR!!
IN THE MIDDLE OF TOWN AGAIN!
RUN!
FSHHT
YOU KNOW IT ISN'T RIGHT TO TAKE THINGS...
...DON'T YOU?
WEISZ TOOK MY MONEY. IF YOU'RE WITH HIM...
PAYO.
...THEN YOU'RE JUST AS GUILTY AS HE IS.

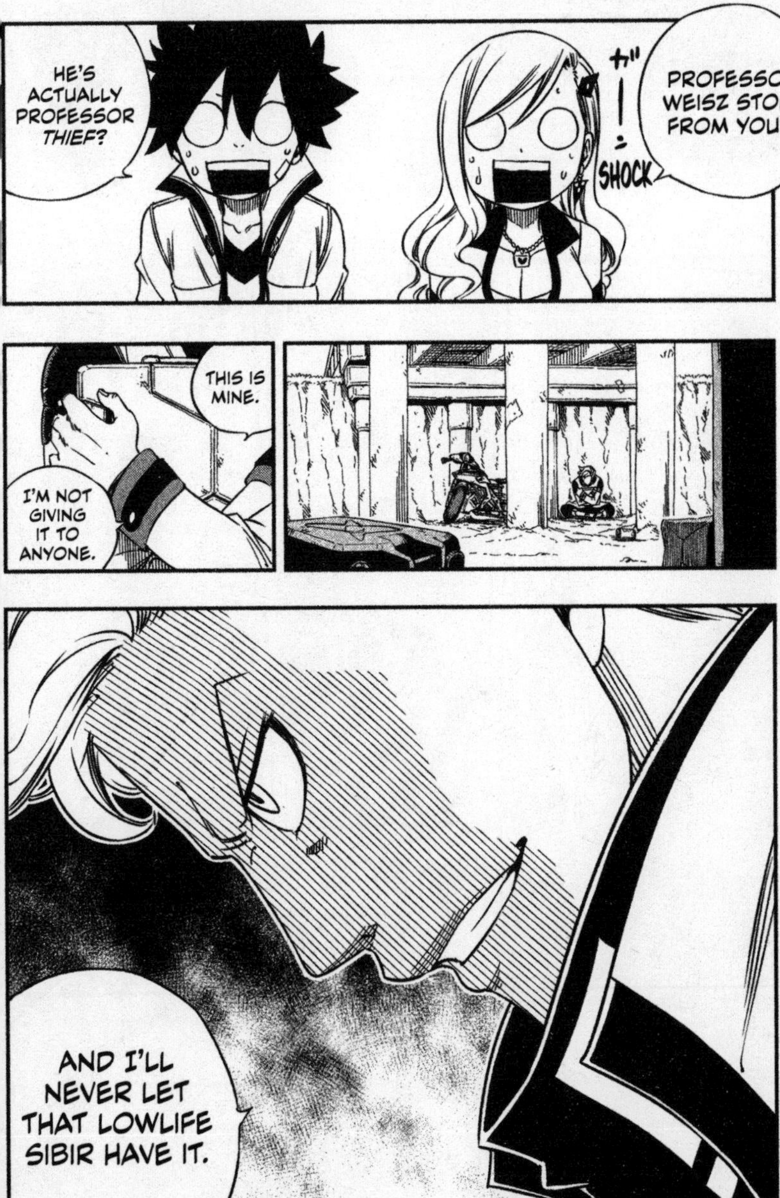
PROFESSOR WEISZ STOLE FROM YOU?!
SHOCK
HE'S ACTUALLY PROFESSOR *THIEF?*
THIS IS MINE.
I'M NOT GIVING IT TO ANYONE.
AND I'LL NEVER LET THAT LOWLIFE SIBIR HAVE IT.

# EDENS ZERO

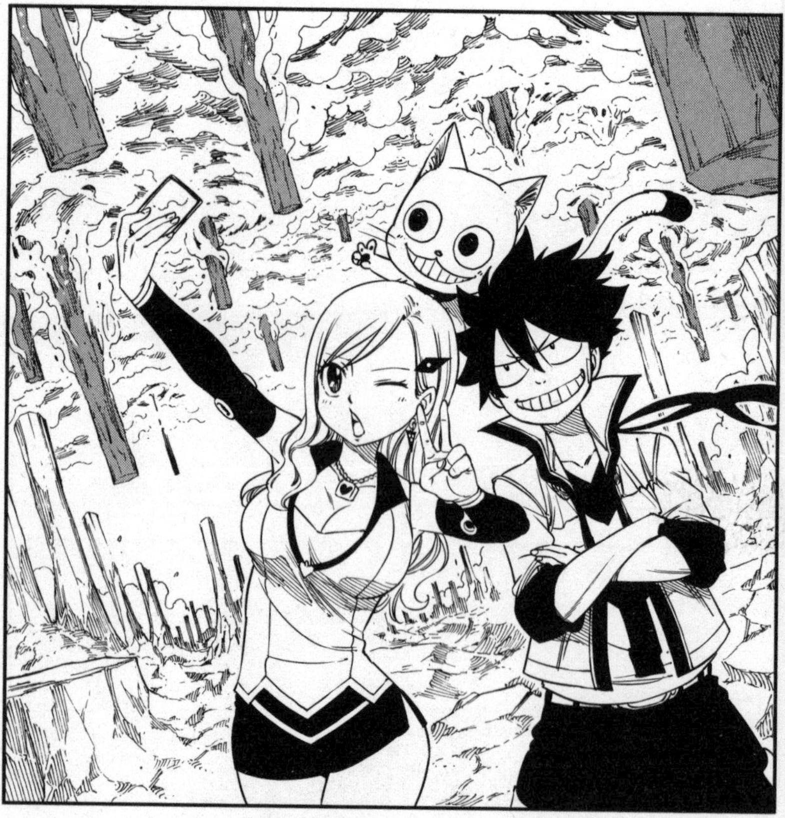

## CHAPTER 6: THIEF

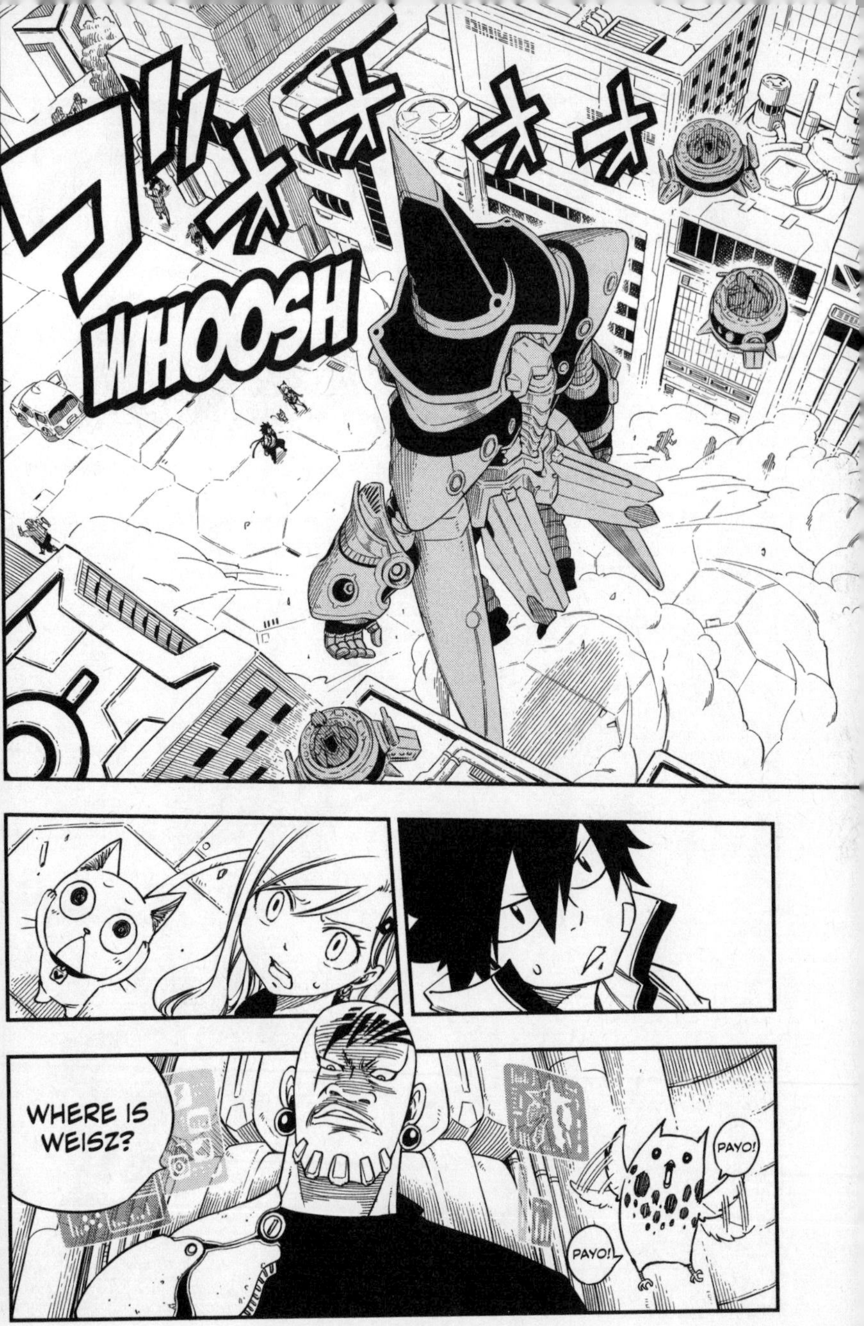
ゴオオオオ
WHOOSH
!
PAYO!
WHERE IS WEISZ?
PAYO!

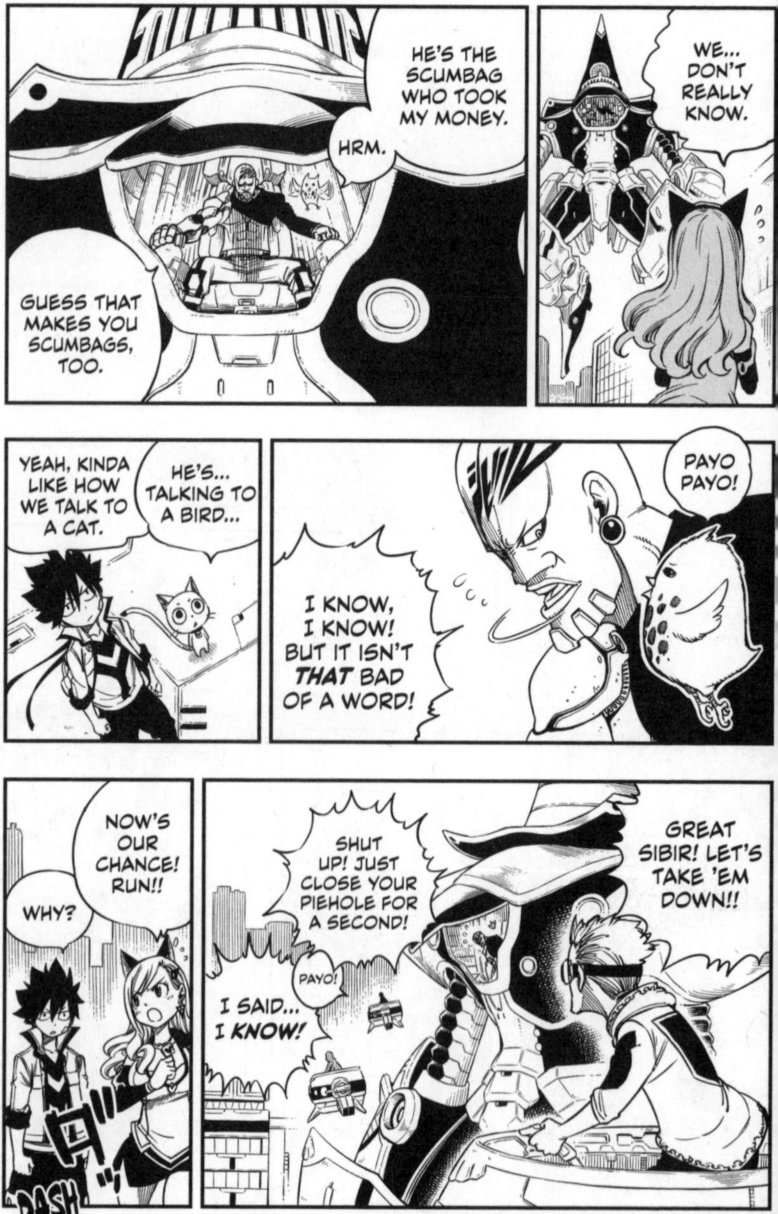
WE... DON'T REALLY KNOW.
HE'S THE SCUMBAG WHO TOOK MY MONEY.
HRM.
GUESS THAT MAKES YOU SCUMBAGS, TOO.
PAYO PAYO!
I KNOW, I KNOW! BUT IT ISN'T THAT BAD OF A WORD!
HE'S... TALKING TO A BIRD...
YEAH, KINDA LIKE HOW WE TALK TO A CAT.
GREAT SIBIR! LET'S TAKE 'EM DOWN!!
SHUT UP! JUST CLOSE YOUR PIEHOLE FOR A SECOND!
PAYO!
I SAID... I KNOW!
NOW'S OUR CHANCE! RUN!!
WHY?
DASH

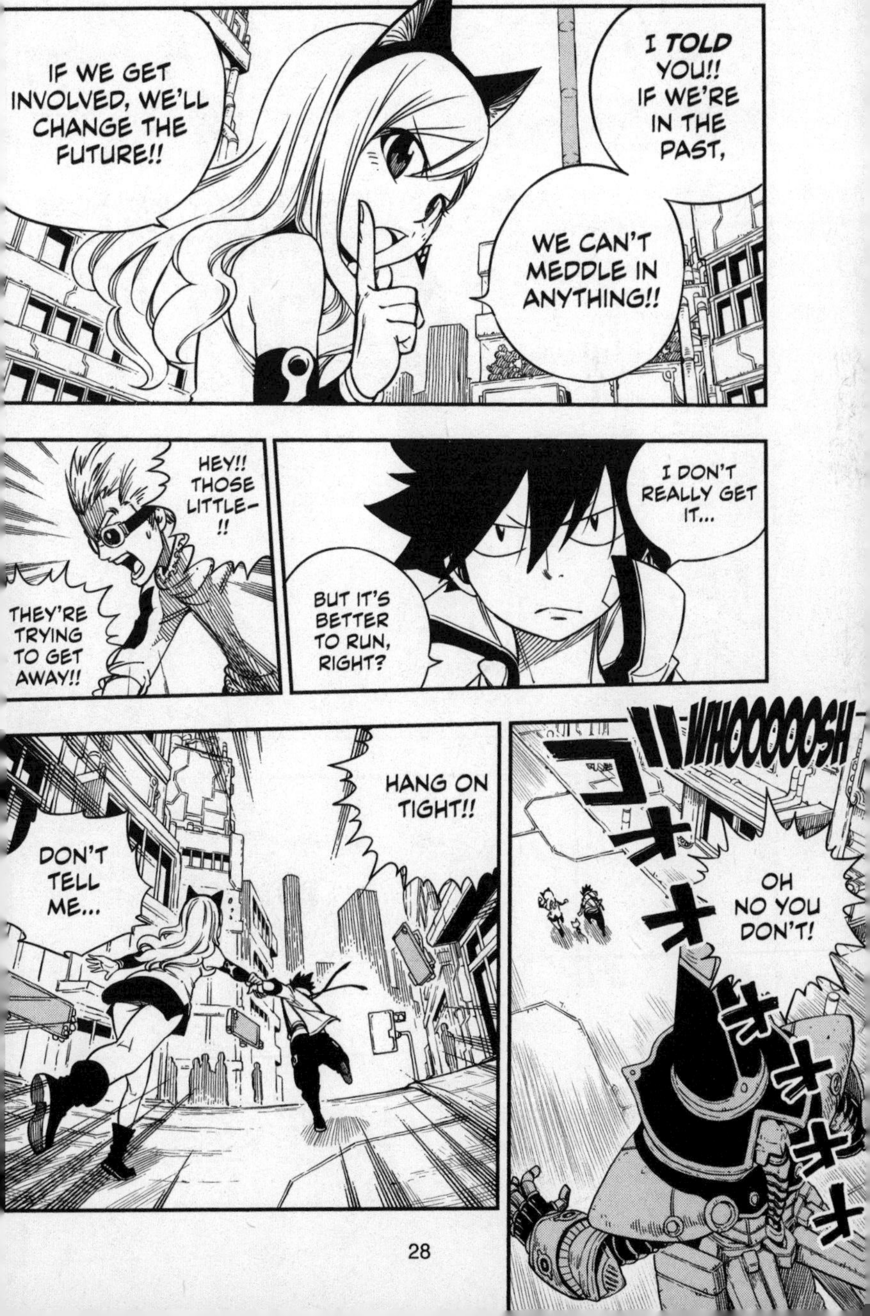
I *TOLD* YOU!! IF WE'RE IN THE PAST,
WE CAN'T MEDDLE IN ANYTHING!!
IF WE GET INVOLVED, WE'LL CHANGE THE FUTURE!!
I DON'T REALLY GET IT...
BUT IT'S BETTER TO RUN, RIGHT?
HEY!! THOSE LITTLE-!!
THEY'RE TRYING TO GET AWAY!!
WHOOOOOOSH
OH NO YOU DON'T!
HANG ON TIGHT!!
DON'T TELL ME...

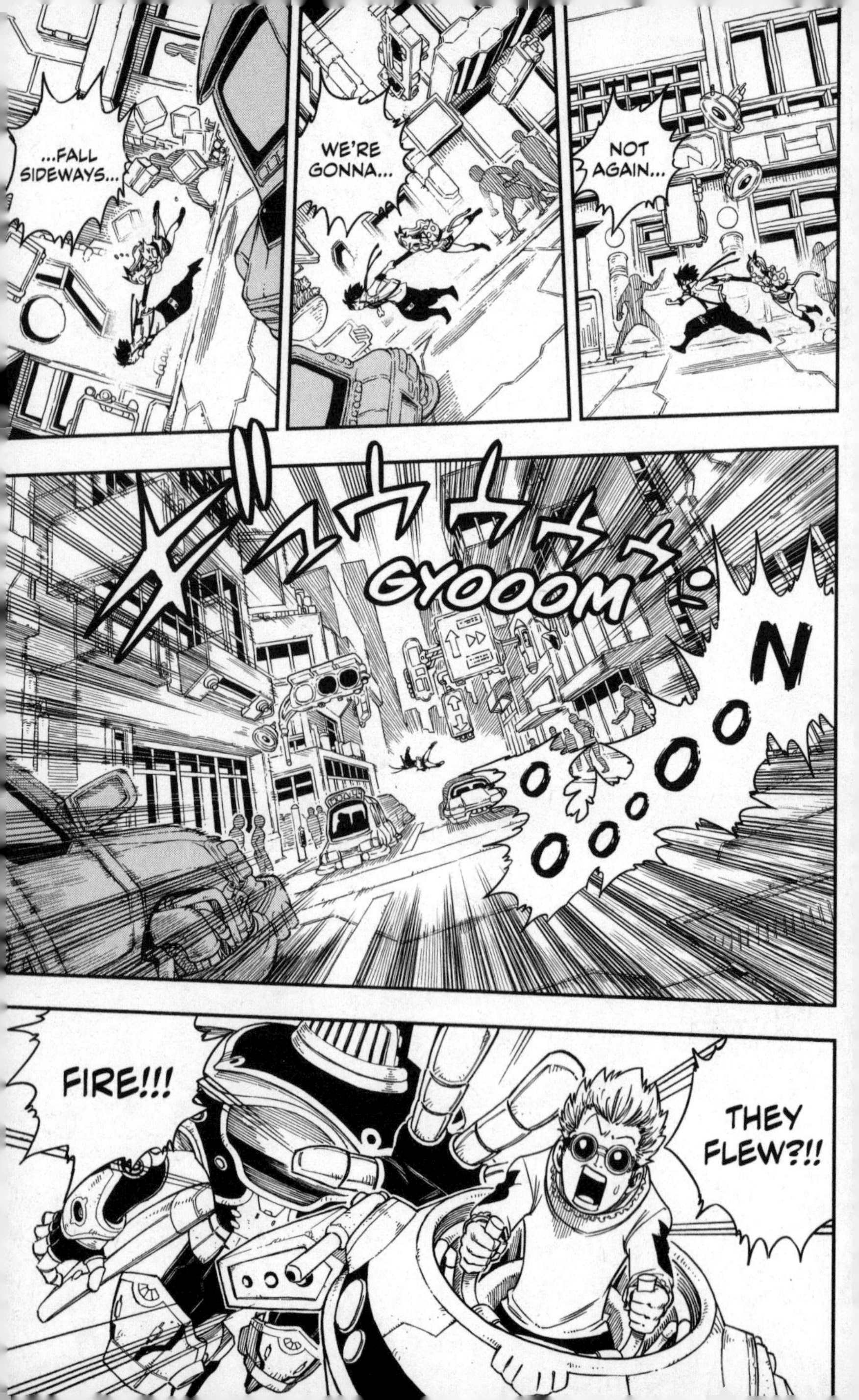
NOT AGAIN...
WE'RE GONNA...
...FALL SIDEWAYS...
GYOOOM
THEY FLEW?!!
FIRE!!!

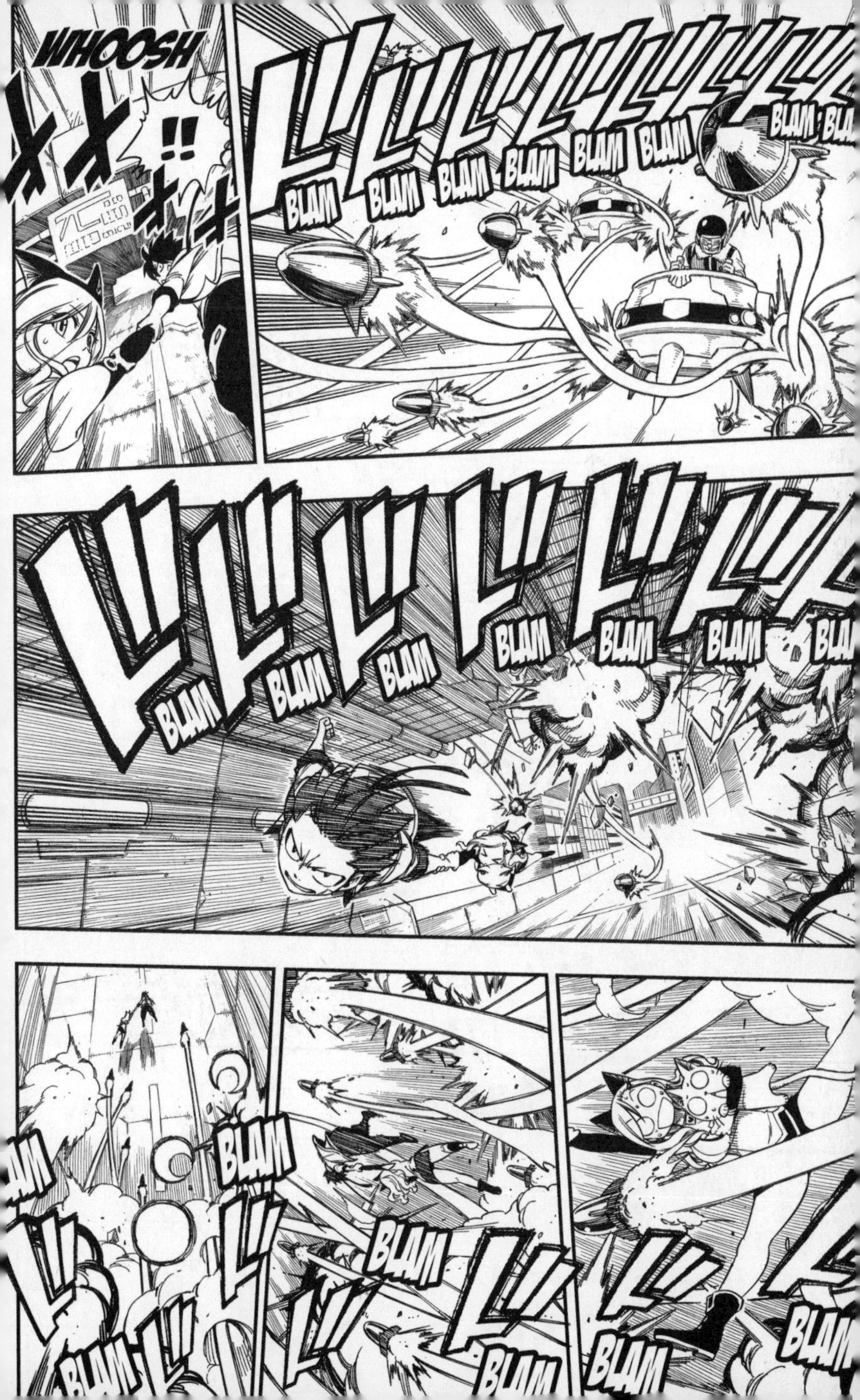

BLAM BLAM BLAM BLAM BLAM BLAM BLAM BLAM
WHOOSH
BLAM BLAM BLAM BLAM BLAM BLAM BLAM
BLAM BLAM
BLAM BLAM
BLAM BLAM

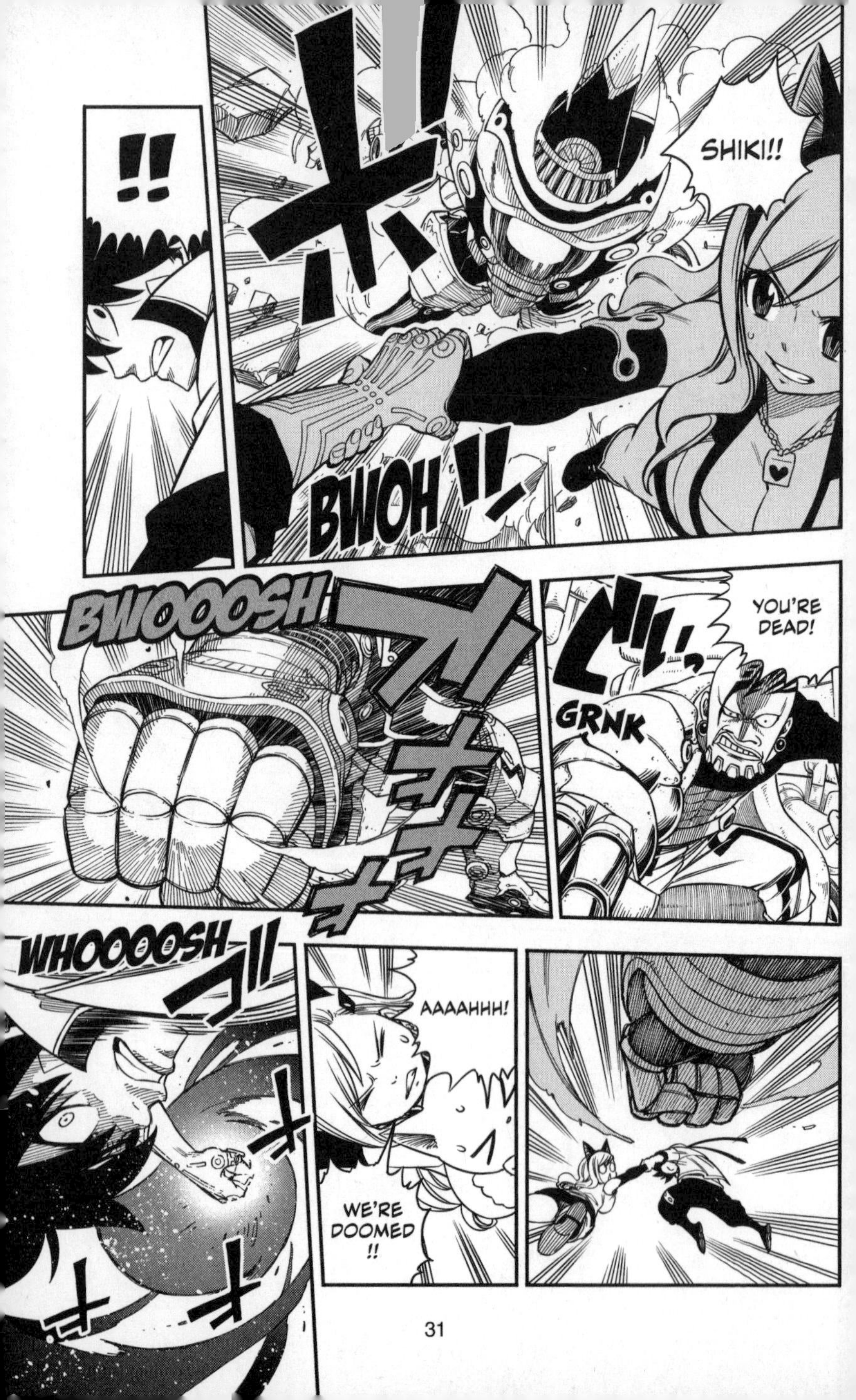
SHIKI!!
!!
BWOH !!
YOU'RE DEAD!
GRNK
BWOOOSH
AAAAHHH!
WE'RE DOOMED !!
WHOOOOSH

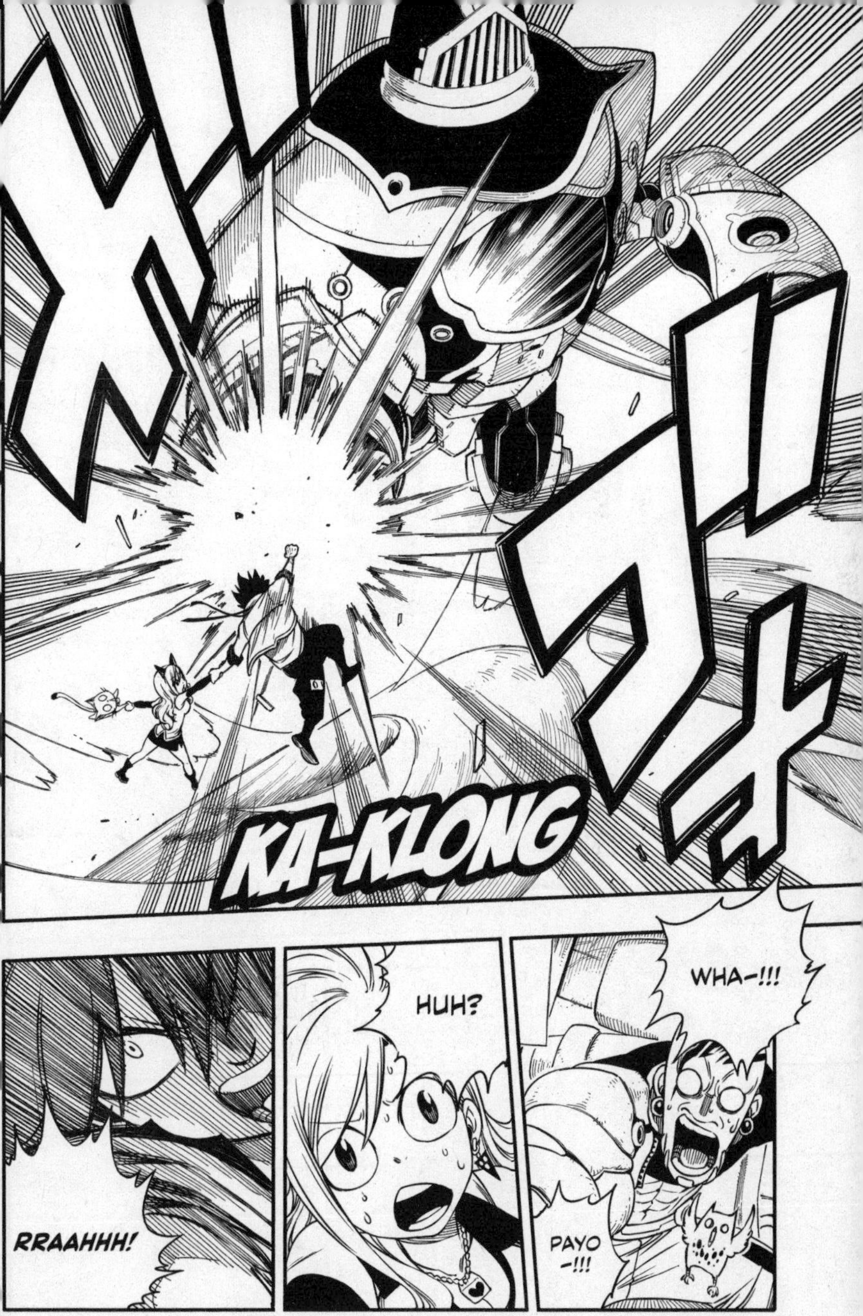
KA-KLONG
WHA-!!!
PAYO
-!!!
HUH?
RRAAHHH!

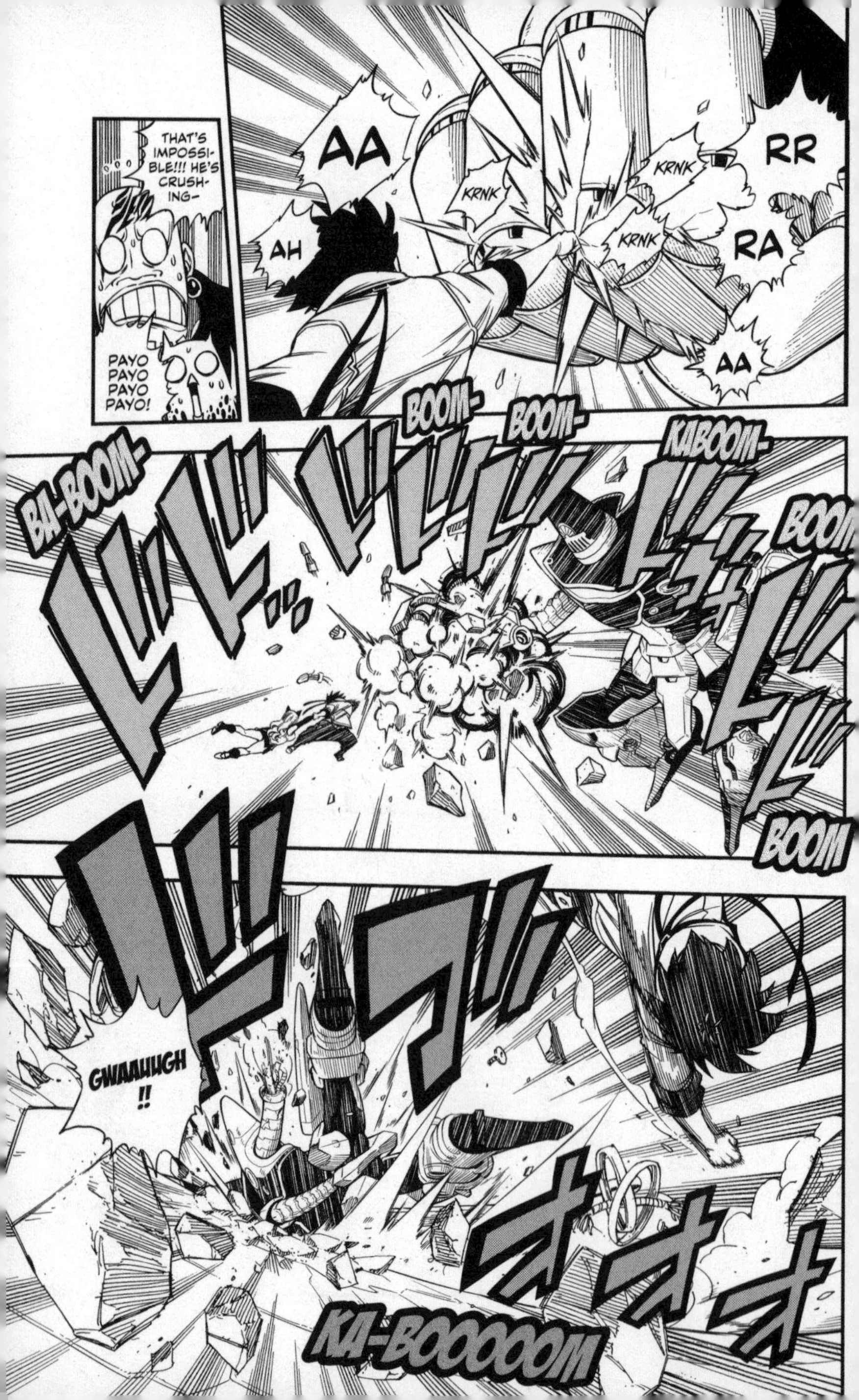

RR
RA
AA
KRNK
KRNK
KRNK
AA
AH
THAT'S IMPOSSI-BLE!!! HE'S CRUSH-ING–
PAYO PAYO PAYO PAYO!
BOOM
KABOOM-
BOOM-
BOOM-
BA-BOOM-
BOOM
GWAAUUGH !!
KA-BOOOOOM

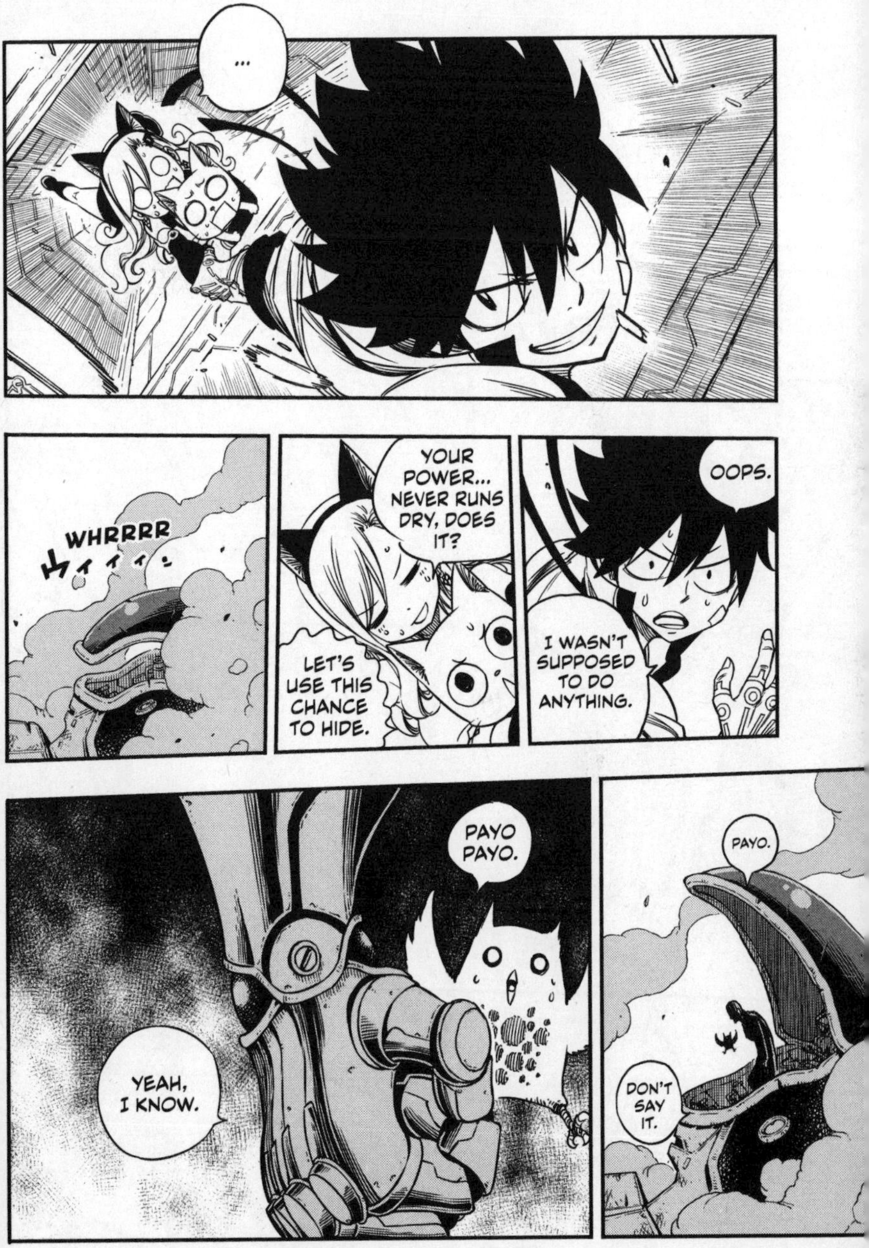
...
OOPS.
I WASN'T SUPPOSED TO DO ANYTHING.
YOUR POWER... NEVER RUNS DRY, DOES IT?
LET'S USE THIS CHANCE TO HIDE.
WHRRRR
PAYO.
DON'T SAY IT.
PAYO PAYO.
YEAH, I KNOW.

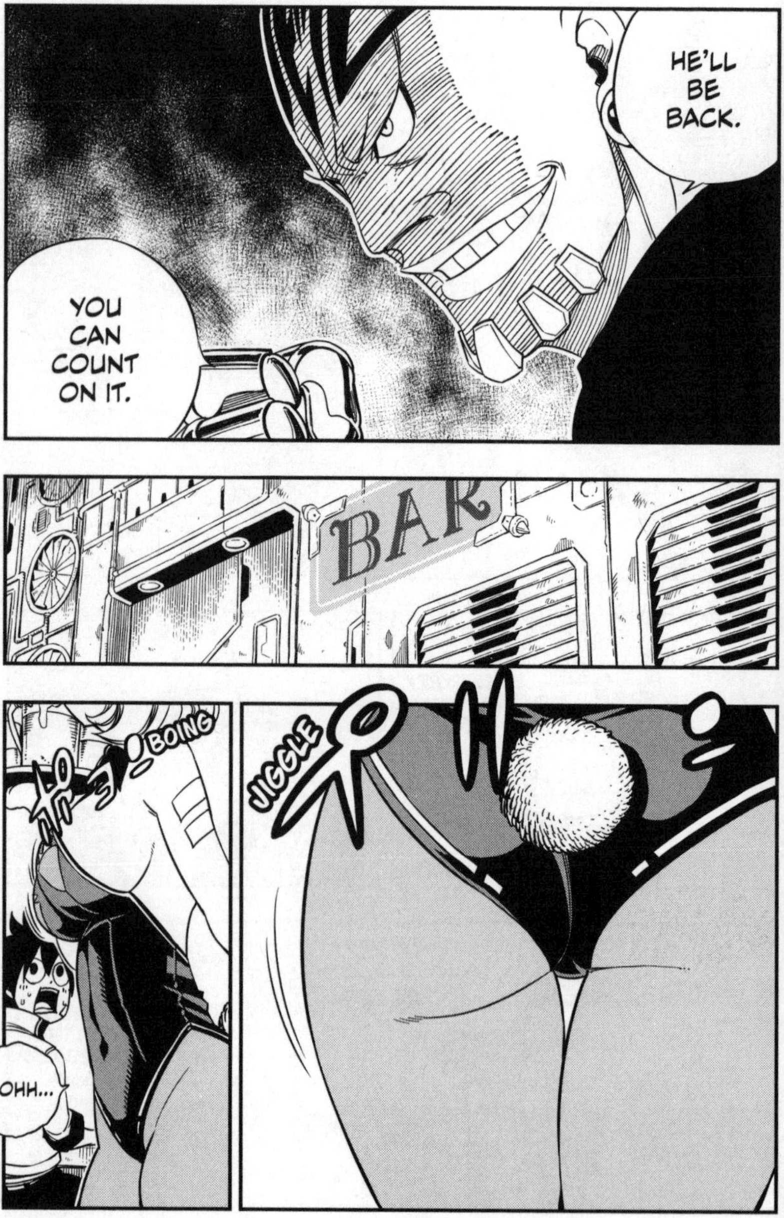
HE'LL BE BACK.
YOU CAN COUNT ON IT.
BAR
JIGGLE
BOING
OOHH...

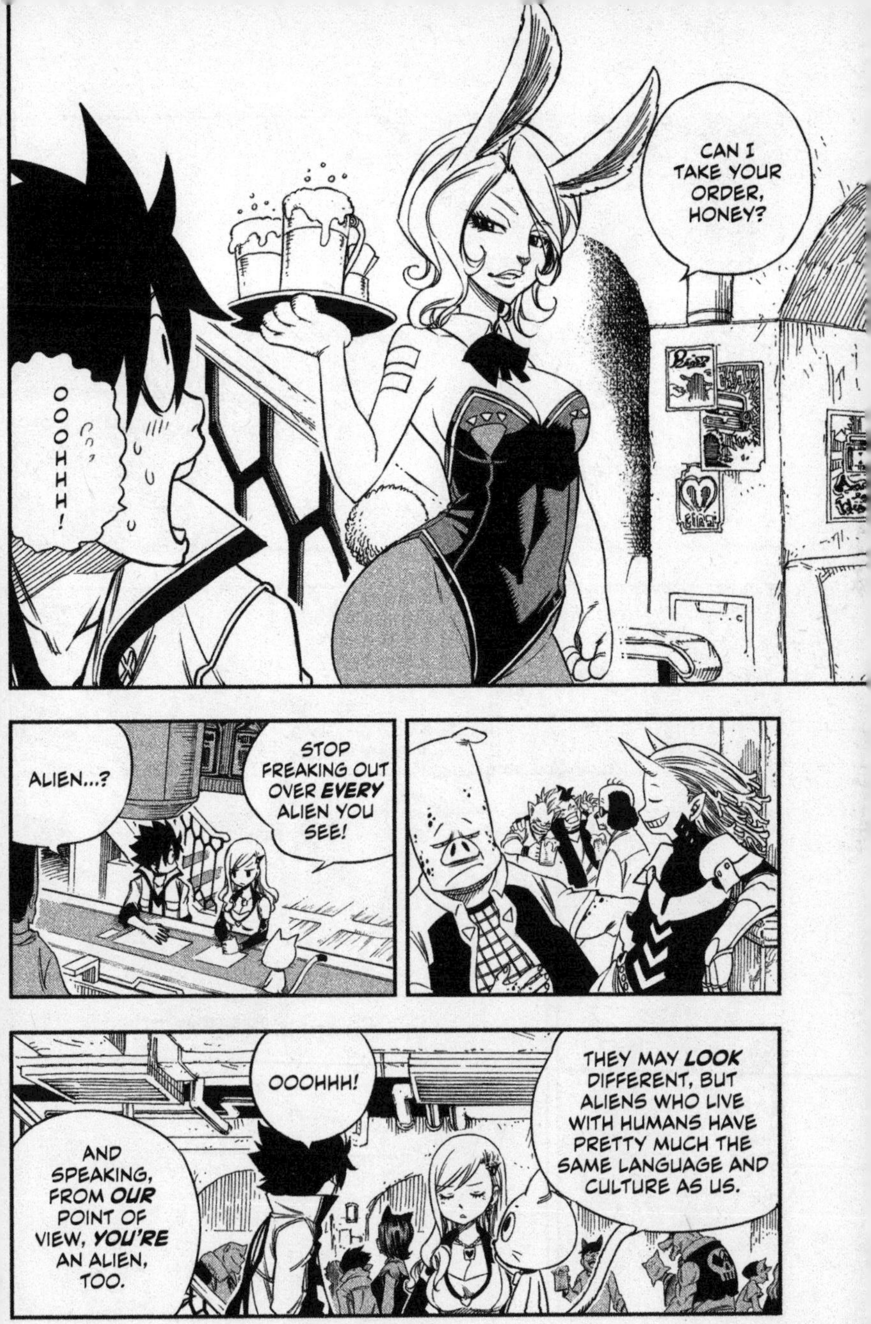
CAN I TAKE YOUR ORDER, HONEY?
OOOOHHH!
STOP FREAKING OUT OVER EVERY ALIEN YOU SEE!
ALIEN...?
THEY MAY LOOK DIFFERENT, BUT ALIENS WHO LIVE WITH HUMANS HAVE PRETTY MUCH THE SAME LANGUAGE AND CULTURE AS US.
OOOHHH!
AND SPEAKING, FROM OUR POINT OF VIEW, YOU'RE AN ALIEN, TOO.

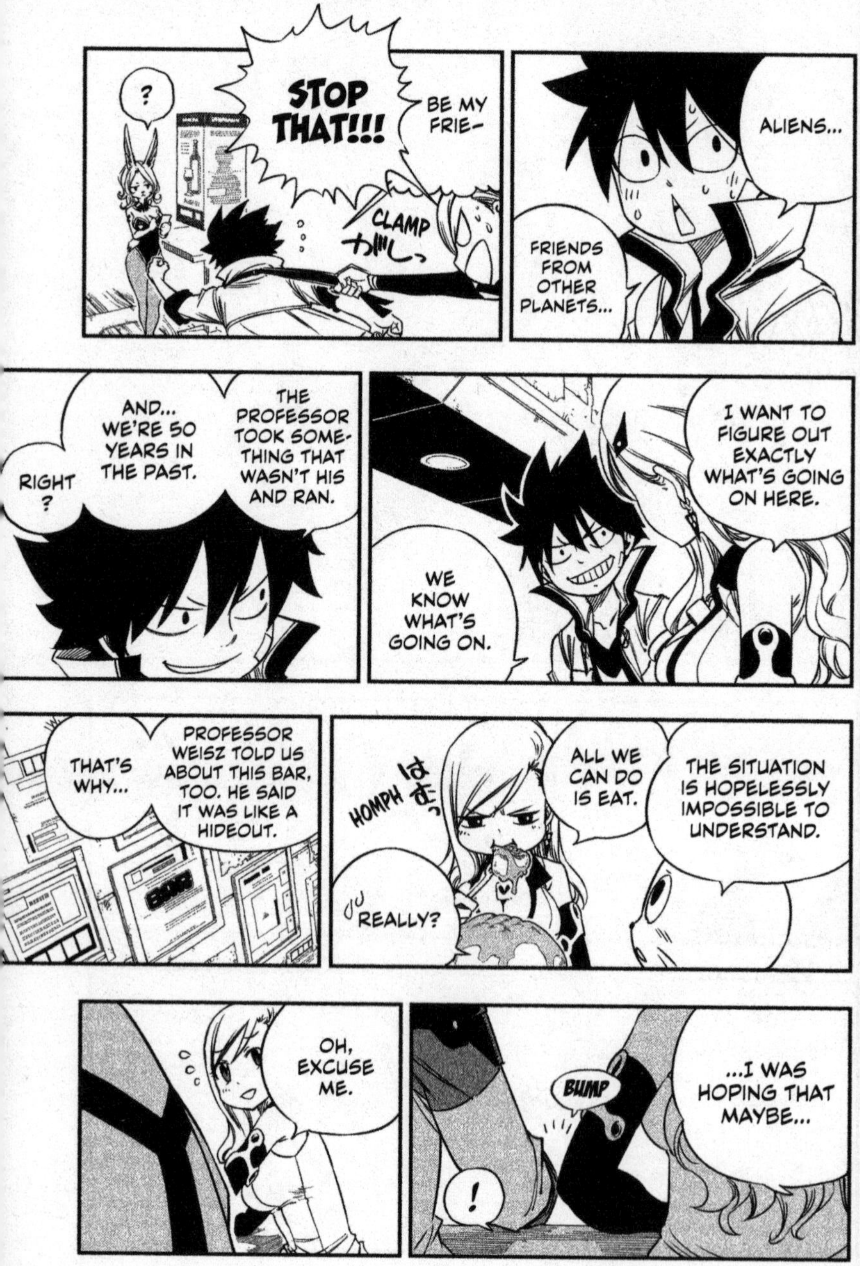
ALIENS...
FRIENDS FROM OTHER PLANETS...
BE MY FRIE-
STOP THAT!!!
?
CLAMP
I WANT TO FIGURE OUT EXACTLY WHAT'S GOING ON HERE.
WE KNOW WHAT'S GOING ON.
THE PROFESSOR TOOK SOMETHING THAT WASN'T HIS AND RAN.
AND... WE'RE 50 YEARS IN THE PAST.
RIGHT?
THE SITUATION IS HOPELESSLY IMPOSSIBLE TO UNDERSTAND.
ALL WE CAN DO IS EAT.
HOMPH
REALLY?
PROFESSOR WEISZ TOLD US ABOUT THIS BAR, TOO. HE SAID IT WAS LIKE A HIDEOUT.
THAT'S WHY...
...I WAS HOPING THAT MAYBE...
BUMP
!
OH, EXCUSE ME.

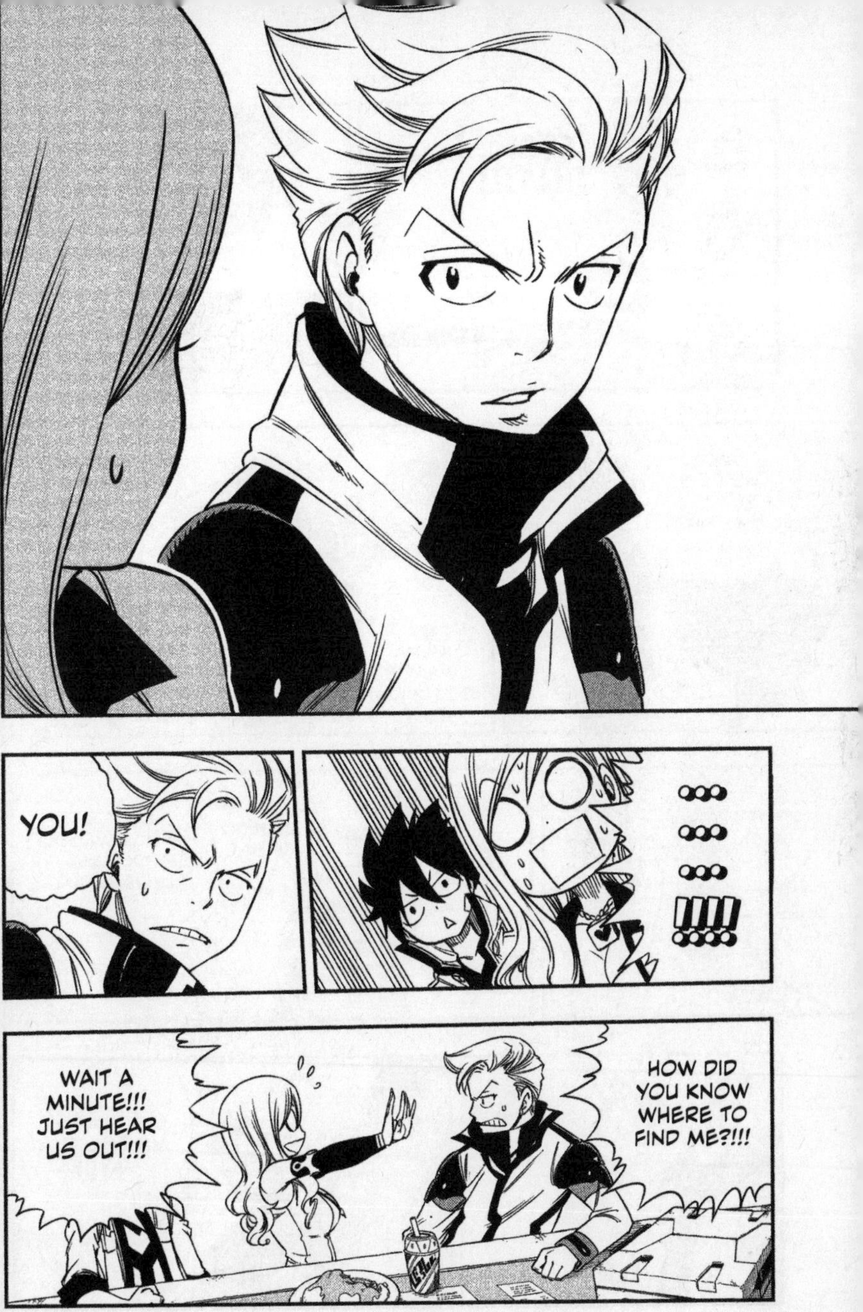
.........!!!!....
YOU!
HOW DID YOU KNOW WHERE TO FIND ME?!!!
WAIT A MINUTE!!! JUST HEAR US OUT!!!

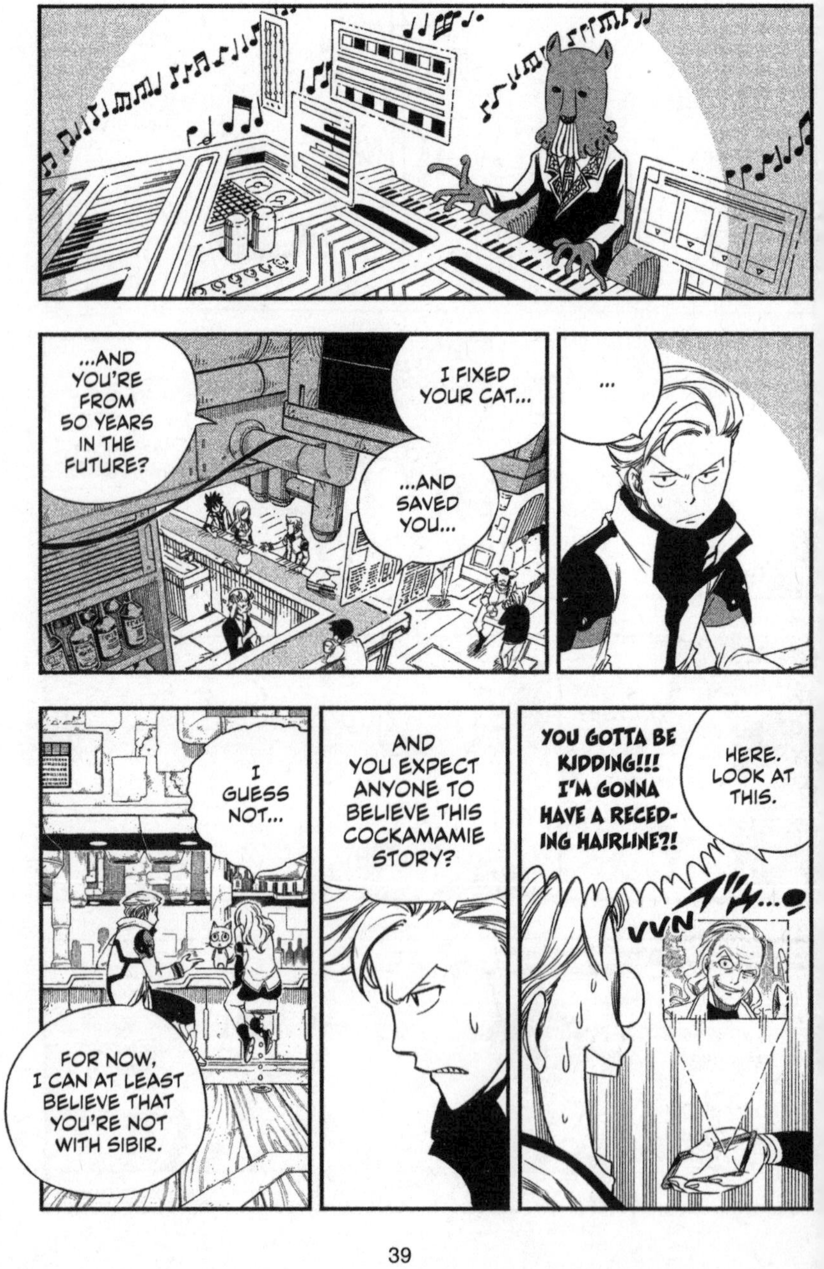
...
I FIXED YOUR CAT...
...AND SAVED YOU...
...AND YOU'RE FROM 50 YEARS IN THE FUTURE?
HERE. LOOK AT THIS.
YOU GOTTA BE KIDDING!!! I'M GONNA HAVE A RECED-ING HAIRLINE?!
VVN
...!
AND YOU EXPECT ANYONE TO BELIEVE THIS COCKAMAMIE STORY?
I GUESS NOT...
FOR NOW, I CAN AT LEAST BELIEVE THAT YOU'RE NOT WITH SIBIR.

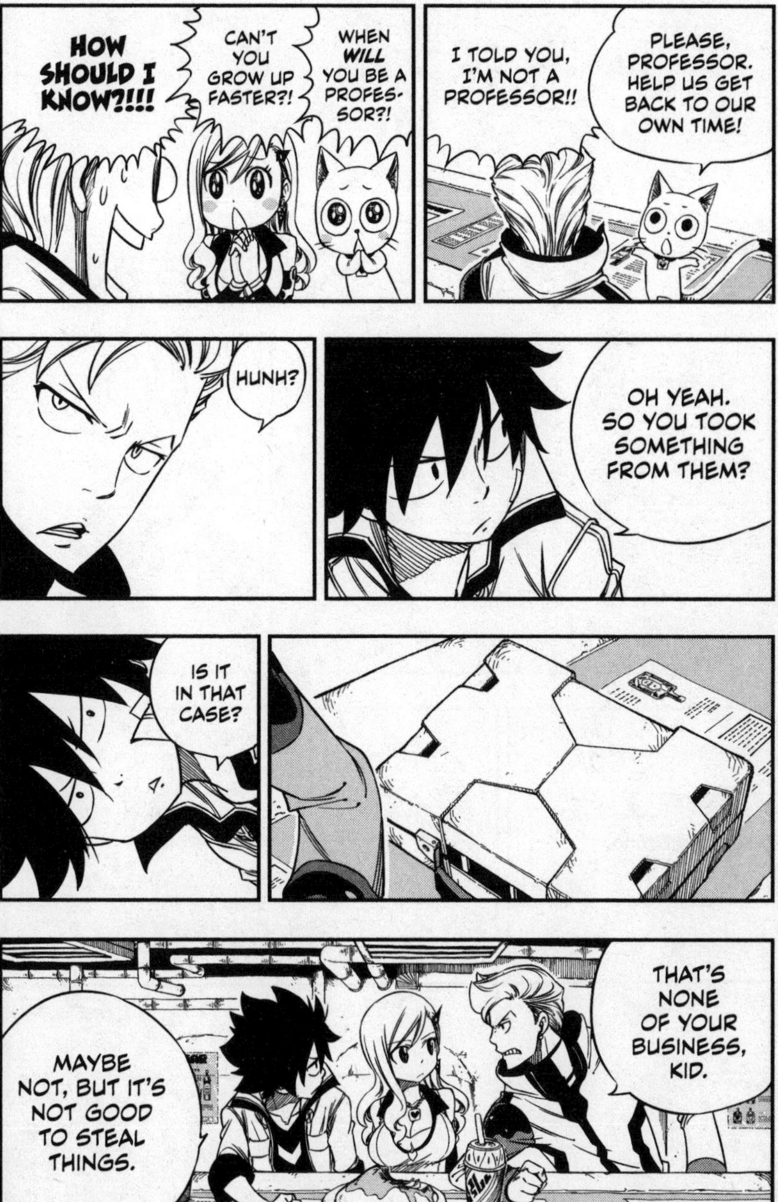
PLEASE, PROFESSOR. HELP US GET BACK TO OUR OWN TIME!
I TOLD YOU, I'M NOT A PROFESSOR!!
WHEN WILL YOU BE A PROFES-SOR?!
CAN'T YOU GROW UP FASTER?!
HOW SHOULD I KNOW?!!!
OH YEAH. SO YOU TOOK SOMETHING FROM THEM?
HUNH?
IS IT IN THAT CASE?
THAT'S NONE OF YOUR BUSINESS, KID.
MAYBE NOT, BUT IT'S NOT GOOD TO STEAL THINGS.

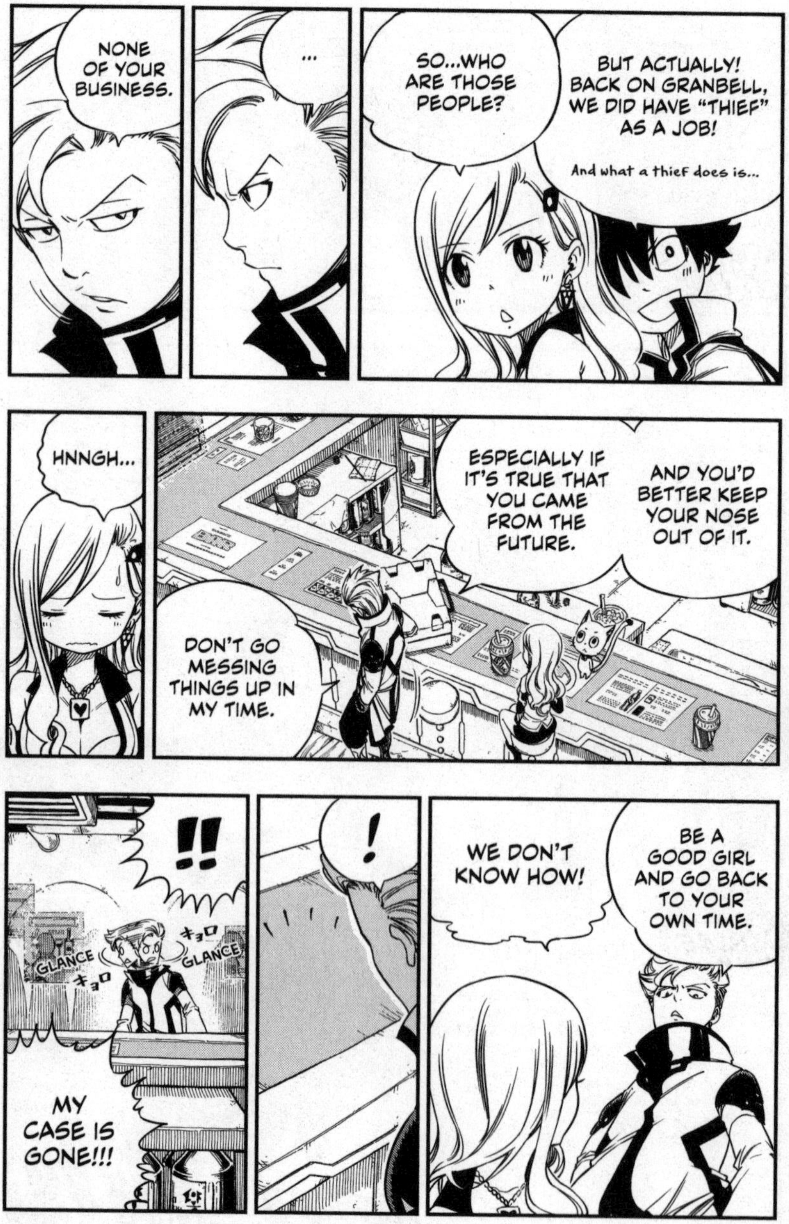
BUT ACTUALLY! BACK ON GRANBELL, WE DID HAVE "THIEF" AS A JOB!
And what a thief does is...
SO...WHO ARE THOSE PEOPLE?
...
NONE OF YOUR BUSINESS.
AND YOU'D BETTER KEEP YOUR NOSE OUT OF IT.
ESPECIALLY IF IT'S TRUE THAT YOU CAME FROM THE FUTURE.
DON'T GO MESSING THINGS UP IN MY TIME.
HNNGH...
BE A GOOD GIRL AND GO BACK TO YOUR OWN TIME.
WE DON'T KNOW HOW!
!
!!
キョロ
GLANCE
GLANCE
キョロ
MY CASE IS GONE!!!

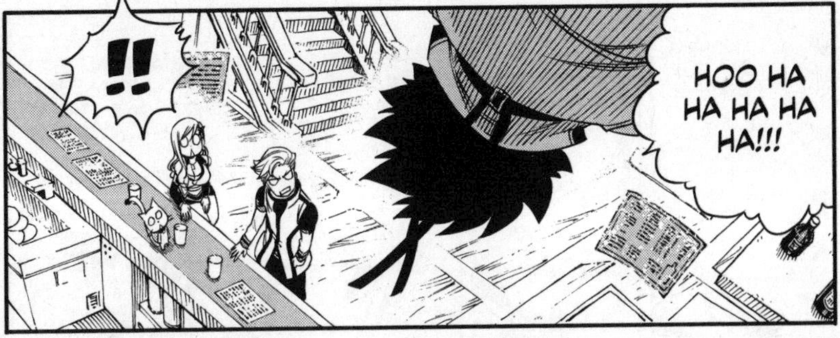
HOO HA HA HA HA HA!!!
!!
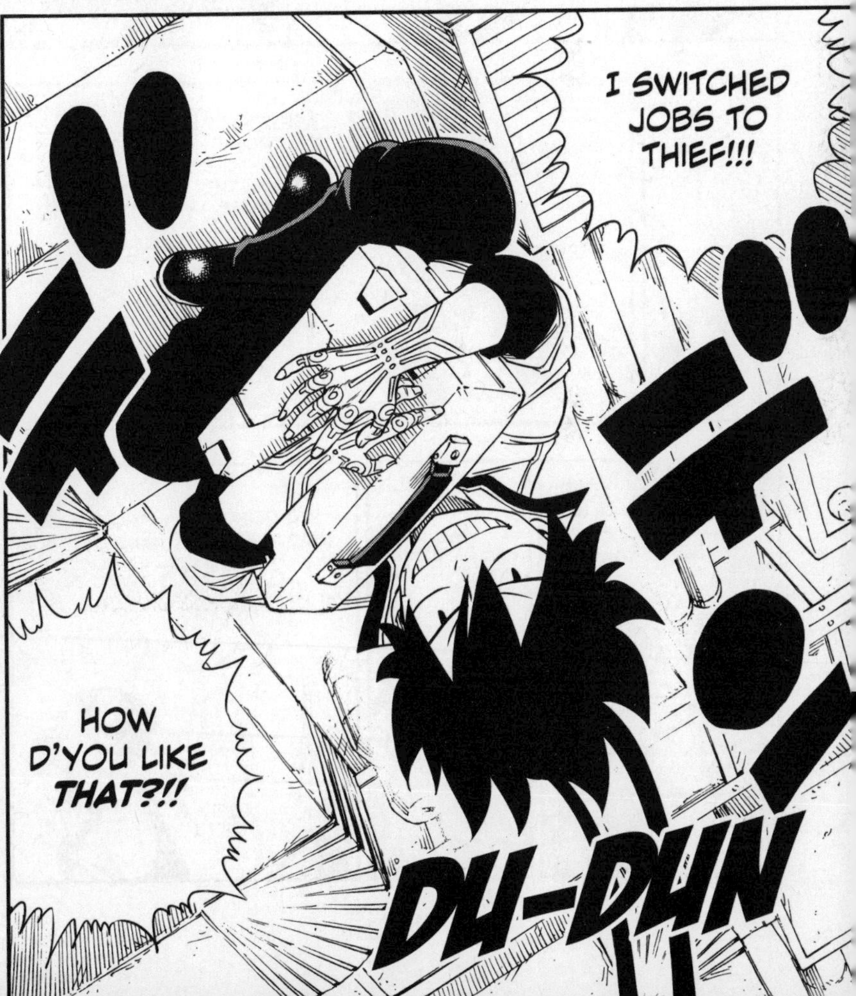
I SWITCHED JOBS TO THIEF!!!
HOW D'YOU LIKE *THAT?!!*
DU-DUN

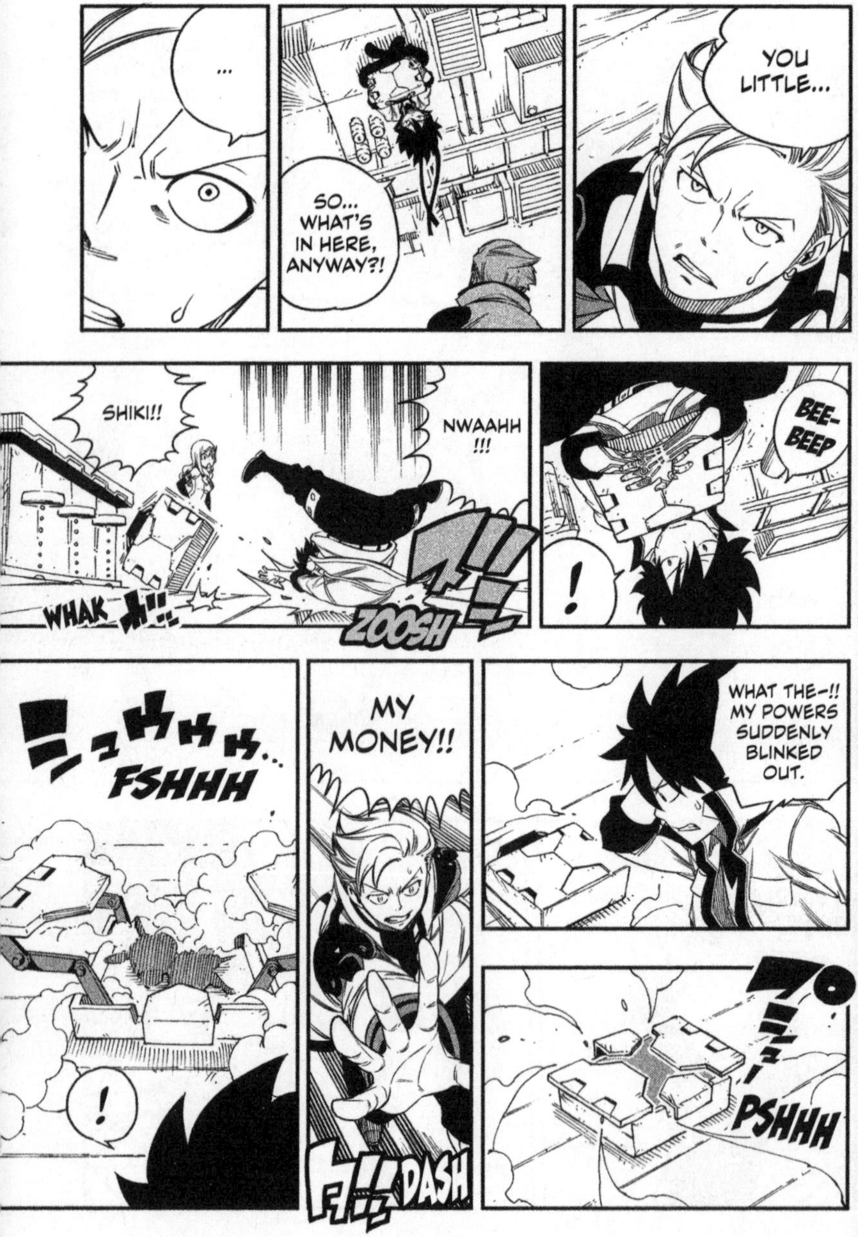
YOU LITTLE...
SO... WHAT'S IN HERE, ANYWAY?!
...
BEE-BEEP
!
NWAAHH!!!
ZOOSH
SHIKI!!
WHAK
WHAT THE-!! MY POWERS SUDDENLY BLINKED OUT.
PSHHH
MY MONEY!!
DASH
FSHHH
!

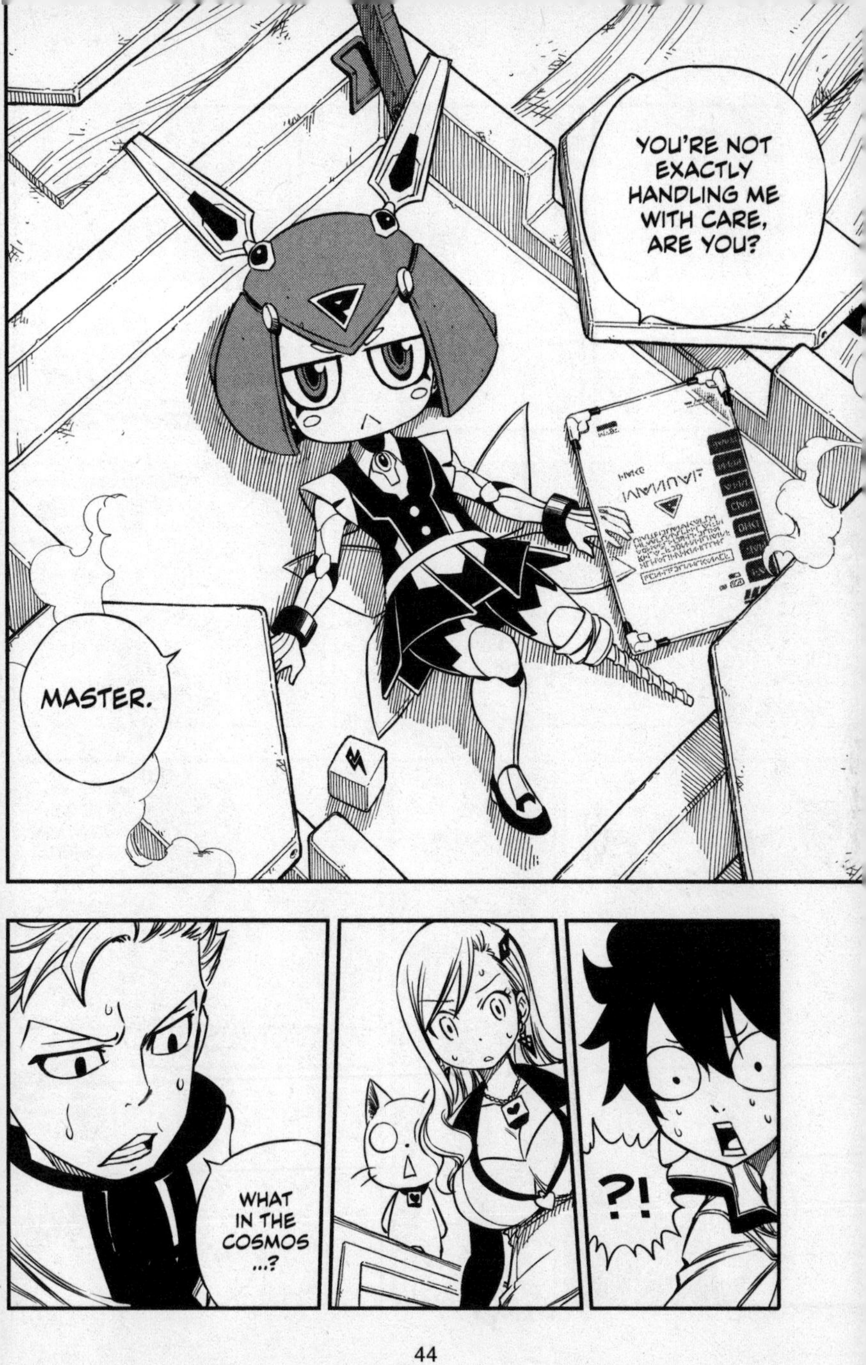
YOU'RE NOT EXACTLY HANDLING ME WITH CARE, ARE YOU?
MASTER.
?!
WHAT IN THE COSMOS ...?

# EDENS ZERO

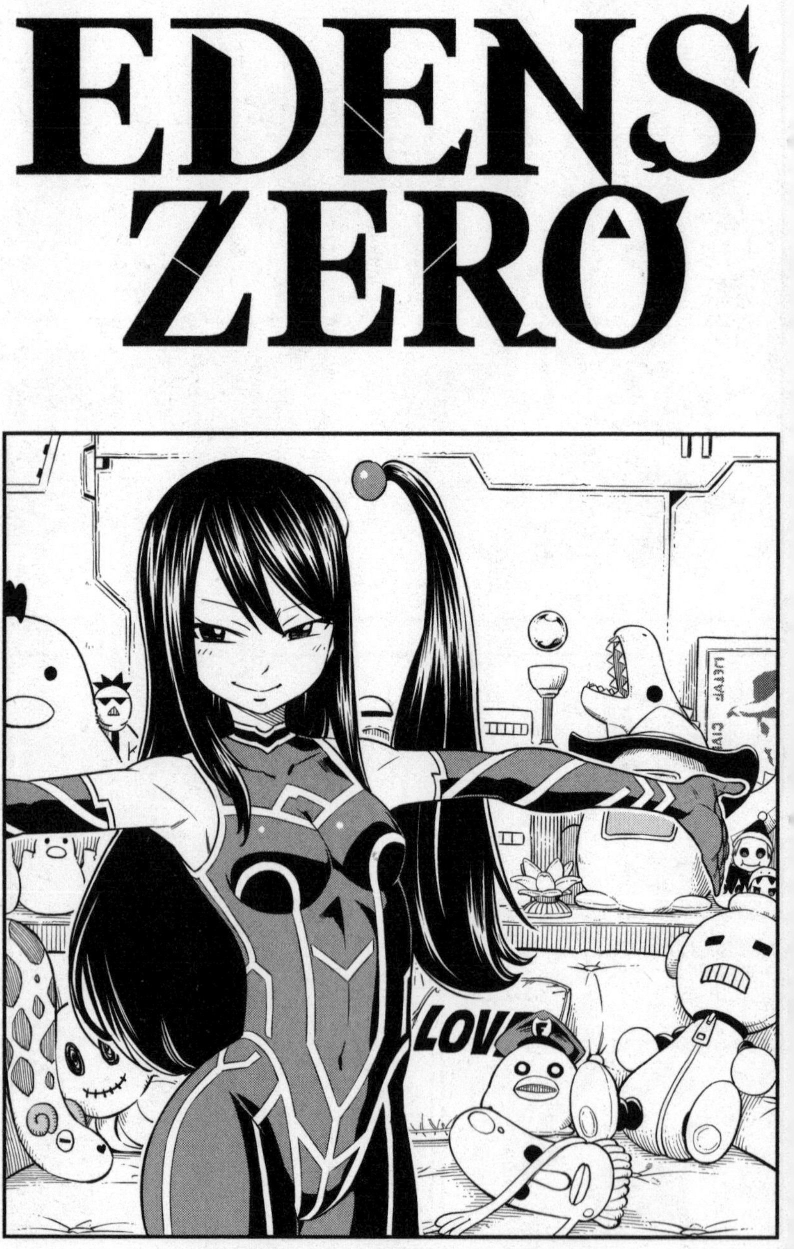

## CHAPTER 7: IRON TEARS

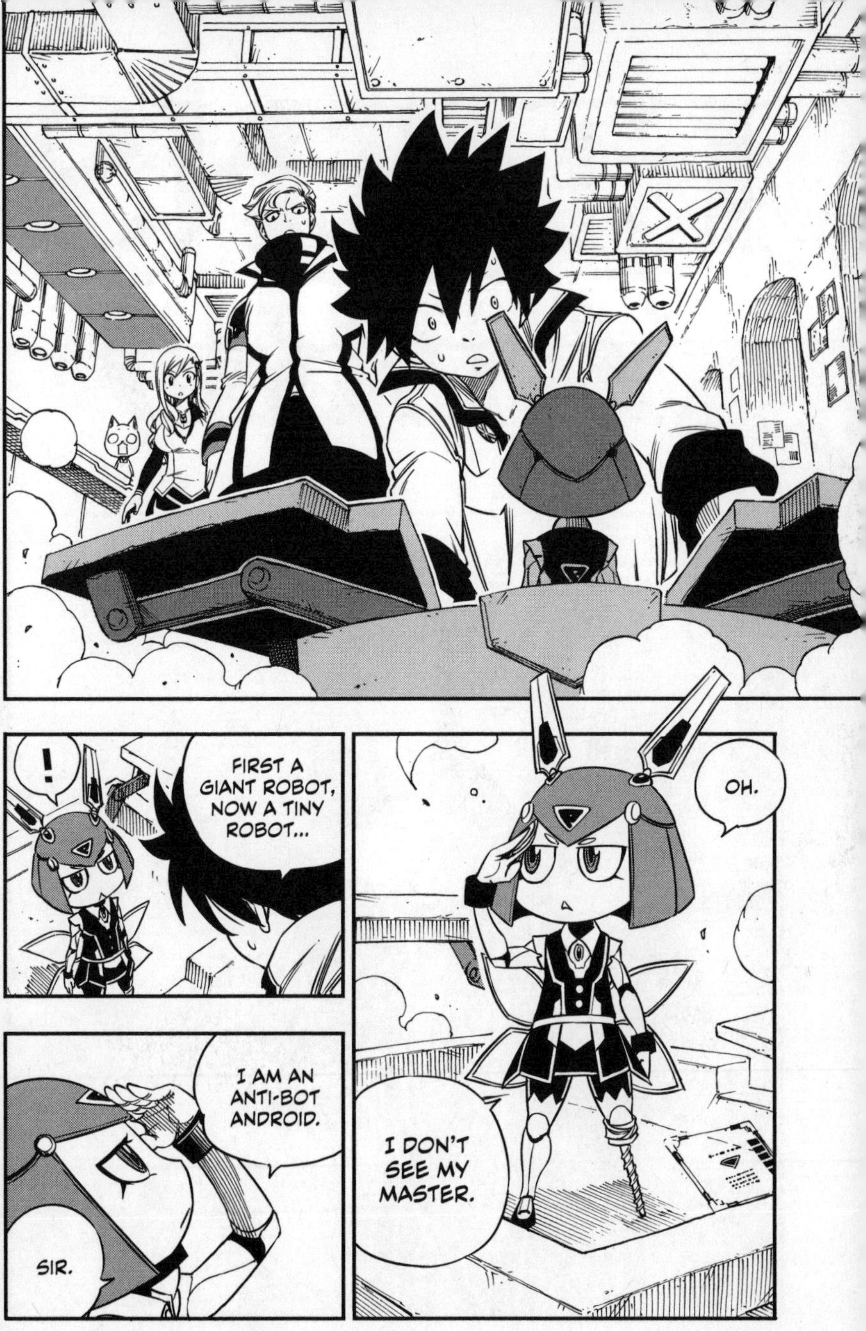
OH.
I DON'T SEE MY MASTER.
FIRST A GIANT ROBOT, NOW A TINY ROBOT...
!
I AM AN ANTI-BOT ANDROID.
SIR.

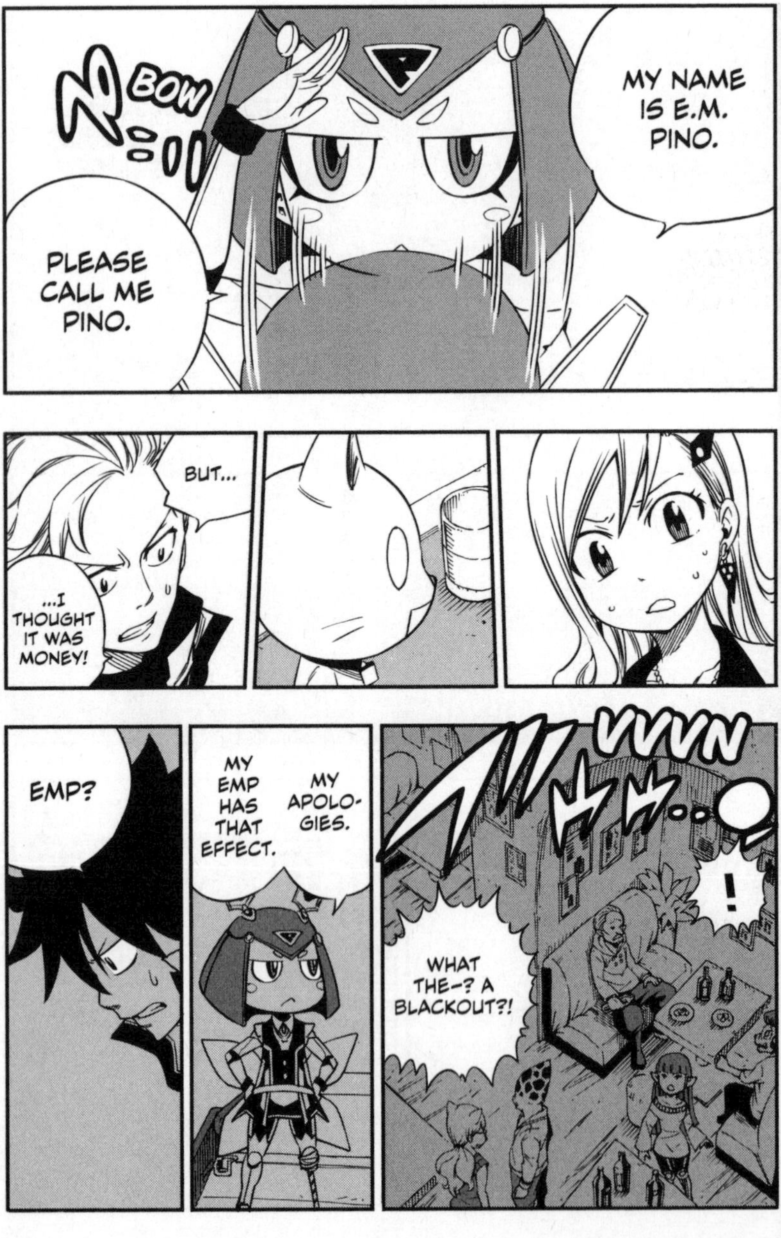
MY NAME IS E.M. PINO.
BOW
PLEASE CALL ME PINO.
BUT...
...I THOUGHT IT WAS MONEY!
VVVN
!
WHAT THE-? A BLACKOUT?!
MY APOLOGIES.
MY EMP HAS THAT EFFECT.
EMP?

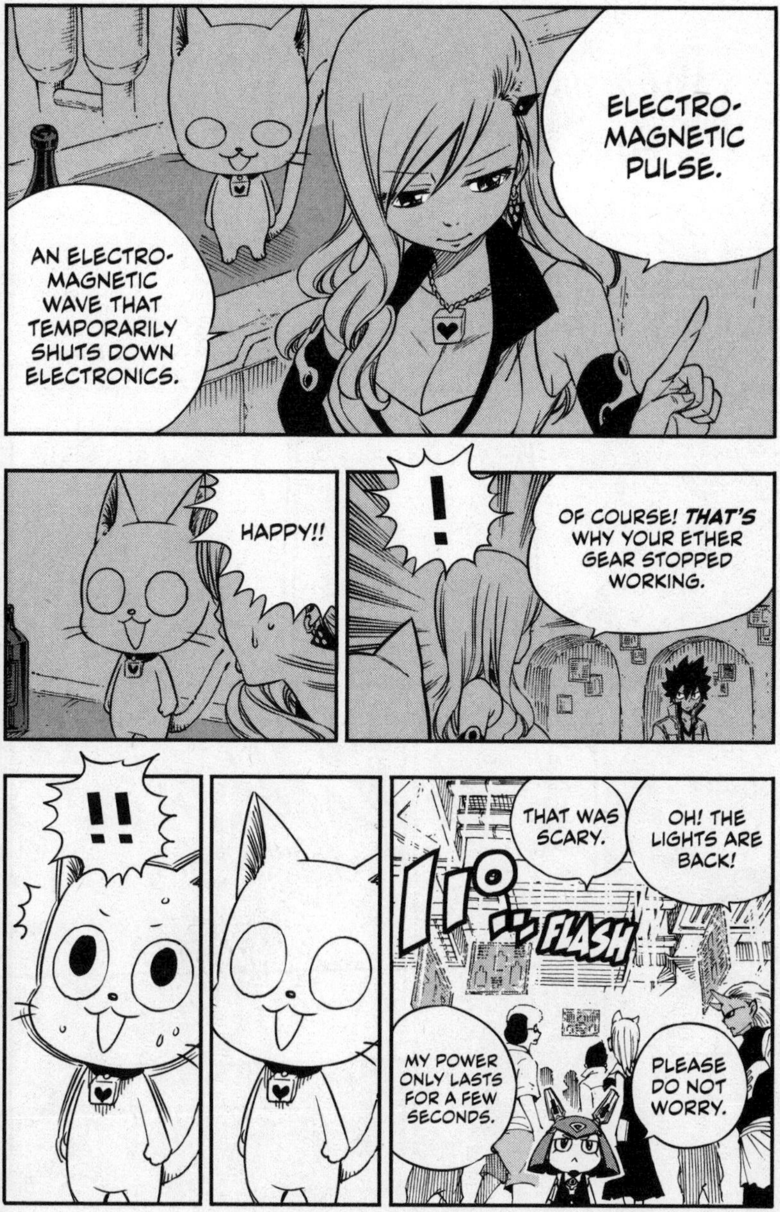
ELECTRO-MAGNETIC PULSE.
AN ELECTRO-MAGNETIC WAVE THAT TEMPORARILY SHUTS DOWN ELECTRONICS.
!
OF COURSE! *THAT'S* WHY YOUR ETHER GEAR STOPPED WORKING.
HAPPY!!
OH! THE LIGHTS ARE BACK!
THAT WAS SCARY.
FLASH
PLEASE DO NOT WORRY.
MY POWER ONLY LASTS FOR A FEW SECONDS.
!!

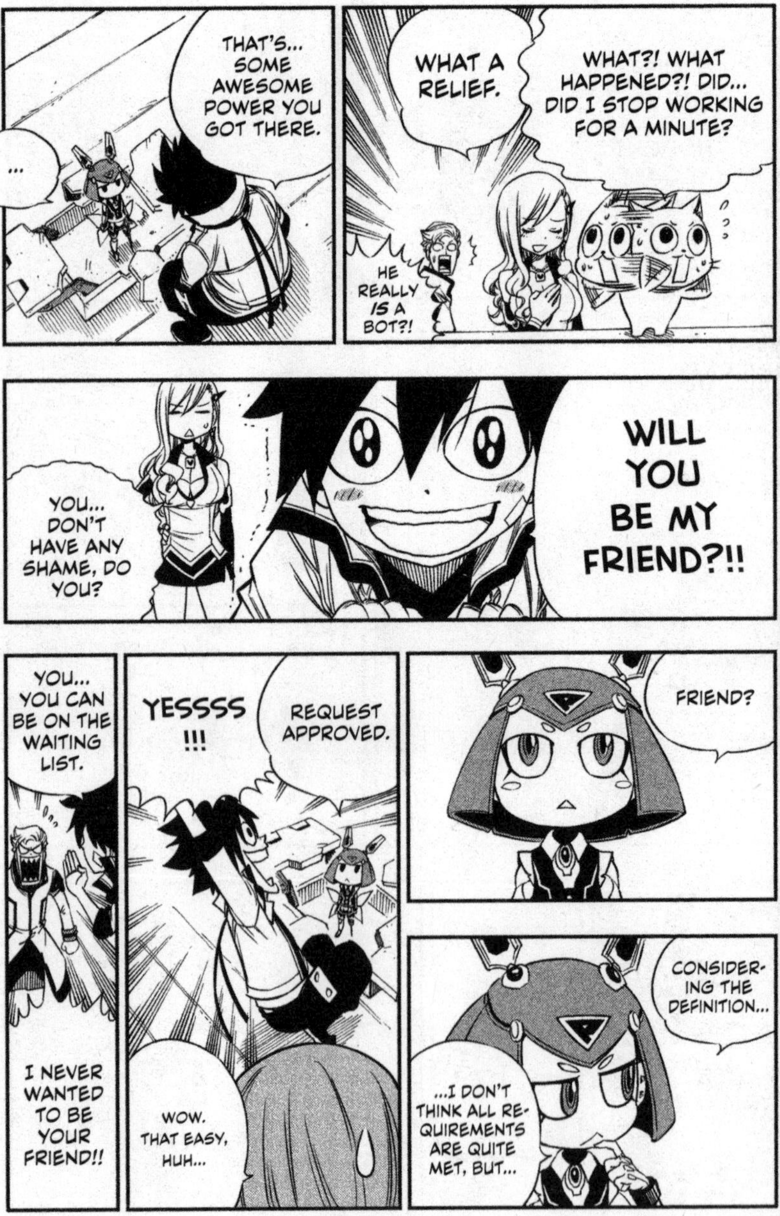
WHAT?! WHAT HAPPENED?! DID... DID I STOP WORKING FOR A MINUTE?
WHAT A RELIEF.
HE REALLY *IS* A BOT?!
THAT'S... SOME AWESOME POWER YOU GOT THERE.
...
WILL YOU BE MY FRIEND?!!
YOU... DON'T HAVE ANY SHAME, DO YOU?
FRIEND?
CONSIDERING THE DEFINITION...
...I DON'T THINK ALL REQUIREMENTS ARE QUITE MET, BUT...
REQUEST APPROVED.
YESSSS!!!
WOW. THAT EASY, HUH...
YOU... YOU CAN BE ON THE WAITING LIST.
I NEVER WANTED TO BE YOUR FRIEND!!

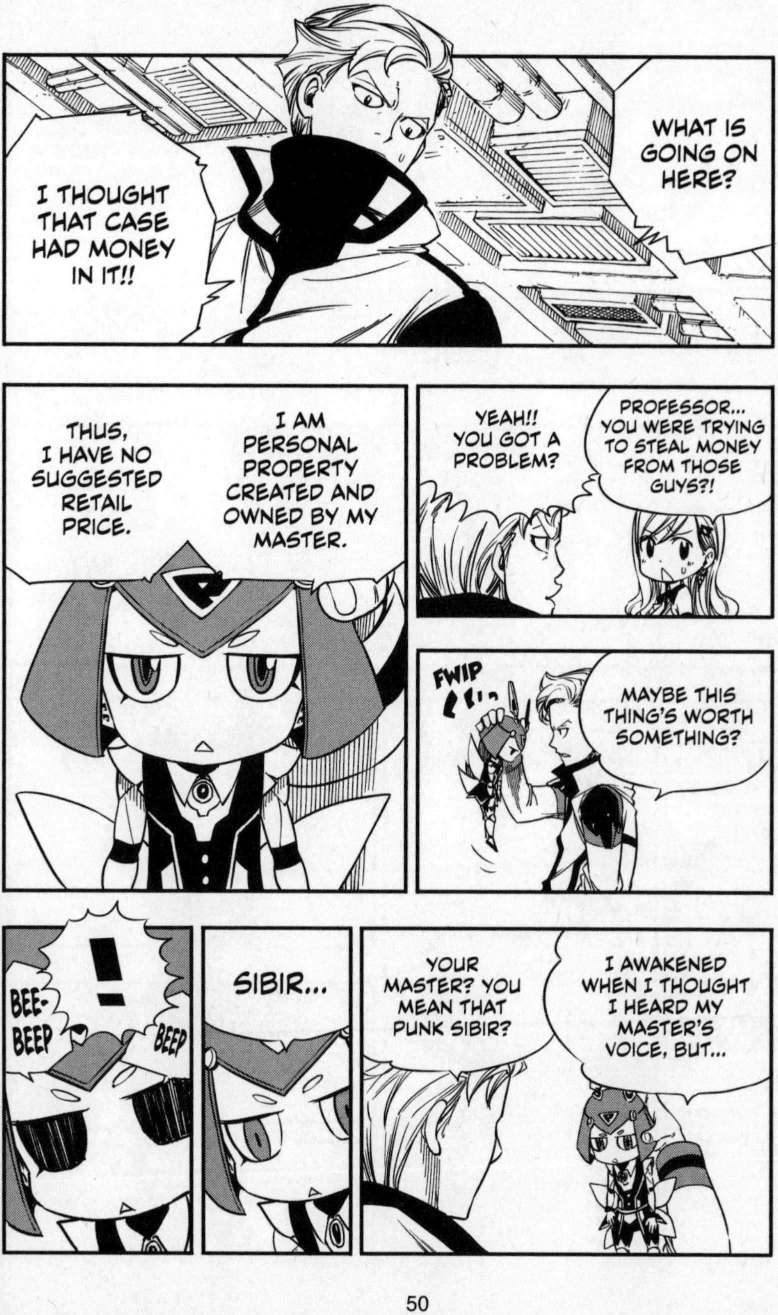
WHAT IS GOING ON HERE?
I THOUGHT THAT CASE HAD MONEY IN IT!!
PROFESSOR... YOU WERE TRYING TO STEAL MONEY FROM THOSE GUYS?!
YEAH!! YOU GOT A PROBLEM?
MAYBE THIS THING'S WORTH SOMETHING?
FWIP
I AM PERSONAL PROPERTY CREATED AND OWNED BY MY MASTER.
THUS, I HAVE NO SUGGESTED RETAIL PRICE.
I AWAKENED WHEN I THOUGHT I HEARD MY MASTER'S VOICE, BUT...
YOUR MASTER? YOU MEAN THAT PUNK SIBIR?
SIBIR...
!
BEEP
BEE-BEEP

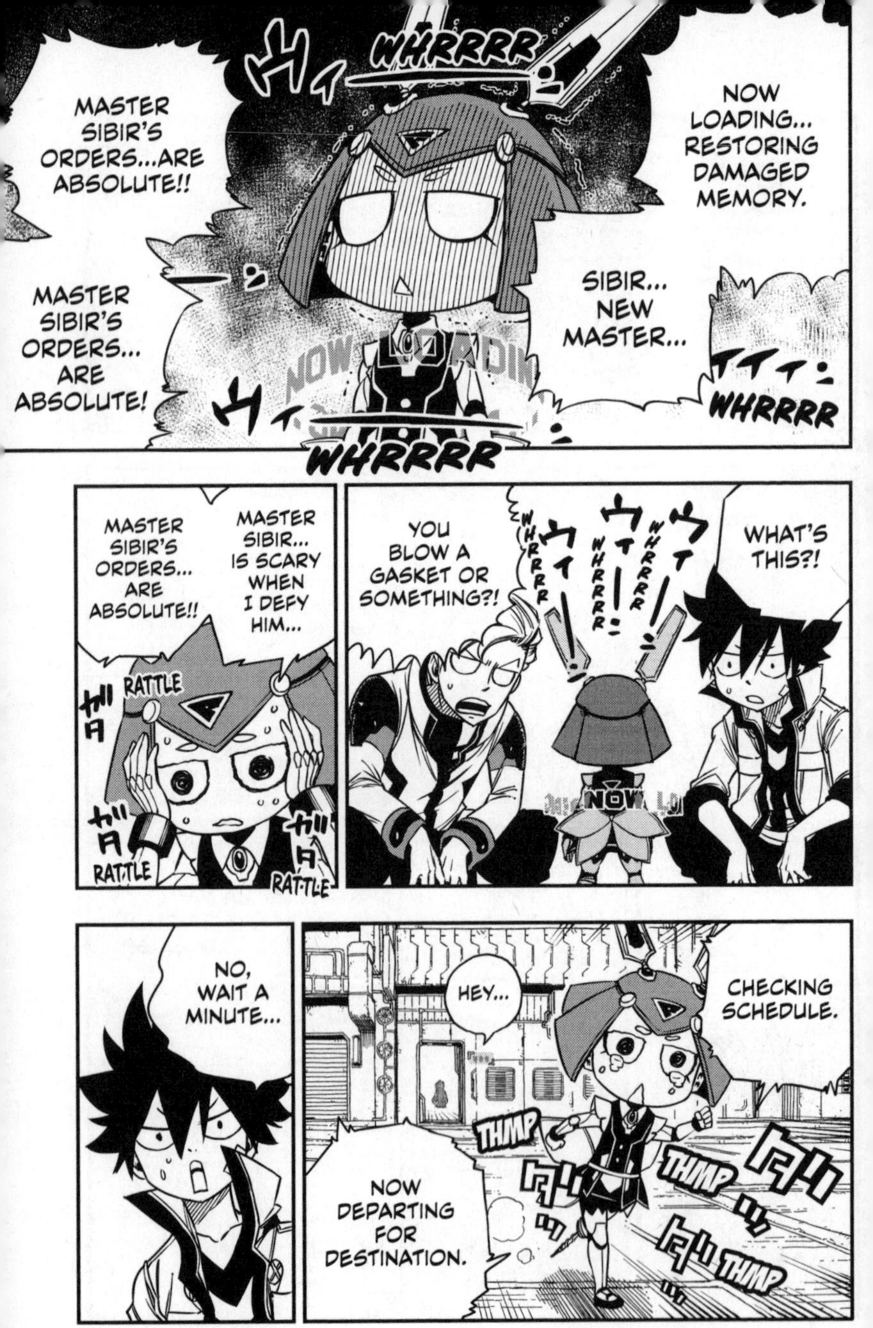
WHRRRR
NOW LOADING... RESTORING DAMAGED MEMORY.
MASTER SIBIR'S ORDERS...ARE ABSOLUTE!!
SIBIR... NEW MASTER...
WHRRRR
MASTER SIBIR'S ORDERS... ARE ABSOLUTE!
WHRRRR
WHAT'S THIS?!
WHRRRR
WHRRRR
WHRRRR
YOU BLOW A GASKET OR SOMETHING?!
NOW LO
MASTER SIBIR... IS SCARY WHEN I DEFY HIM...
MASTER SIBIR'S ORDERS... ARE ABSOLUTE!!
RATTLE
RATTLE
RATTLE
CHECKING SCHEDULE.
HEY...
THMP
THMP
THMP
NOW DEPARTING FOR DESTINATION.
NO, WAIT A MINUTE...

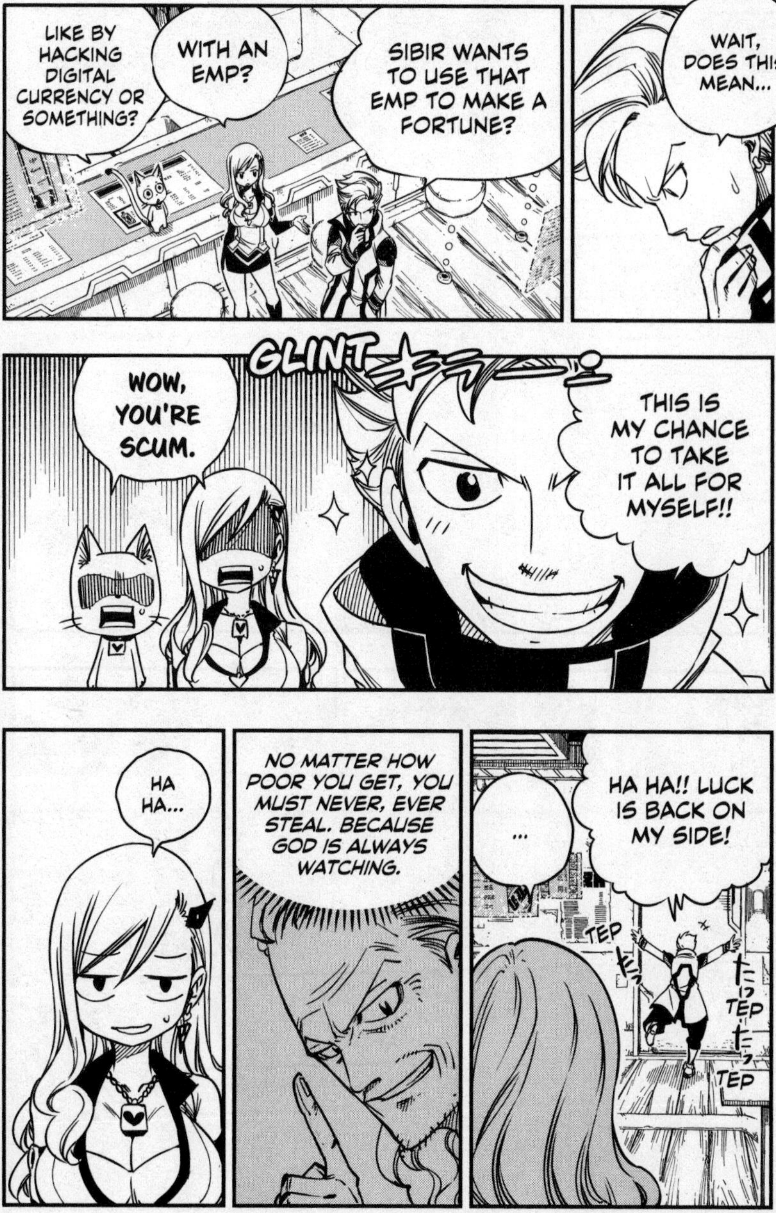
WAIT, DOES THIS MEAN...
SIBIR WANTS TO USE THAT EMP TO MAKE A FORTUNE?
WITH AN EMP?
LIKE BY HACKING DIGITAL CURRENCY OR SOMETHING?
GLINT
THIS IS MY CHANCE TO TAKE IT ALL FOR MYSELF!!
WOW, YOU'RE SCUM.
HA HA!! LUCK IS BACK ON MY SIDE!
...
TEP
TEP
TEP
NO MATTER HOW POOR YOU GET, YOU MUST NEVER, EVER STEAL. BECAUSE GOD IS ALWAYS WATCHING.
HA HA...

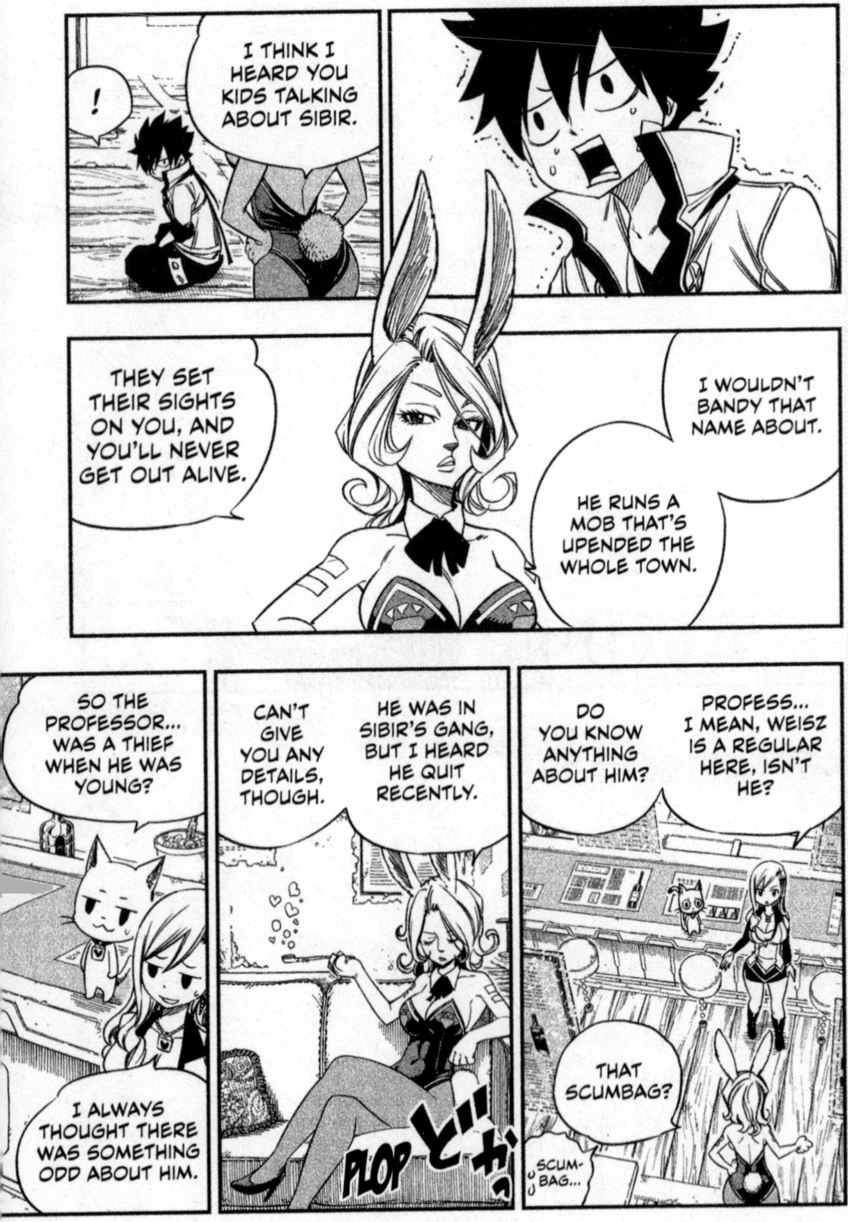
I THINK I HEARD YOU KIDS TALKING ABOUT SIBIR.
!
I WOULDN'T BANDY THAT NAME ABOUT.
HE RUNS A MOB THAT'S UPENDED THE WHOLE TOWN.
THEY SET THEIR SIGHTS ON YOU, AND YOU'LL NEVER GET OUT ALIVE.
PROFESS... I MEAN, WEISZ IS A REGULAR HERE, ISN'T HE?
DO YOU KNOW ANYTHING ABOUT HIM?
THAT SCUMBAG?
SCUM-BAG...
HE WAS IN SIBIR'S GANG, BUT I HEARD HE QUIT RECENTLY.
CAN'T GIVE YOU ANY DETAILS, THOUGH.
PLOP
SO THE PROFESSOR... WAS A THIEF WHEN HE WAS YOUNG?
I ALWAYS THOUGHT THERE WAS SOMETHING ODD ABOUT HIM.

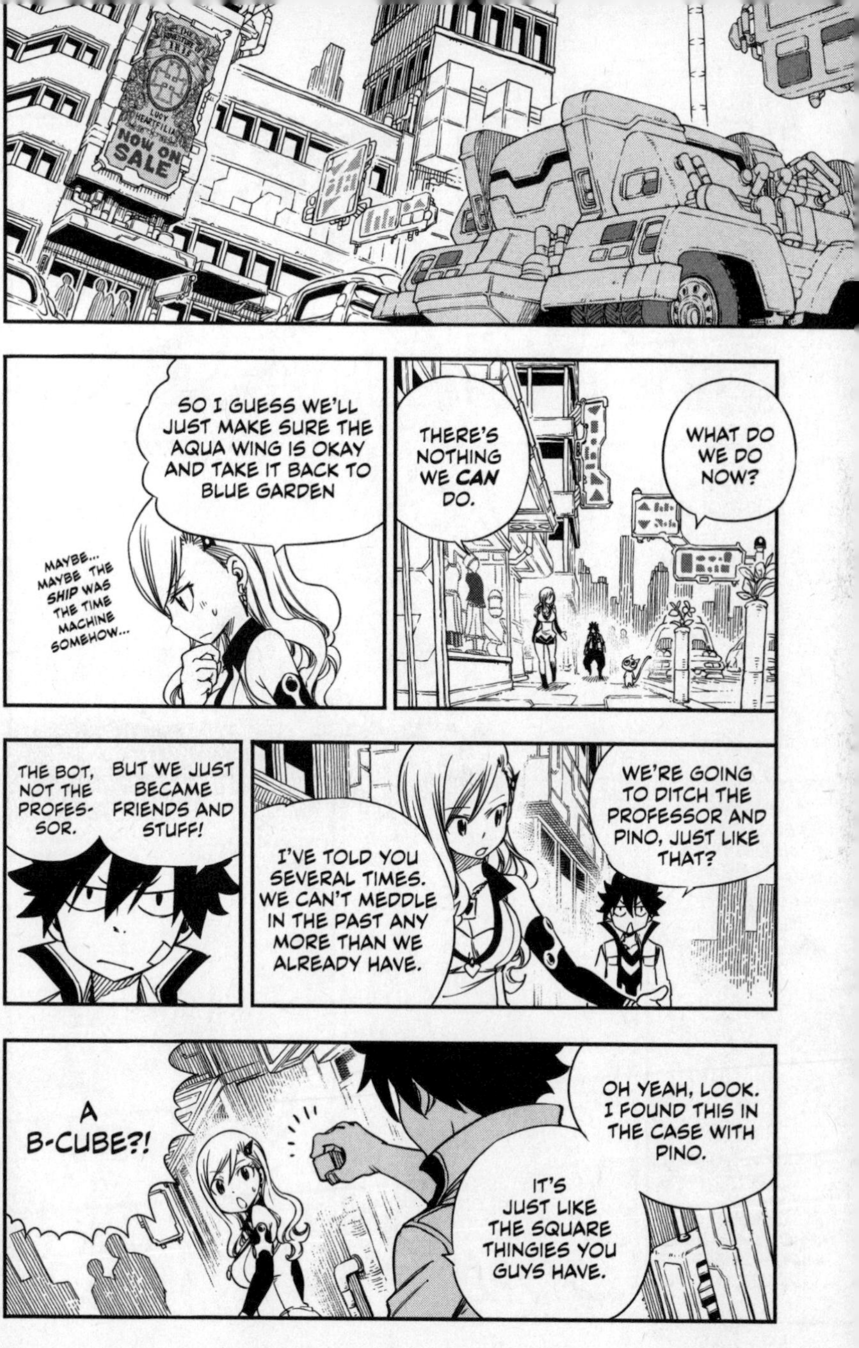
LUCY HEARTFILIA
NOW ON SALE
WHAT DO WE DO NOW?
THERE'S NOTHING WE **CAN** DO.
SO I GUESS WE'LL JUST MAKE SURE THE AQUA WING IS OKAY AND TAKE IT BACK TO BLUE GARDEN
MAYBE... MAYBE THE **SHIP** WAS THE TIME MACHINE SOMEHOW...
WE'RE GOING TO DITCH THE PROFESSOR AND PINO, JUST LIKE THAT?
I'VE TOLD YOU SEVERAL TIMES. WE CAN'T MEDDLE IN THE PAST ANY MORE THAN WE ALREADY HAVE.
BUT WE JUST BECAME FRIENDS AND STUFF!
THE BOT, NOT THE PROFES-SOR.
OH YEAH, LOOK. I FOUND THIS IN THE CASE WITH PINO.
IT'S JUST LIKE THE SQUARE THINGIES YOU GUYS HAVE.
A B-CUBE?!

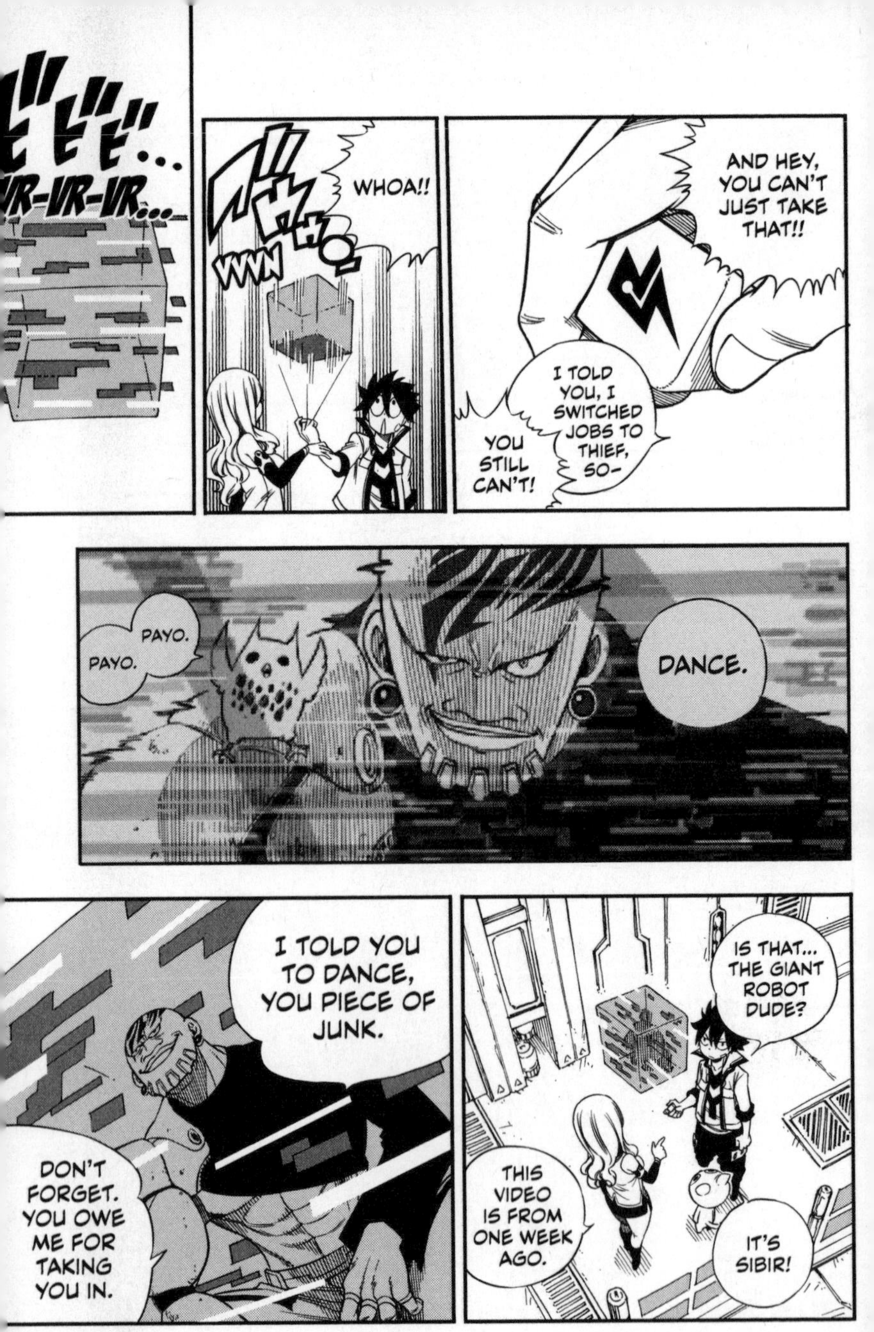
AND HEY, YOU CAN'T JUST TAKE THAT!!
I TOLD YOU, I SWITCHED JOBS TO THIEF, SO-
YOU STILL CAN'T!
WHOA!!
VVVN
VR-VR-VR...
DANCE.
PAYO.
PAYO.
IS THAT... THE GIANT ROBOT DUDE?
IT'S SIBIR!
THIS VIDEO IS FROM ONE WEEK AGO.
I TOLD YOU TO DANCE, YOU PIECE OF JUNK.
DON'T FORGET. YOU OWE ME FOR TAKING YOU IN.

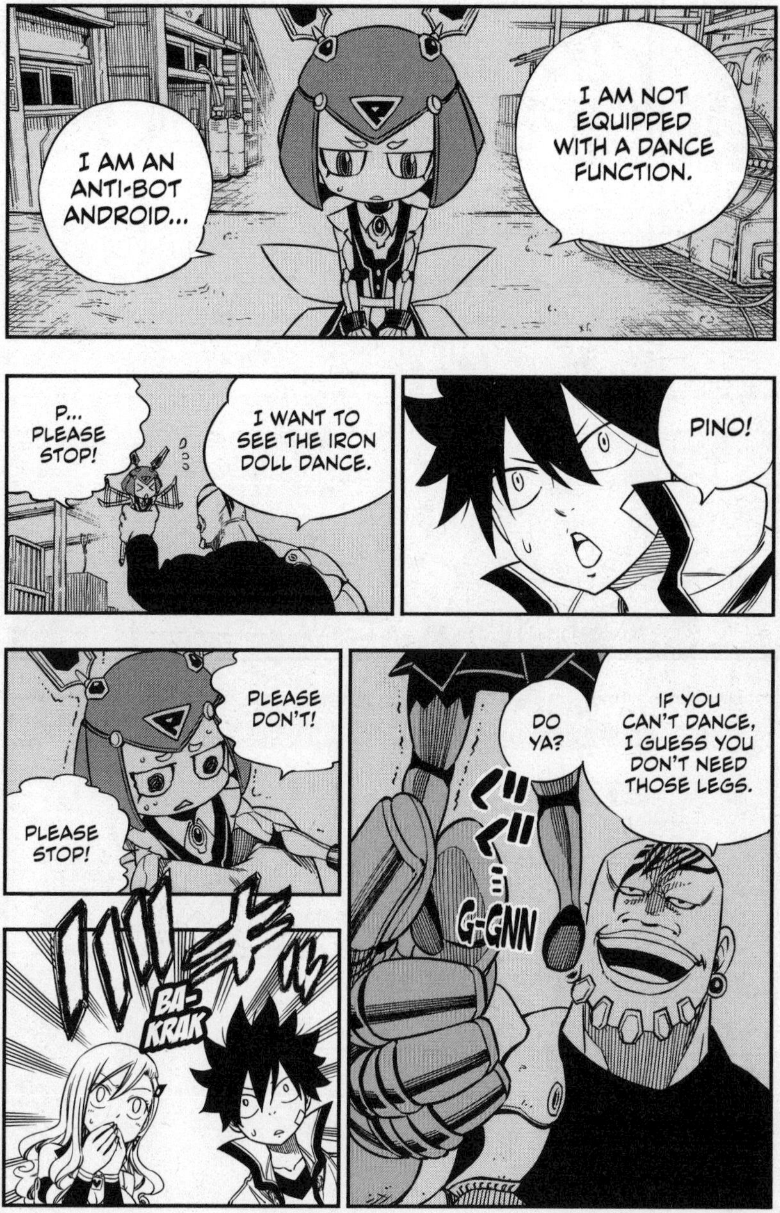
I AM NOT EQUIPPED WITH A DANCE FUNCTION.
I AM AN ANTI-BOT ANDROID...
PINO!
I WANT TO SEE THE IRON DOLL DANCE.
P... PLEASE STOP!
IF YOU CAN'T DANCE, I GUESS YOU DON'T NEED THOSE LEGS.
DO YA?
G-GNN
PLEASE DON'T!
PLEASE STOP!
BA-KRAK

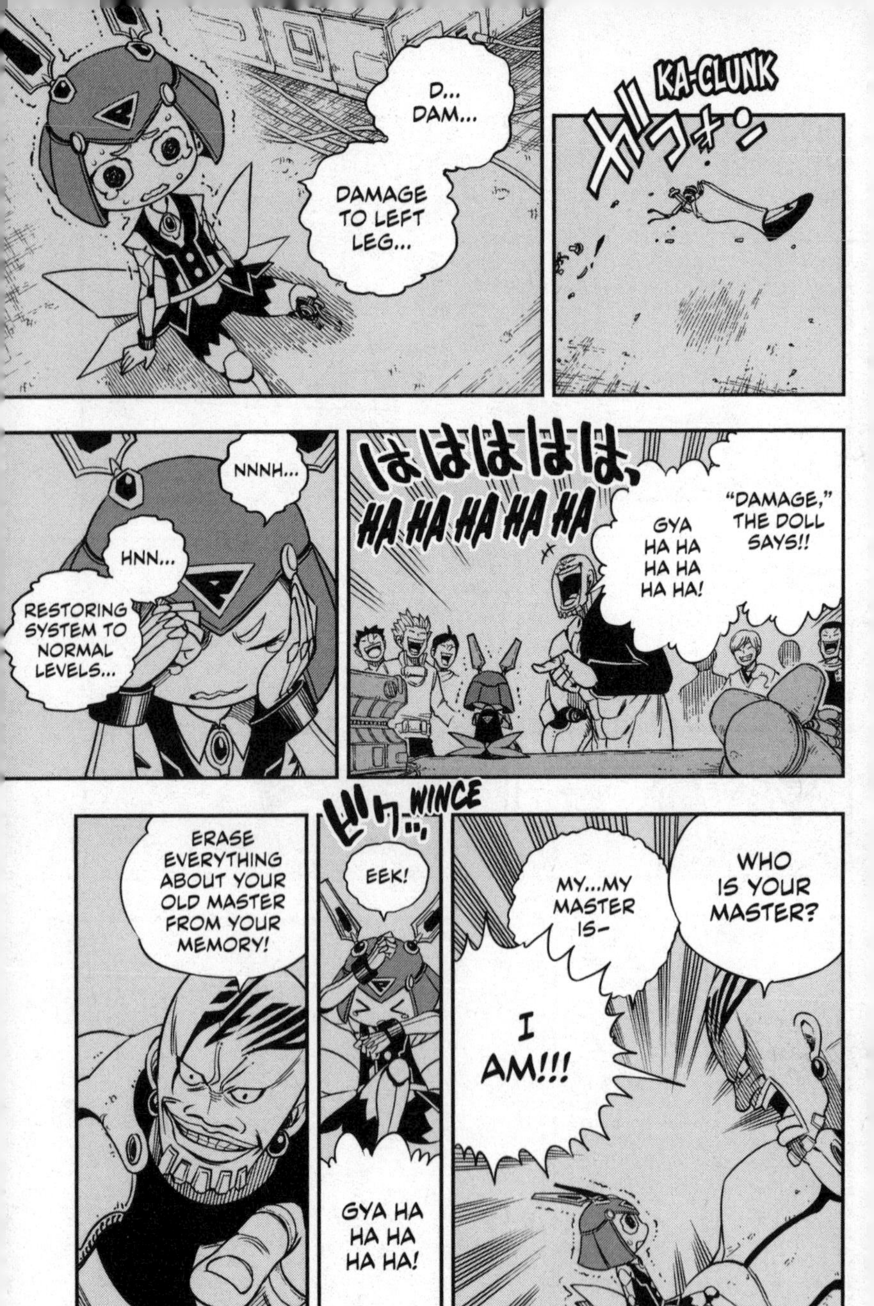
KA-CLUNK
D... DAM...
DAMAGE TO LEFT LEG...
ははははは,
HA HA HA HA HA
"DAMAGE," THE DOLL SAYS!!
GYA HA HA HA HA HA HA!
NNNH...
HNN...
RESTORING SYSTEM TO NORMAL LEVELS...
WHO IS YOUR MASTER?
MY...MY MASTER IS-
I AM!!!
ビクッ
WINCE
EEK!
GYA HA HA HA HA HA!
ERASE EVERYTHING ABOUT YOUR OLD MASTER FROM YOUR MEMORY!

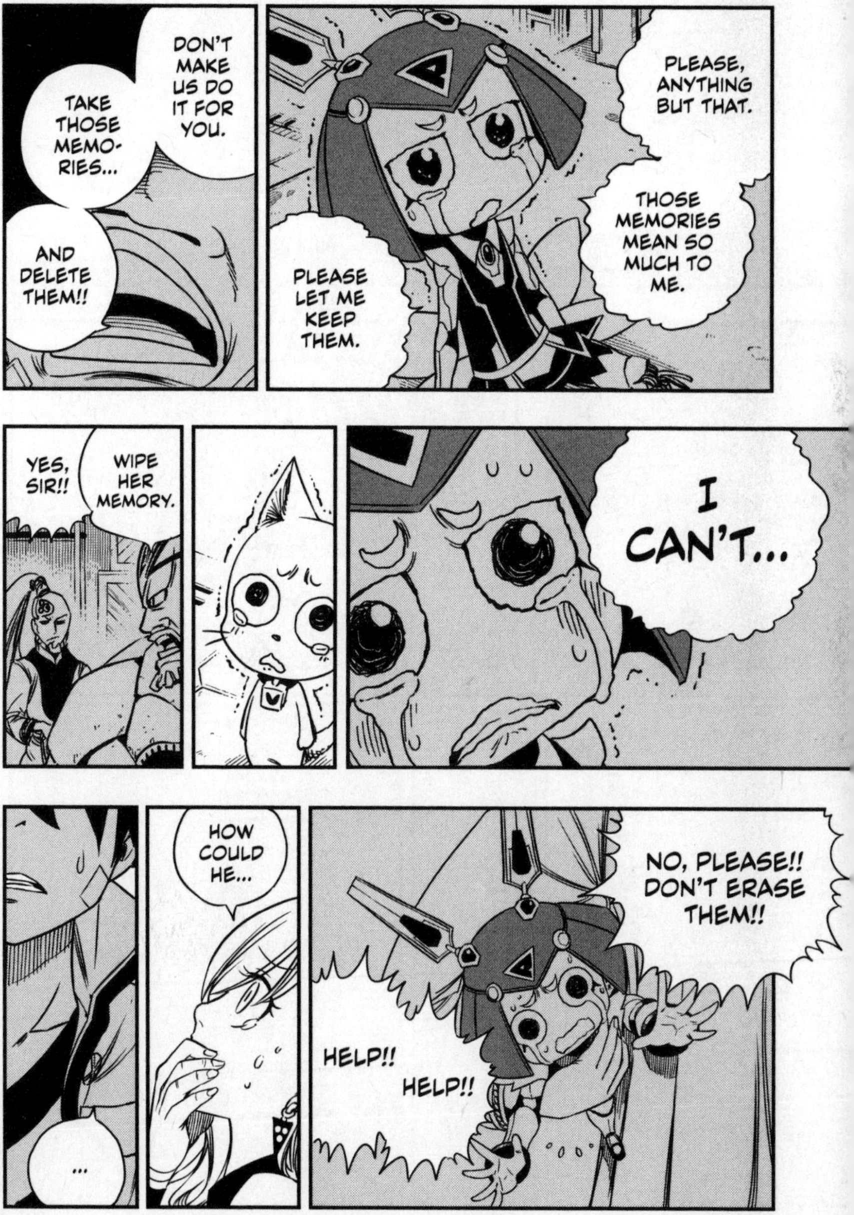
PLEASE, ANYTHING BUT THAT.
THOSE MEMORIES MEAN SO MUCH TO ME.
PLEASE LET ME KEEP THEM.
DON'T MAKE US DO IT FOR YOU.
TAKE THOSE MEMORIES...
AND DELETE THEM!!
I CAN'T...
WIPE HER MEMORY.
YES, SIR!!
NO, PLEASE!! DON'T ERASE THEM!!
HELP!!
HELP!!
HOW COULD HE...
...

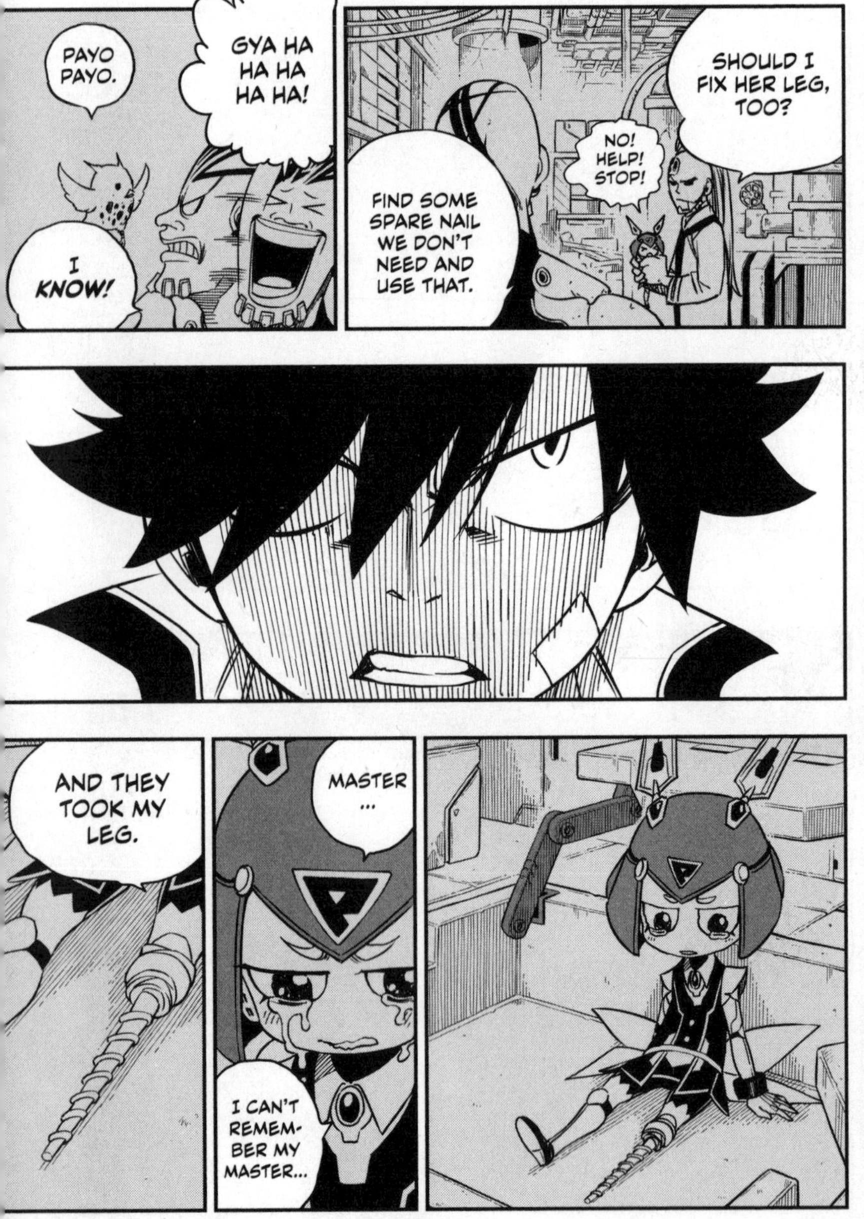
SHOULD I FIX HER LEG, TOO?
NO! HELP! STOP!
FIND SOME SPARE NAIL WE DON'T NEED AND USE THAT.
GYA HA HA HA HA HA!
PAYO PAYO.
I KNOW!
MASTER ...
I CAN'T REMEM-BER MY MASTER...
AND THEY TOOK MY LEG.

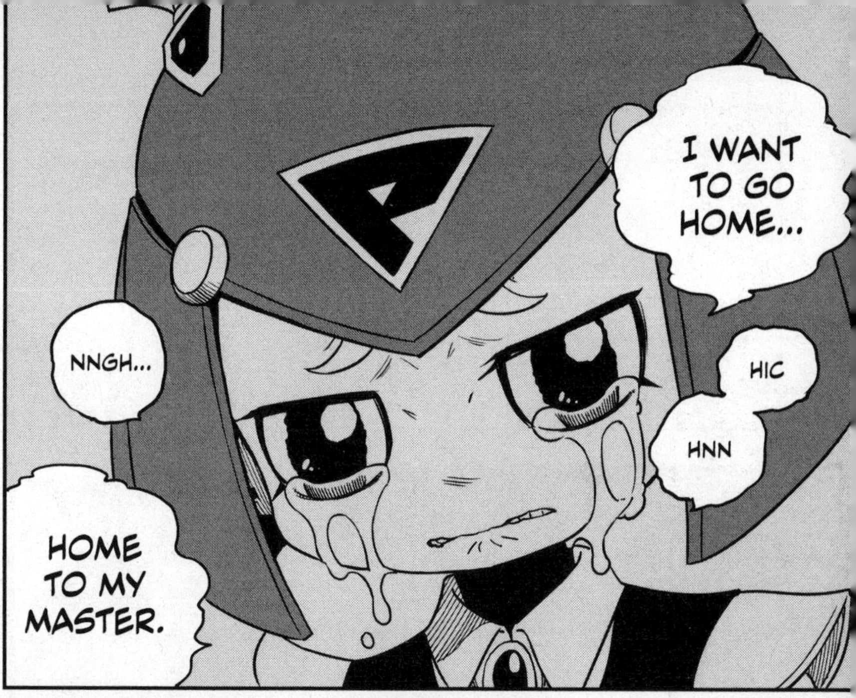
I WANT TO GO HOME...
HIC
HNN
NNGH...
HOME TO MY MASTER.

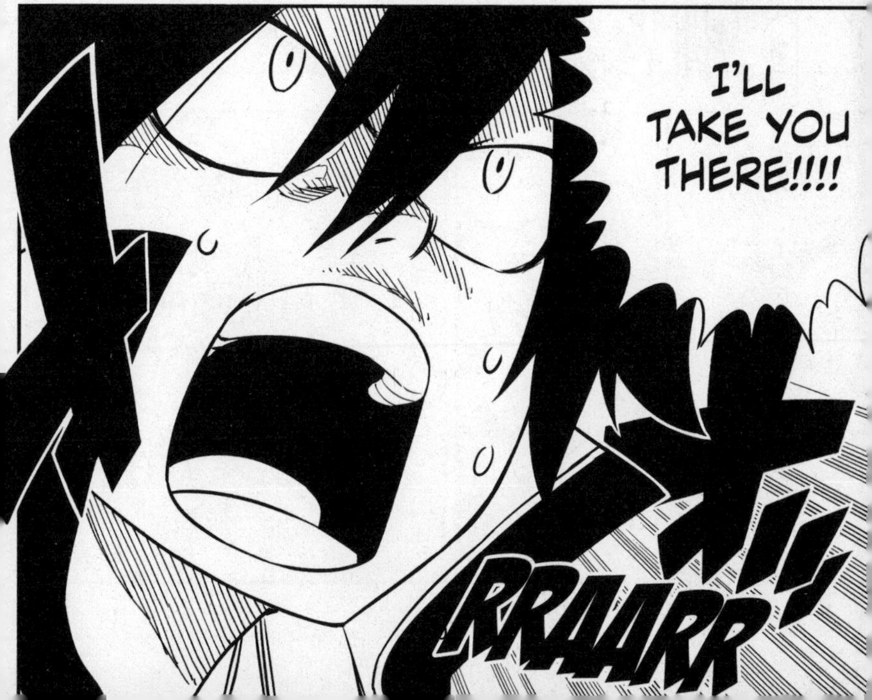
I'LL TAKE YOU THERE!!!!
CRRAARR!!

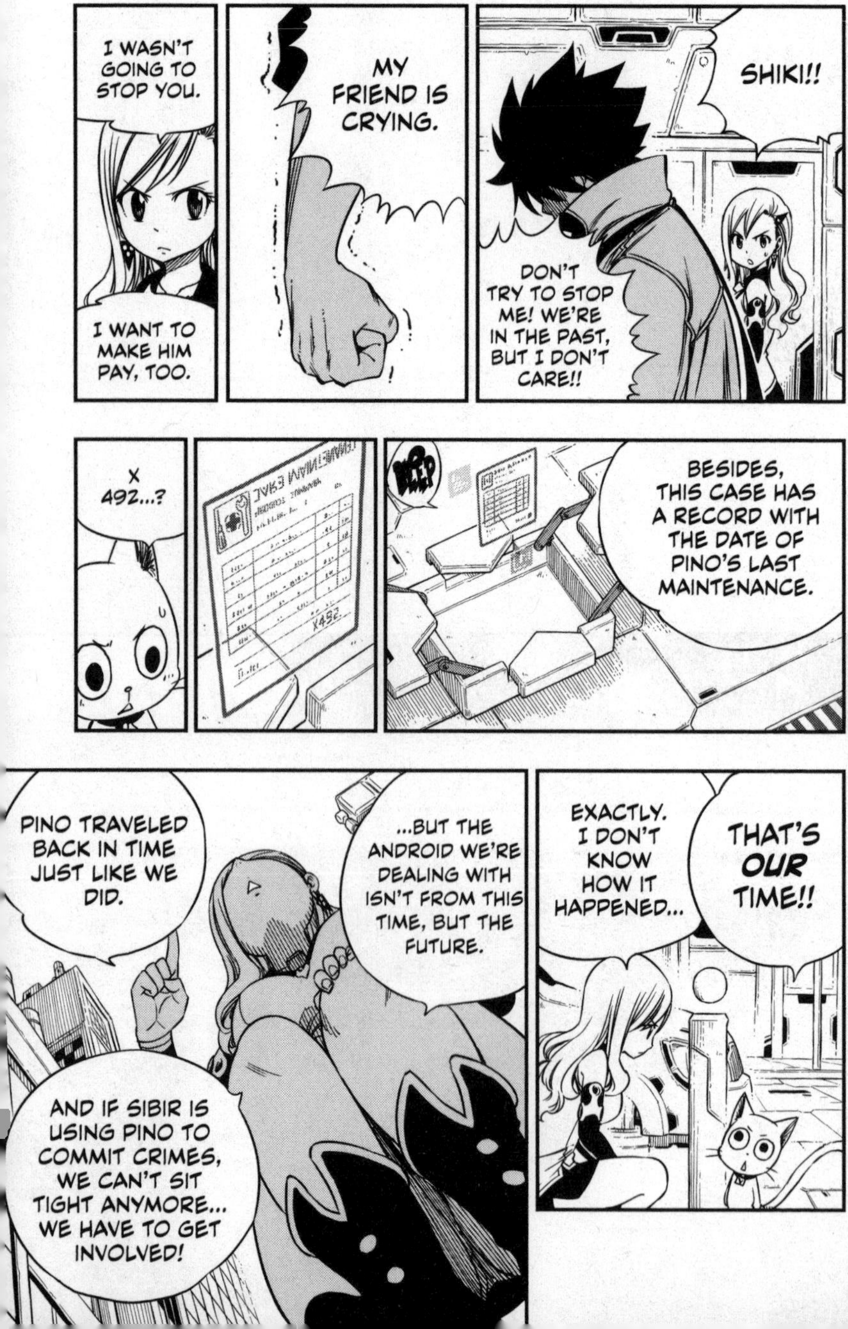
SHIKI!!
DON'T TRY TO STOP ME! WE'RE IN THE PAST, BUT I DON'T CARE!!
MY FRIEND IS CRYING.
I WASN'T GOING TO STOP YOU.
I WANT TO MAKE HIM PAY, TOO.
BEEP
BESIDES, THIS CASE HAS A RECORD WITH THE DATE OF PINO'S LAST MAINTENANCE.
X492
X 492...?
THAT'S OUR TIME!!
EXACTLY. I DON'T KNOW HOW IT HAPPENED...
...BUT THE ANDROID WE'RE DEALING WITH ISN'T FROM THIS TIME, BUT THE FUTURE.
PINO TRAVELED BACK IN TIME JUST LIKE WE DID.
AND IF SIBIR IS USING PINO TO COMMIT CRIMES, WE CAN'T SIT TIGHT ANYMORE... WE HAVE TO GET INVOLVED!

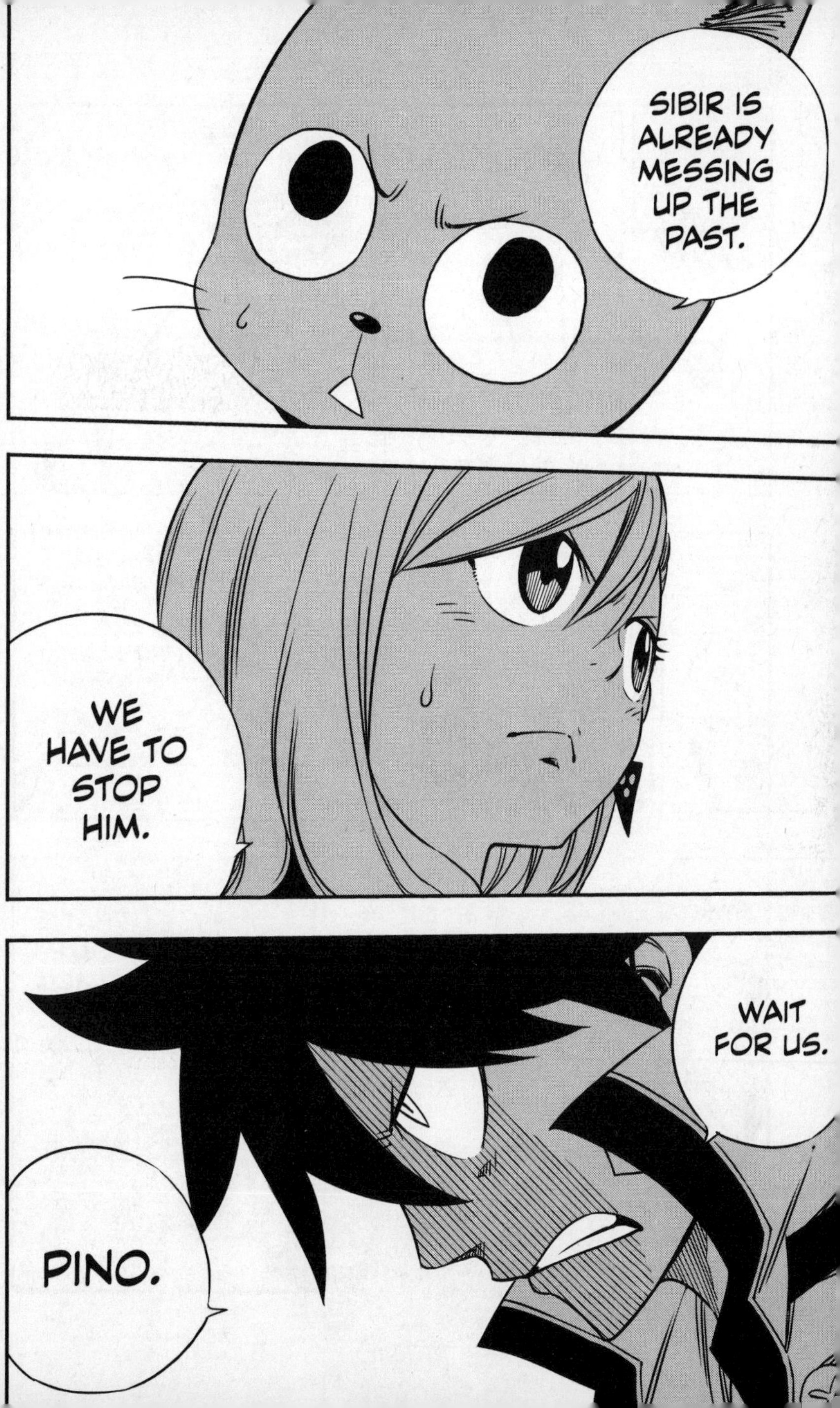
SIBIR IS ALREADY MESSING UP THE PAST.
WE HAVE TO STOP HIM.
WAIT FOR US.
PINO.

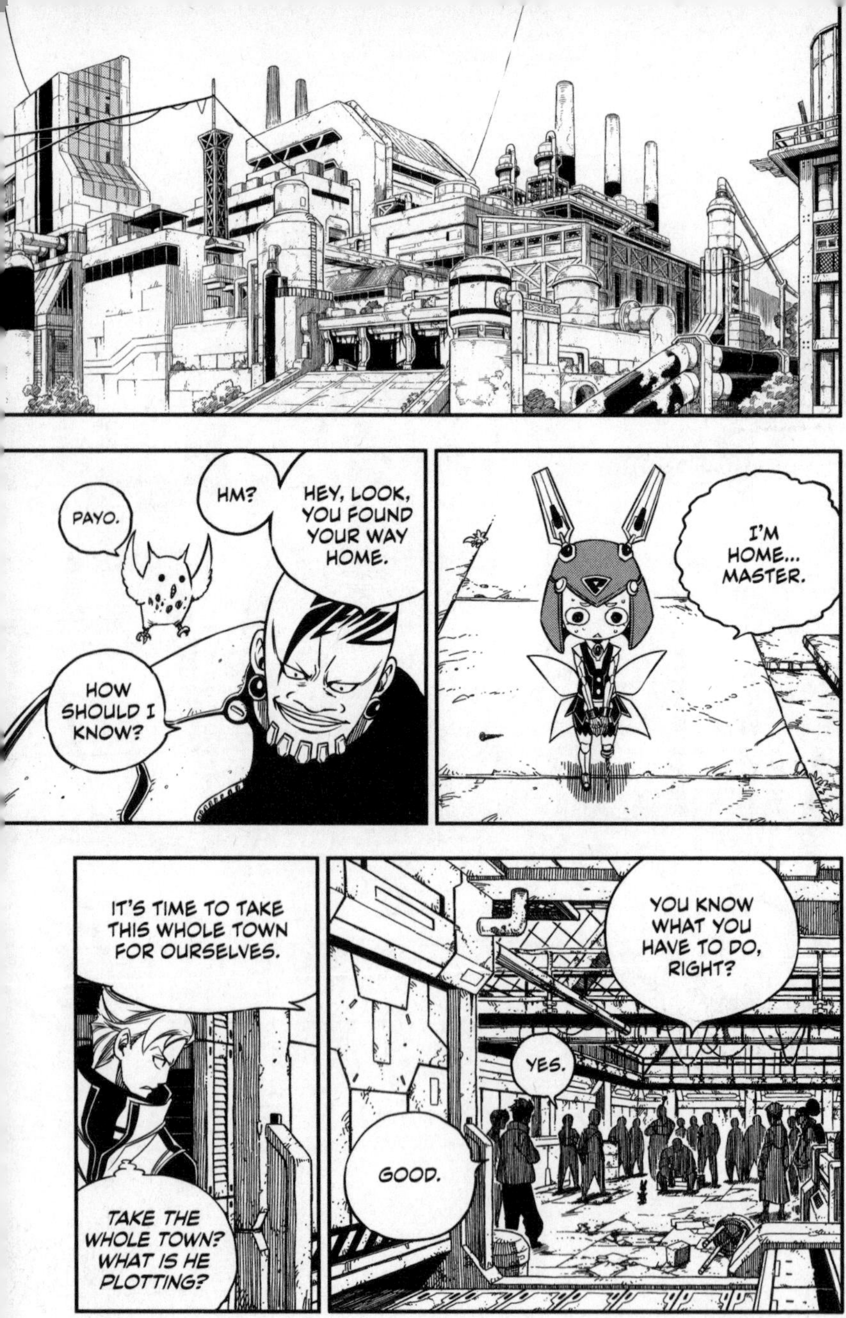
I'M HOME... MASTER.
HEY, LOOK, YOU FOUND YOUR WAY HOME.
HM?
PAYO.
HOW SHOULD I KNOW?
YOU KNOW WHAT YOU HAVE TO DO, RIGHT?
YES.
GOOD.
IT'S TIME TO TAKE THIS WHOLE TOWN FOR OURSELVES.
TAKE THE WHOLE TOWN? WHAT IS HE PLOTTING?

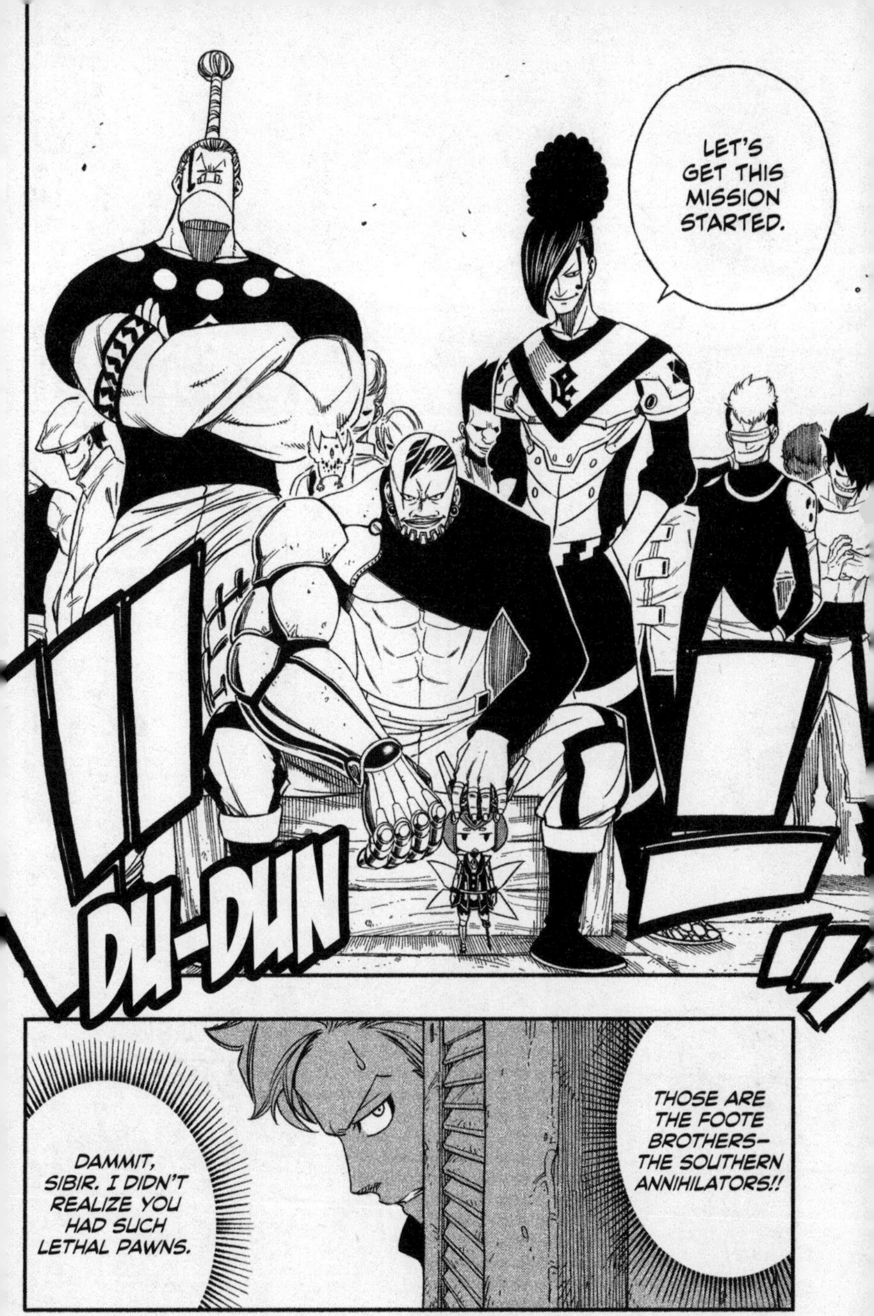
LET'S GET THIS MISSION STARTED.
DU-DUN
THOSE ARE THE FOOTE BROTHERS—THE SOUTHERN ANNIHILATORS!!
DAMMIT, SIBIR. I DIDN'T REALIZE YOU HAD SUCH LETHAL PAWNS.

# EDENS ZERO

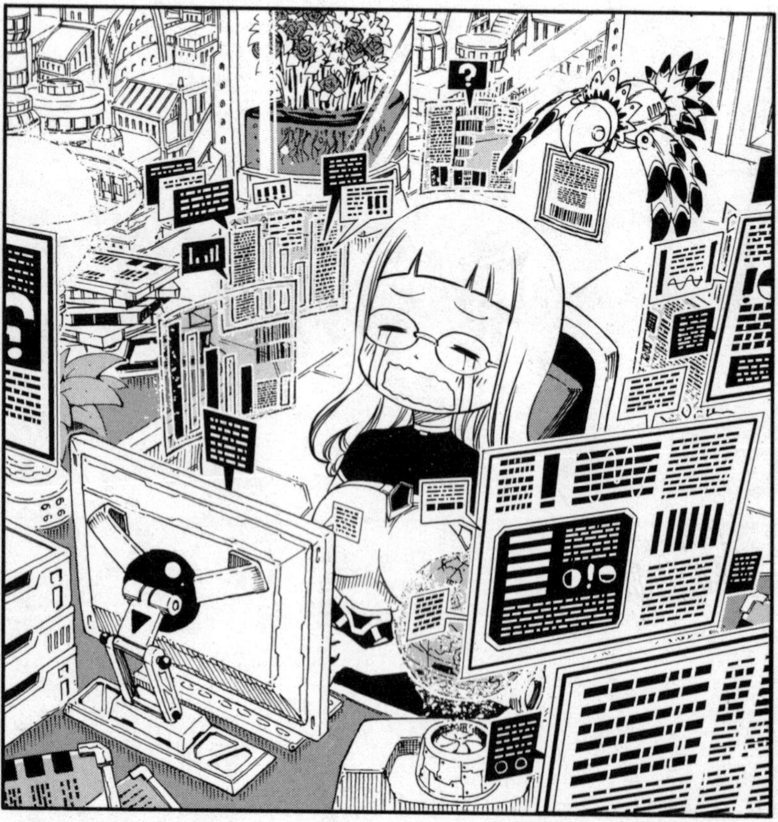

## CHAPTER 8: CLASH!! THE SIBIR FAMILY

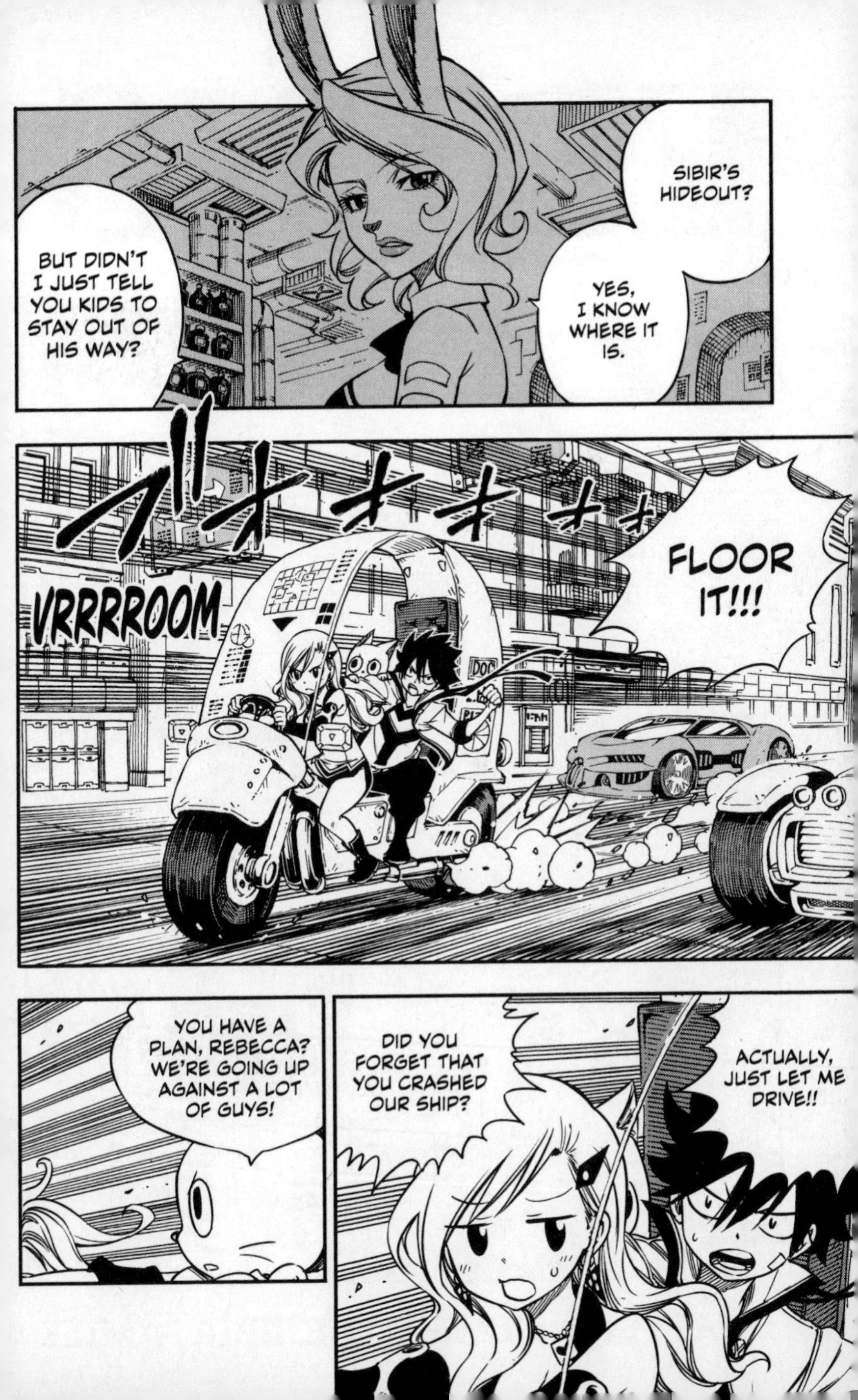
SIBIR'S HIDEOUT?
YES, I KNOW WHERE IT IS.
BUT DIDN'T I JUST TELL YOU KIDS TO STAY OUT OF HIS WAY?
FLOOR IT!!!
VRRRROOM
ACTUALLY, JUST LET ME DRIVE!!
DID YOU FORGET THAT YOU CRASHED OUR SHIP?
YOU HAVE A PLAN, REBECCA? WE'RE GOING UP AGAINST A LOT OF GUYS!

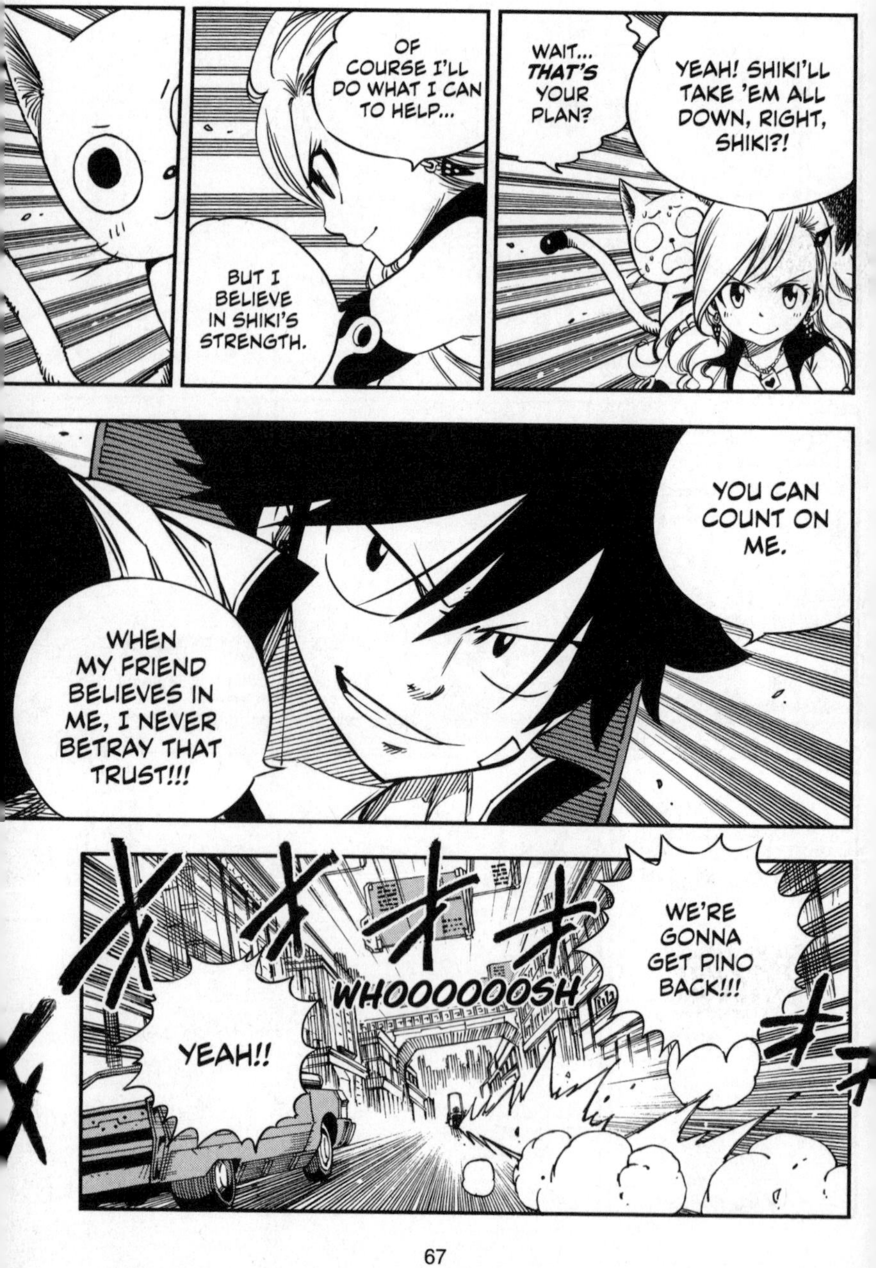
YEAH! SHIKI'LL TAKE 'EM ALL DOWN, RIGHT, SHIKI?!
WAIT... *THAT'S* YOUR PLAN?
OF COURSE I'LL DO WHAT I CAN TO HELP...
BUT I BELIEVE IN SHIKI'S STRENGTH.
YOU CAN COUNT ON ME.
WHEN MY FRIEND BELIEVES IN ME, I NEVER BETRAY THAT TRUST!!!
WE'RE GONNA GET PINO BACK!!!
WHOOOOOOOSH
YEAH!!

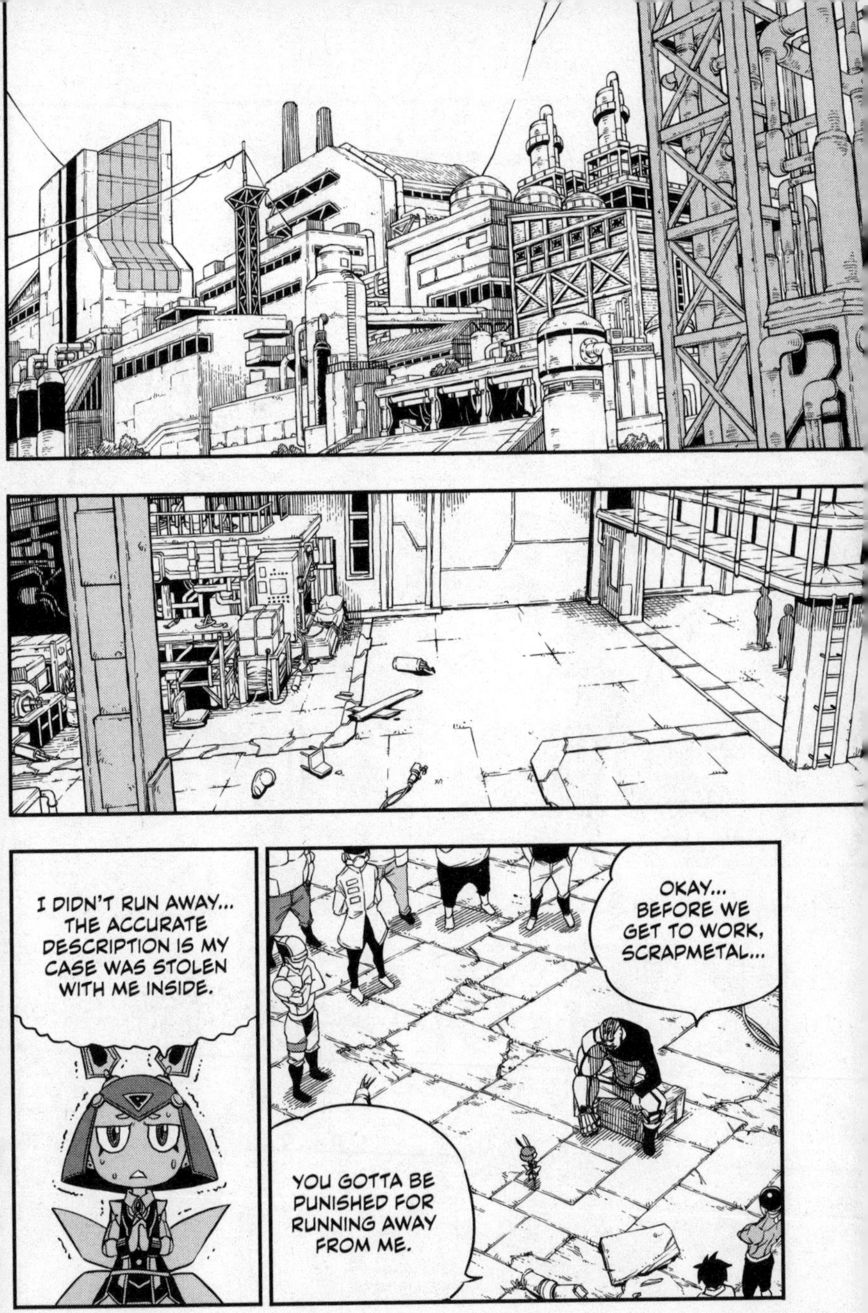
OKAY... BEFORE WE GET TO WORK, SCRAPMETAL...
YOU GOTTA BE PUNISHED FOR RUNNING AWAY FROM ME.
I DIDN'T RUN AWAY... THE ACCURATE DESCRIPTION IS MY CASE WAS STOLEN WITH ME INSIDE.

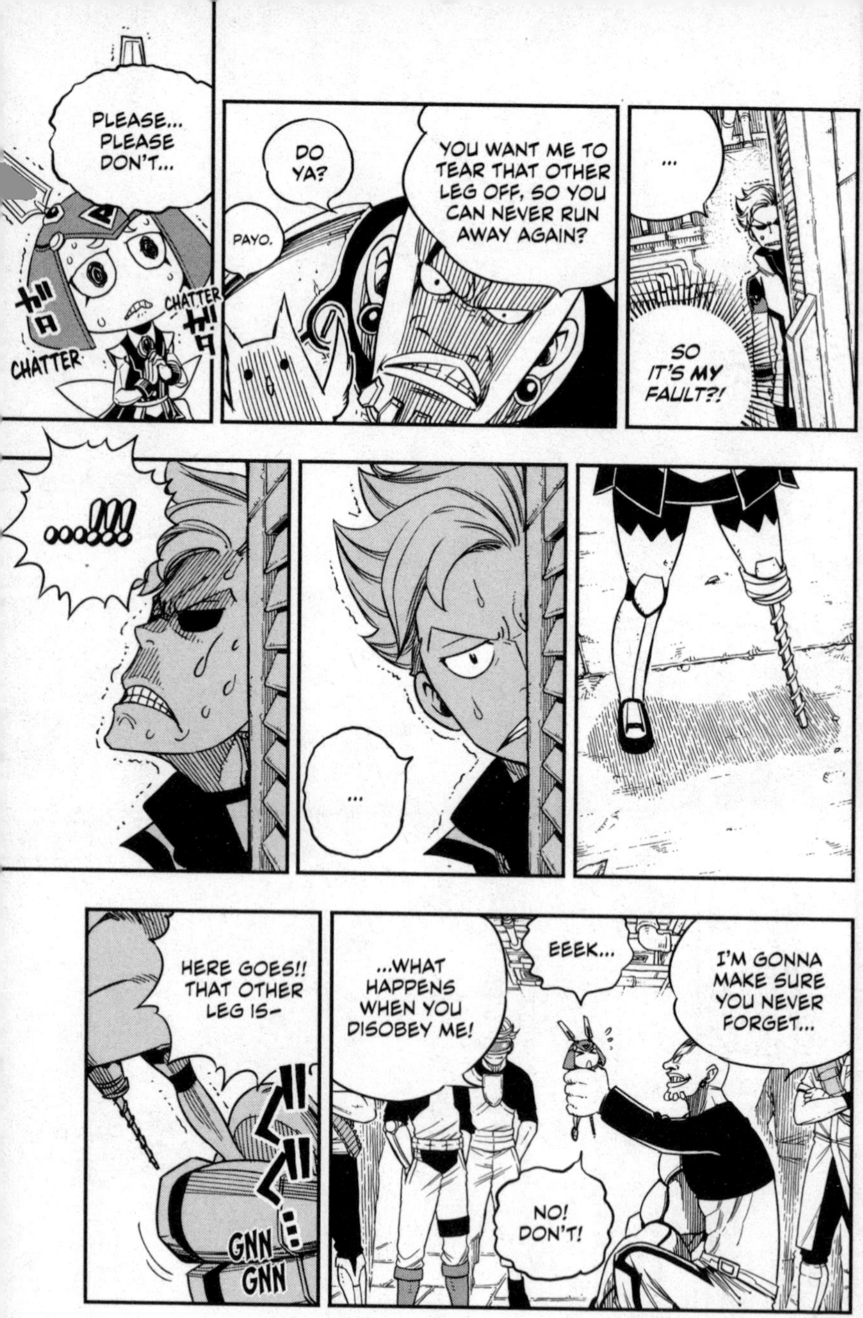
...
SO IT'S MY FAULT?!
YOU WANT ME TO TEAR THAT OTHER LEG OFF, SO YOU CAN NEVER RUN AWAY AGAIN?
DO YA?
PAYO.
PLEASE... PLEASE DON'T...
CHATTER
CHATTER
...
...!!!
I'M GONNA MAKE SURE YOU NEVER FORGET...
EEEK...
...WHAT HAPPENS WHEN YOU DISOBEY ME!
NO! DON'T!
HERE GOES!! THAT OTHER LEG IS–
GNN GNN

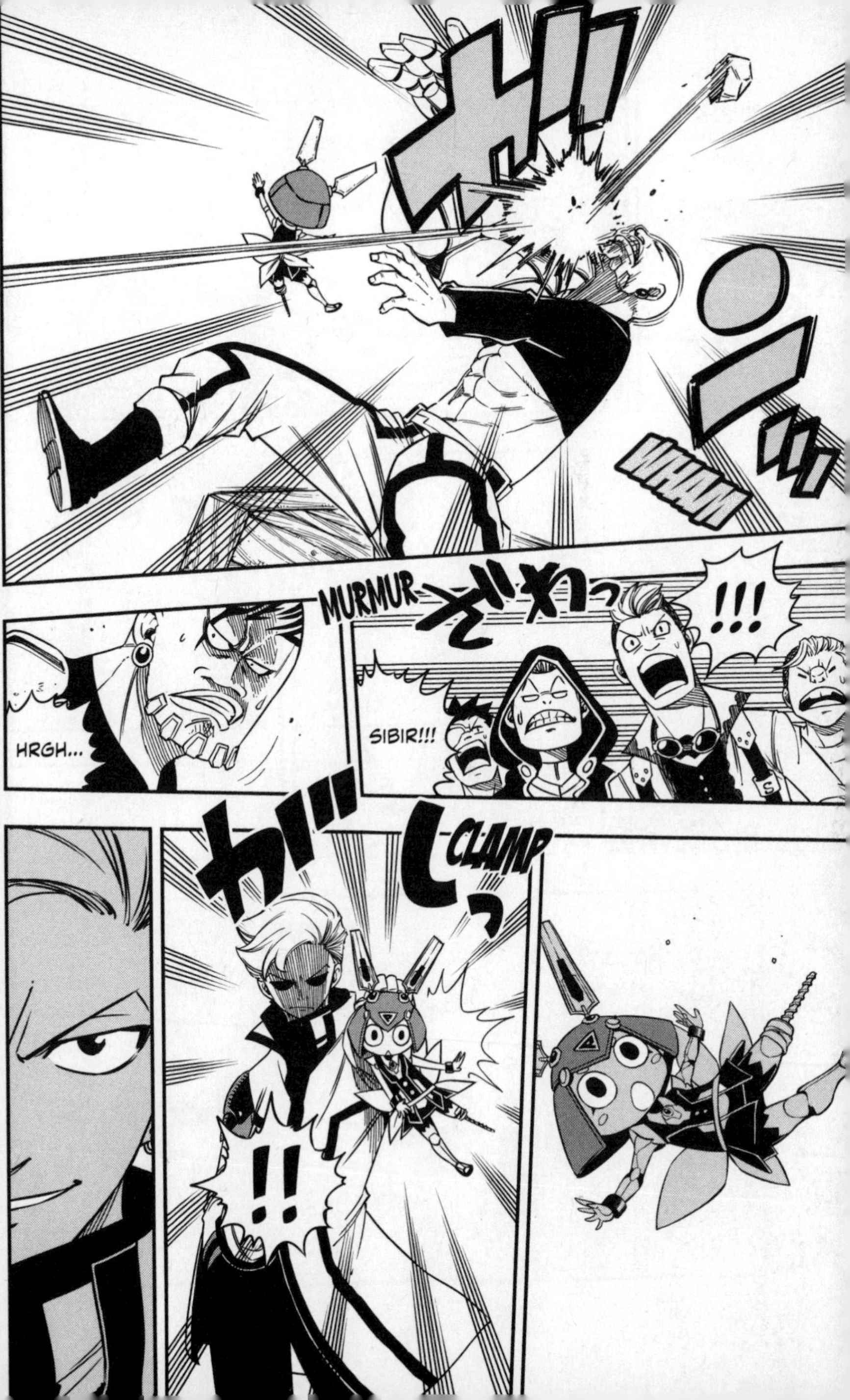
WHAM
MURMUR
!!!
SIBIR!!!
HRGH...
CLAMP
!!

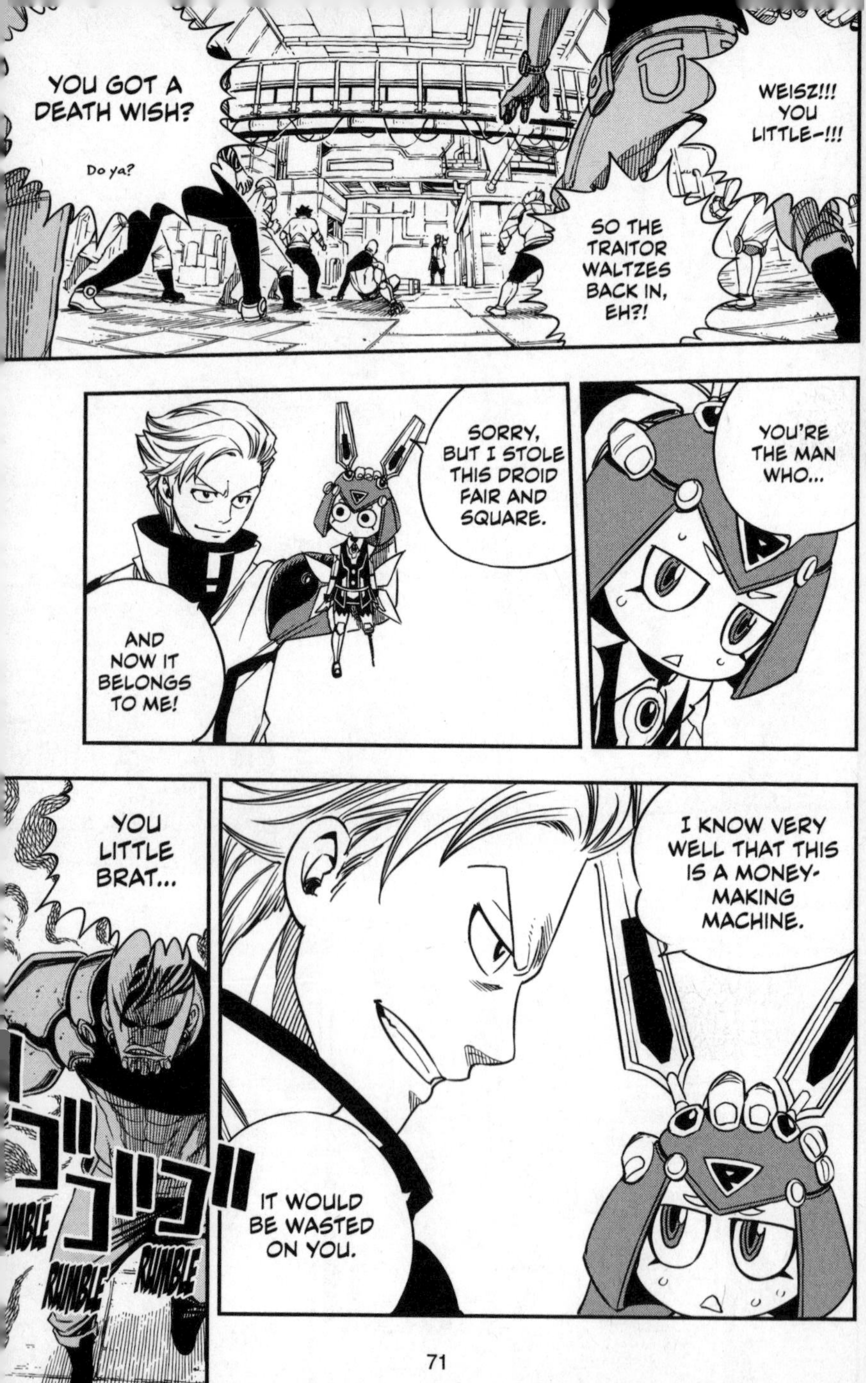
WEISZ!!! YOU LITTLE-!!!
SO THE TRAITOR WALTZES BACK IN, EH?!
YOU GOT A DEATH WISH?
Do ya?
YOU'RE THE MAN WHO...
SORRY, BUT I STOLE THIS DROID FAIR AND SQUARE.
AND NOW IT BELONGS TO ME!
I KNOW VERY WELL THAT THIS IS A MONEY-MAKING MACHINE.
IT WOULD BE WASTED ON YOU.
YOU LITTLE BRAT...
RUMBLE
RUMBLE

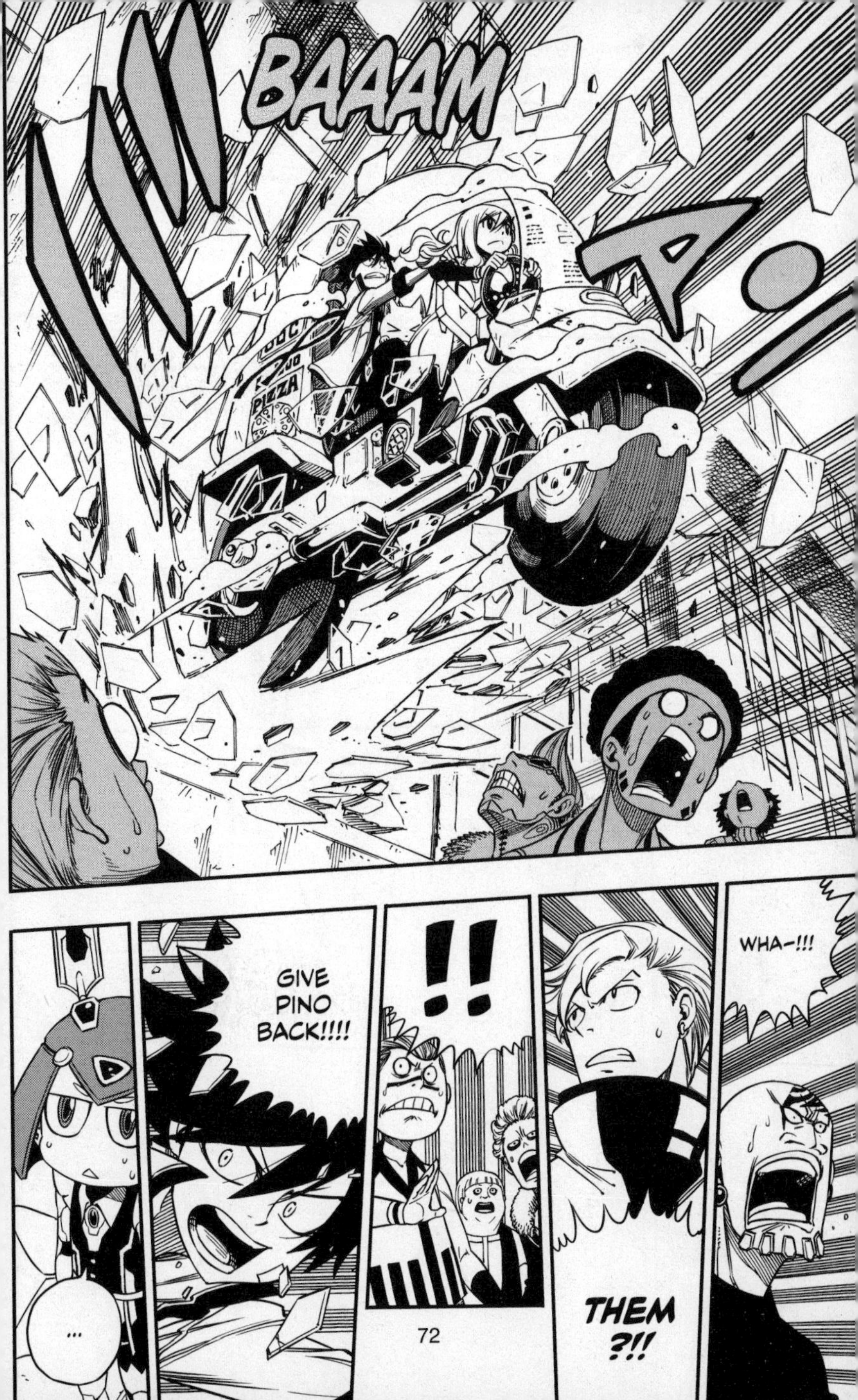
BAAAM
WHA-!!!
THEM ?!!
!!
GIVE PINO BACK!!!!
...

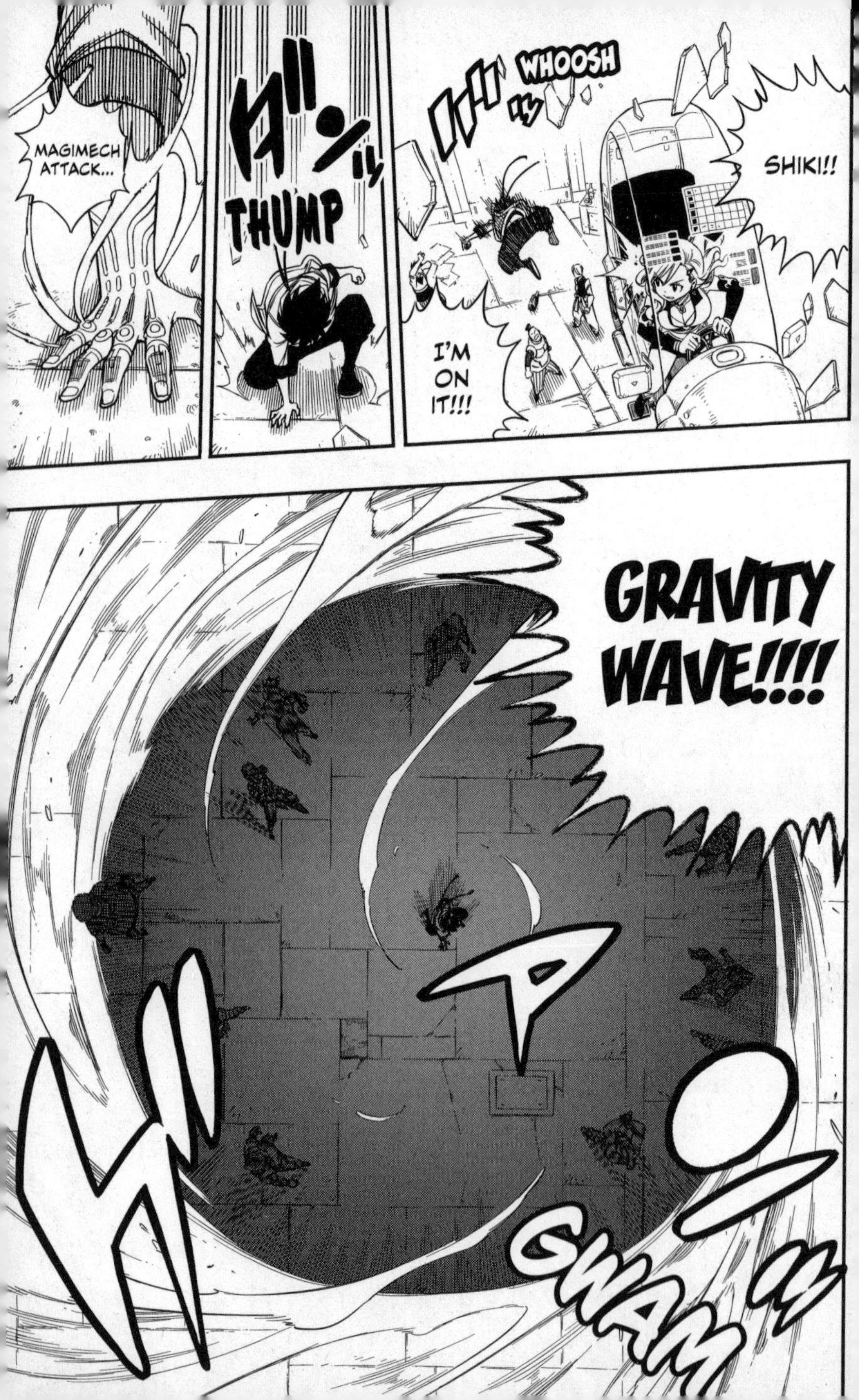
SHIKI!!
WHOOSH
I'M ON IT!!!
THUMP
MAGIMECH ATTACK...
GRAVITY WAVE!!!!
GWAM

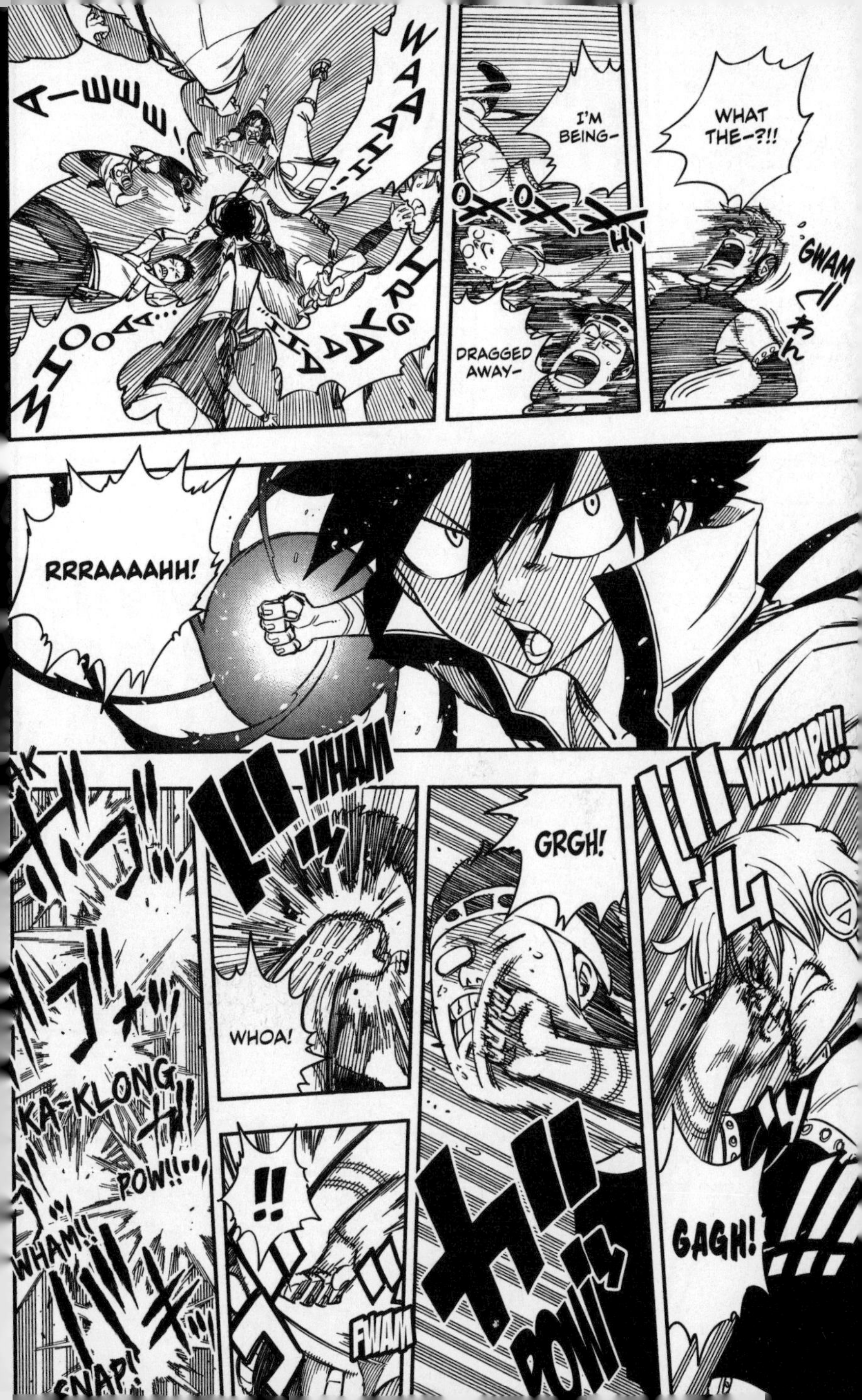

WHAT THE-?!!
GWAM
I'M BEING-
DRAGGED AWAY-
WAAAHHH!!
RRRAAAAHH!
WHUMP!!!
GAGH!
GRGH!
WHAM
WHOA!
FWAM
KA-KLONG
POW!!
WHAM!!
SNAP!

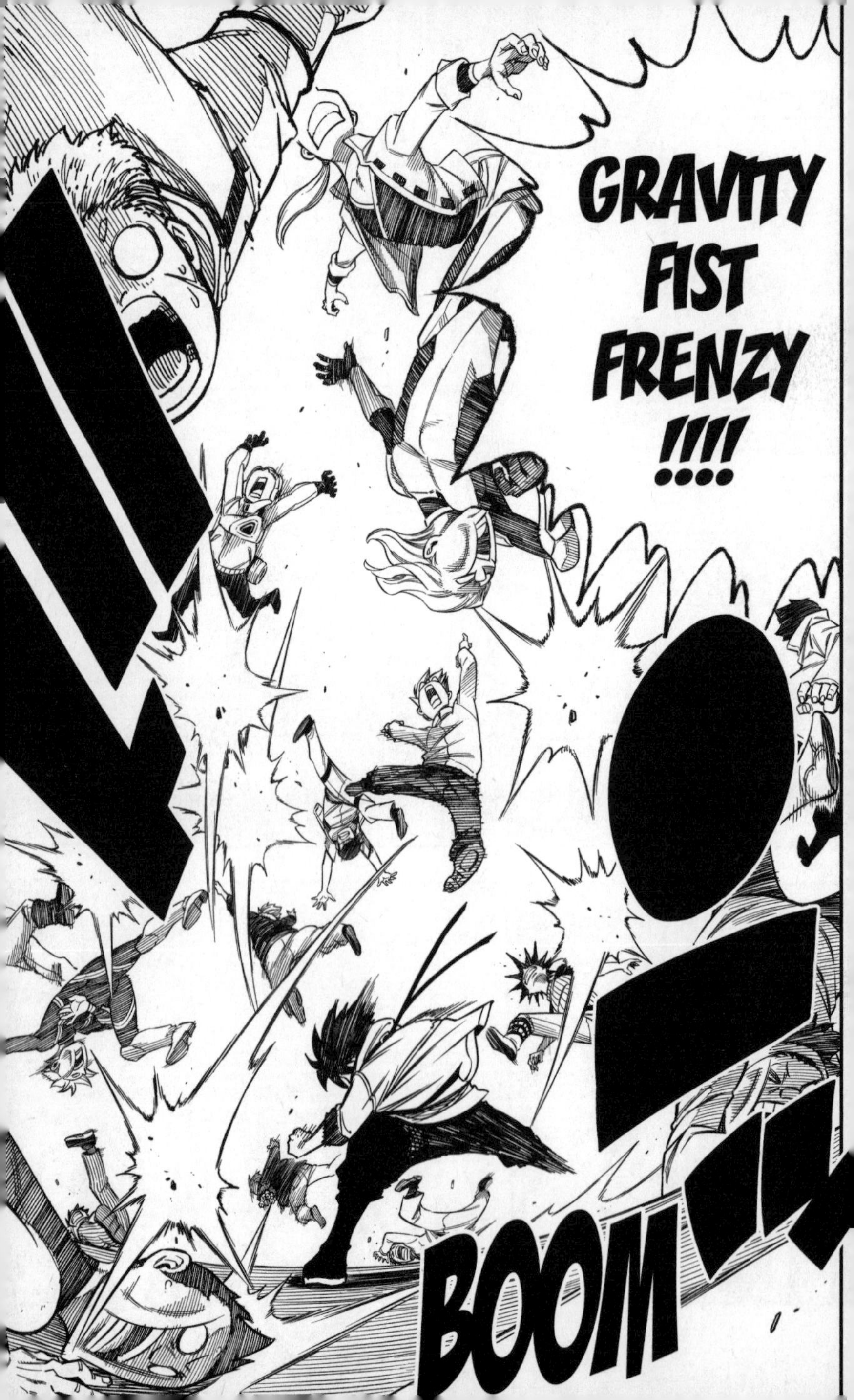
GRAVITY FIST FRENZY!!!!
BOOM

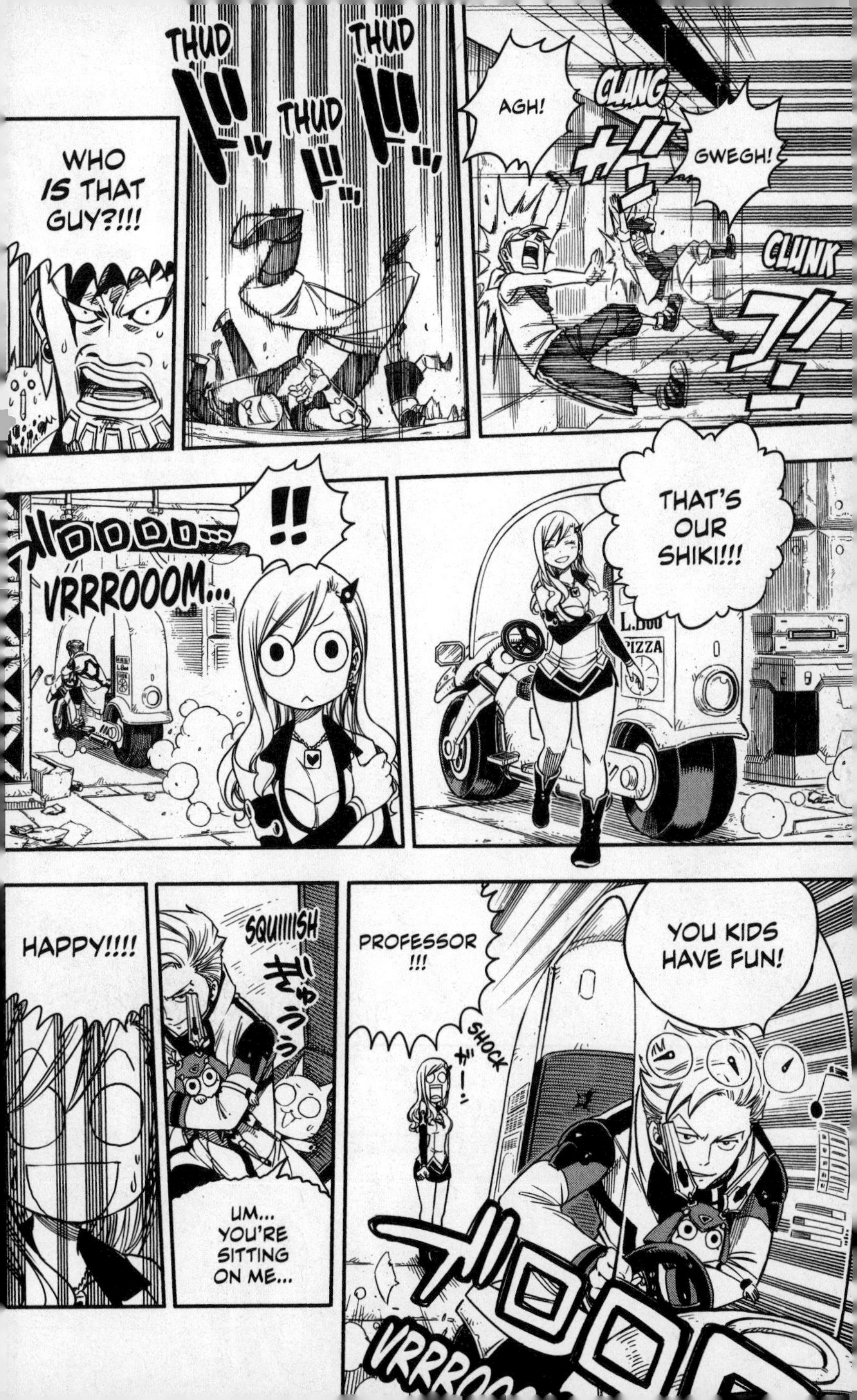
AGH!
CLANG
GWEGH!
CLUNK
THUD
THUD
THUD
WHO IS THAT GUY?!!!
THAT'S OUR SHIKI!!!
!!
VRRROOOM...
YOU KIDS HAVE FUN!
PROFESSOR!!!
SHOCK
SQUIIIISH
UM... YOU'RE SITTING ON ME...
HAPPY!!!!

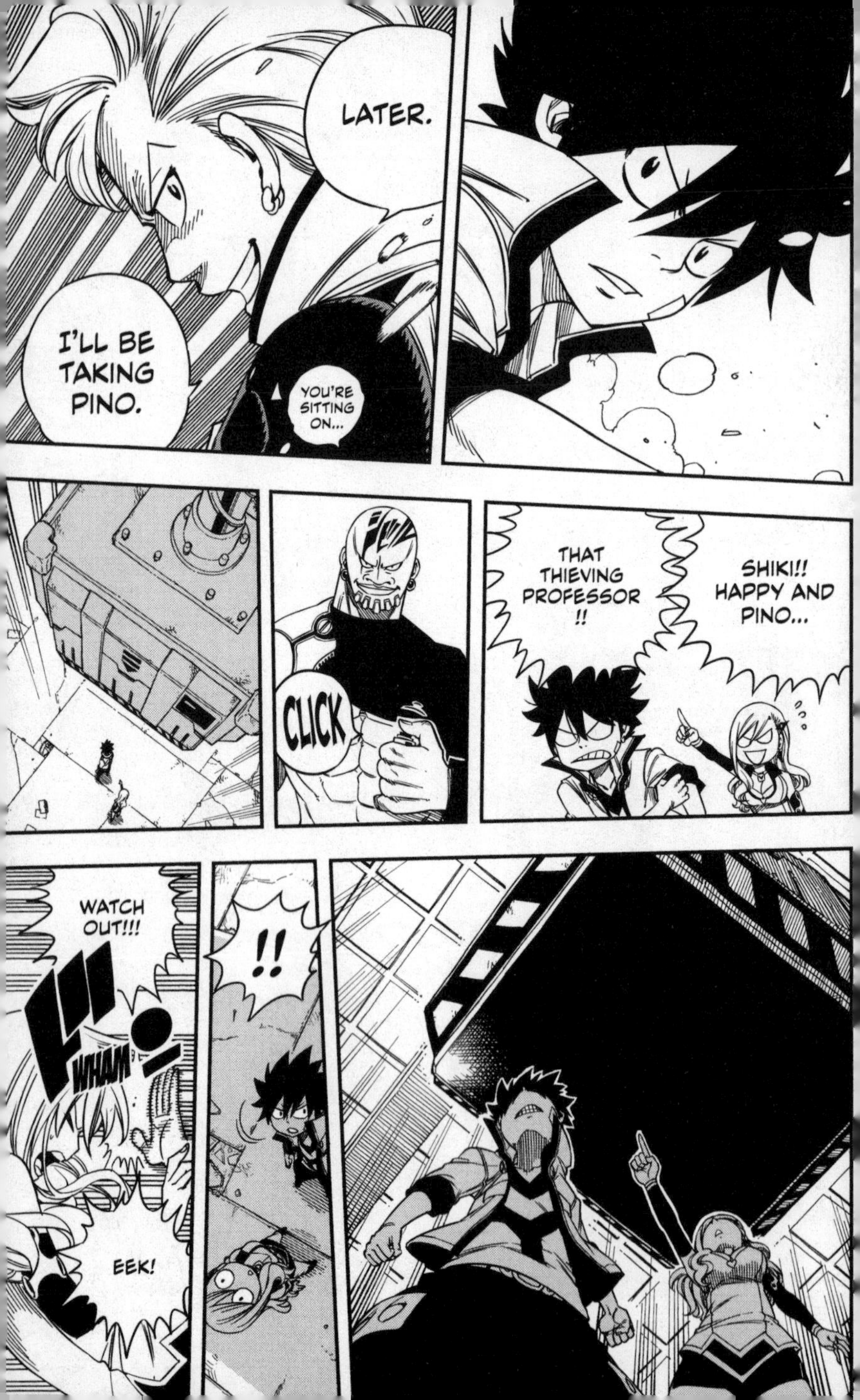
LATER.
I'LL BE TAKING PINO.
YOU'RE SITTING ON...
SHIKI!! HAPPY AND PINO...
THAT THIEVING PROFESSOR !!
CLICK
!!
WATCH OUT!!!
WHAM
EEK!

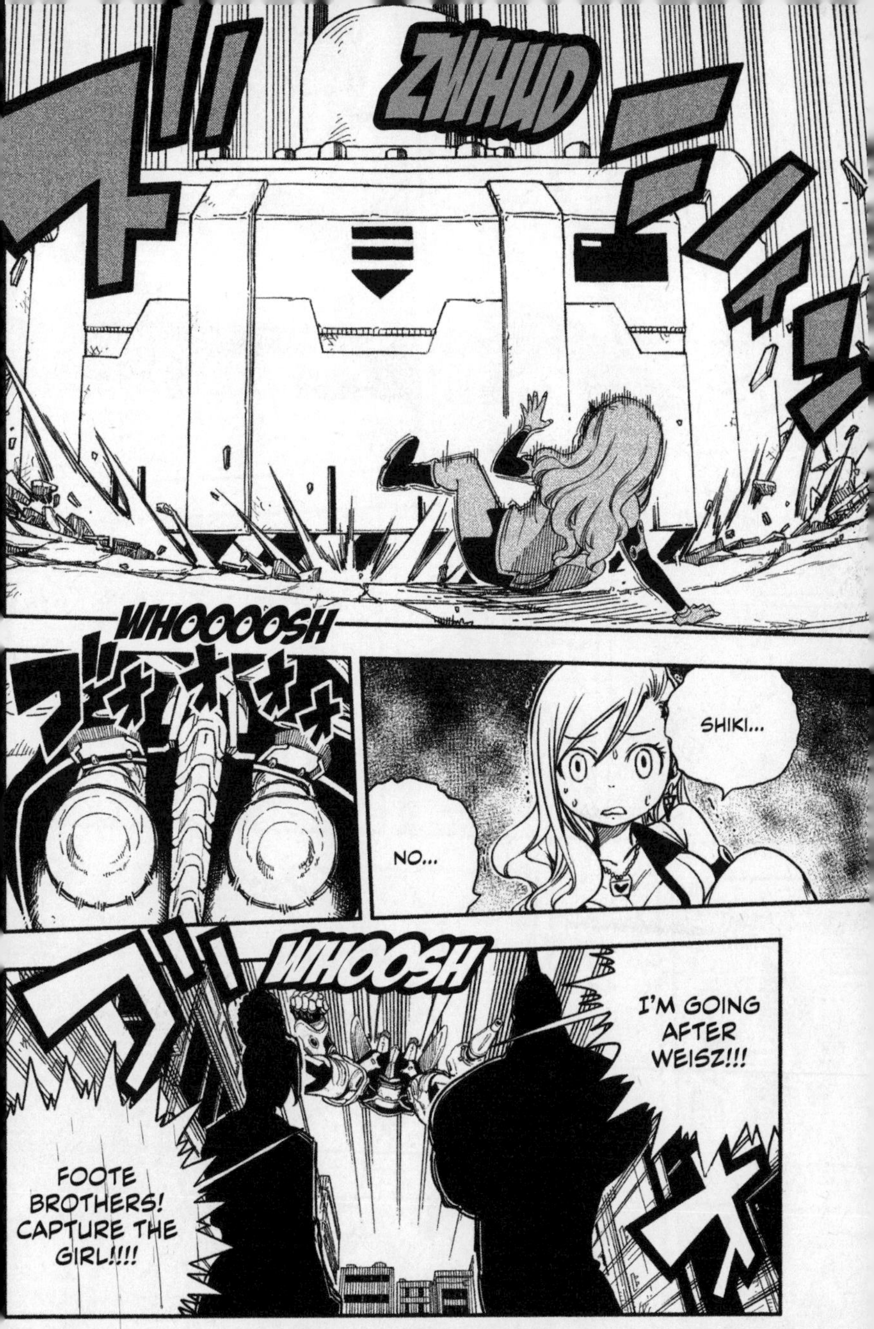
ZWHUD
SHIKI...
NO...
WHOOOOSH
I'M GOING AFTER WEISZ!!!
WHOOSH
FOOTE BROTHERS! CAPTURE THE GIRL!!!!

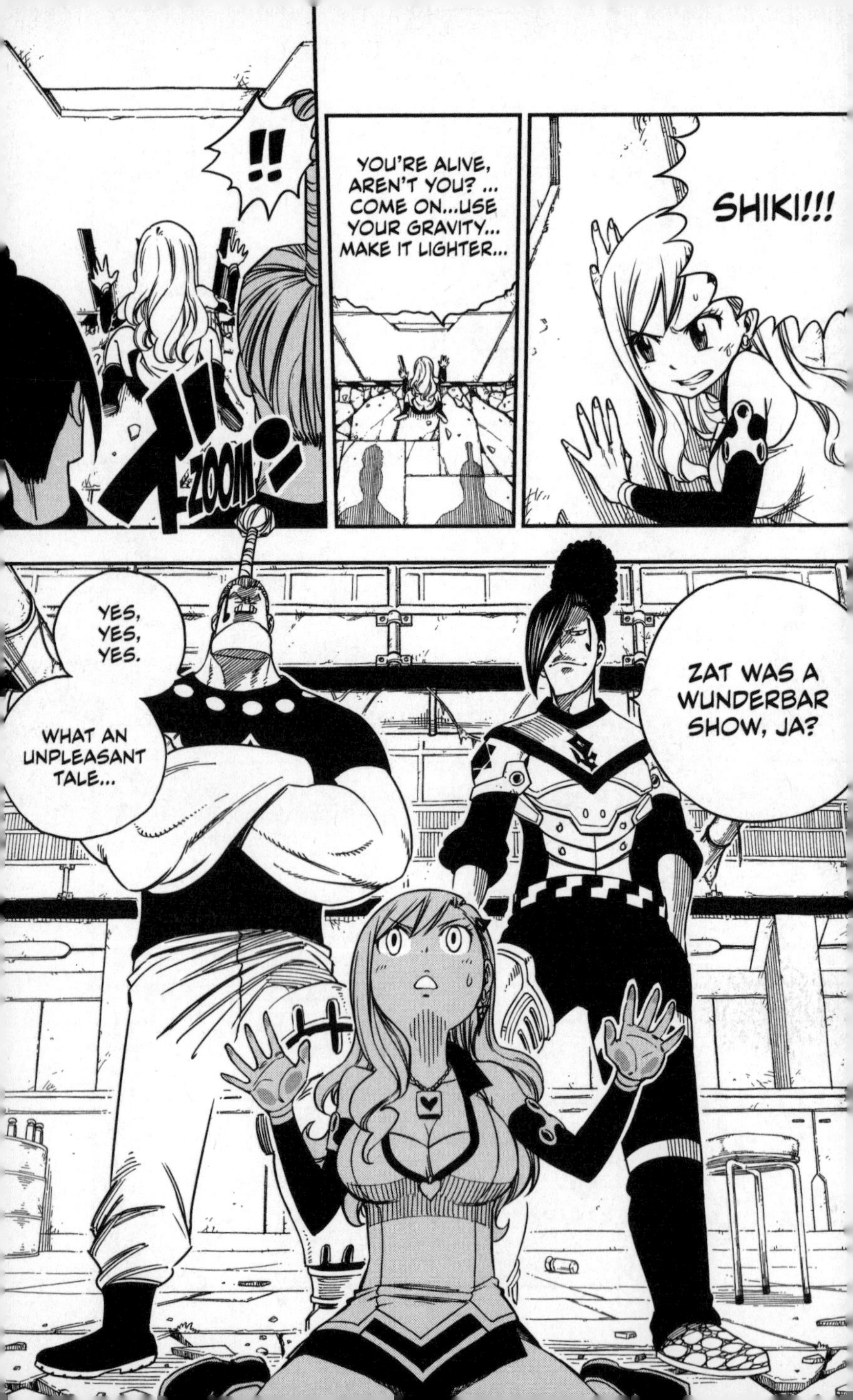
SHIKI!!!
YOU'RE ALIVE, AREN'T YOU? ... COME ON...USE YOUR GRAVITY... MAKE IT LIGHTER...
!!
ZOOM
ZAT WAS A WUNDERBAR SHOW, JA?
YES, YES, YES.
WHAT AN UNPLEASANT TALE...

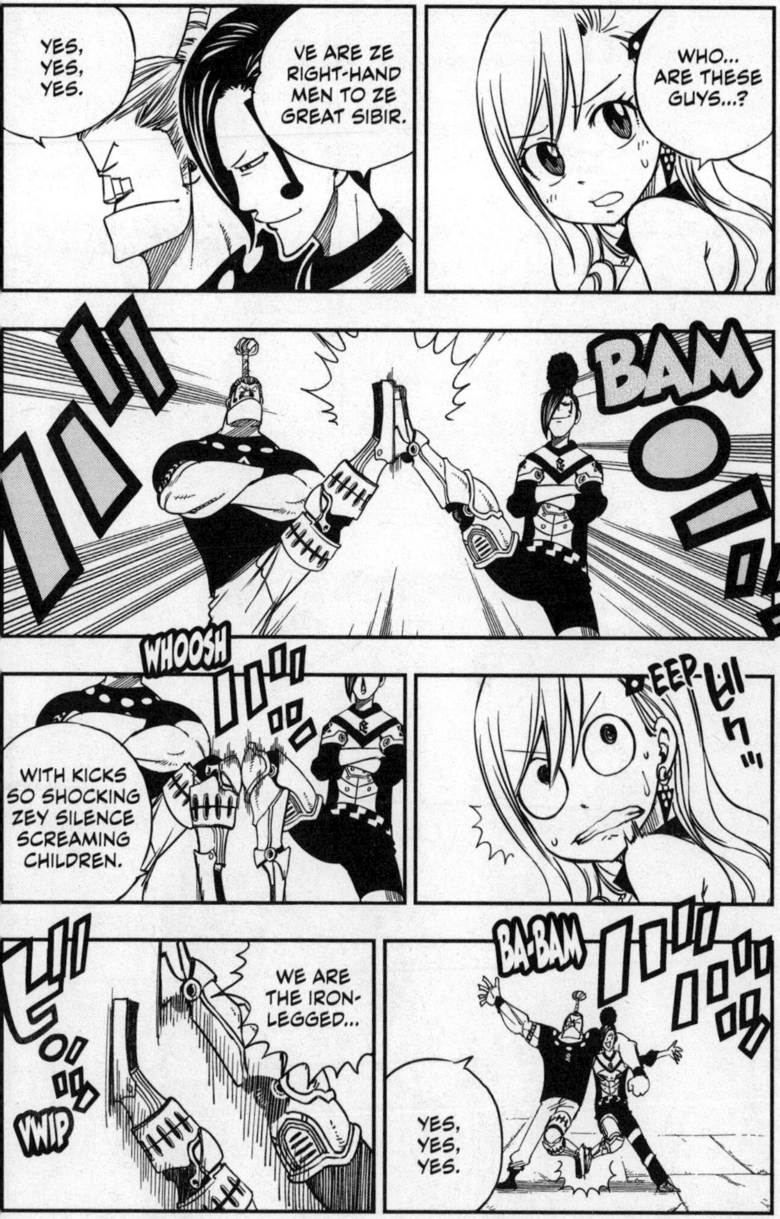
WHO... ARE THESE GUYS...?
VE ARE ZE RIGHT-HAND MEN TO ZE GREAT SIBIR.
YES, YES, YES.
BAM
EEP
WHOOSH
WITH KICKS SO SHOCKING ZEY SILENCE SCREAMING CHILDREN.
BA-BAM
YES, YES, YES.
WE ARE THE IRON-LEGGED...
VWIP

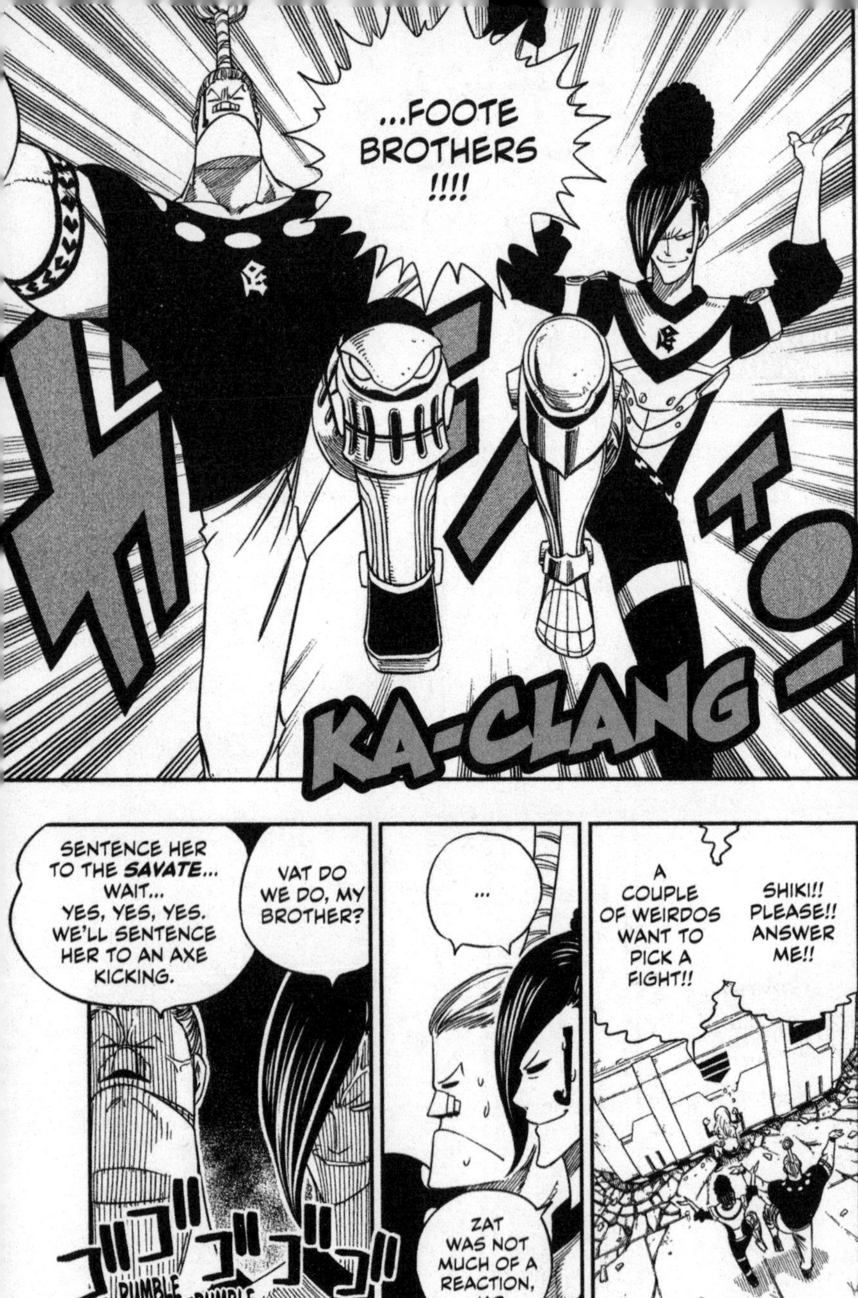
...FOOTE BROTHERS !!!!
KA-CLANG
SHIKI!! PLEASE!! ANSWER ME!!
A COUPLE OF WEIRDOS WANT TO PICK A FIGHT!!
...
ZAT WAS NOT MUCH OF A REACTION, JA?
VAT DO WE DO, MY BROTHER?
SENTENCE HER TO THE *SAVATE*... WAIT... YES, YES, YES. WE'LL SENTENCE HER TO AN AXE KICKING.
RUMBLE RUMBLE RUMBLE RUMBLE RUMBLE

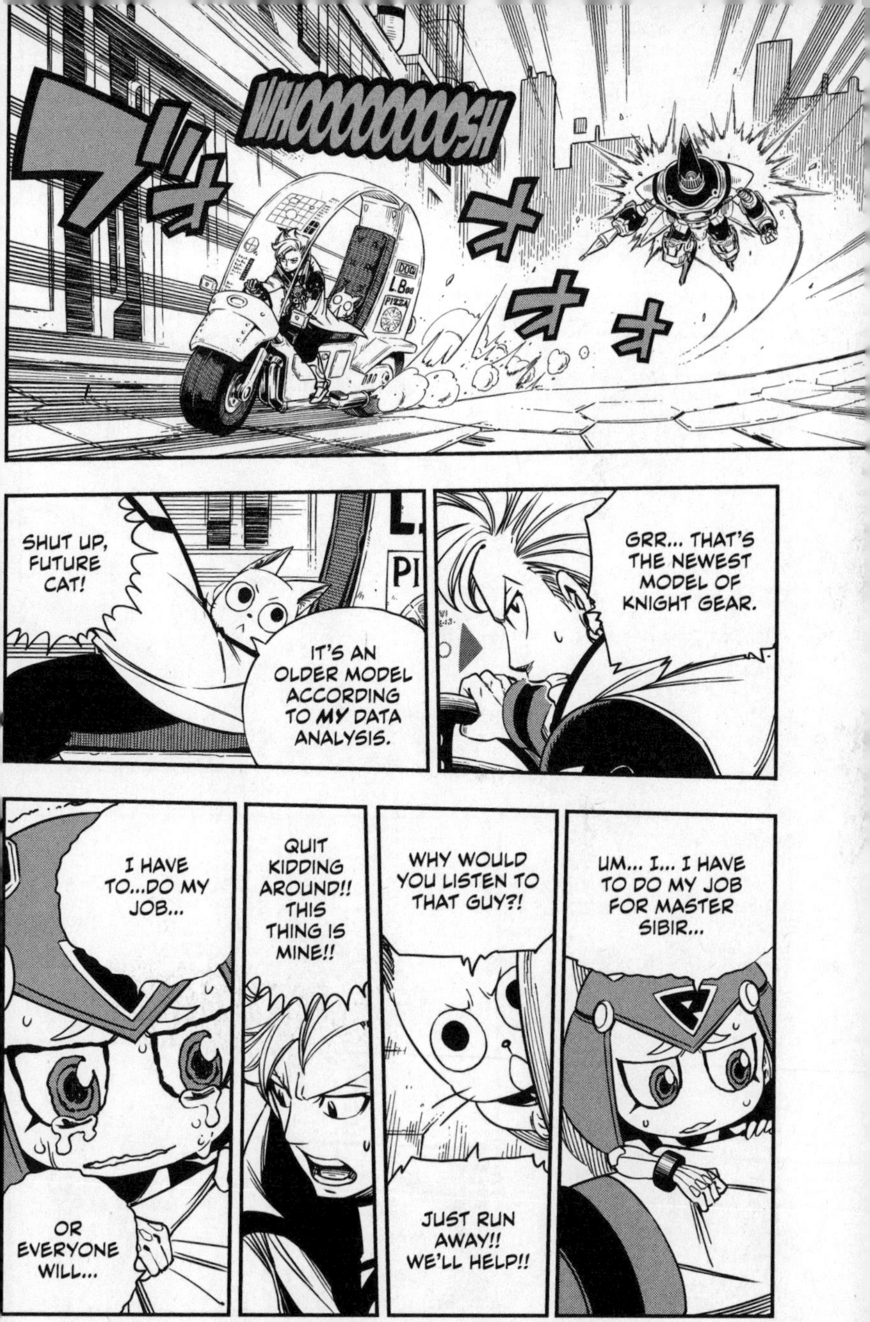
WHOOOOOOOOOSH
ブォォォォ
GRR... THAT'S THE NEWEST MODEL OF KNIGHT GEAR.
IT'S AN OLDER MODEL ACCORDING TO MY DATA ANALYSIS.
SHUT UP, FUTURE CAT!
UM... I... I HAVE TO DO MY JOB FOR MASTER SIBIR...
WHY WOULD YOU LISTEN TO THAT GUY?!
JUST RUN AWAY!! WE'LL HELP!!
QUIT KIDDING AROUND!! THIS THING IS MINE!!
I HAVE TO...DO MY JOB...
OR EVERYONE WILL...

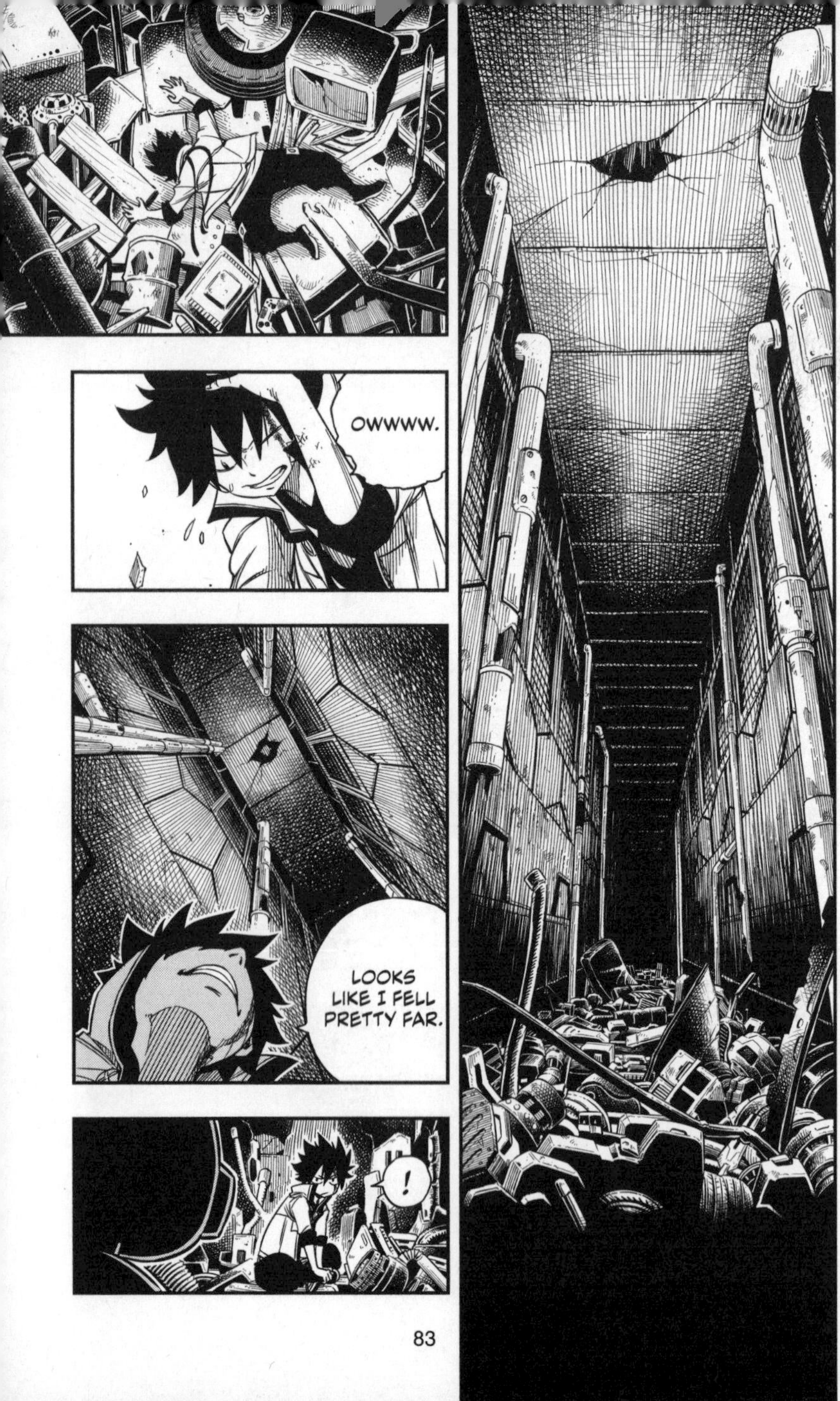
OWWWW.
LOOKS LIKE I FELL PRETTY FAR.
!

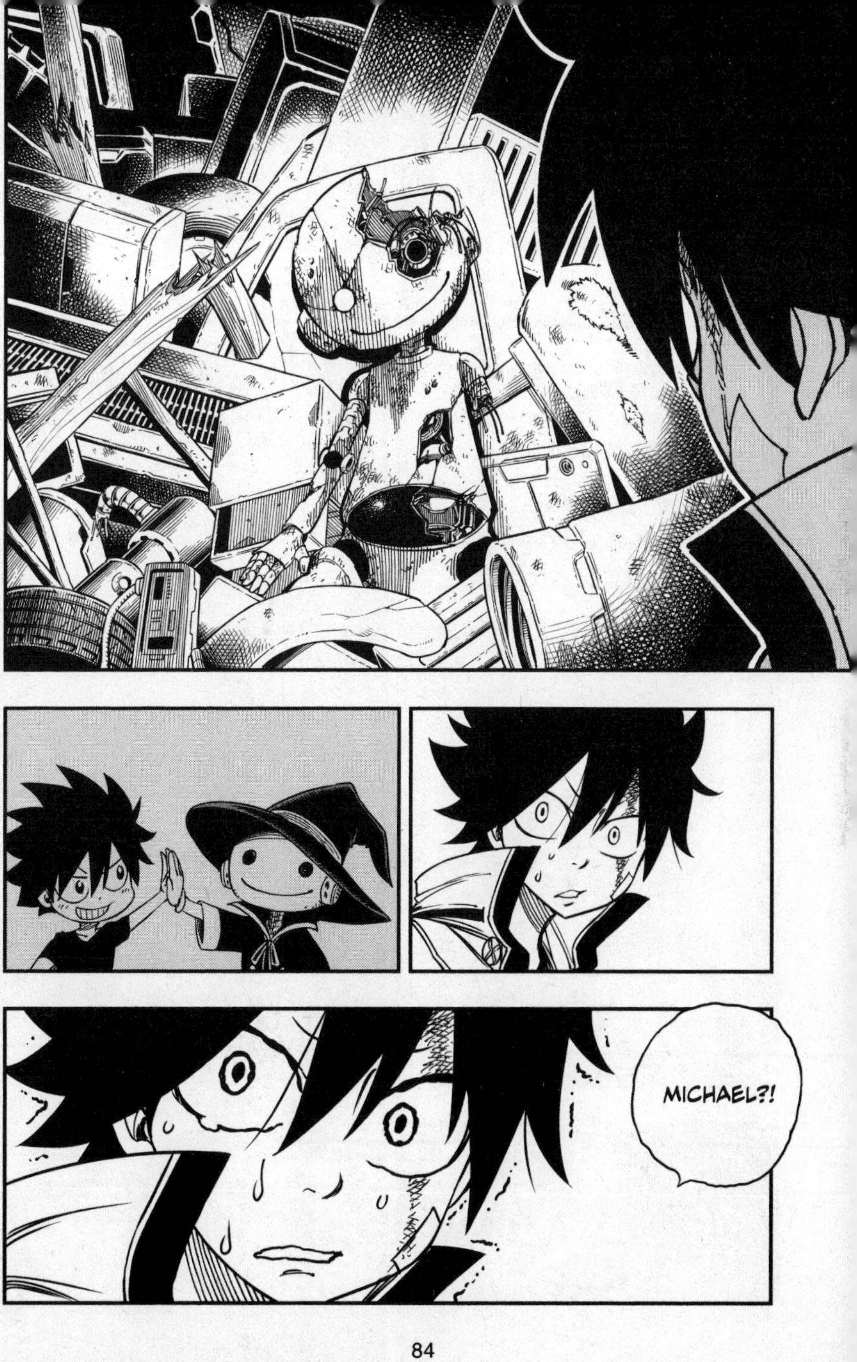
MICHAEL?!

# EDENS ZERO

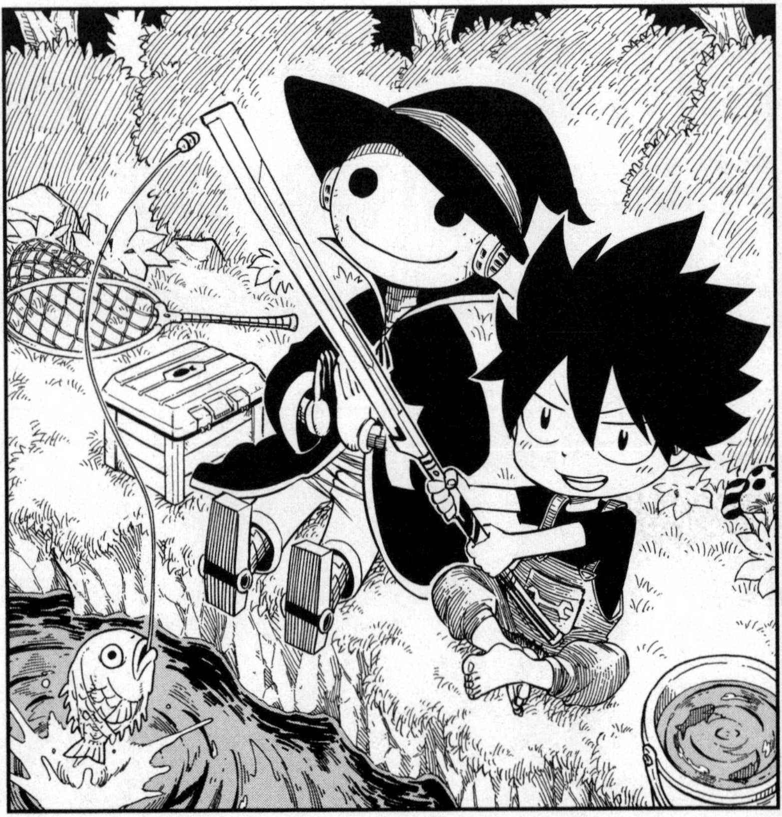

## CHAPTER 9: VS. THE FOOTE BROTHERS

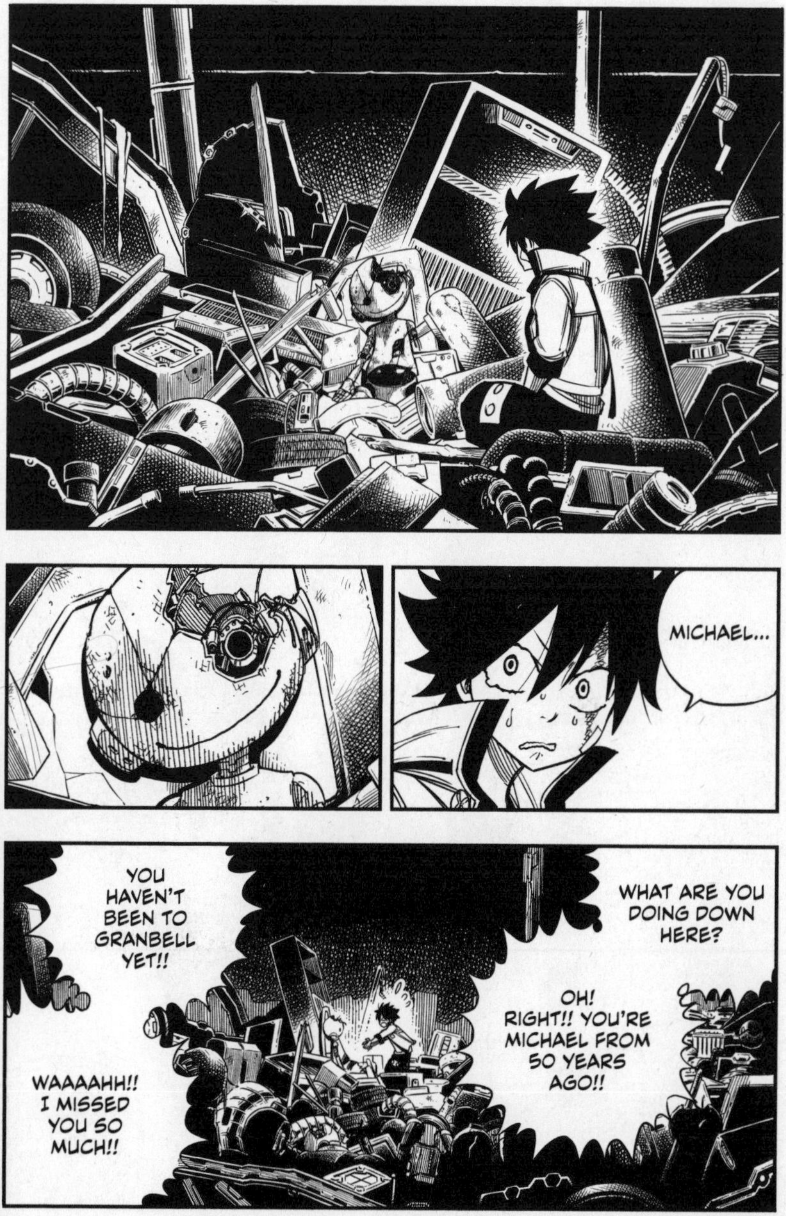
MICHAEL...
WHAT ARE YOU DOING DOWN HERE?
OH! RIGHT!! YOU'RE MICHAEL FROM 50 YEARS AGO!!
YOU HAVEN'T BEEN TO GRANBELL YET!!
WAAAAHH!! I MISSED YOU SO MUCH!!

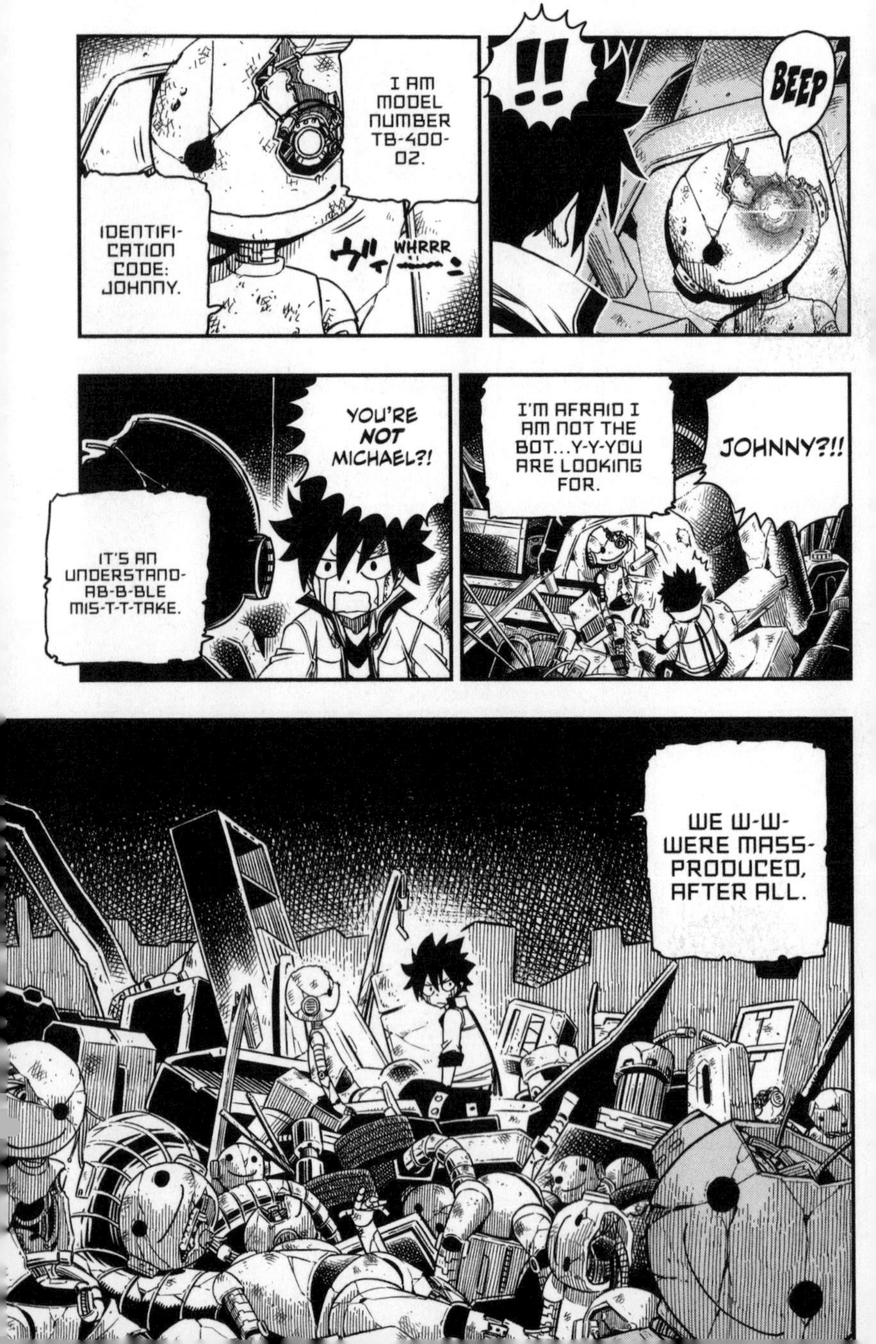
!!
BEEP
I AM MODEL NUMBER TB-400-02.
IDENTIFICATION CODE: JOHNNY.
WHRRR
JOHNNY?!!
I'M AFRAID I AM NOT THE BOT...Y-Y-YOU ARE LOOKING FOR.
YOU'RE *NOT* MICHAEL?!
IT'S AN UNDERSTANDAB-B-BLE MIS-T-T-TAKE.
WE W-W-WERE MASS-PRODUCED, AFTER ALL.

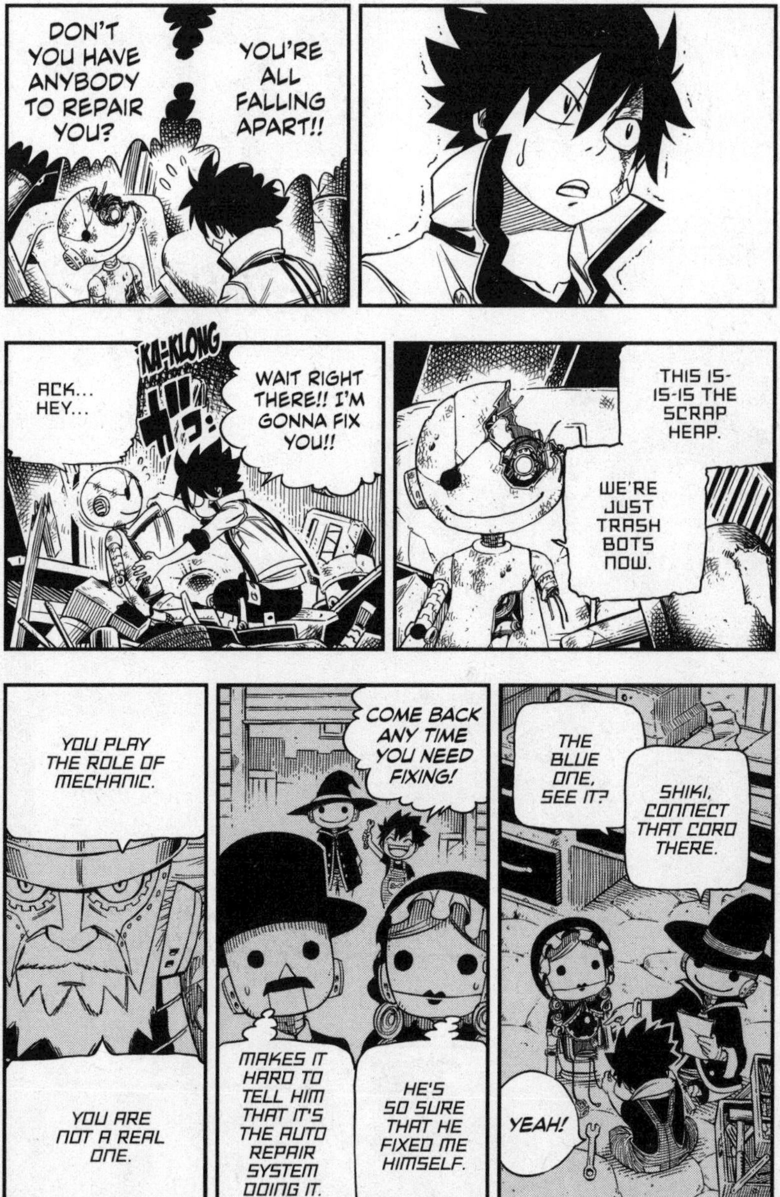
YOU'RE ALL FALLING APART!!
DON'T YOU HAVE ANYBODY TO REPAIR YOU?
THIS IS-IS-IS THE SCRAP HEAP.
WE'RE JUST TRASH BOTS NOW.
WAIT RIGHT THERE!! I'M GONNA FIX YOU!!
KA-KLONG
ACK... HEY...
SHIKI, CONNECT THAT CORD THERE.
THE BLUE ONE, SEE IT?
YEAH!
COME BACK ANY TIME YOU NEED FIXING!
HE'S SO SURE THAT HE FIXED ME HIMSELF.
MAKES IT HARD TO TELL HIM THAT IT'S THE AUTO REPAIR SYSTEM DOING IT.
YOU PLAY THE ROLE OF MECHANIC.
YOU ARE NOT A REAL ONE.

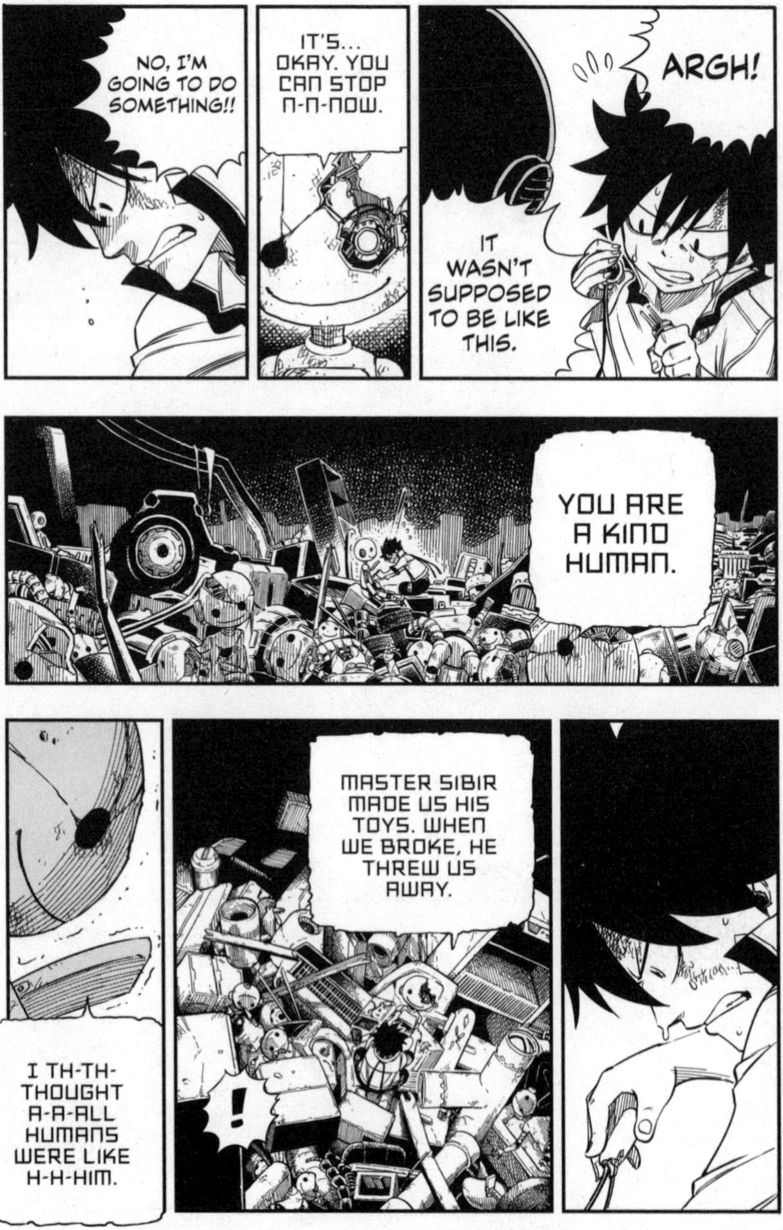
ARGH!
IT WASN'T SUPPOSED TO BE LIKE THIS.
IT'S... OKAY. YOU CAN STOP N-N-NOW.
NO, I'M GOING TO DO SOMETHING!!
YOU ARE A KIND HUMAN.
MASTER SIBIR MADE US HIS TOYS. WHEN WE BROKE, HE THREW US AWAY.
!
I TH-TH-THOUGHT A-A-ALL HUMANS WERE LIKE H-H-HIM.

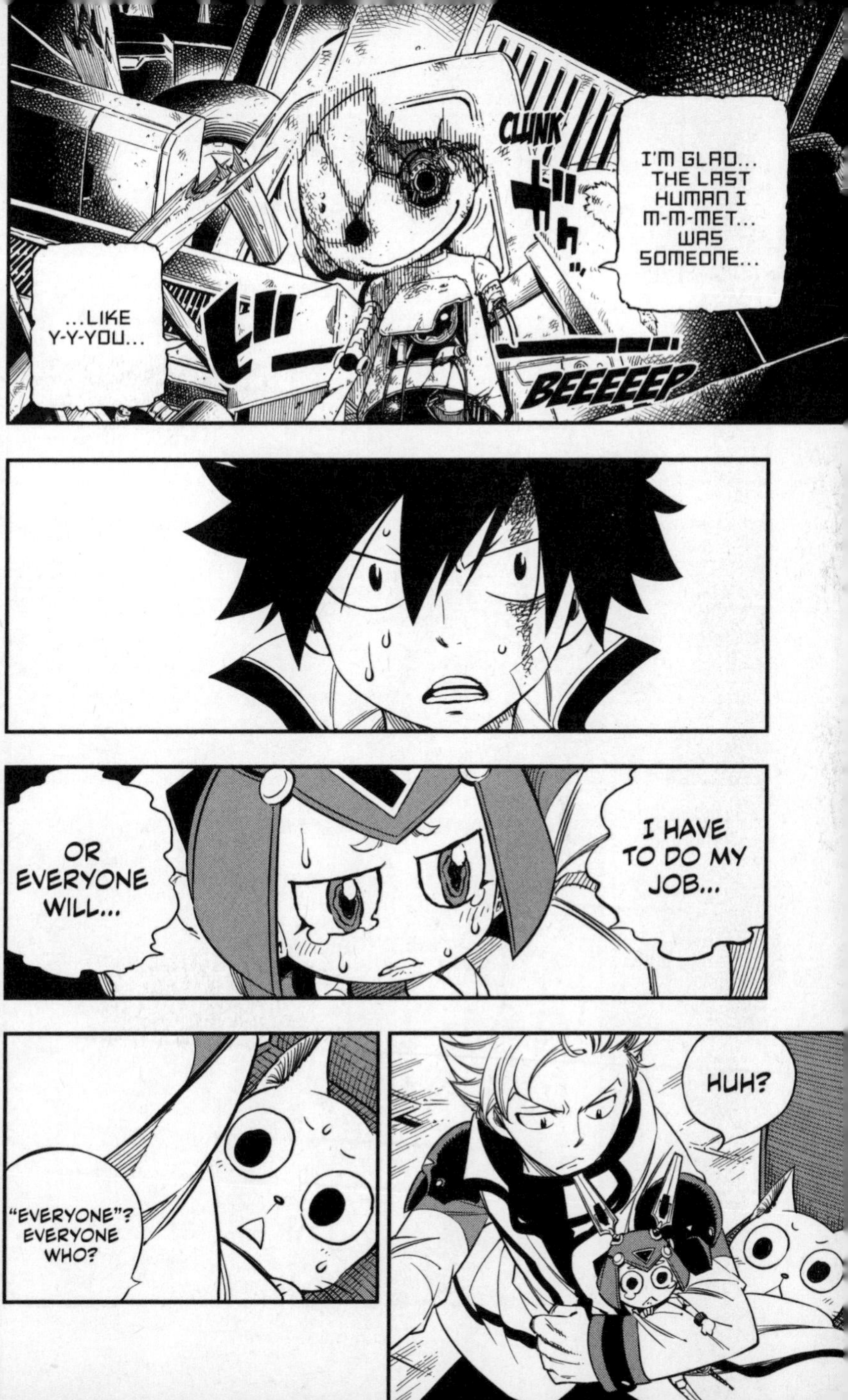
I'M GLAD... THE LAST HUMAN I M-M-MET... WAS SOMEONE...
CLUNK
...LIKE Y-Y-YOU...
BEEEEEP
I HAVE TO DO MY JOB...
OR EVERYONE WILL...
HUH?
"EVERYONE"? EVERYONE WHO?

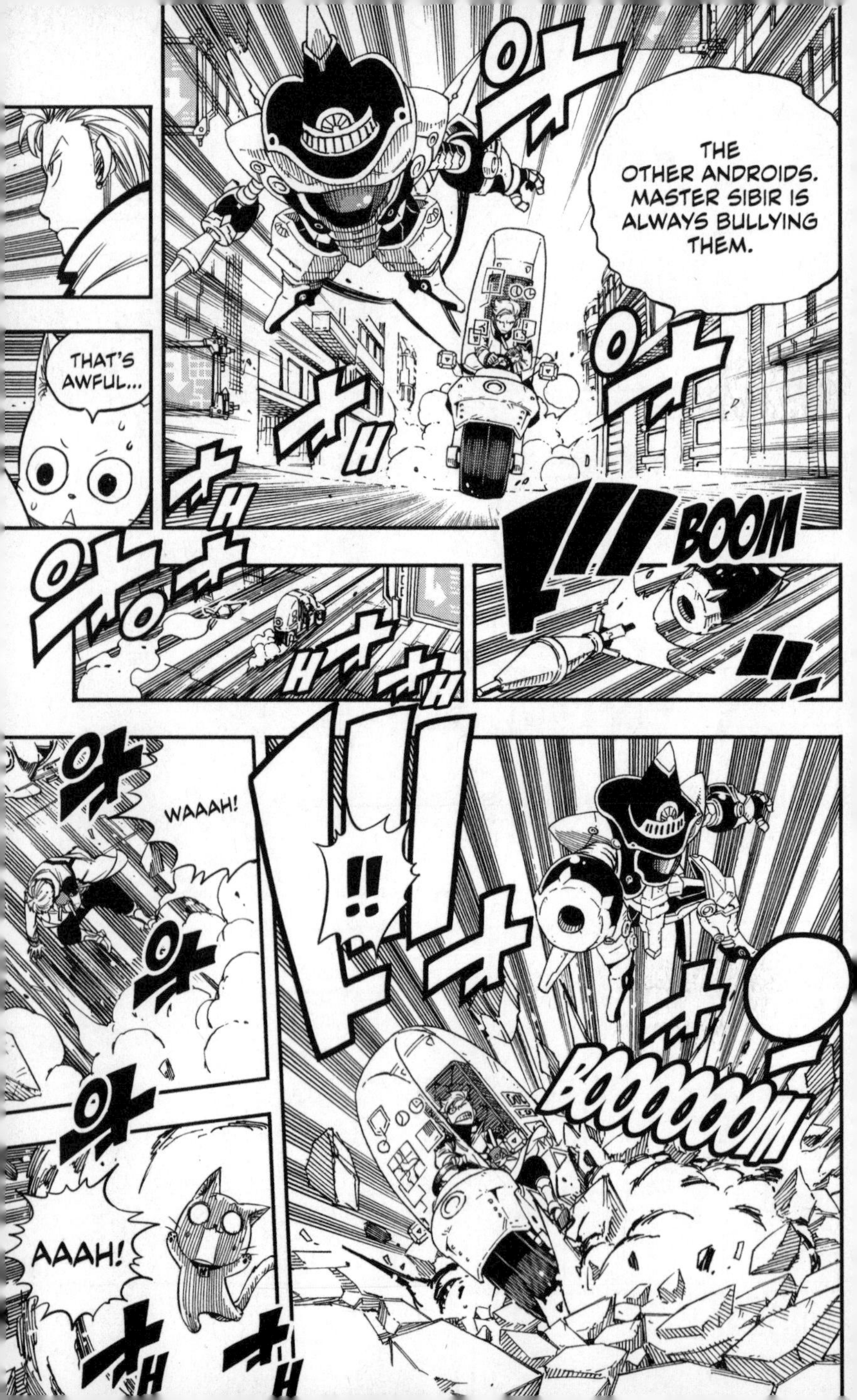
THE OTHER ANDROIDS. MASTER SIBIR IS ALWAYS BULLYING THEM.
THAT'S AWFUL...
BOOM
BOOOOOOM
WAAAH!
AAAH!

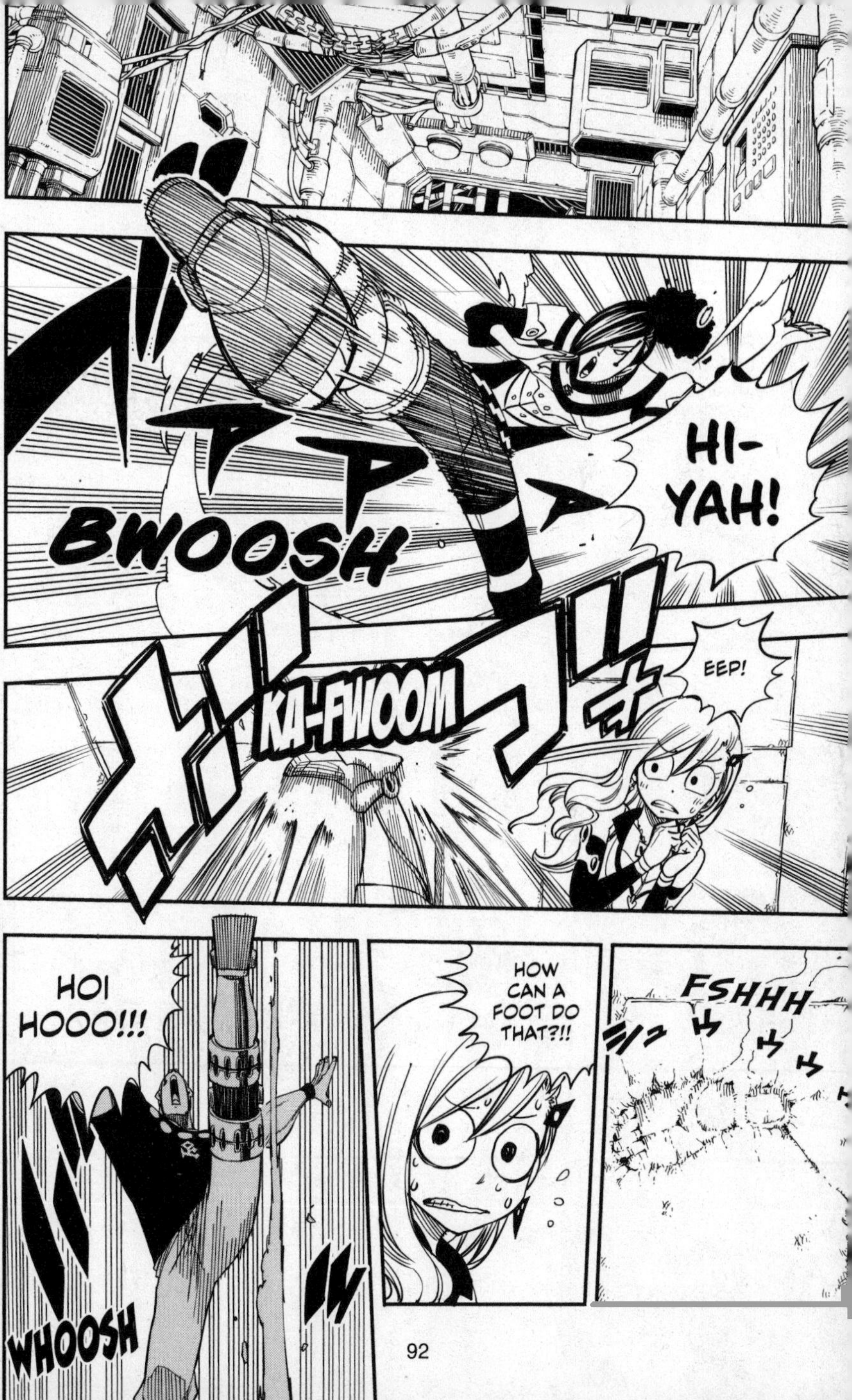
BWOOSH
HI-YAH!
KA-FWOOM
EEP!
FSHHH
HOW CAN A FOOT DO THAT?!!
HOI HOOO!!!
WHOOSH

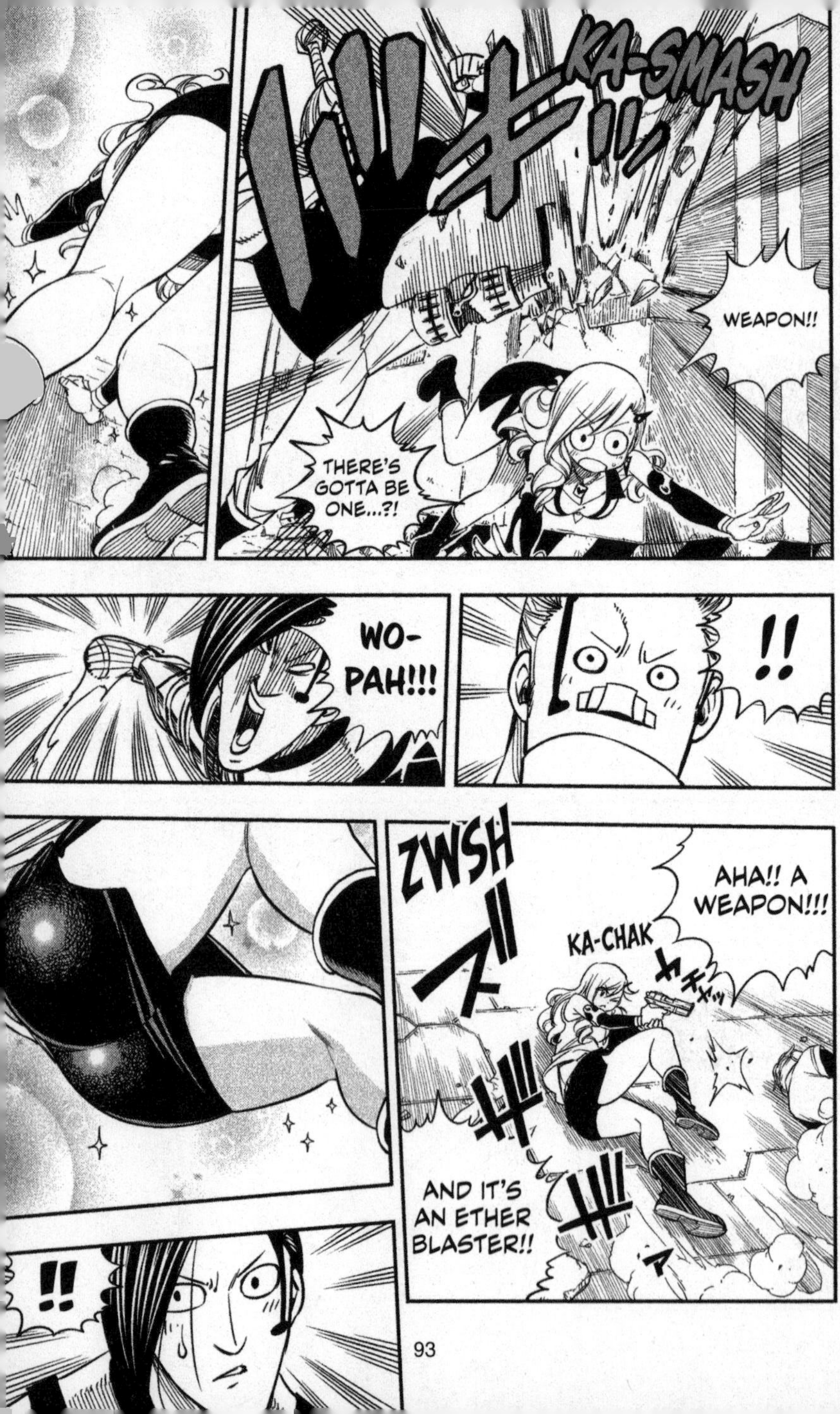
KA-SMASH
WEAPON!!
THERE'S GOTTA BE ONE...?!
!!
WO-PAH!!!
ZWSH
AHA!! A WEAPON!!!
KA-CHAK
AND IT'S AN ETHER BLASTER!!
!!

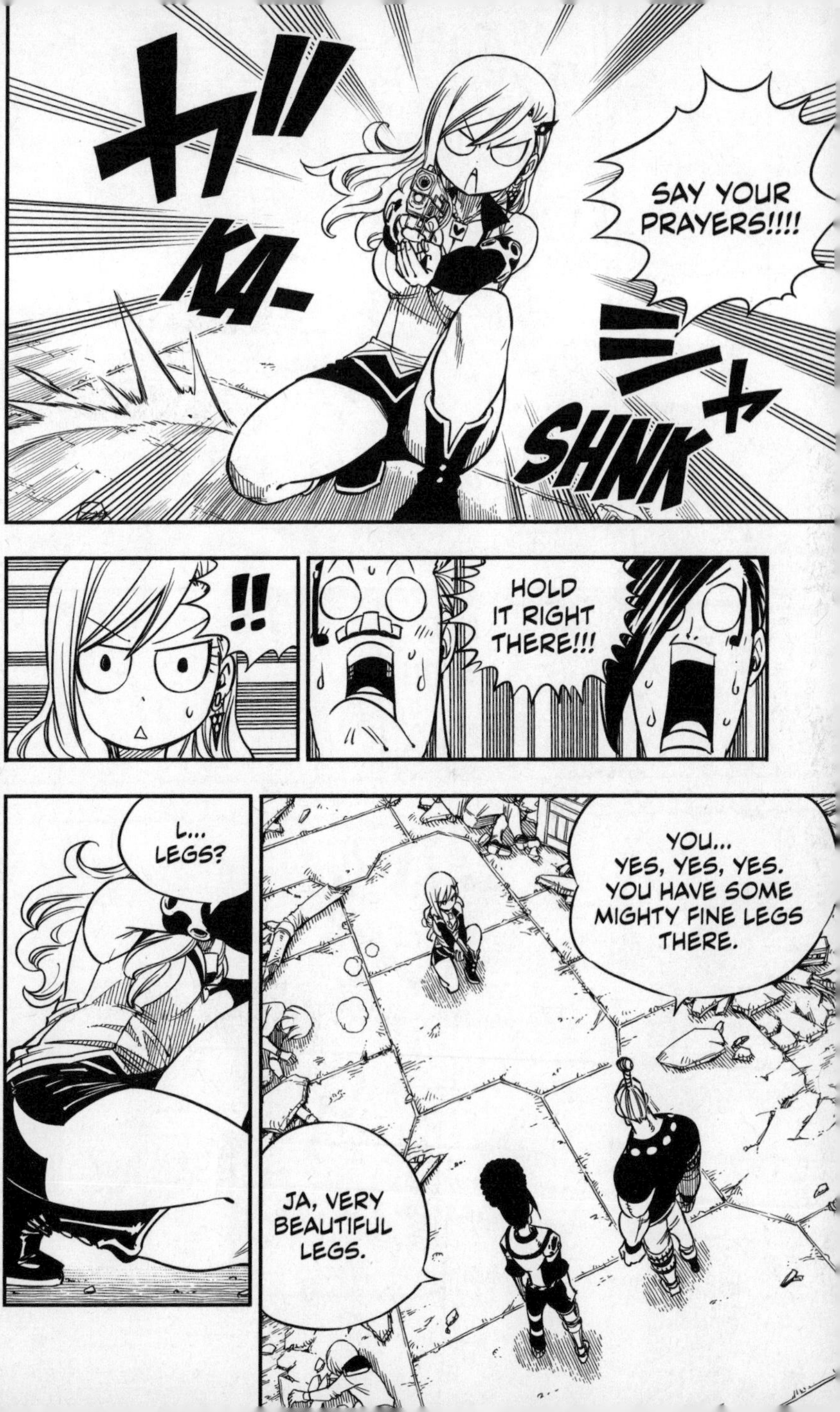
SAY YOUR PRAYERS!!!!
KA-
SHNK
HOLD IT RIGHT THERE!!!
!!
YOU... YES, YES, YES. YOU HAVE SOME MIGHTY FINE LEGS THERE.
JA, VERY BEAUTIFUL LEGS.
L... LEGS?

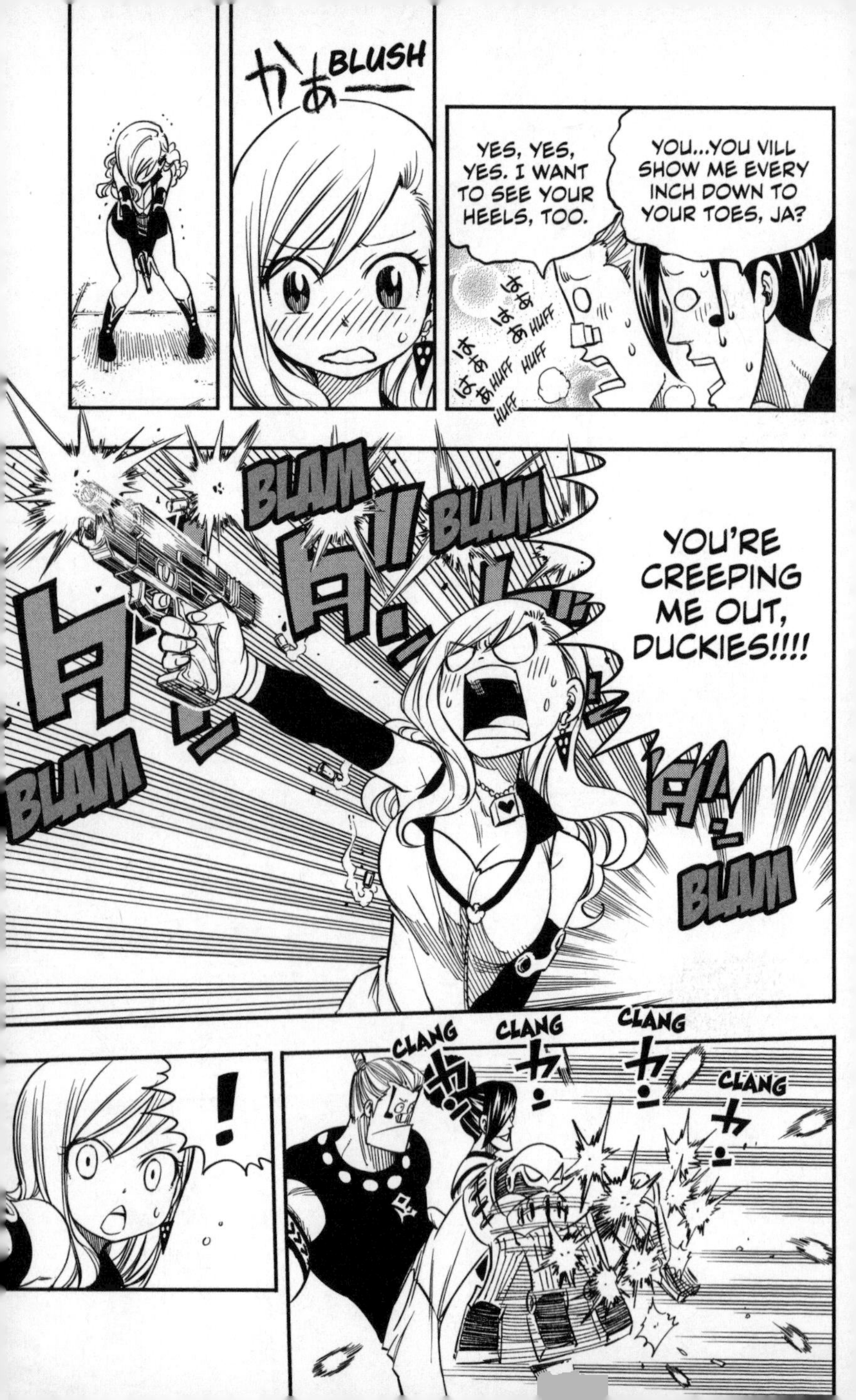
YOU...YOU VILL SHOW ME EVERY INCH DOWN TO YOUR TOES, JA?
YES, YES, YES. I WANT TO SEE YOUR HEELS, TOO.
HUFF HUFF HUFF HUFF
かあー BLUSH
YOU'RE CREEPING ME OUT, DUCKIES!!!!
BLAM BLAM BLAM BLAM
CLANG CLANG CLANG CLANG
!

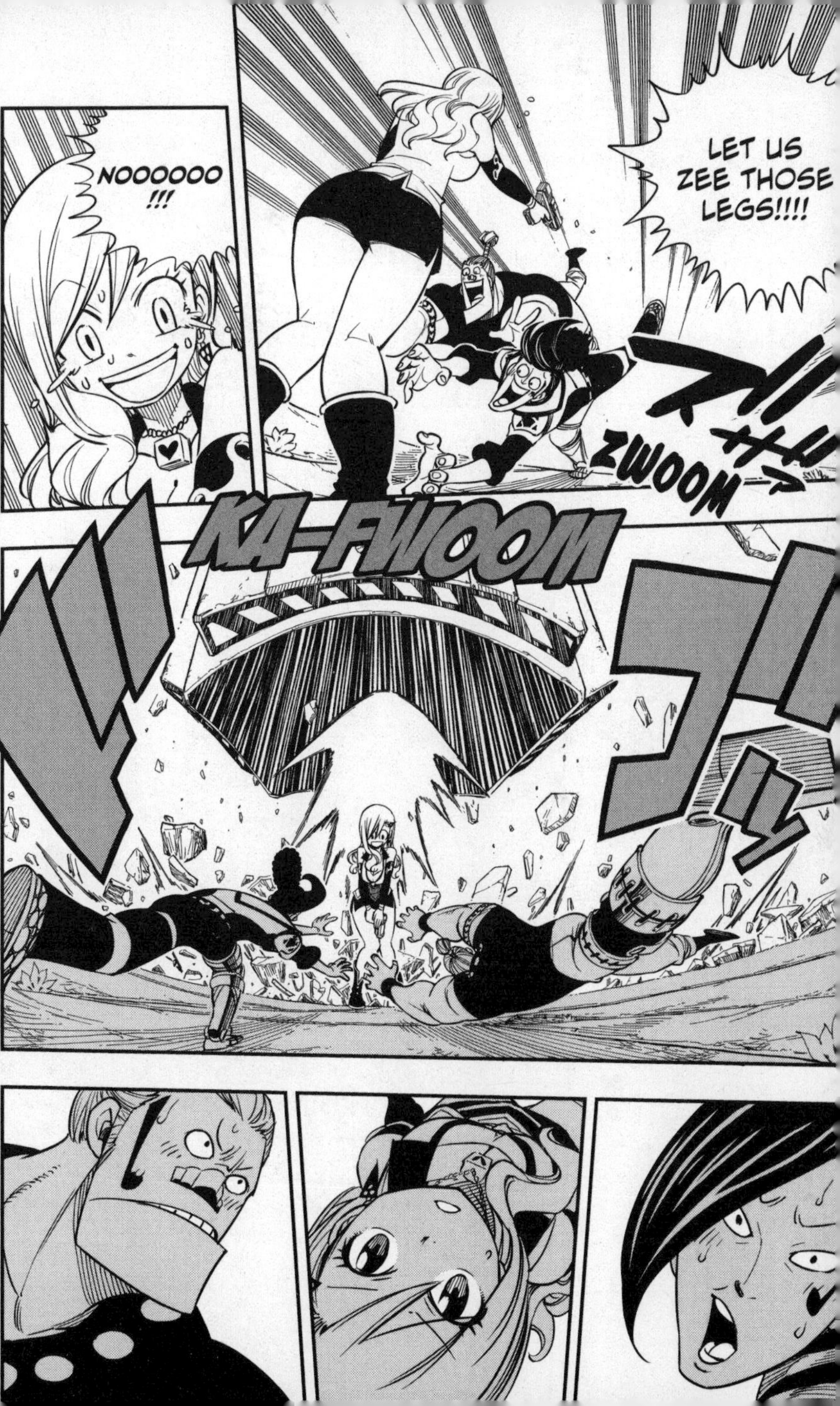
LET US ZEE THOSE LEGS!!!!
ZWOOM
NOOOOOO !!!
KA-FWOOM

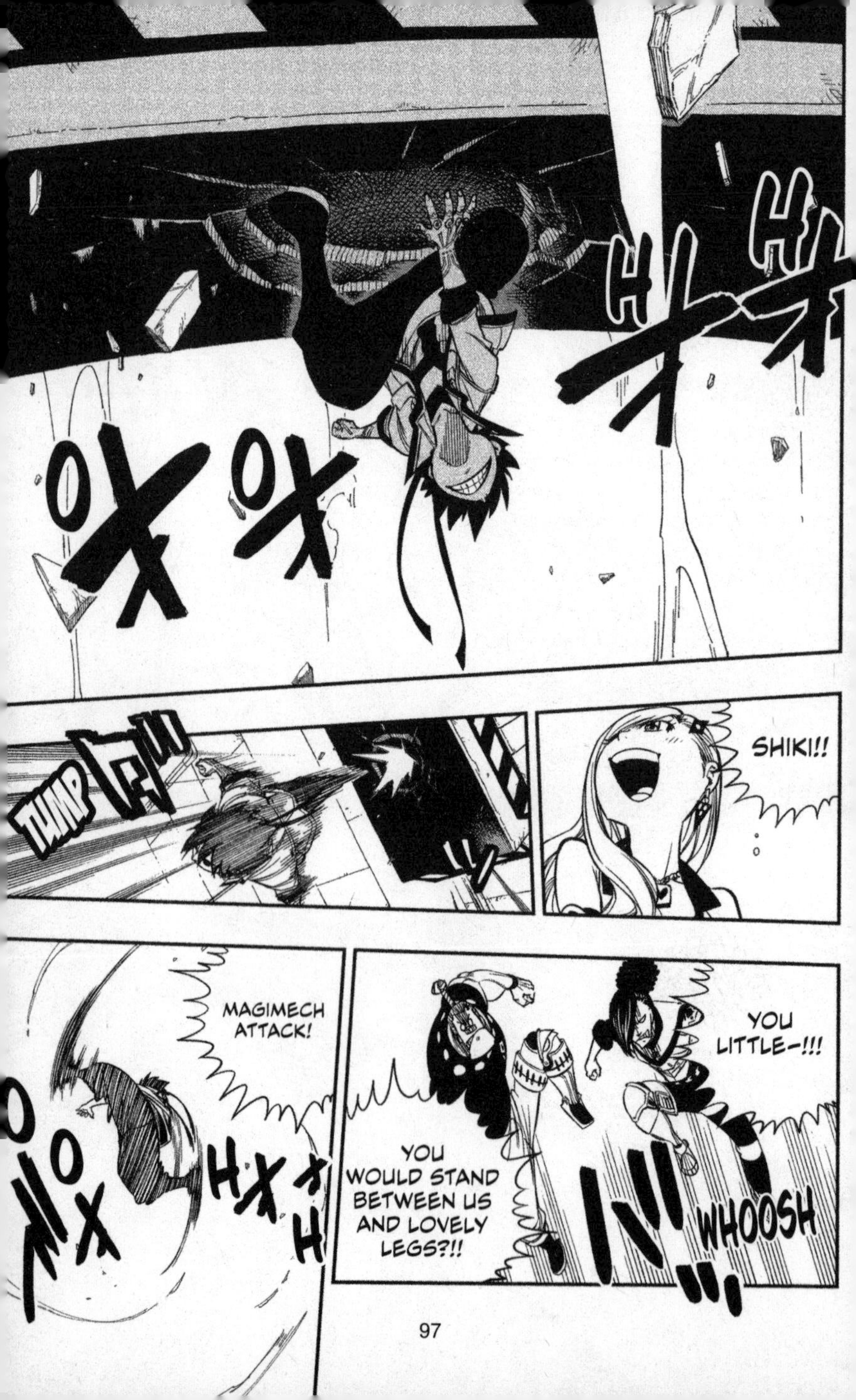
SHIKI!!!
TUMP
YOU LITTLE-!!!
YOU WOULD STAND BETWEEN US AND LOVELY LEGS?!!
WHOOSH
MAGIMECH ATTACK!

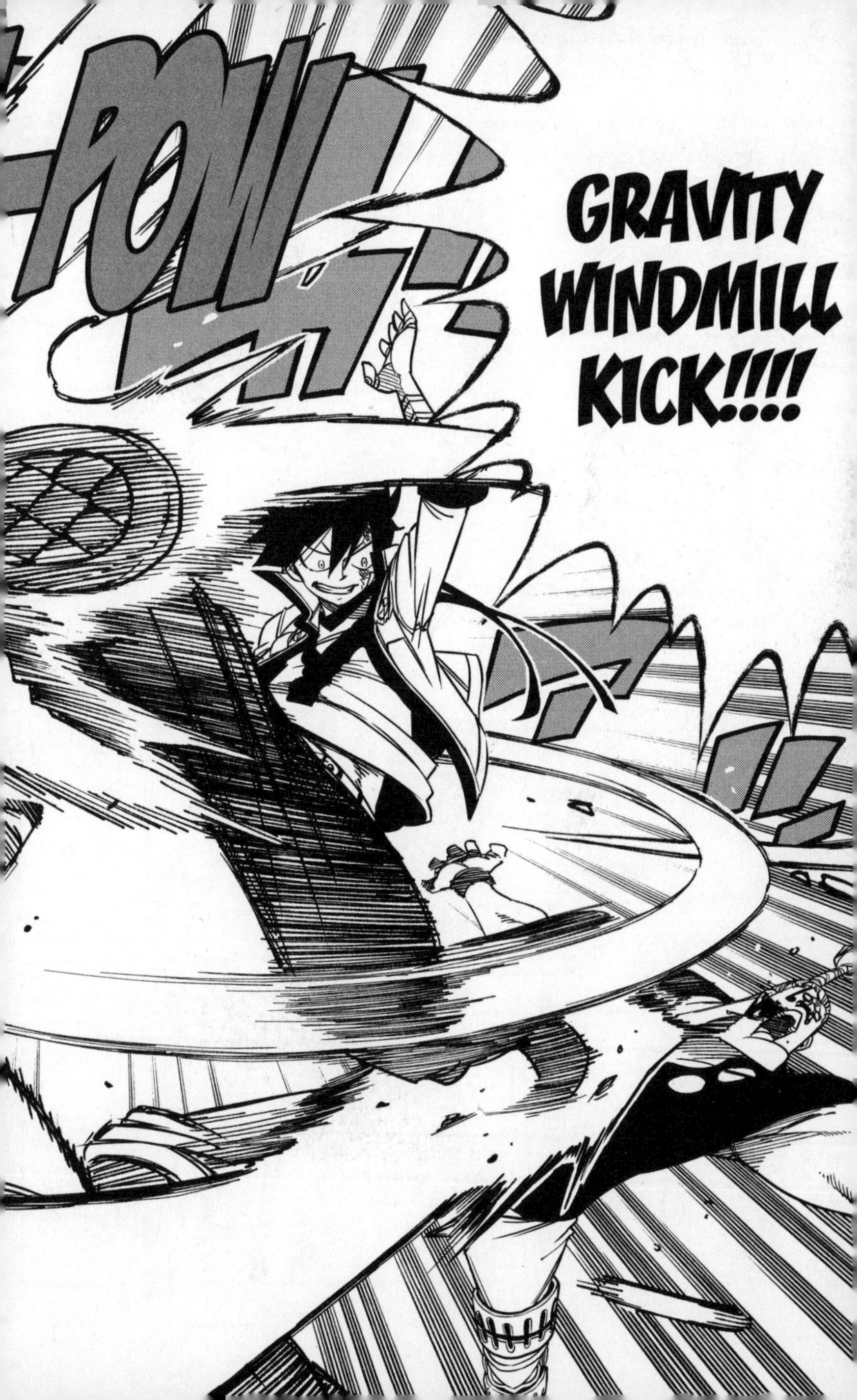
POW
GRAVITY WINDMILL KICK!!!!

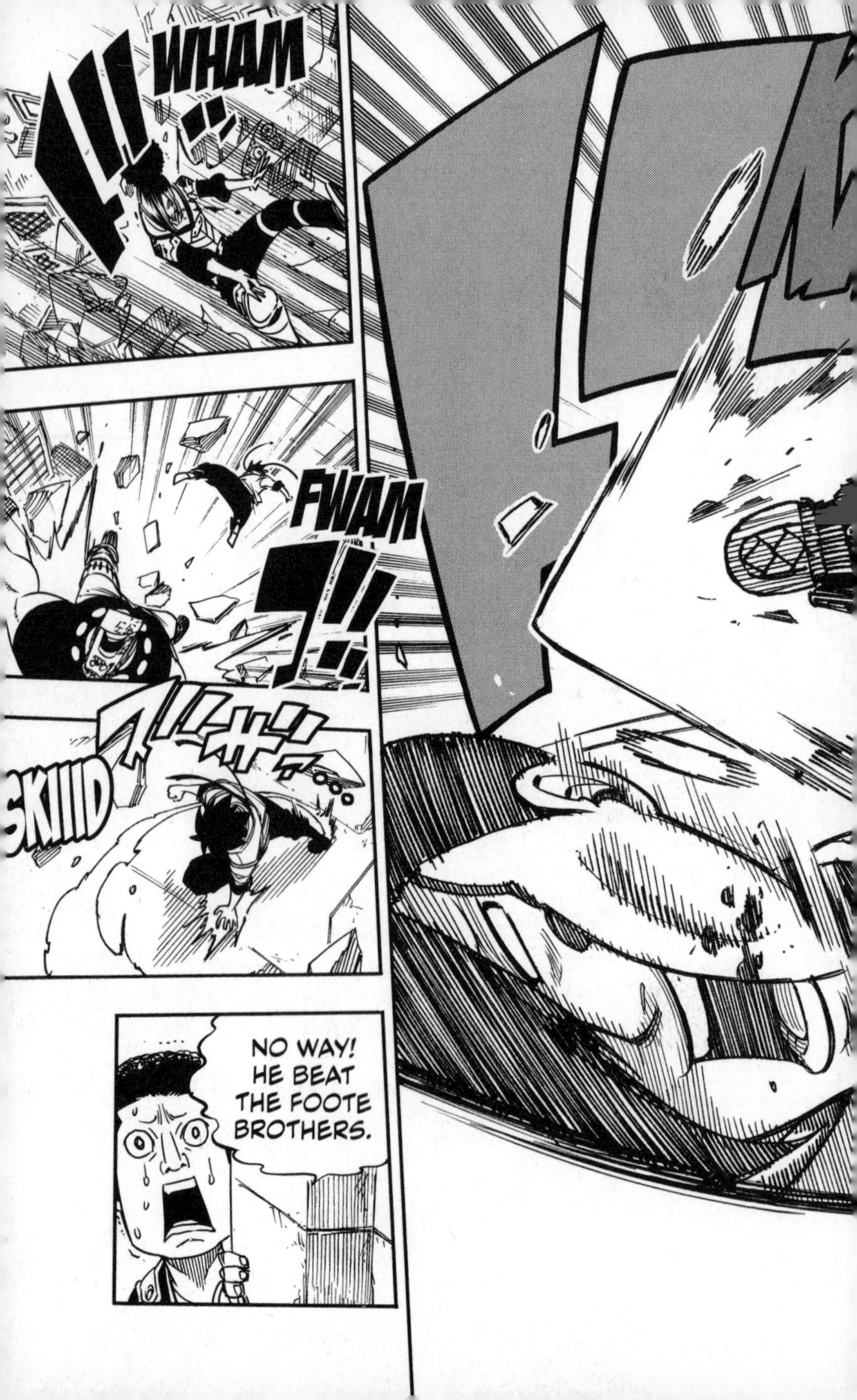
WHAM!!
FWAM!!
SKIIID
NO WAY! HE BEAT THE FOOTE BROTHERS.

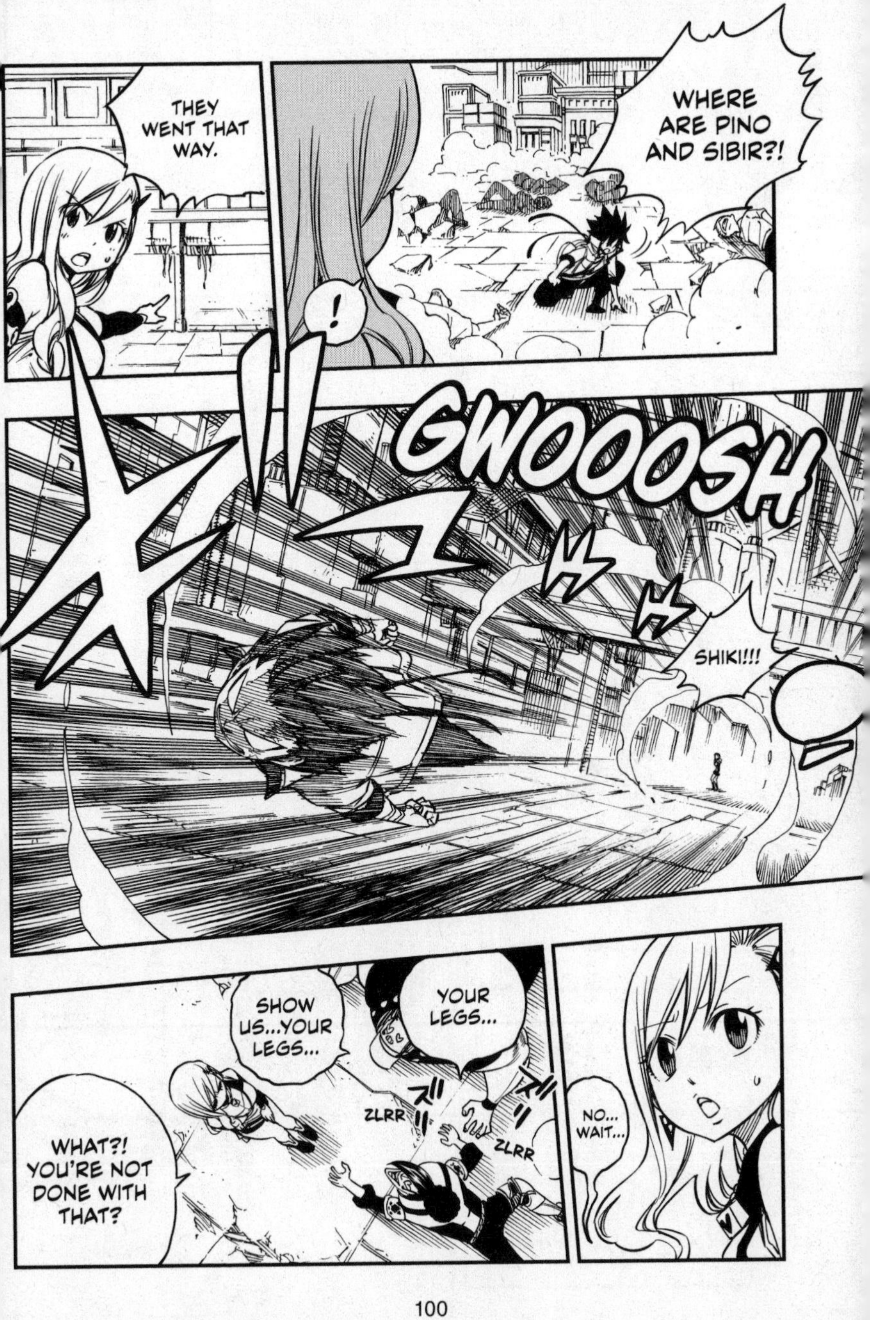
WHERE ARE PINO AND SIBIR?!
!
THEY WENT THAT WAY.
GWOOOSH
SHIKI!!!
NO... WAIT...
YOUR LEGS...
SHOW US...YOUR LEGS...
ZLRR
ZLRR
WHAT?! YOU'RE NOT DONE WITH THAT?

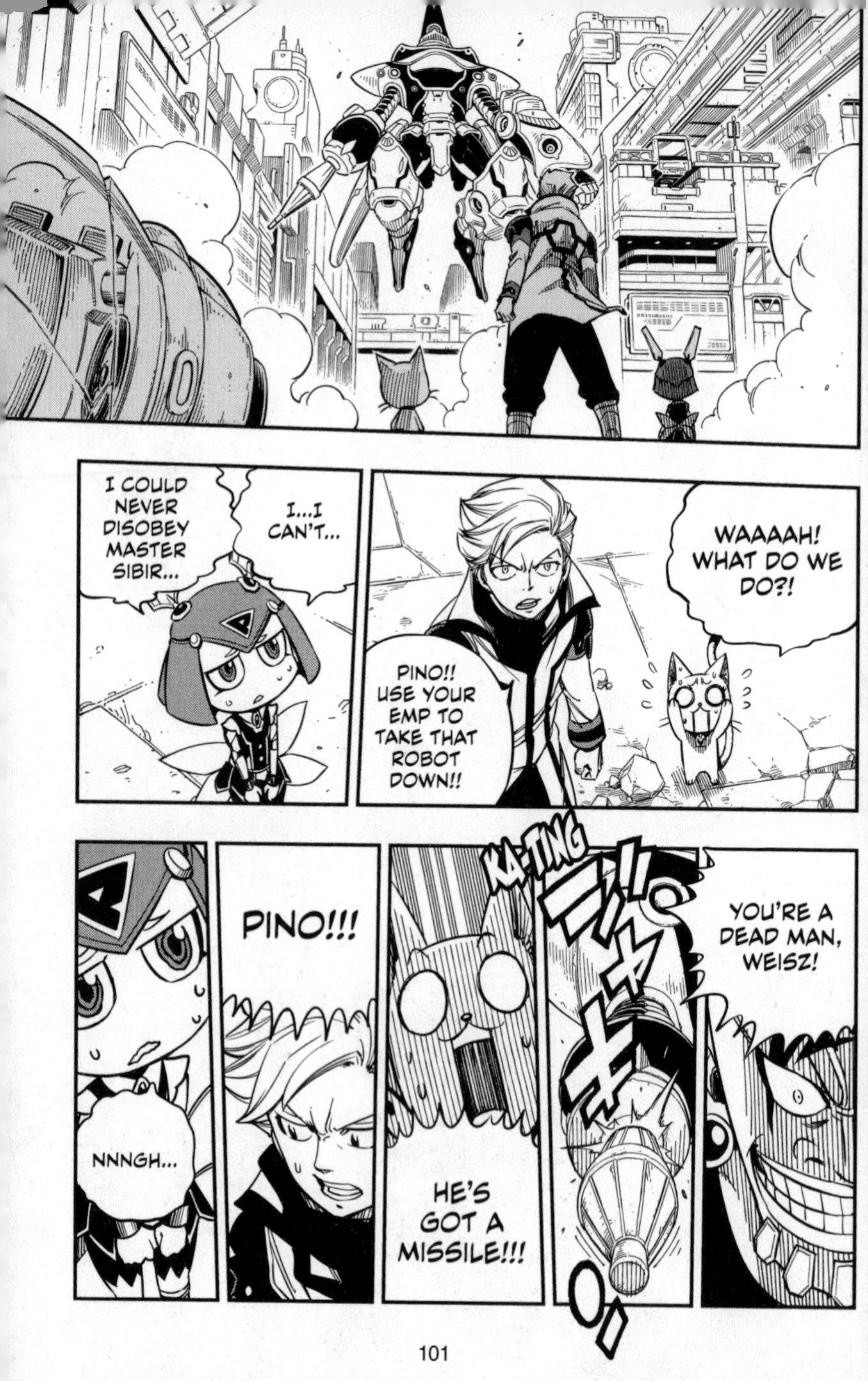
WAAAAH! WHAT DO WE DO?!
PINO!! USE YOUR EMP TO TAKE THAT ROBOT DOWN!!
I...I CAN'T...
I COULD NEVER DISOBEY MASTER SIBIR...
YOU'RE A DEAD MAN, WEISZ!
KA-TING
HE'S GOT A MISSILE!!!
PINO!!!
NNNGH...

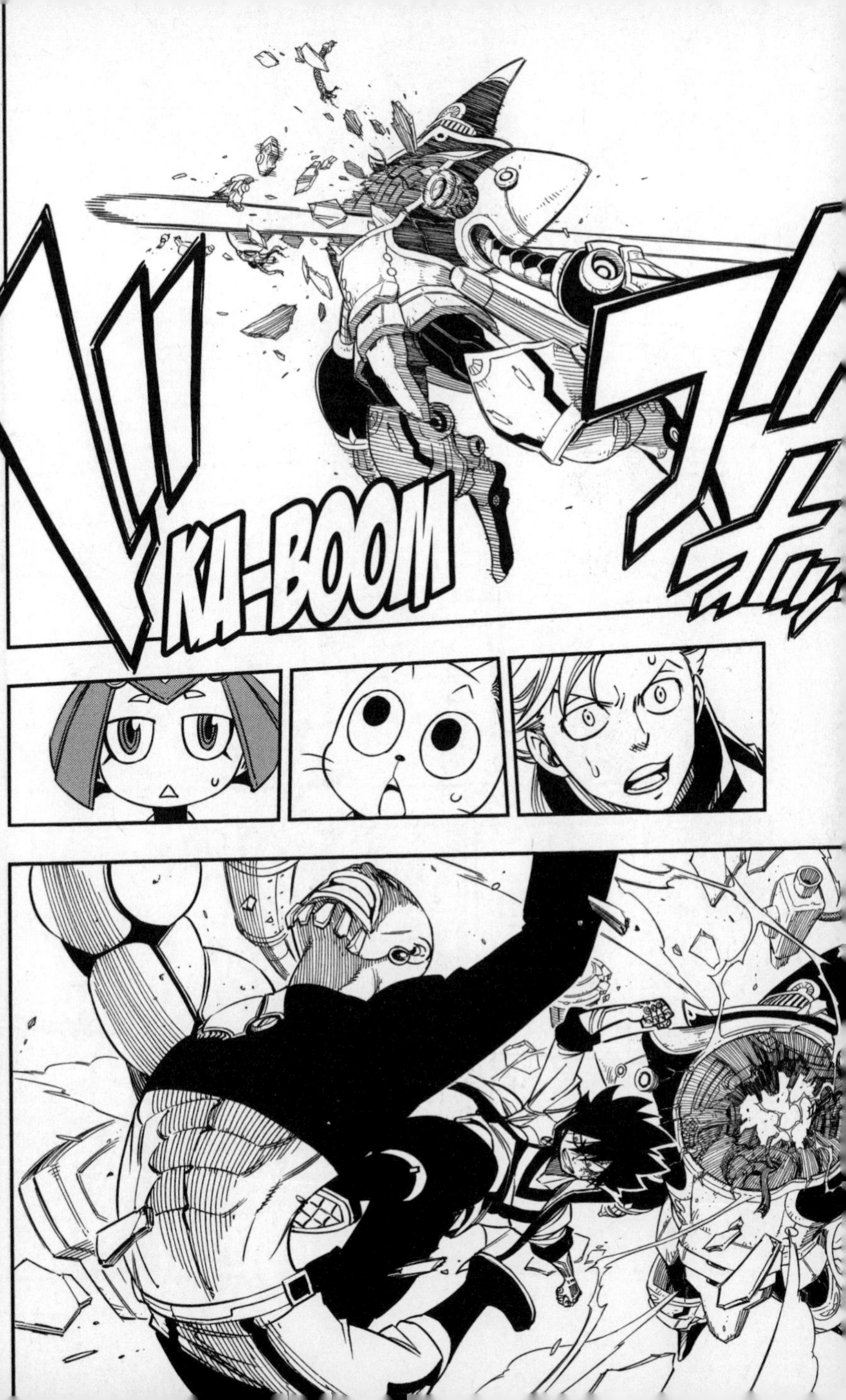
KA-BOOM

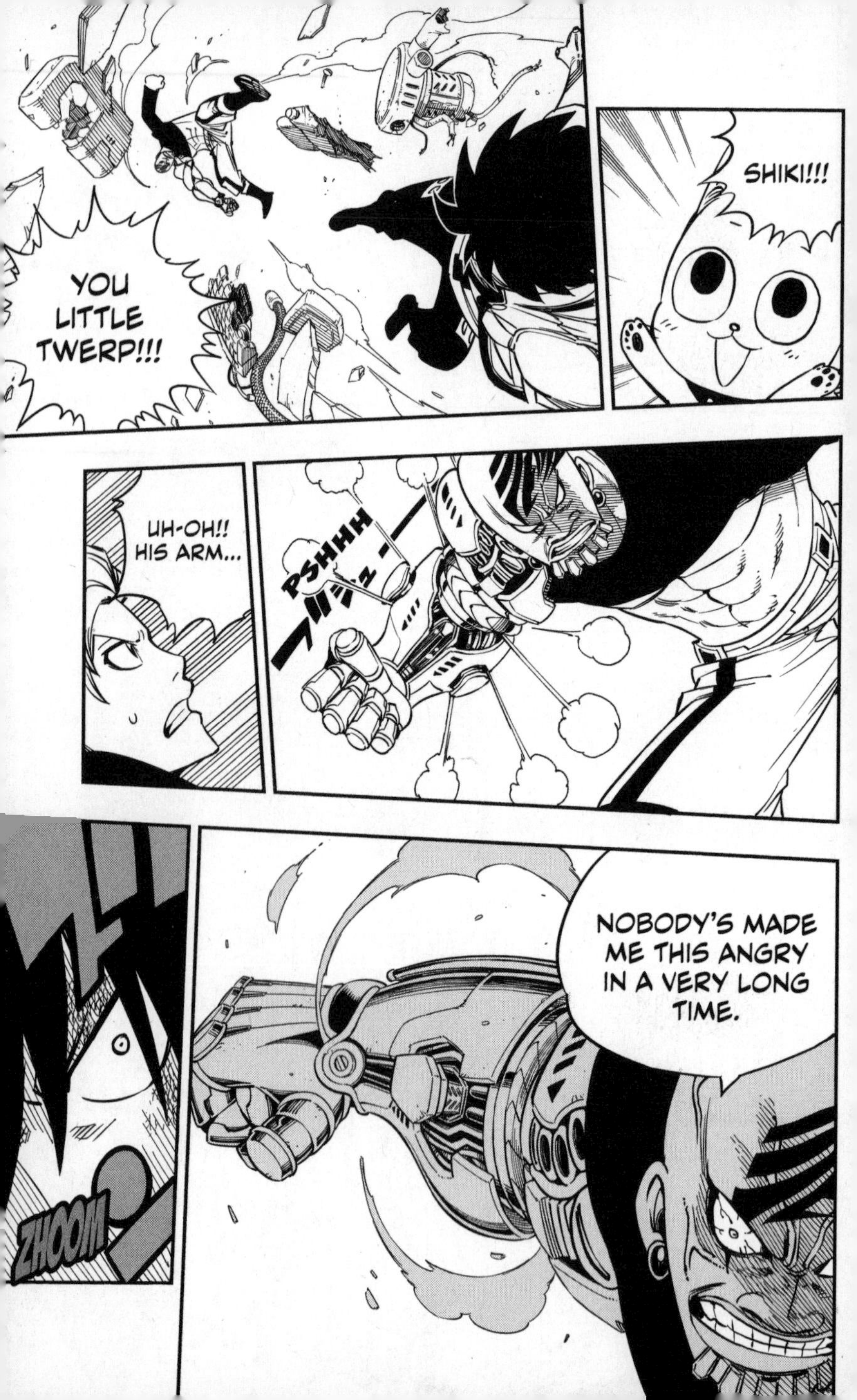
SHIKI!!!
YOU LITTLE TWERP!!!
PSHHH
UH-OH!! HIS ARM...
NOBODY'S MADE ME THIS ANGRY IN A VERY LONG TIME.
ZHOOM

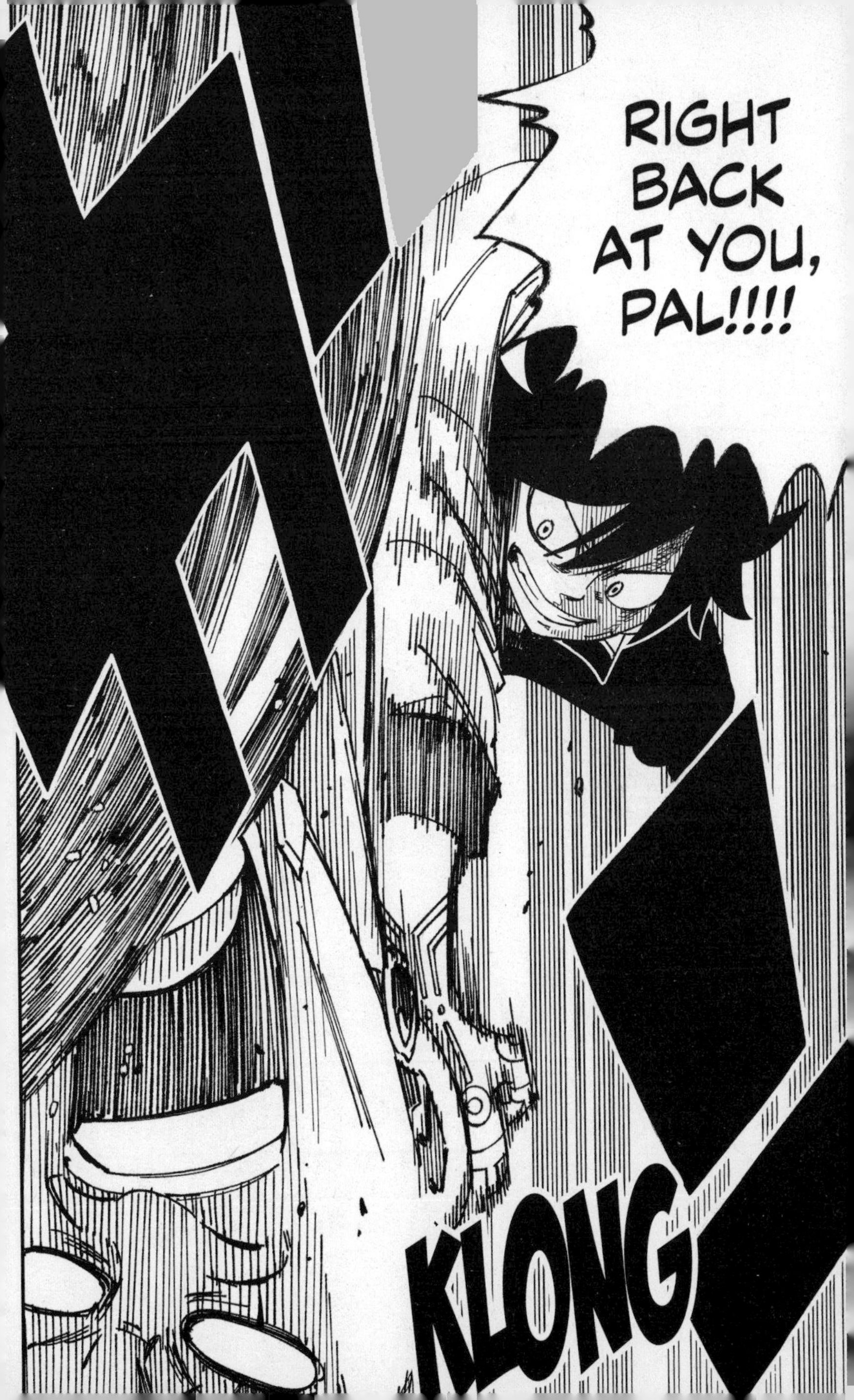
RIGHT BACK AT YOU, PAL!!!!
KLONG

# EDENS ZERO

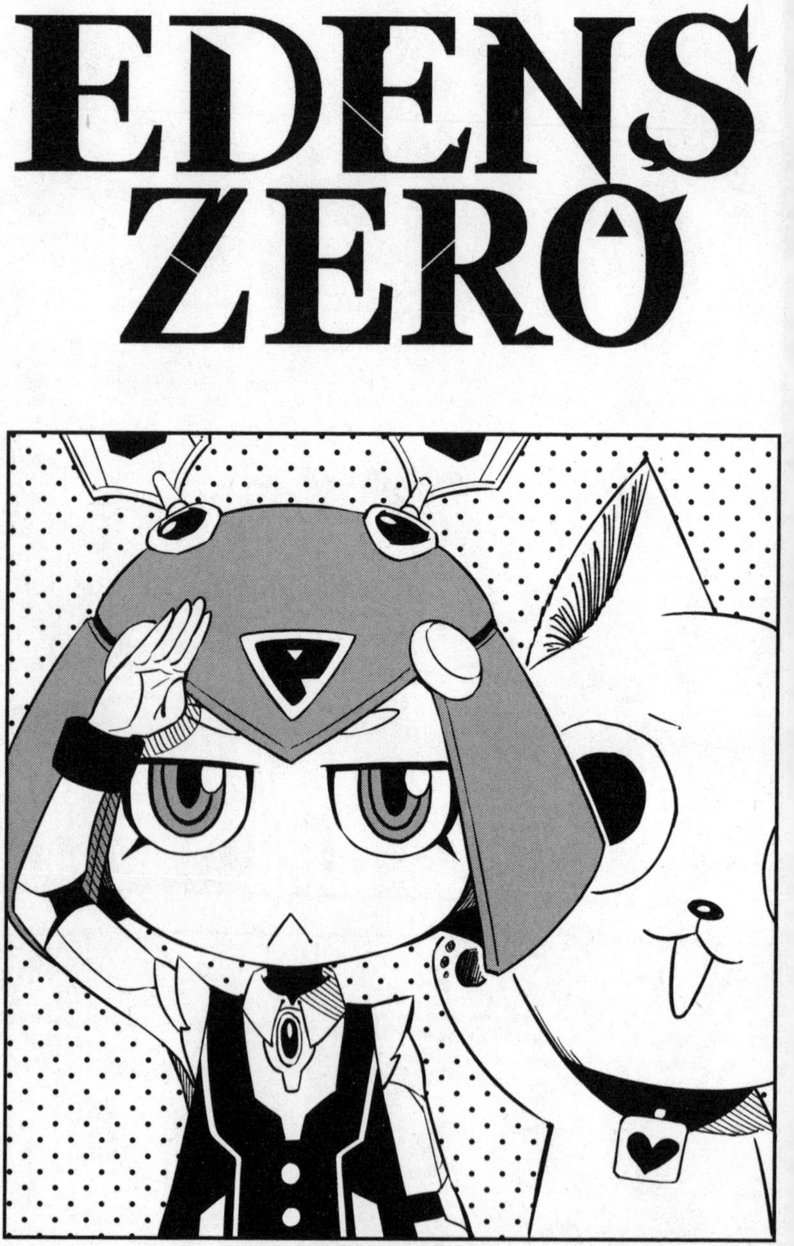

## CHAPTER 10: WE'RE FRIENDS, AREN'T WE?

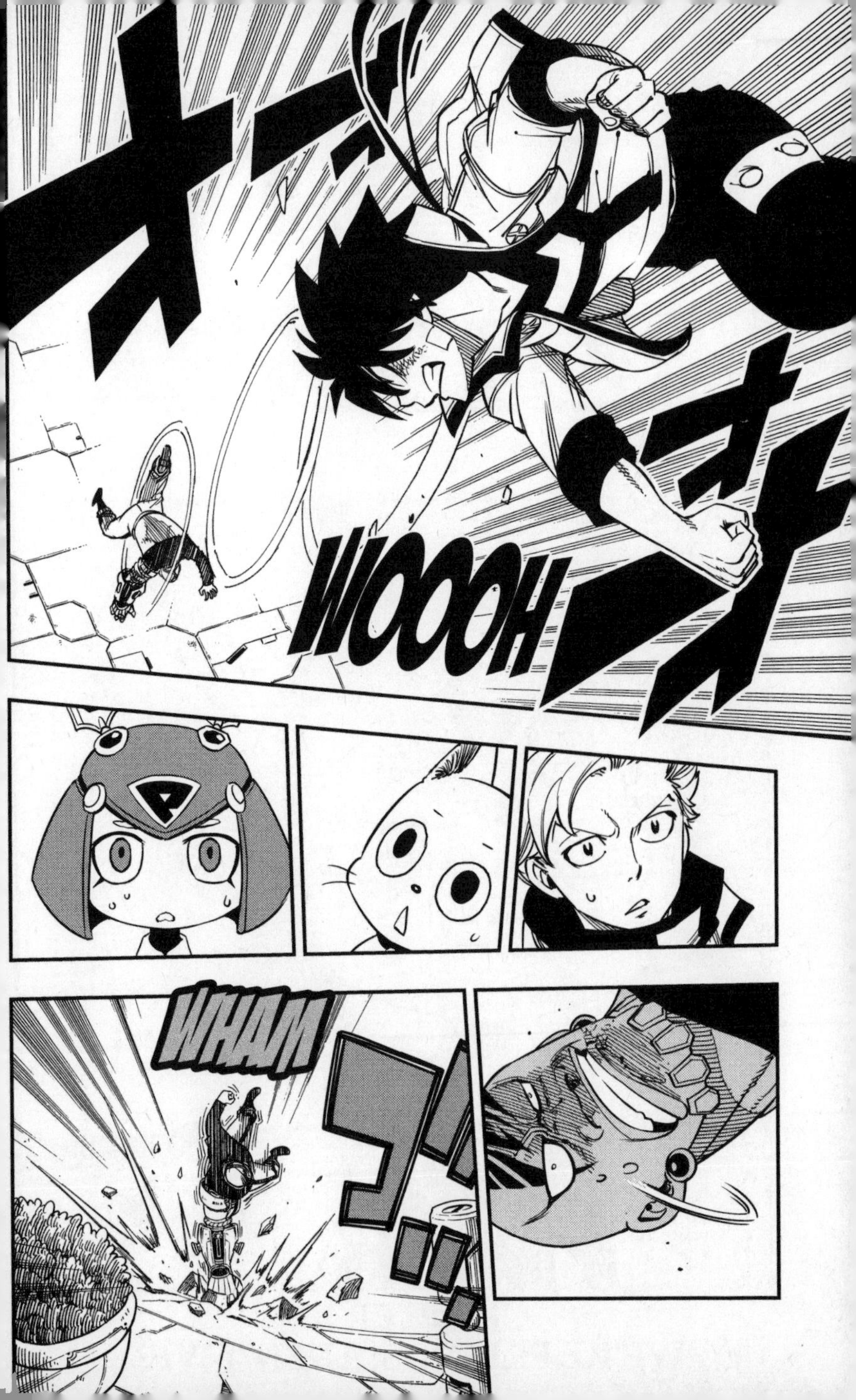
WOOOH
WHAM

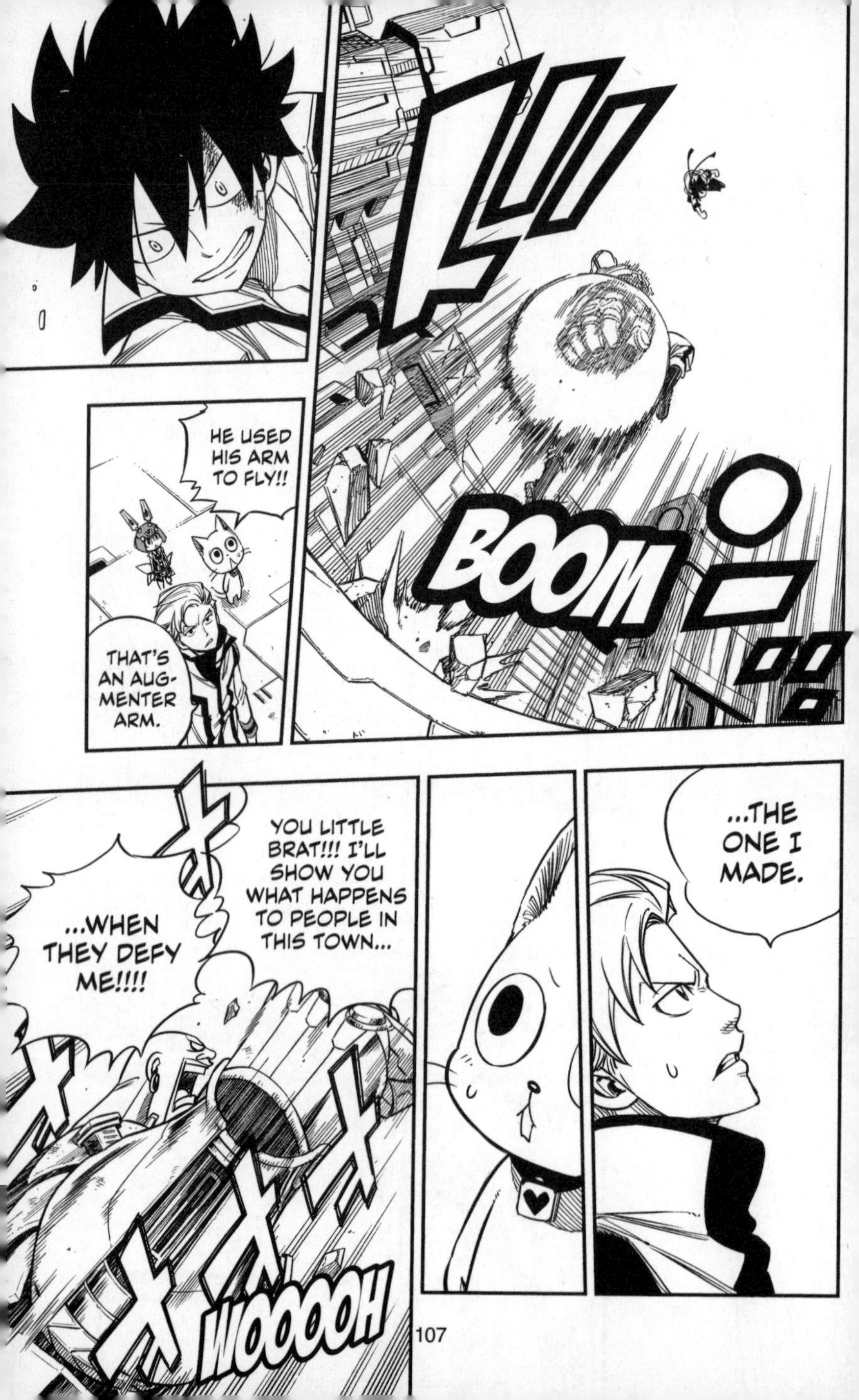
BOOM
HE USED HIS ARM TO FLY!!
THAT'S AN AUG-MENTER ARM.
...THE ONE I MADE.
YOU LITTLE BRAT!!! I'LL SHOW YOU WHAT HAPPENS TO PEOPLE IN THIS TOWN...
...WHEN THEY DEFY ME!!!!
WOOOOH

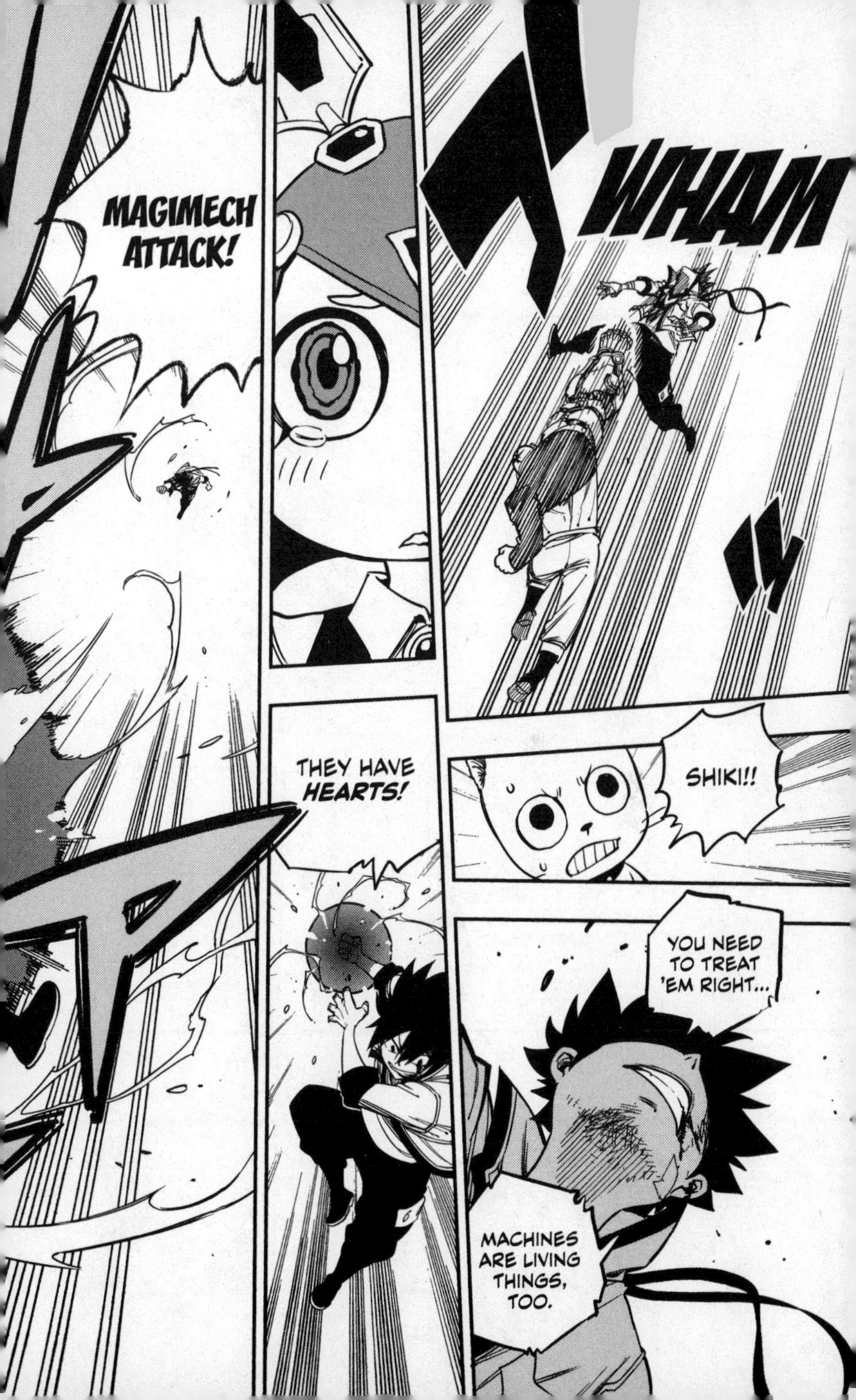
WHAM
SHIKI!!
YOU NEED TO TREAT 'EM RIGHT...
MACHINES ARE LIVING THINGS, TOO.
THEY HAVE HEARTS!
MAGIMECH ATTACK!

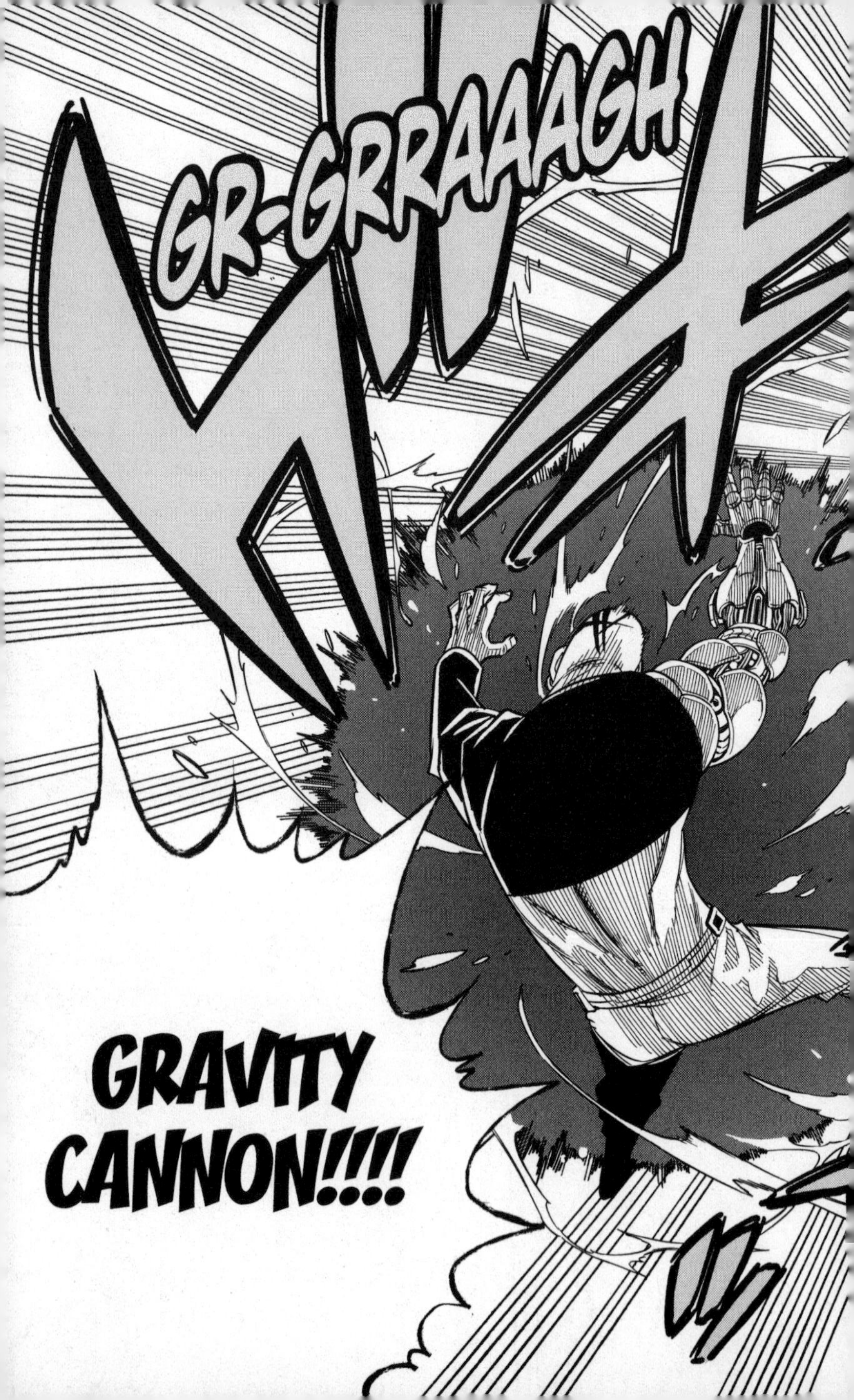
GR-GRRAAAGH
GRAVITY CANNON!!!!

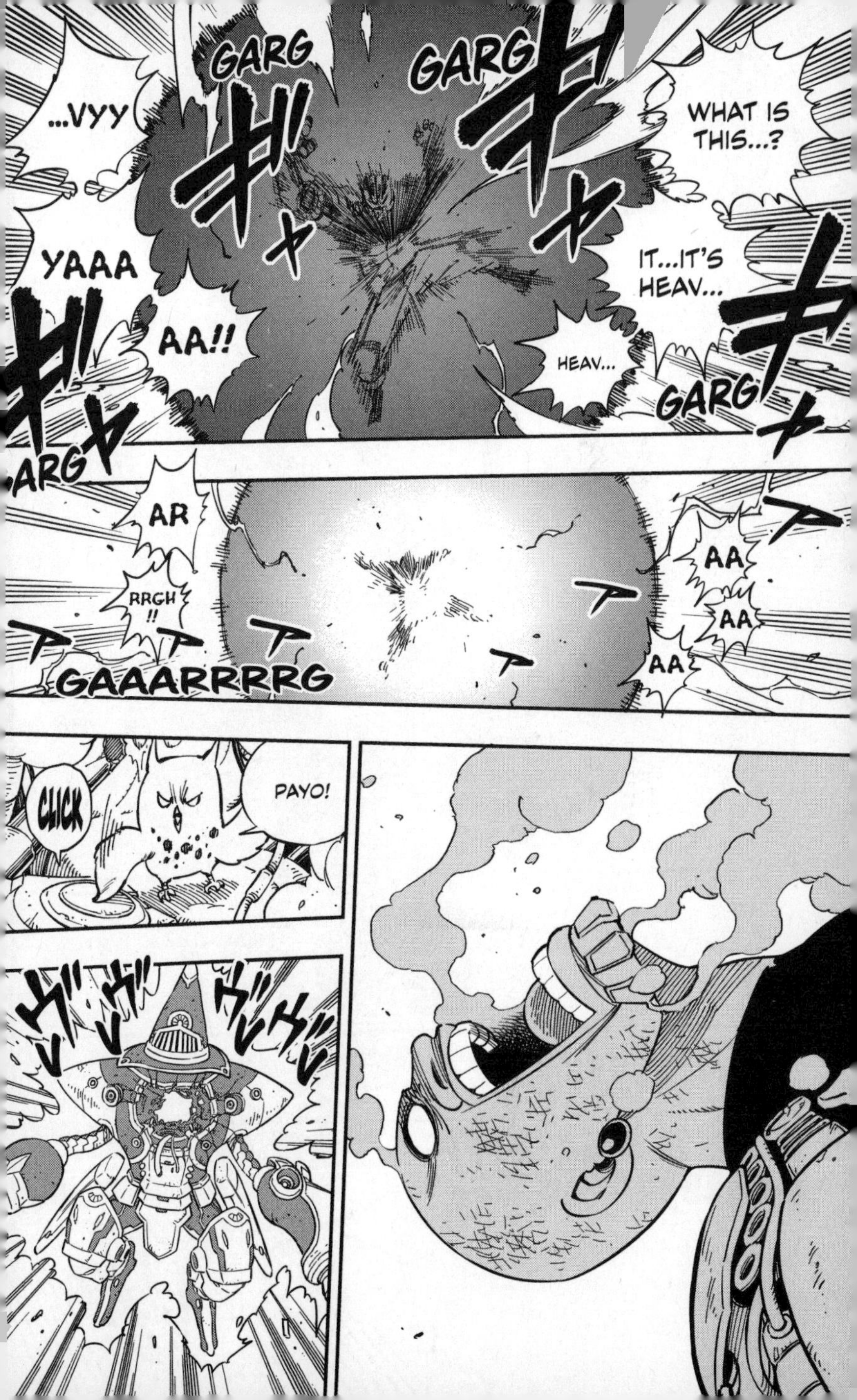
WHAT IS THIS...?
GARG
GARG
...VYY
IT...IT'S HEAV...
HEAV...
GARG
YAAA
AA!!
ARG
AA
AA
AA
AR
RRGH !!
GAAARRRRG
PAYO!
CLICK

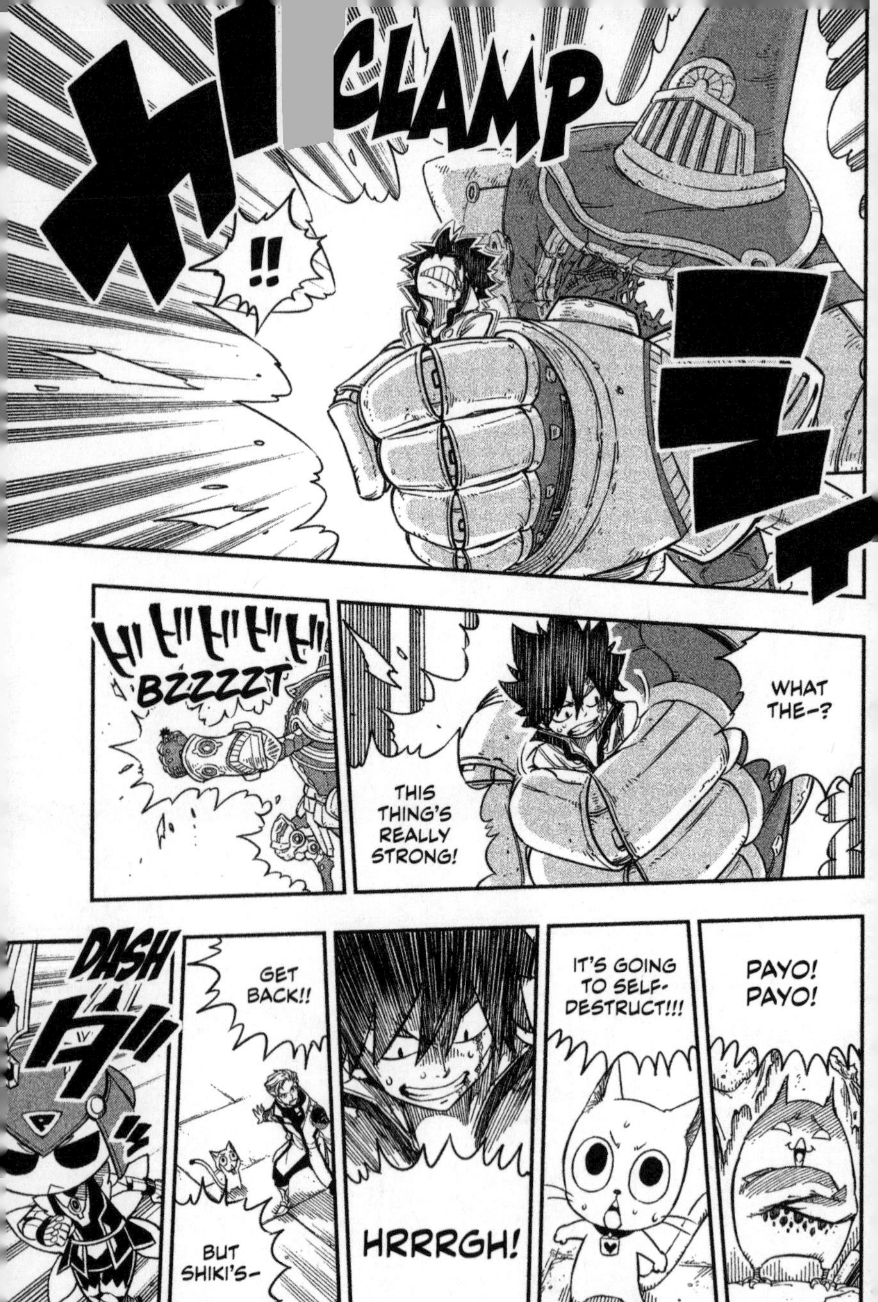
CLAMP
!!
WHAT THE-?
THIS THING'S REALLY STRONG!
BZZZZT
PAYO! PAYO!
IT'S GOING TO SELF-DESTRUCT!!!
HRRRGH!
GET BACK!!
BUT SHIKI'S-
DASH

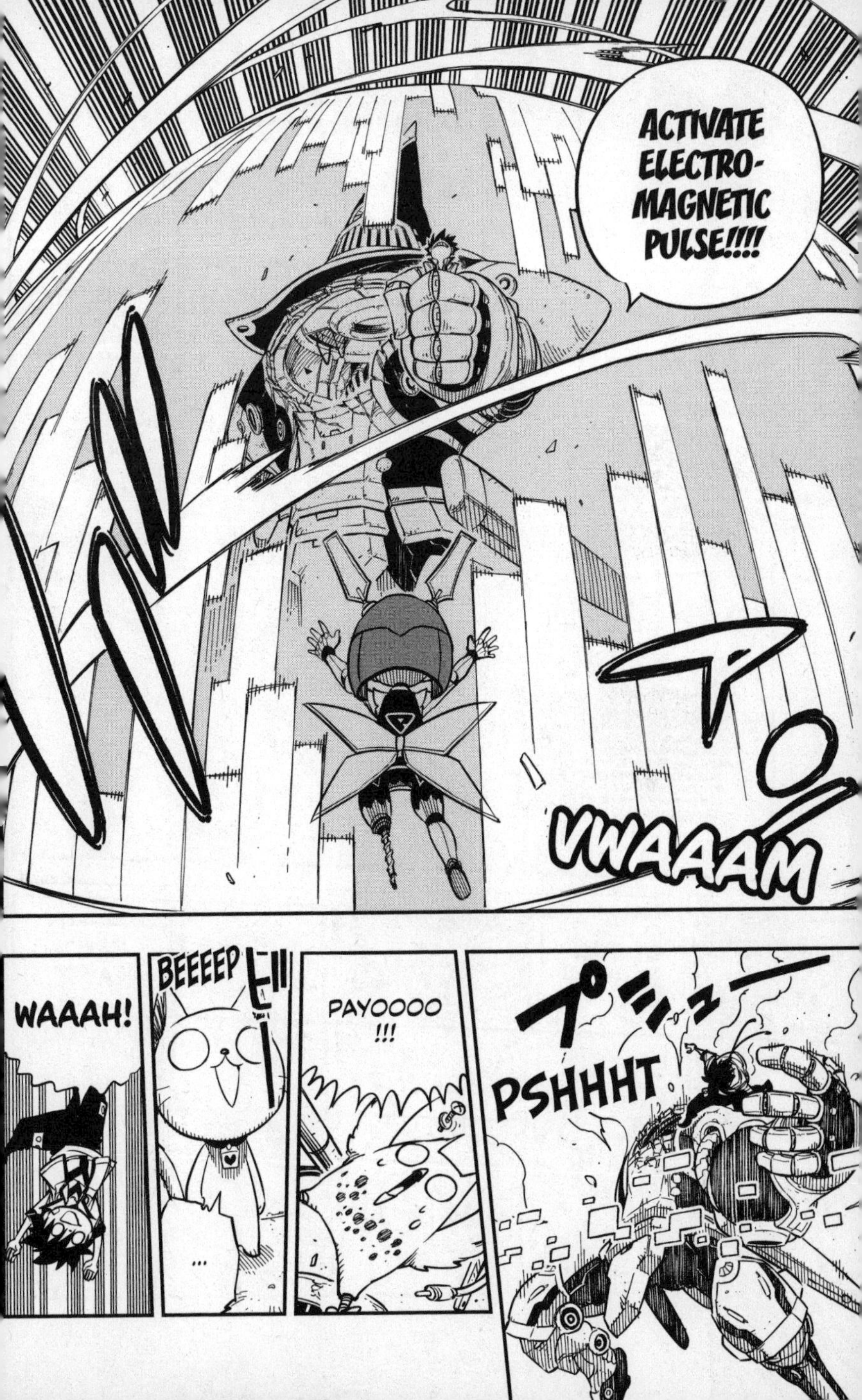
ACTIVATE ELECTRO-MAGNETIC PULSE!!!!
VWAAAM
PSHHHT
PAYOOOO !!!
BEEEEP
...
WAAAH!

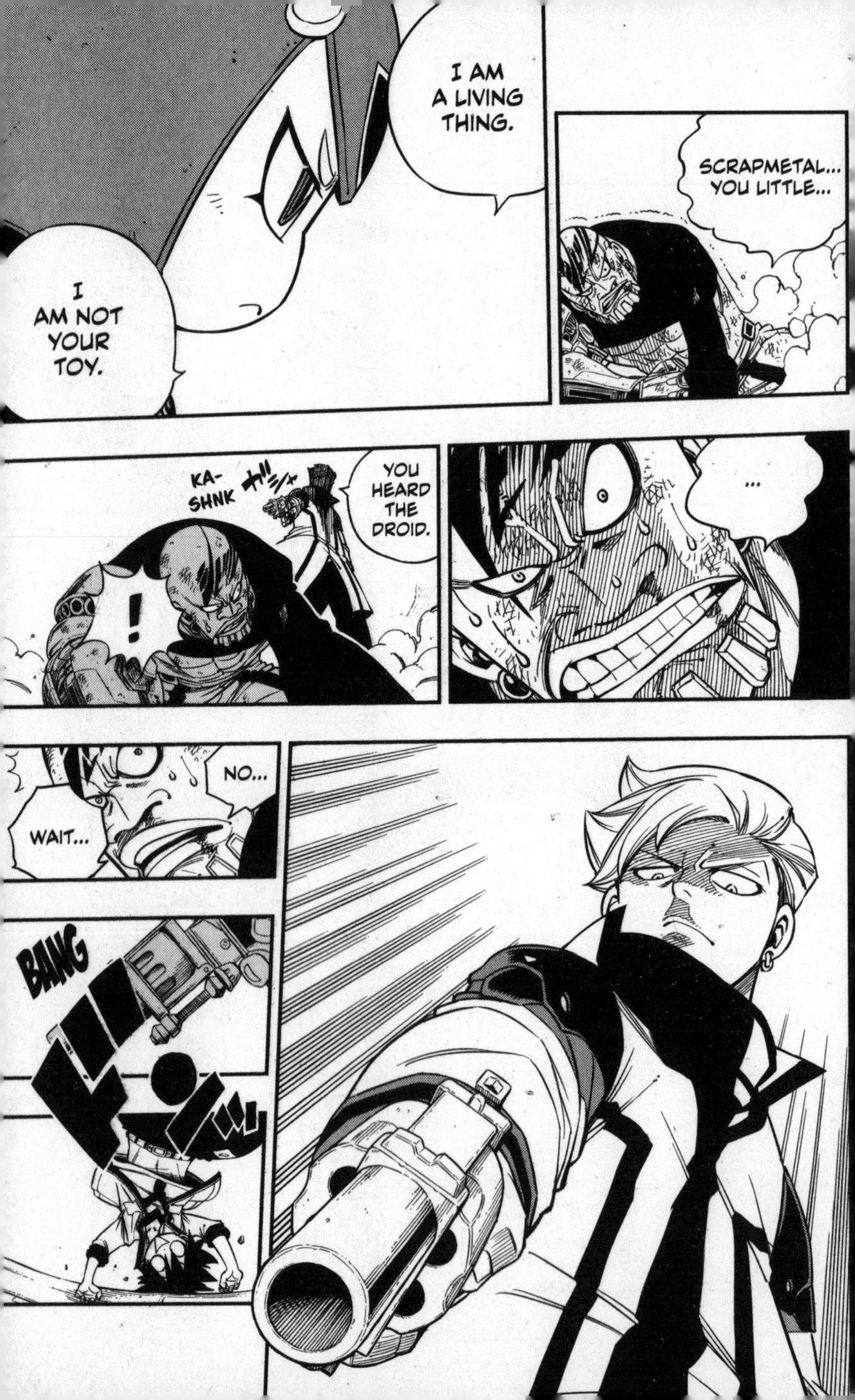
I AM A LIVING THING.
I AM NOT YOUR TOY.
SCRAPMETAL... YOU LITTLE...
...
YOU HEARD THE DROID.
KA-SHNK
!
NO...
WAIT...
BANG

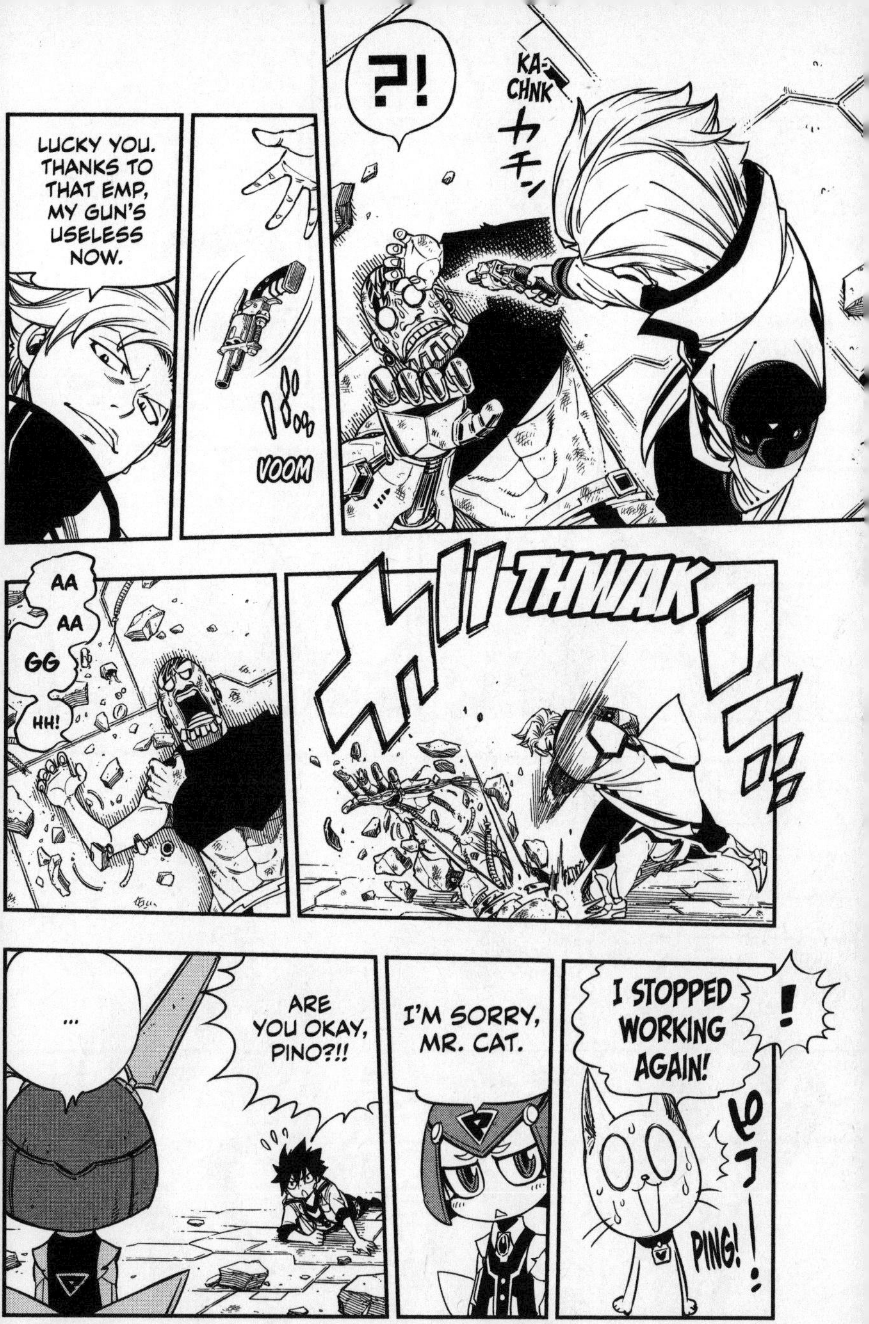

KA-CHNK
カチン
?!
VOOM
LUCKY YOU. THANKS TO THAT EMP, MY GUN'S USELESS NOW.
THWAK
AA AA GG HH!
I STOPPED WORKING AGAIN!
!
PING!
I'M SORRY, MR. CAT.
ARE YOU OKAY, PINO?!!
...

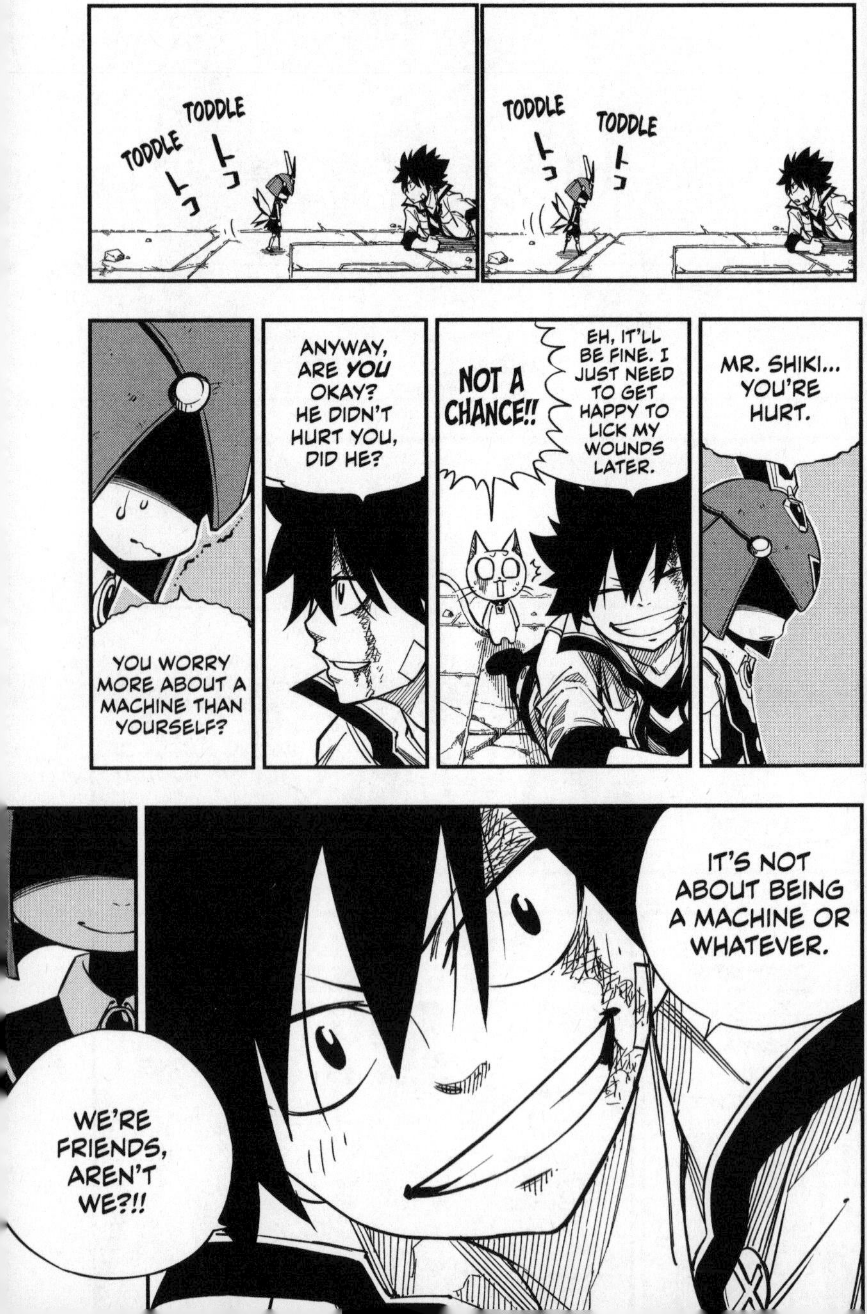
TODDLE
TODDLE
トコ
トコ
TODDLE
TODDLE
トコ
トコ
MR. SHIKI... YOU'RE HURT.
EH, IT'LL BE FINE. I JUST NEED TO GET HAPPY TO LICK MY WOUNDS LATER.
NOT A CHANCE!!
ANYWAY, ARE YOU OKAY? HE DIDN'T HURT YOU, DID HE?
YOU WORRY MORE ABOUT A MACHINE THAN YOURSELF?
IT'S NOT ABOUT BEING A MACHINE OR WHATEVER.
WE'RE FRIENDS, AREN'T WE?!!

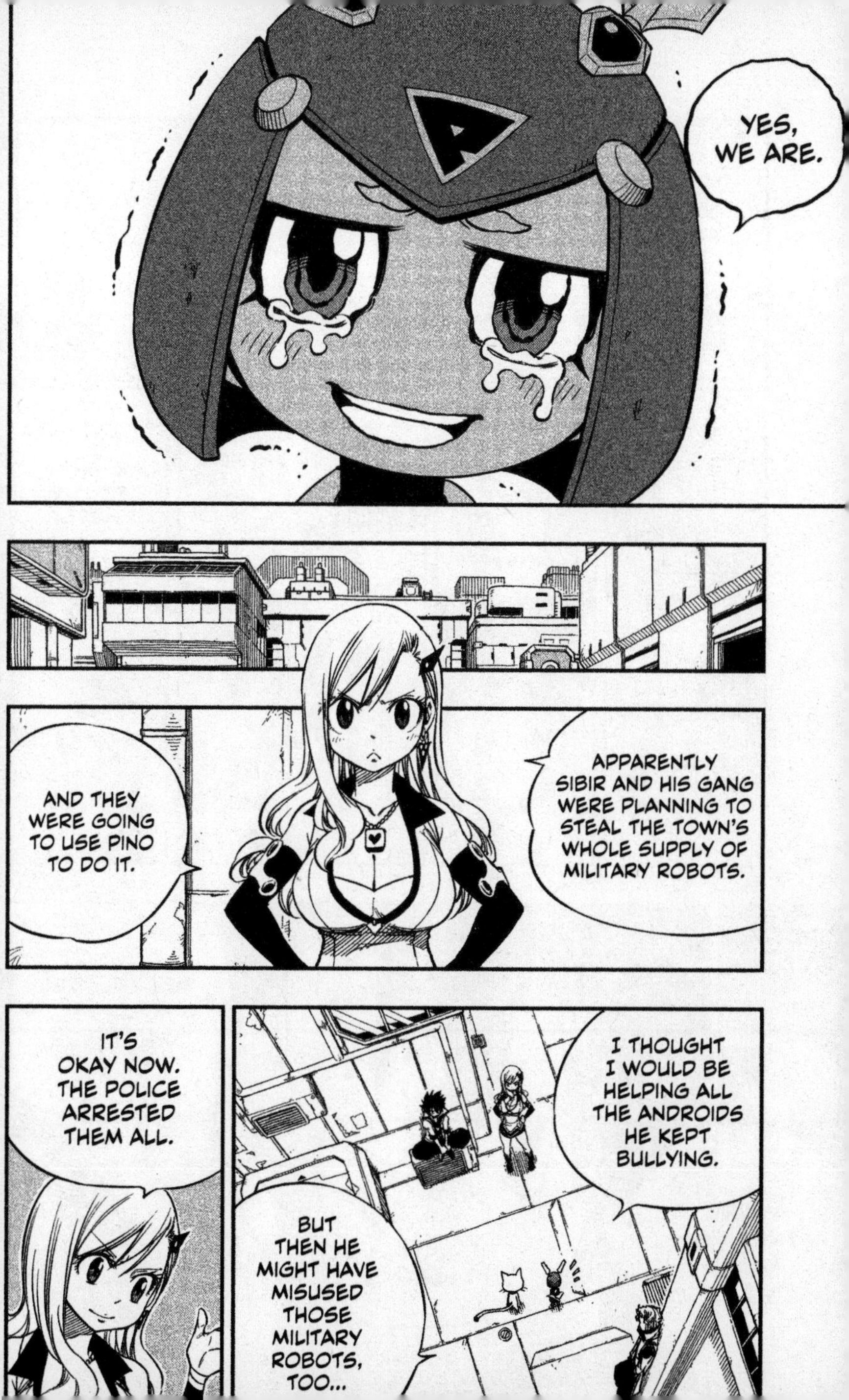
YES, WE ARE.
APPARENTLY SIBIR AND HIS GANG WERE PLANNING TO STEAL THE TOWN'S WHOLE SUPPLY OF MILITARY ROBOTS.
AND THEY WERE GOING TO USE PINO TO DO IT.
I THOUGHT I WOULD BE HELPING ALL THE ANDROIDS HE KEPT BULLYING.
BUT THEN HE MIGHT HAVE MISUSED THOSE MILITARY ROBOTS, TOO...
IT'S OKAY NOW. THE POLICE ARRESTED THEM ALL.

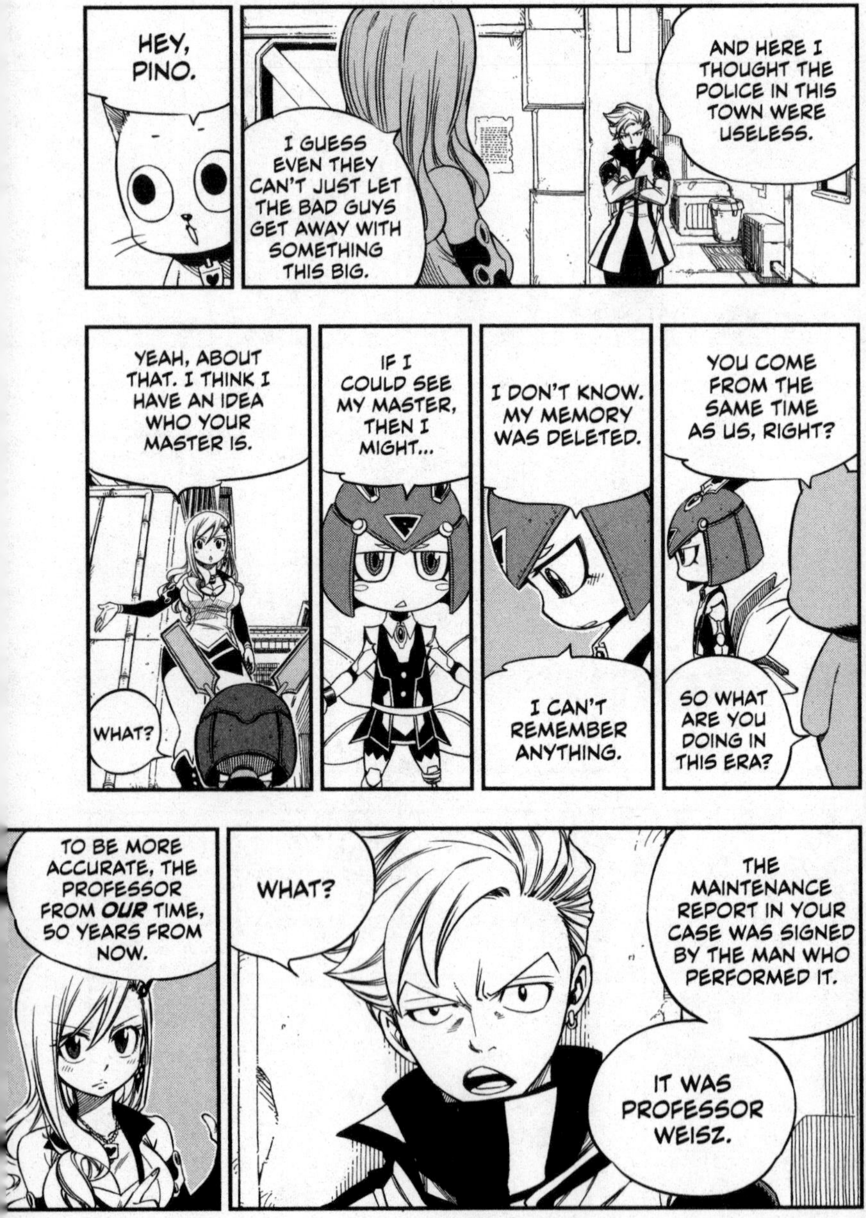

AND HERE I THOUGHT THE POLICE IN THIS TOWN WERE USELESS.
I GUESS EVEN THEY CAN'T JUST LET THE BAD GUYS GET AWAY WITH SOMETHING THIS BIG.
HEY, PINO.
YOU COME FROM THE SAME TIME AS US, RIGHT?
SO WHAT ARE YOU DOING IN THIS ERA?
I DON'T KNOW. MY MEMORY WAS DELETED.
I CAN'T REMEMBER ANYTHING.
IF I COULD SEE MY MASTER, THEN I MIGHT...
YEAH, ABOUT THAT. I THINK I HAVE AN IDEA WHO YOUR MASTER IS.
WHAT?
THE MAINTENANCE REPORT IN YOUR CASE WAS SIGNED BY THE MAN WHO PERFORMED IT.
IT WAS PROFESSOR WEISZ.
WHAT?
TO BE MORE ACCURATE, THE PROFESSOR FROM ***OUR*** TIME, 50 YEARS FROM NOW.

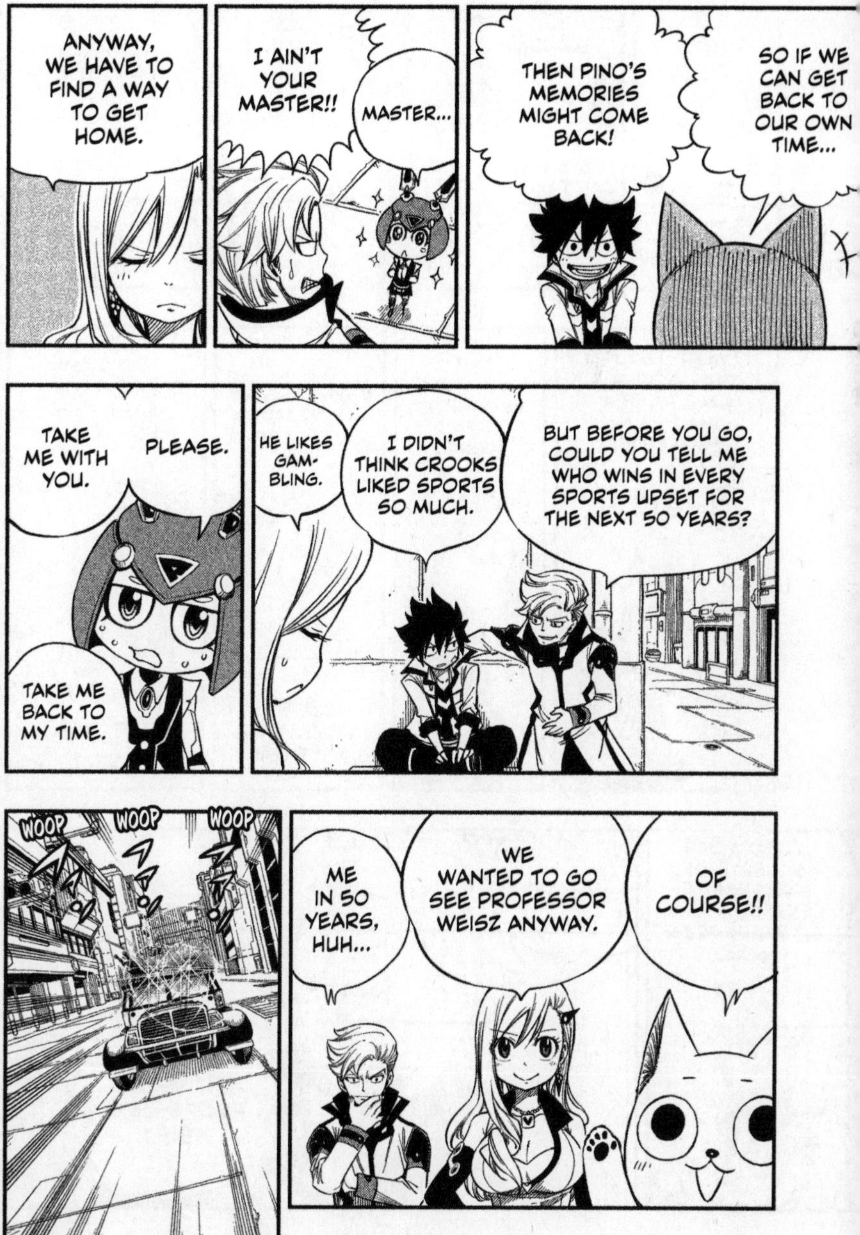
SO IF WE CAN GET BACK TO OUR OWN TIME...
THEN PINO'S MEMORIES MIGHT COME BACK!
MASTER...
I AIN'T YOUR MASTER!!
ANYWAY, WE HAVE TO FIND A WAY TO GET HOME.
BUT BEFORE YOU GO, COULD YOU TELL ME WHO WINS IN EVERY SPORTS UPSET FOR THE NEXT 50 YEARS?
I DIDN'T THINK CROOKS LIKED SPORTS SO MUCH.
HE LIKES GAM-BLING.
PLEASE.
TAKE ME WITH YOU.
TAKE ME BACK TO MY TIME.
OF COURSE!!
WE WANTED TO GO SEE PROFESSOR WEISZ ANYWAY.
ME IN 50 YEARS, HUH...
WOOP
WOOP
WOOP

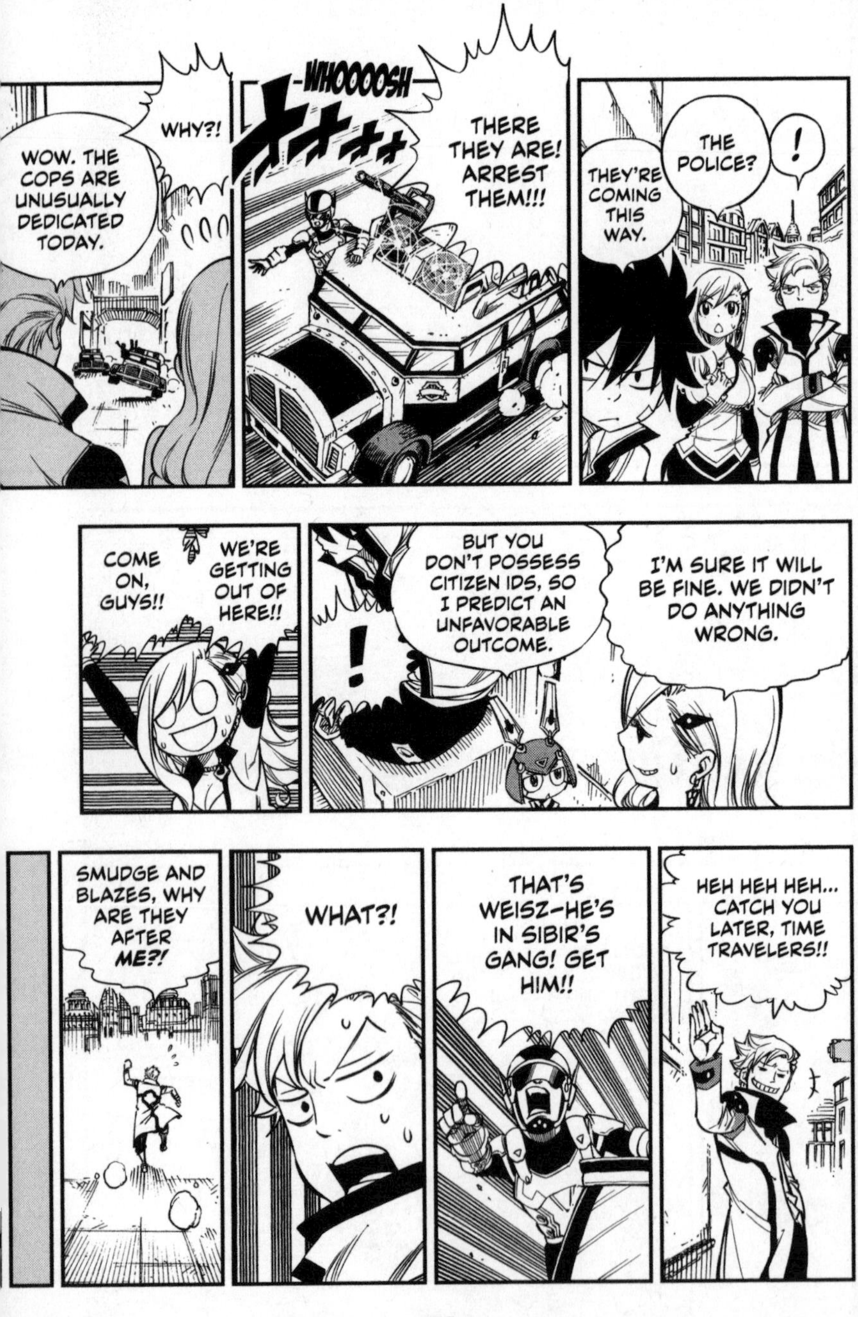
!
THE POLICE?
THEY'RE COMING THIS WAY.
THERE THEY ARE! ARREST THEM!!!
-WHOOOOSH-
WHY?!
WOW. THE COPS ARE UNUSUALLY DEDICATED TODAY.
I'M SURE IT WILL BE FINE. WE DIDN'T DO ANYTHING WRONG.
BUT YOU DON'T POSSESS CITIZEN IDS, SO I PREDICT AN UNFAVORABLE OUTCOME.
!
WE'RE GETTING OUT OF HERE!!
COME ON, GUYS!!
HEH HEH HEH... CATCH YOU LATER, TIME TRAVELERS!!
THAT'S WEISZ—HE'S IN SIBIR'S GANG! GET HIM!!
WHAT?!
SMUDGE AND BLAZES, WHY ARE THEY AFTER *ME*?!

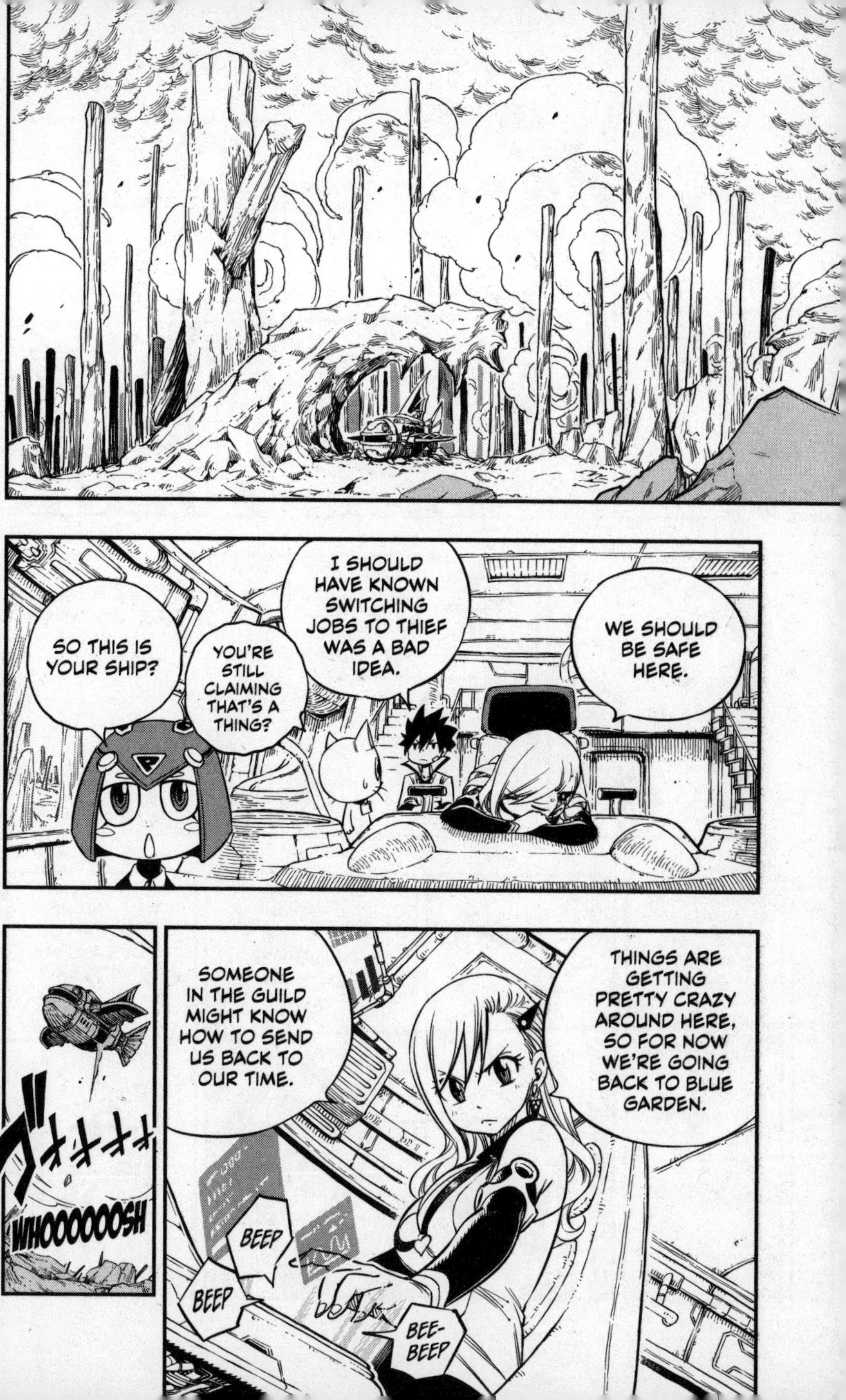
WE SHOULD BE SAFE HERE.
I SHOULD HAVE KNOWN SWITCHING JOBS TO THIEF WAS A BAD IDEA.
YOU'RE STILL CLAIMING THAT'S A THING?
SO THIS IS YOUR SHIP?
THINGS ARE GETTING PRETTY CRAZY AROUND HERE, SO FOR NOW WE'RE GOING BACK TO BLUE GARDEN.
SOMEONE IN THE GUILD MIGHT KNOW HOW TO SEND US BACK TO OUR TIME.
BEEP
BEEP
BEE-BEEP
WHOOOOOOSH

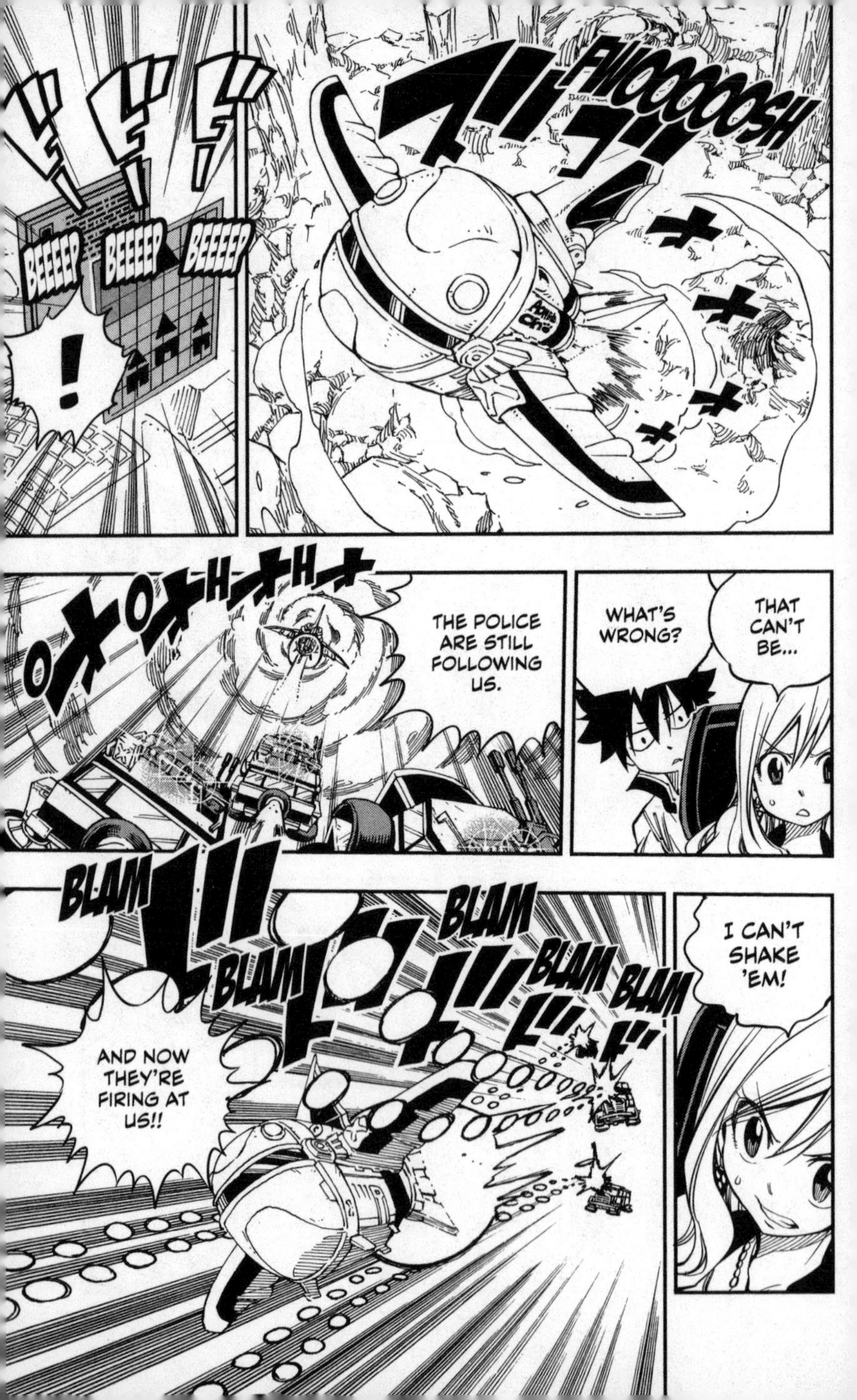
FWOOOOOSH
BEEEEP
BEEEEP
BEEEEP
!
THAT CAN'T BE...
WHAT'S WRONG?
THE POLICE ARE STILL FOLLOWING US.
I CAN'T SHAKE 'EM!
BLAM
BLAM
BLAM
BLAM
BLAM
AND NOW THEY'RE FIRING AT US!!

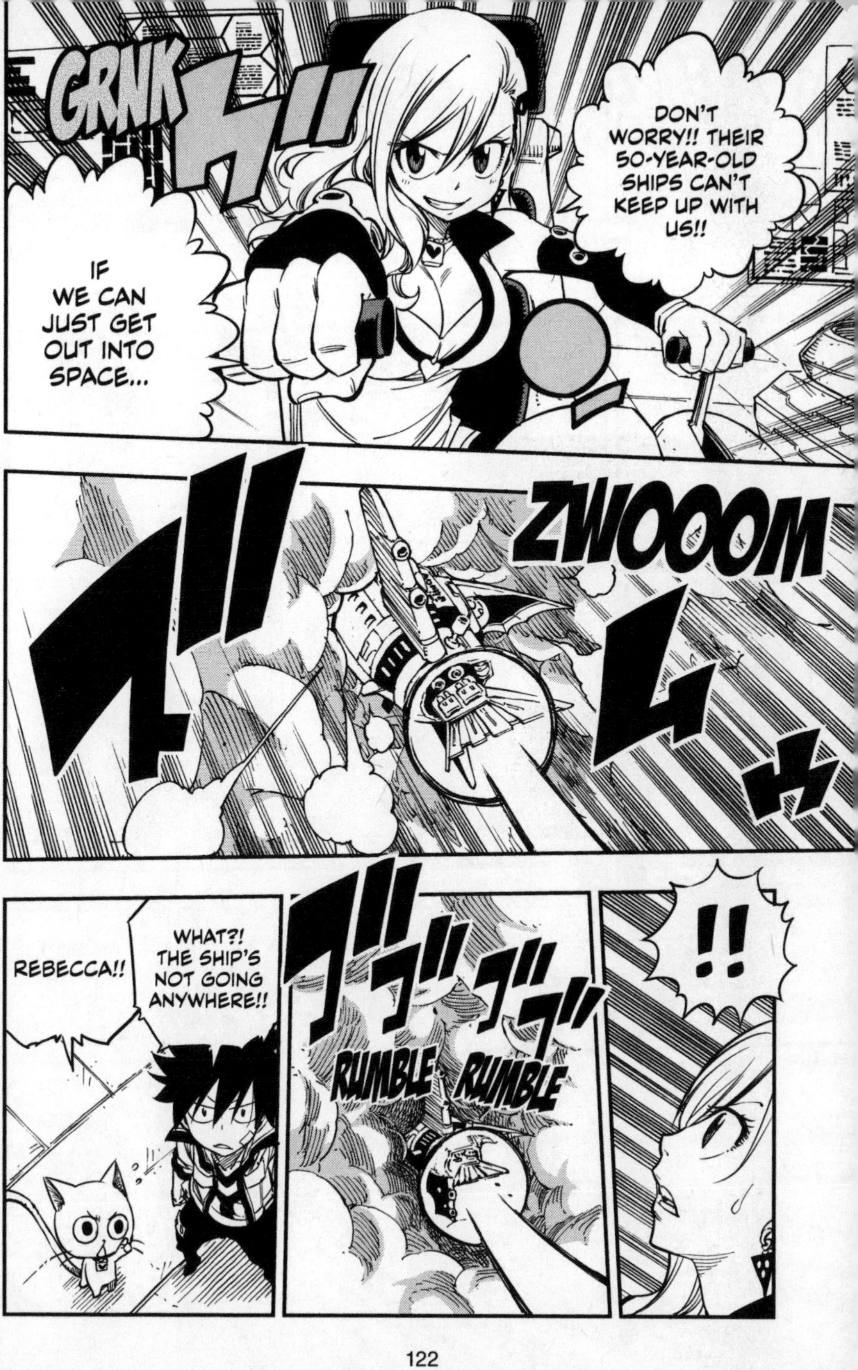
DON'T WORRY!! THEIR 50-YEAR-OLD SHIPS CAN'T KEEP UP WITH US!!
GRNK
IF WE CAN JUST GET OUT INTO SPACE...
ZWOOOM
!!
RUMBLE
RUMBLE
WHAT?! THE SHIP'S NOT GOING ANYWHERE!!
REBECCA!!

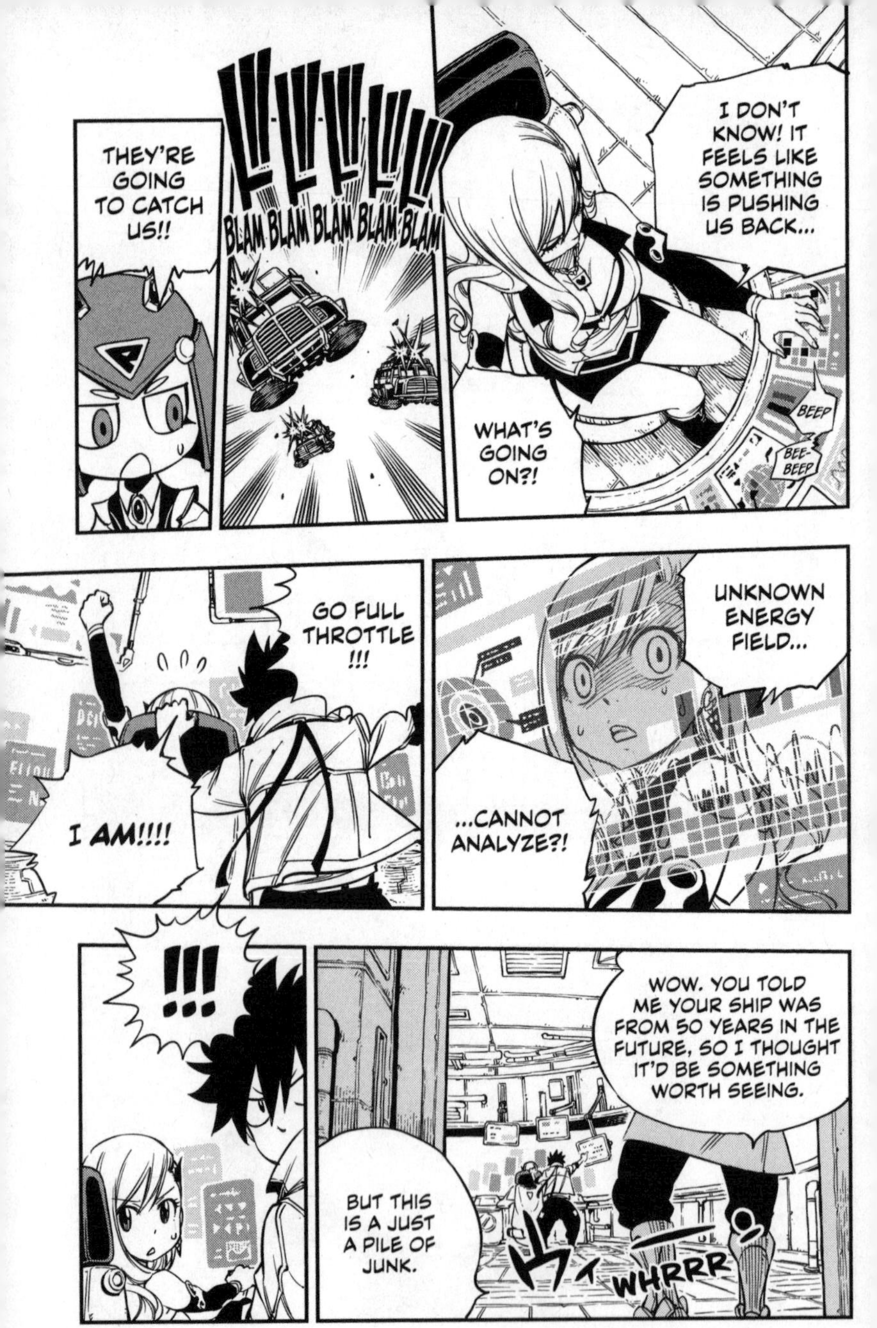

I DON'T KNOW! IT FEELS LIKE SOMETHING IS PUSHING US BACK...
BEEP
BEE-BEEP
WHAT'S GOING ON?!
BLAM BLAM BLAM BLAM BLAM
THEY'RE GOING TO CATCH US!!
UNKNOWN ENERGY FIELD...
...CANNOT ANALYZE?!
GO FULL THROTTLE!!!
I AM!!!!
WOW. YOU TOLD ME YOUR SHIP WAS FROM 50 YEARS IN THE FUTURE, SO I THOUGHT IT'D BE SOMETHING WORTH SEEING.
WHRRR
BUT THIS IS A JUST A PILE OF JUNK.
!!!

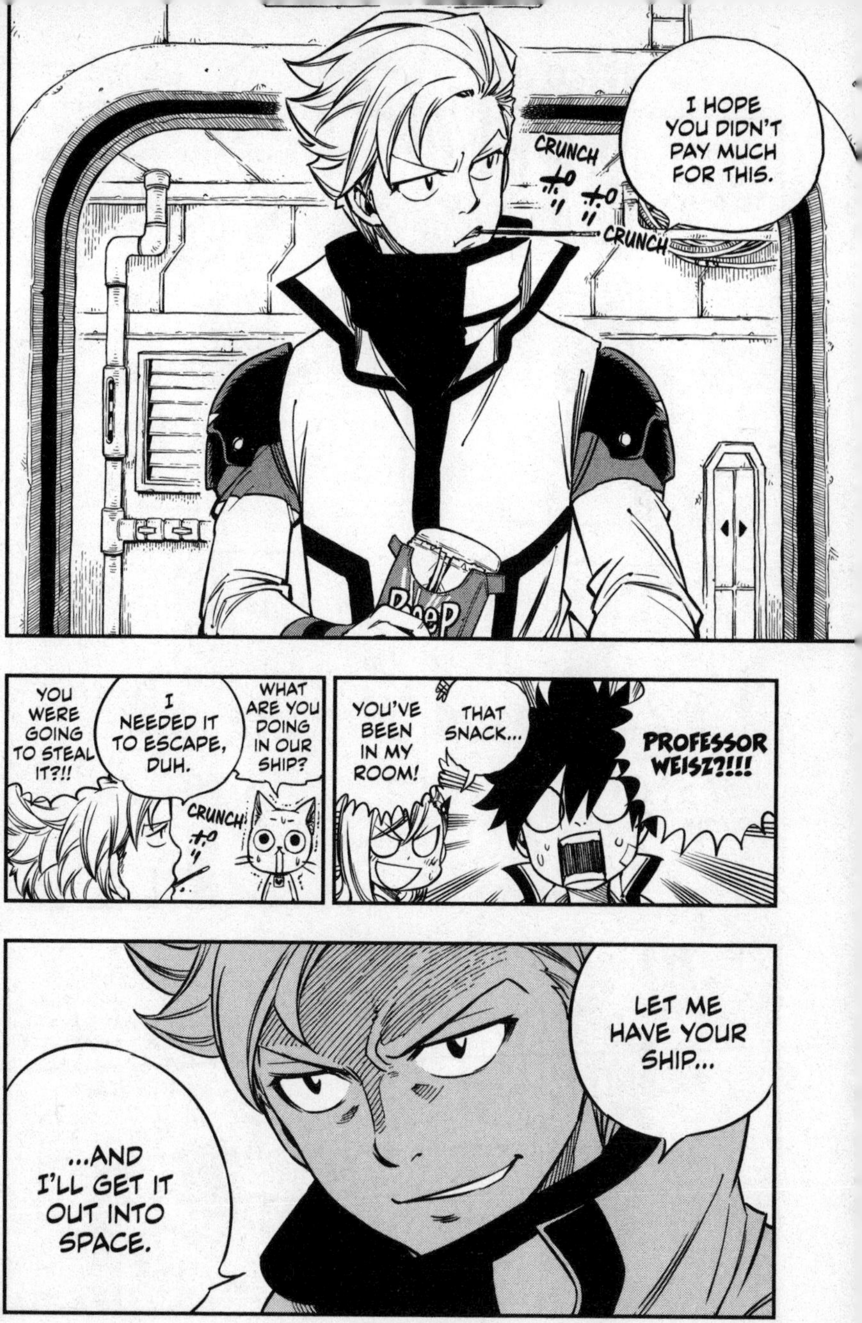
I HOPE YOU DIDN'T PAY MUCH FOR THIS.
CRUNCH
CRUNCH
PROFESSOR WEISZ?!!!
THAT SNACK...
YOU'VE BEEN IN MY ROOM!
WHAT ARE YOU DOING IN OUR SHIP?
I NEEDED IT TO ESCAPE, DUH.
CRUNCH
YOU WERE GOING TO STEAL IT?!!
LET ME HAVE YOUR SHIP...
...AND I'LL GET IT OUT INTO SPACE.

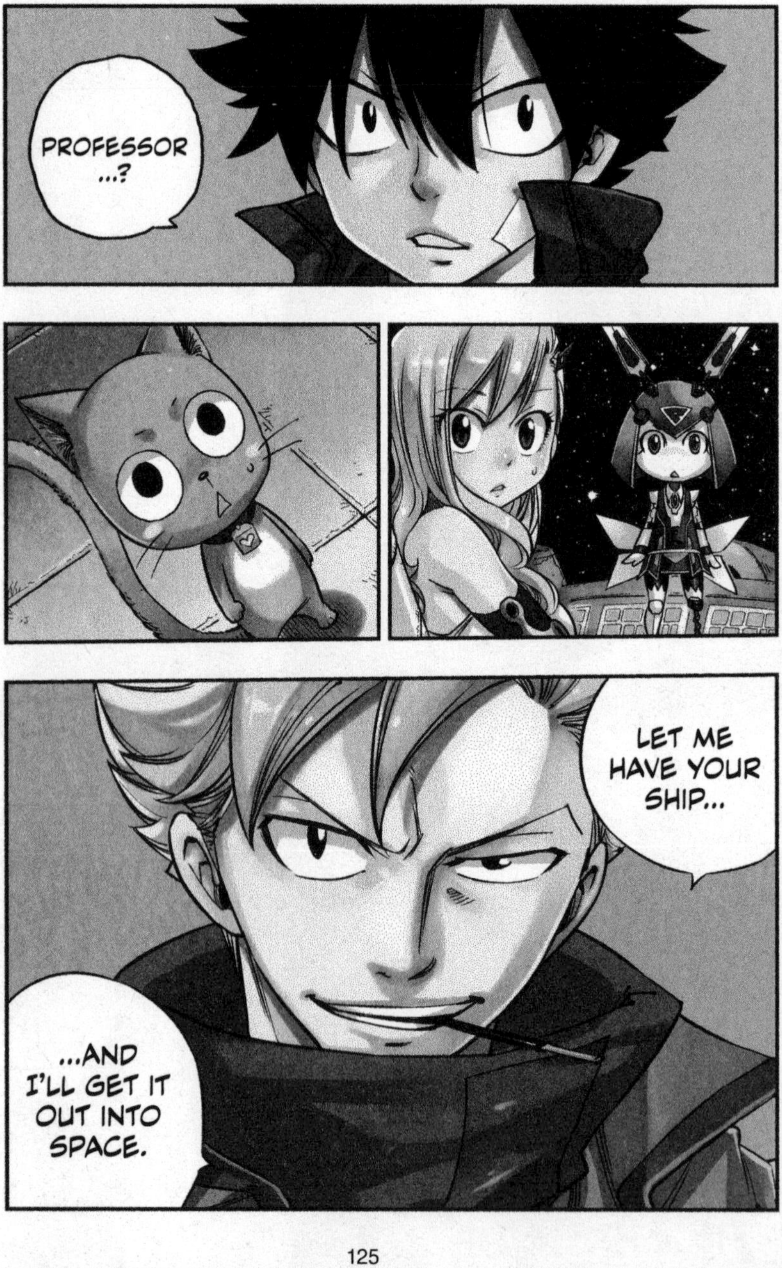
PROFESSOR ...?
LET ME HAVE YOUR SHIP...
...AND I'LL GET IT OUT INTO SPACE.

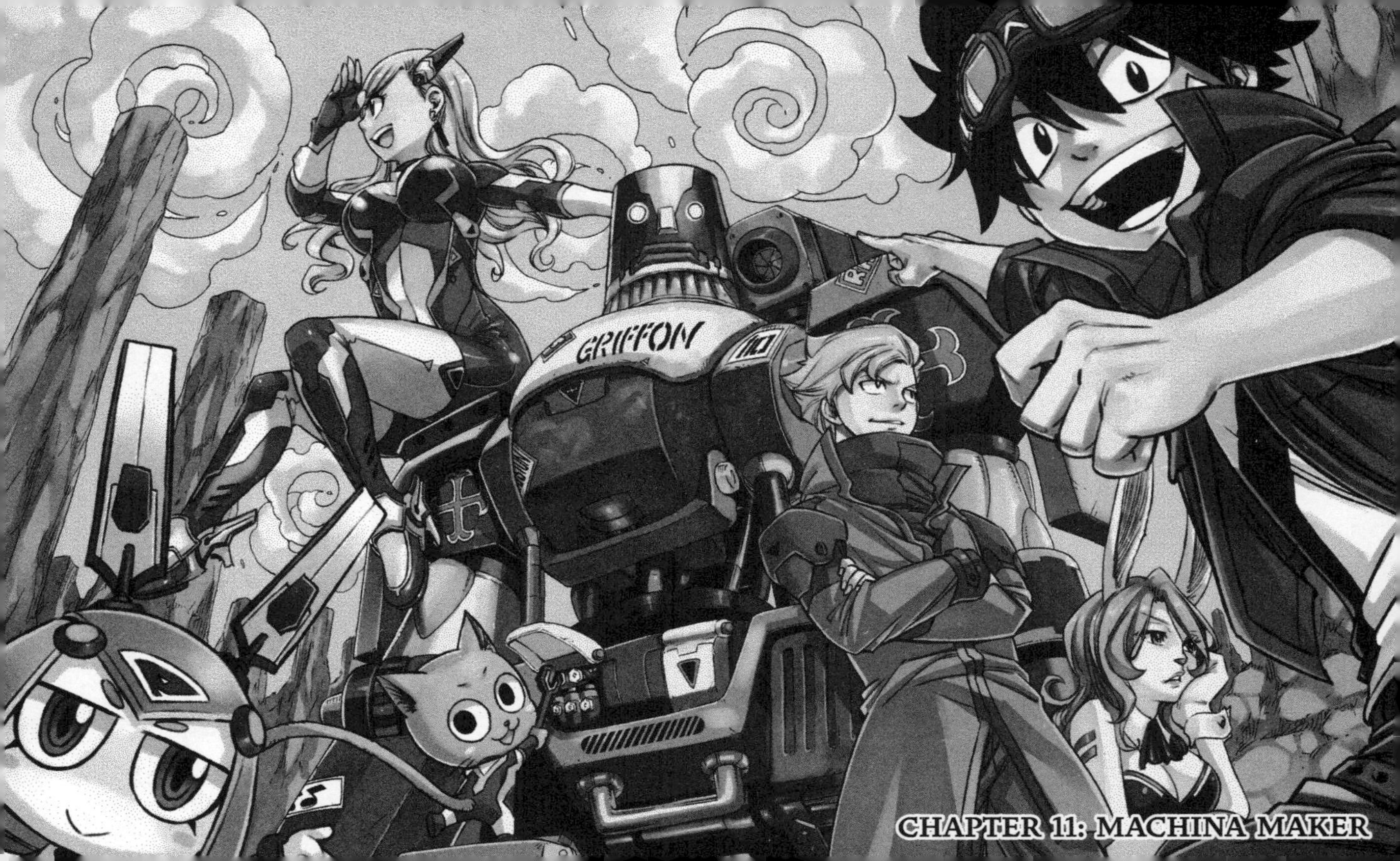
GRIFFON
GRIFFON

# CHAPTER 11: MACHINA MAKER

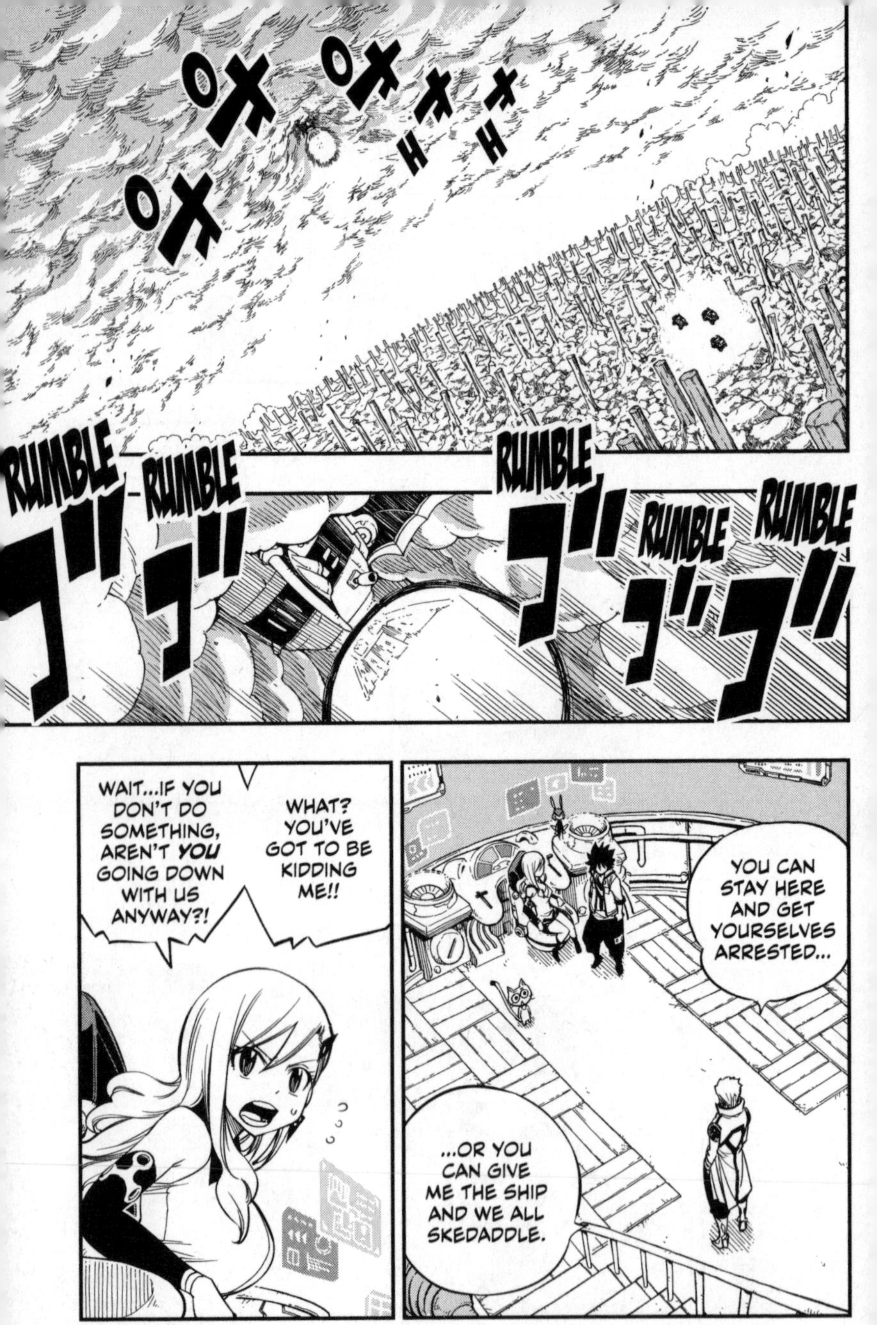
RUMBLE
RUMBLE
RUMBLE
RUMBLE
RUMBLE
YOU CAN STAY HERE AND GET YOURSELVES ARRESTED...
...OR YOU CAN GIVE ME THE SHIP AND WE ALL SKEDADDLE.
WHAT? YOU'VE GOT TO BE KIDDING ME!!
WAIT...IF YOU DON'T DO SOMETHING, AREN'T *YOU* GOING DOWN WITH US ANYWAY?!

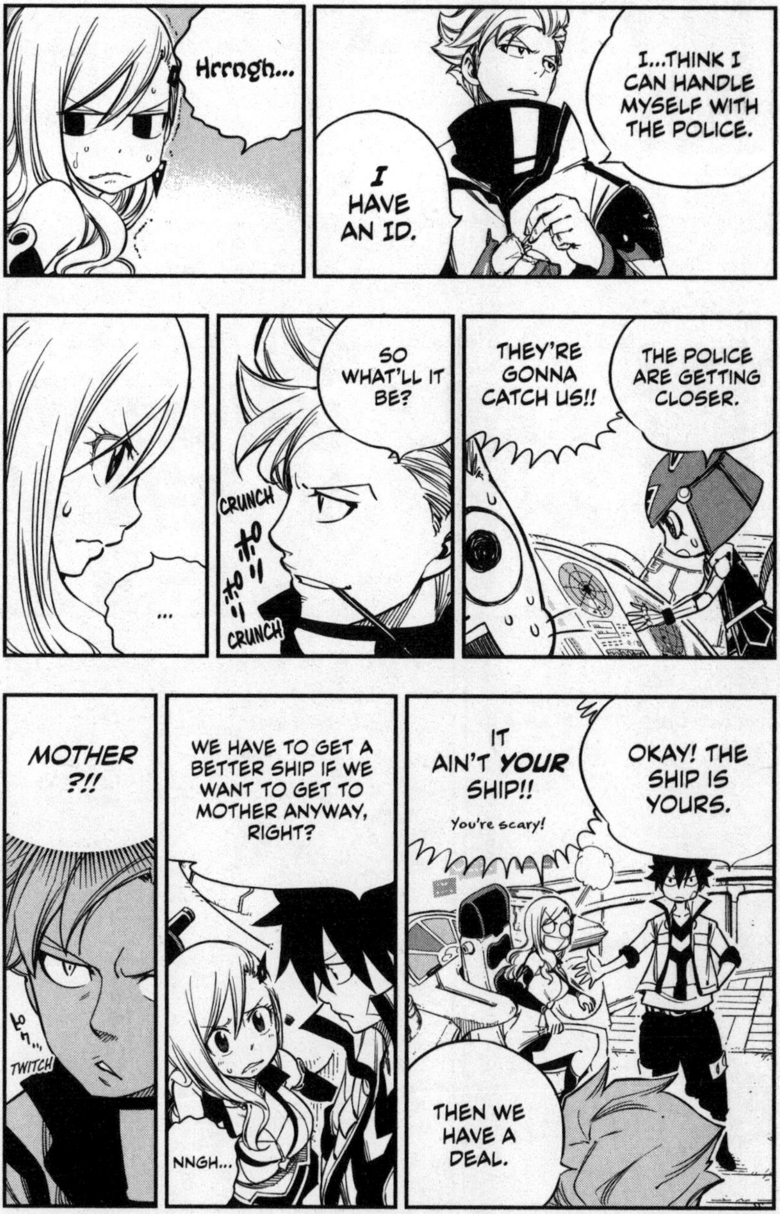
I...THINK I CAN HANDLE MYSELF WITH THE POLICE.
I HAVE AN ID.
Hrrngh...
THE POLICE ARE GETTING CLOSER.
THEY'RE GONNA CATCH US!!
SO WHAT'LL IT BE?
CRUNCH
CRUNCH
...
OKAY! THE SHIP IS YOURS.
IT AIN'T YOUR SHIP!!
You're scary!
THEN WE HAVE A DEAL.
WE HAVE TO GET A BETTER SHIP IF WE WANT TO GET TO MOTHER ANYWAY, RIGHT?
NNGH...
MOTHER ?!!
TWITCH

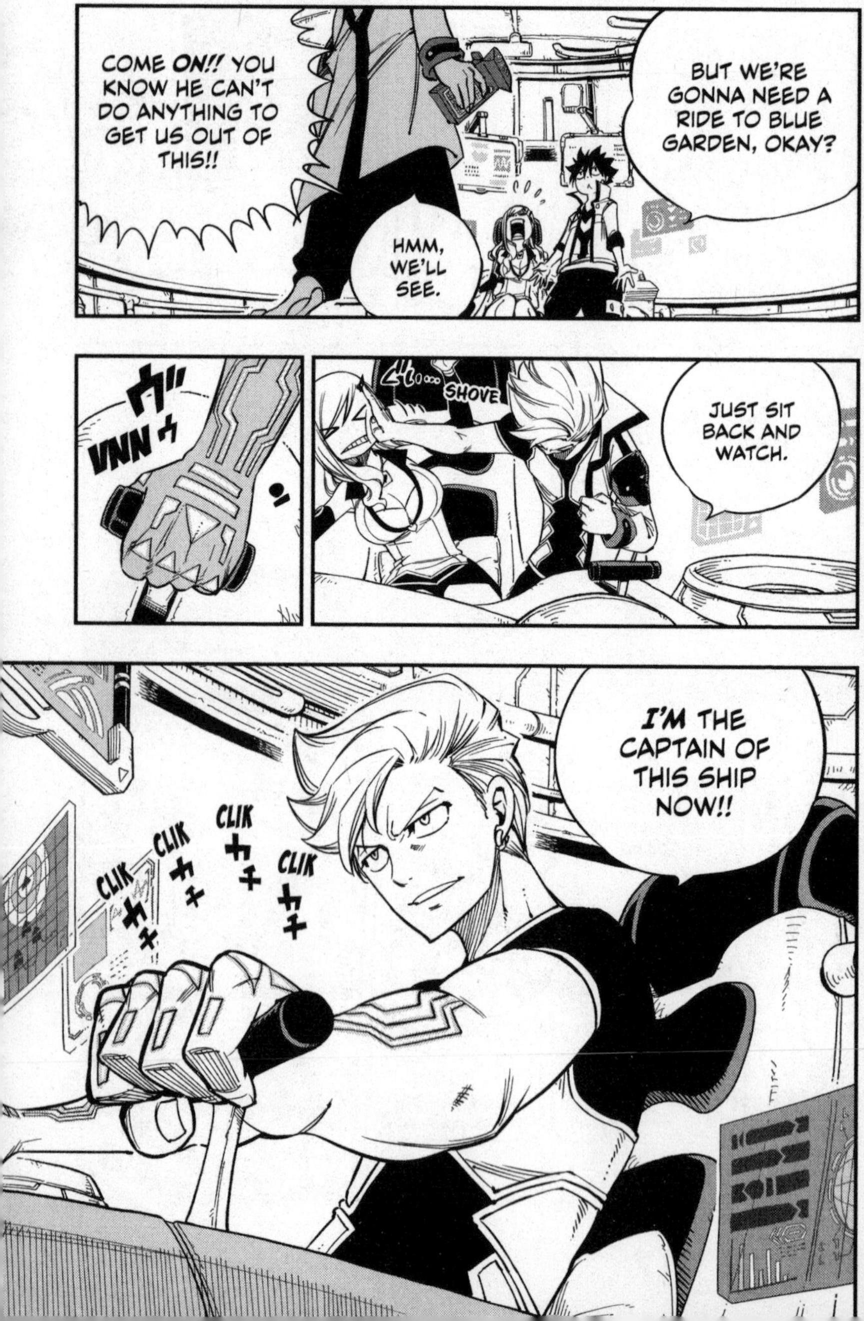
BUT WE'RE GONNA NEED A RIDE TO BLUE GARDEN, OKAY?
HMM, WE'LL SEE.
COME ON!! YOU KNOW HE CAN'T DO ANYTHING TO GET US OUT OF THIS!!
SHOVE
JUST SIT BACK AND WATCH.
VNN
I'M THE CAPTAIN OF THIS SHIP NOW!!
CLIK
CLIK
CLIK
CLIK

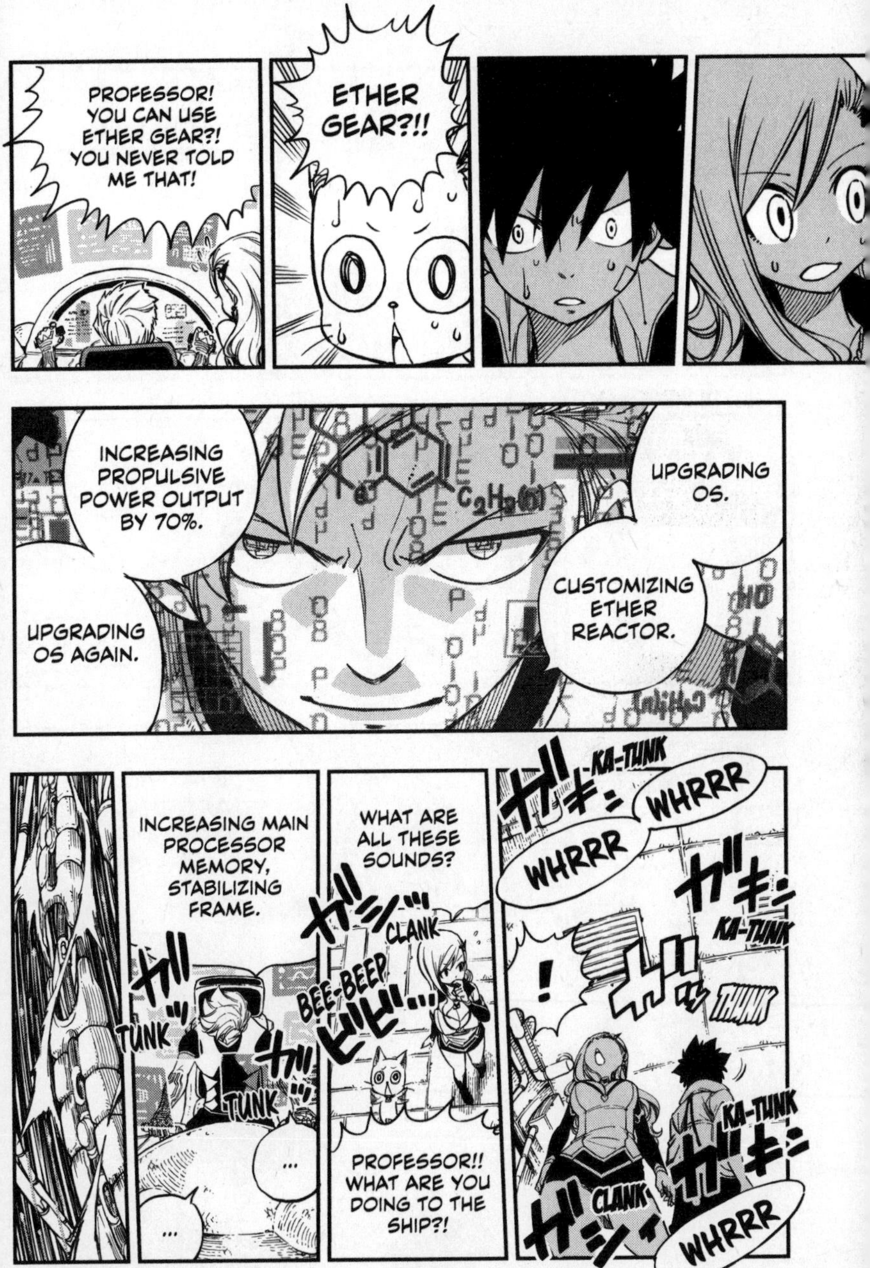
ETHER GEAR?!!
PROFESSOR! YOU CAN USE ETHER GEAR?! YOU NEVER TOLD ME THAT!
UPGRADING OS.
INCREASING PROPULSIVE POWER OUTPUT BY 70%.
CUSTOMIZING ETHER REACTOR.
UPGRADING OS AGAIN.
KA-TUNK
WHRRR
WHRRR
KA-TUNK
!
THUNK
KA-TUNK
CLANK
WHRRR
WHAT ARE ALL THESE SOUNDS?
CLANK
BEE-BEEP
PROFESSOR!! WHAT ARE YOU DOING TO THE SHIP?!
INCREASING MAIN PROCESSOR MEMORY, STABILIZING FRAME.
TUNK
TUNK
...
...

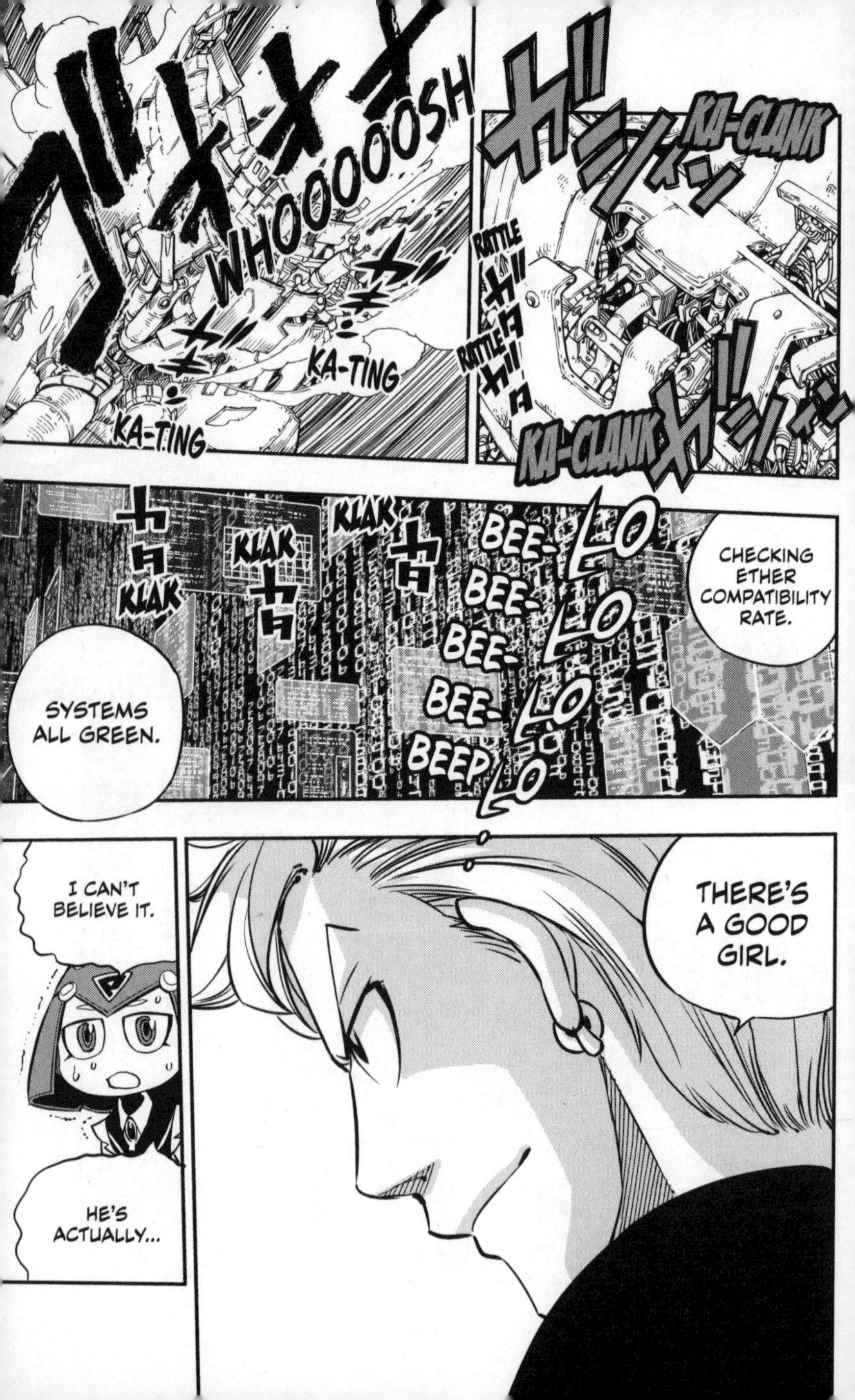
KA-CLANK
RATTLE
RATTLE
KA-CLANK
WHOOOOOSH
KA-TING
KA-TING
CHECKING ETHER COMPATIBILITY RATE.
BEE-
BEE-
BEE-
BEE-
BEEP
KLAK
KLAK
KLAK
SYSTEMS ALL GREEN.
THERE'S A GOOD GIRL.
I CAN'T BELIEVE IT.
HE'S ACTUALLY...

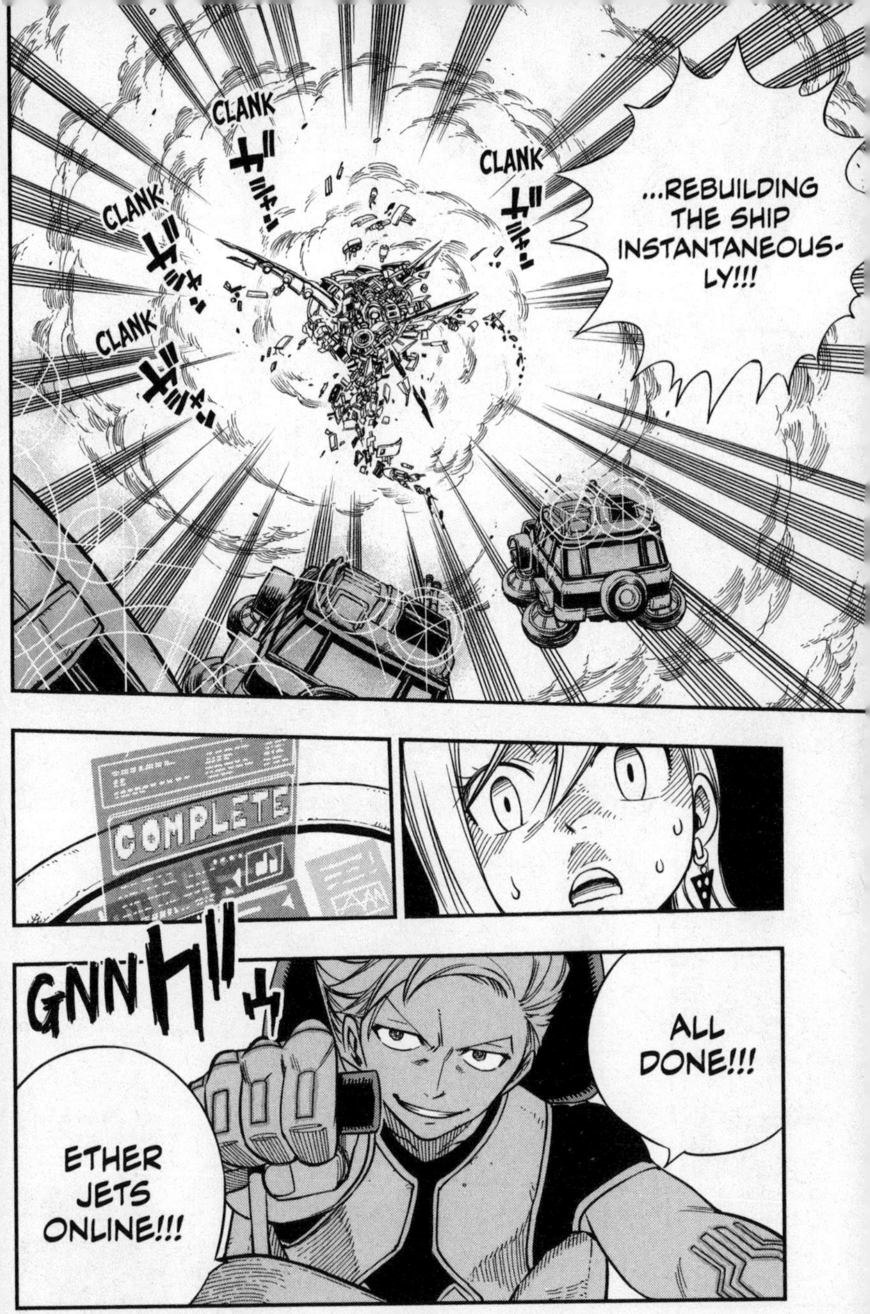
...REBUILDING THE SHIP INSTANTANEOUS-LY!!!
CLANK
CLANK
CLANK
CLANK
COMPLETE
ALL DONE!!!
GNN
ETHER JETS ONLINE!!!

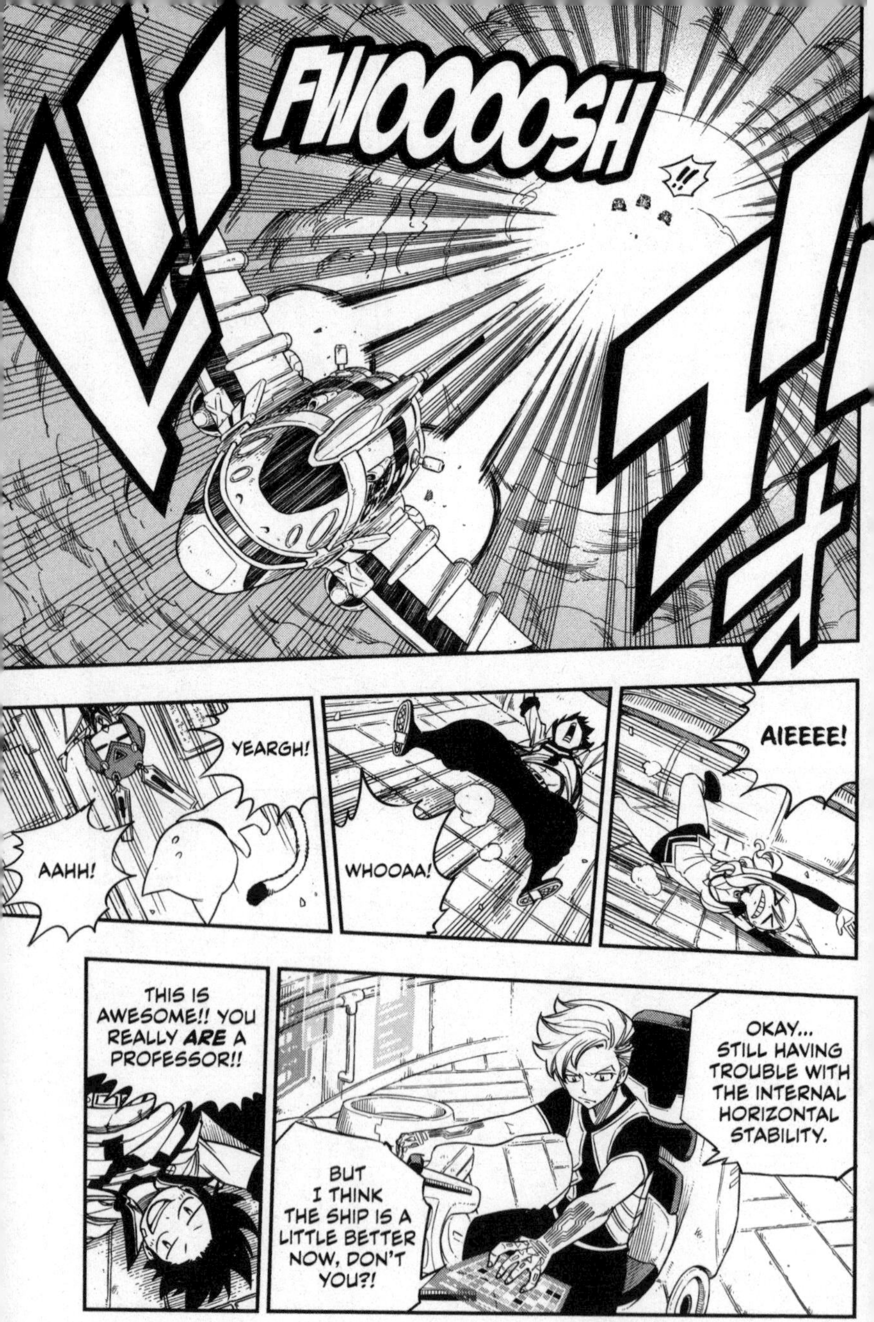
FWOOOOSH
!!
AIEEEE!
WHOOAA!
YEARGH!
AAHH!
OKAY... STILL HAVING TROUBLE WITH THE INTERNAL HORIZONTAL STABILITY.
BUT I THINK THE SHIP IS A LITTLE BETTER NOW, DON'T YOU?!
THIS IS AWESOME!! YOU REALLY **ARE** A PROFESSOR!!

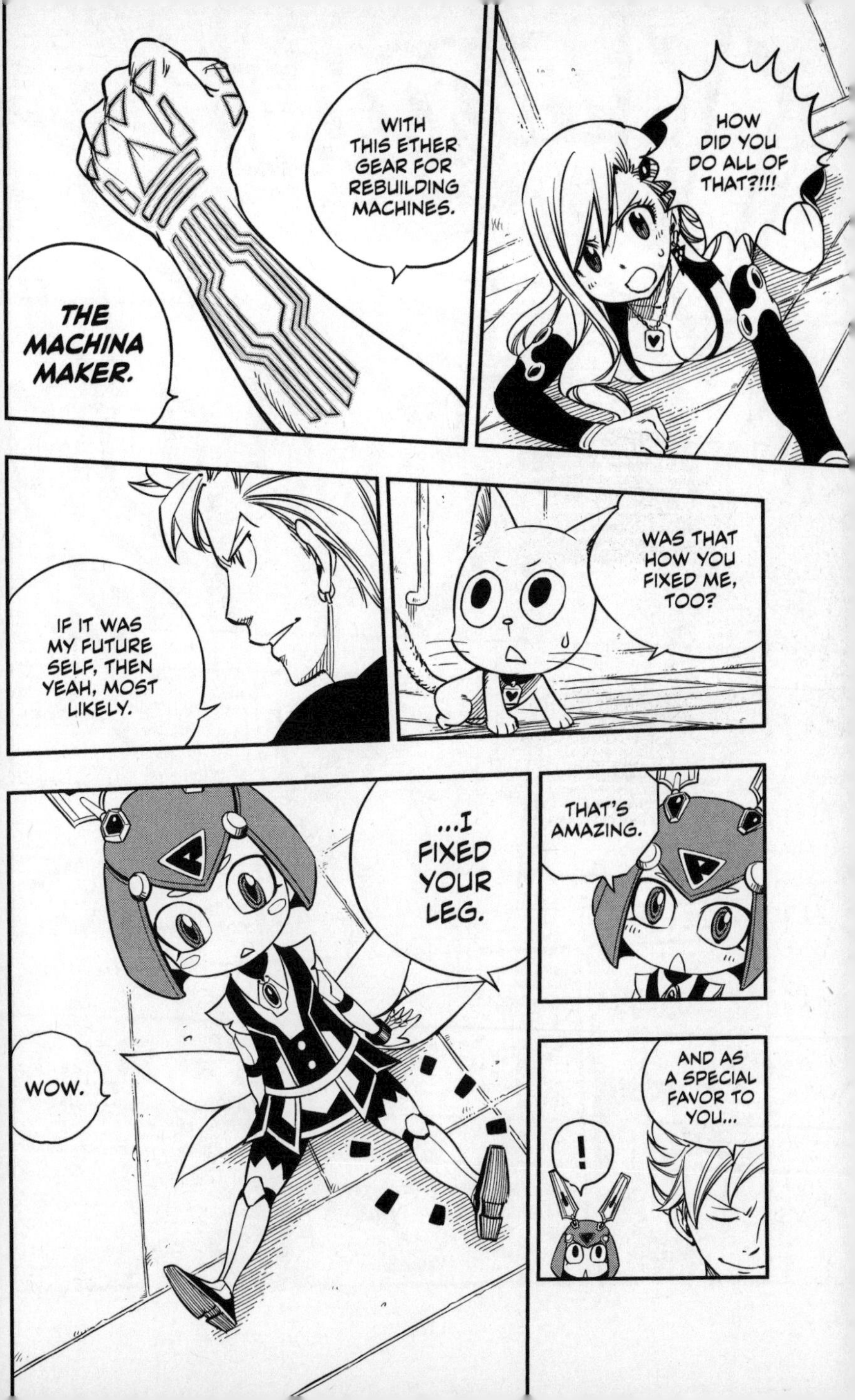
HOW DID YOU DO ALL OF THAT?!!!
WITH THIS ETHER GEAR FOR REBUILDING MACHINES.
THE MACHINA MAKER.
WAS THAT HOW YOU FIXED ME, TOO?
IF IT WAS MY FUTURE SELF, THEN YEAH, MOST LIKELY.
THAT'S AMAZING.
AND AS A SPECIAL FAVOR TO YOU...
!
...I FIXED YOUR LEG.
WOW.

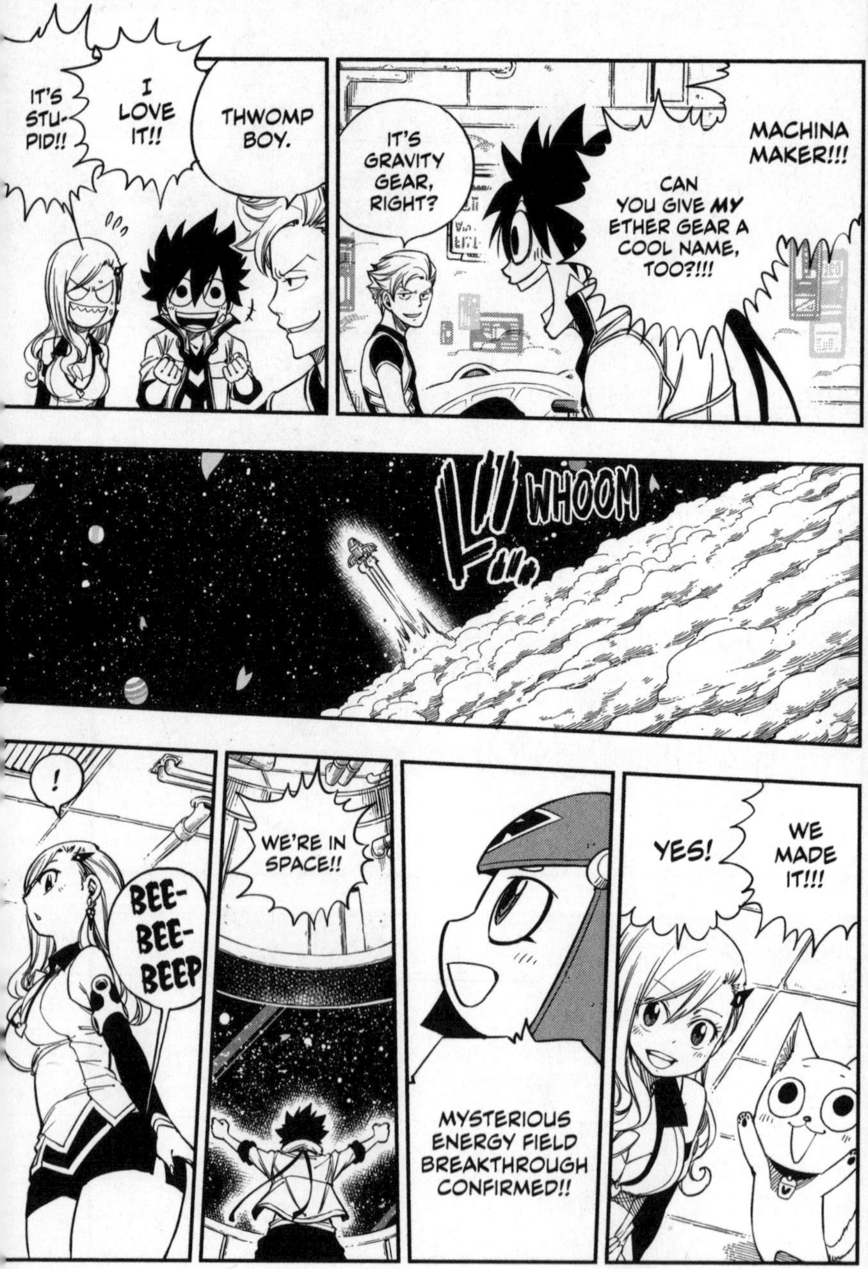
MACHINA MAKER!!!
CAN YOU GIVE MY ETHER GEAR A COOL NAME, TOO?!!!
IT'S GRAVITY GEAR, RIGHT?
THWOMP BOY.
I LOVE IT!!
IT'S STU-PID!!
WHOOM
WE MADE IT!!!
YES!
MYSTERIOUS ENERGY FIELD BREAKTHROUGH CONFIRMED!!
WE'RE IN SPACE!!
!
BEE-BEE-BEEP

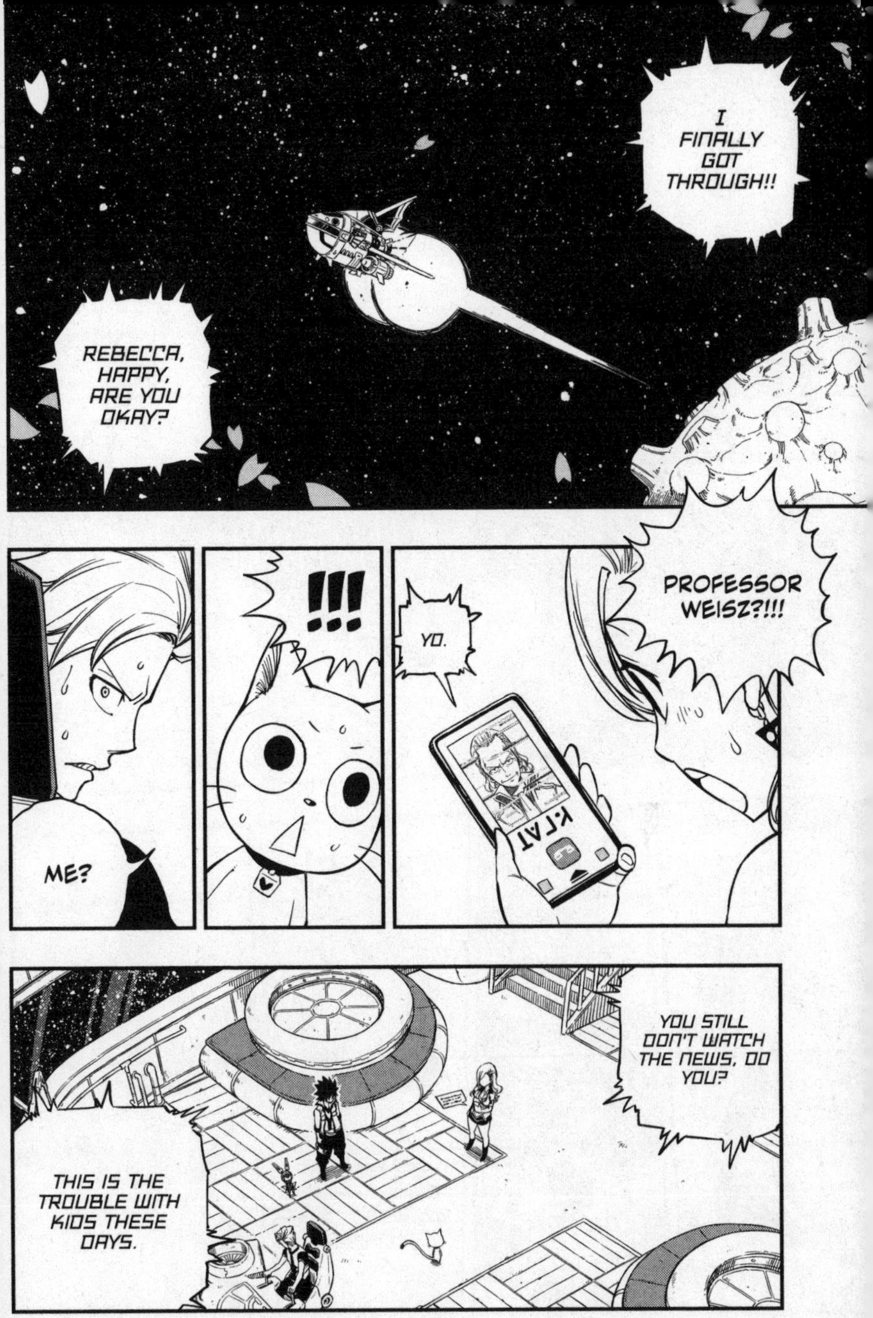
I FINALLY GOT THROUGH!!
REBECCA, HAPPY, ARE YOU OKAY?
PROFESSOR WEISZ?!!!
YO.
!!!
ME?
YOU STILL DON'T WATCH THE NEWS, DO YOU?
THIS IS THE TROUBLE WITH KIDS THESE DAYS.

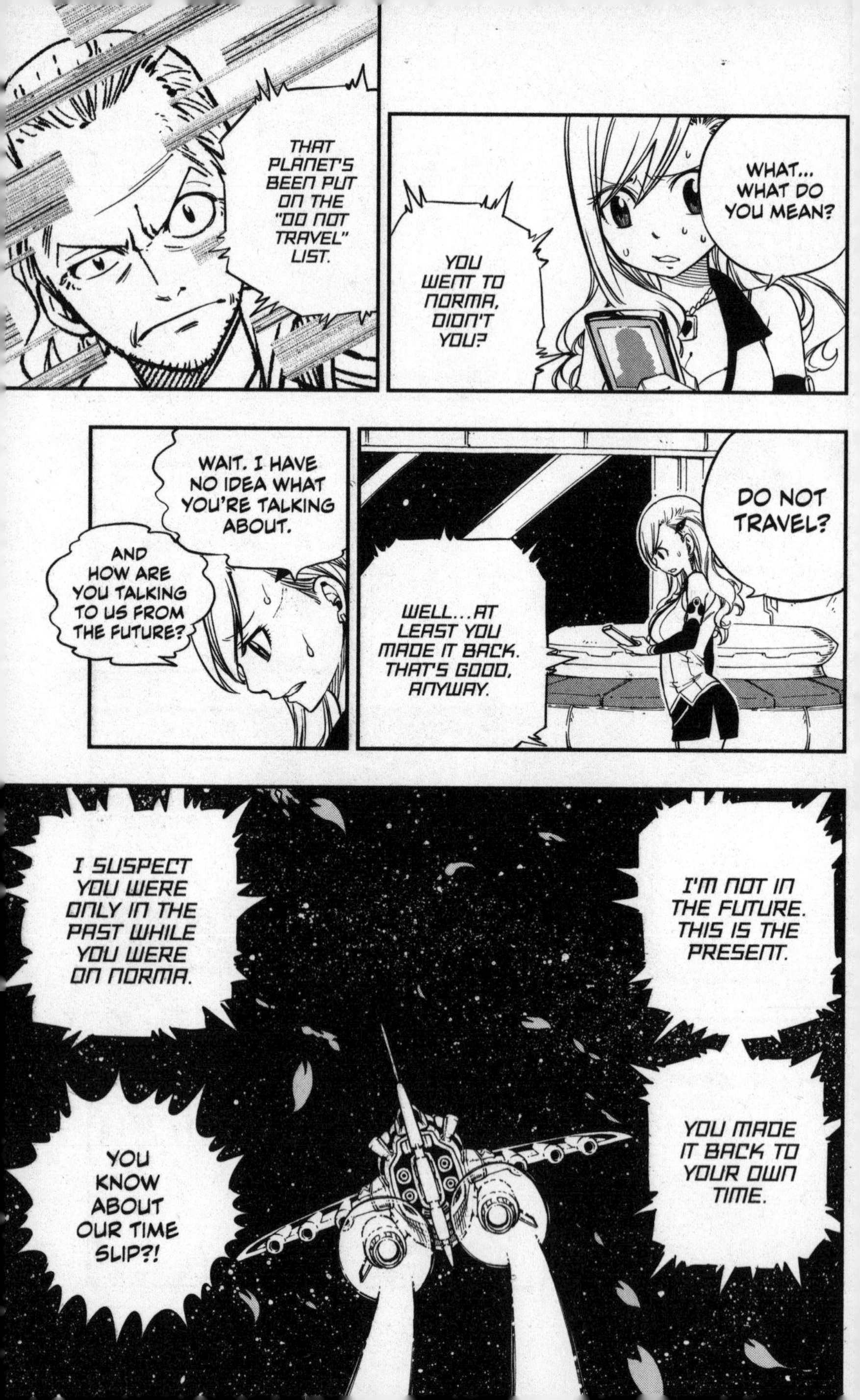
WHAT... WHAT DO YOU MEAN?
YOU WENT TO NORMA, DIDN'T YOU?
THAT PLANET'S BEEN PUT ON THE "DO NOT TRAVEL" LIST.
DO NOT TRAVEL?
WELL...AT LEAST YOU MADE IT BACK. THAT'S GOOD, ANYWAY.
WAIT. I HAVE NO IDEA WHAT YOU'RE TALKING ABOUT.
AND HOW ARE YOU TALKING TO US FROM THE FUTURE?
I'M NOT IN THE FUTURE. THIS IS THE PRESENT.
I SUSPECT YOU WERE ONLY IN THE PAST WHILE YOU WERE ON NORMA.
YOU MADE IT BACK TO YOUR OWN TIME.
YOU KNOW ABOUT OUR TIME SLIP?!

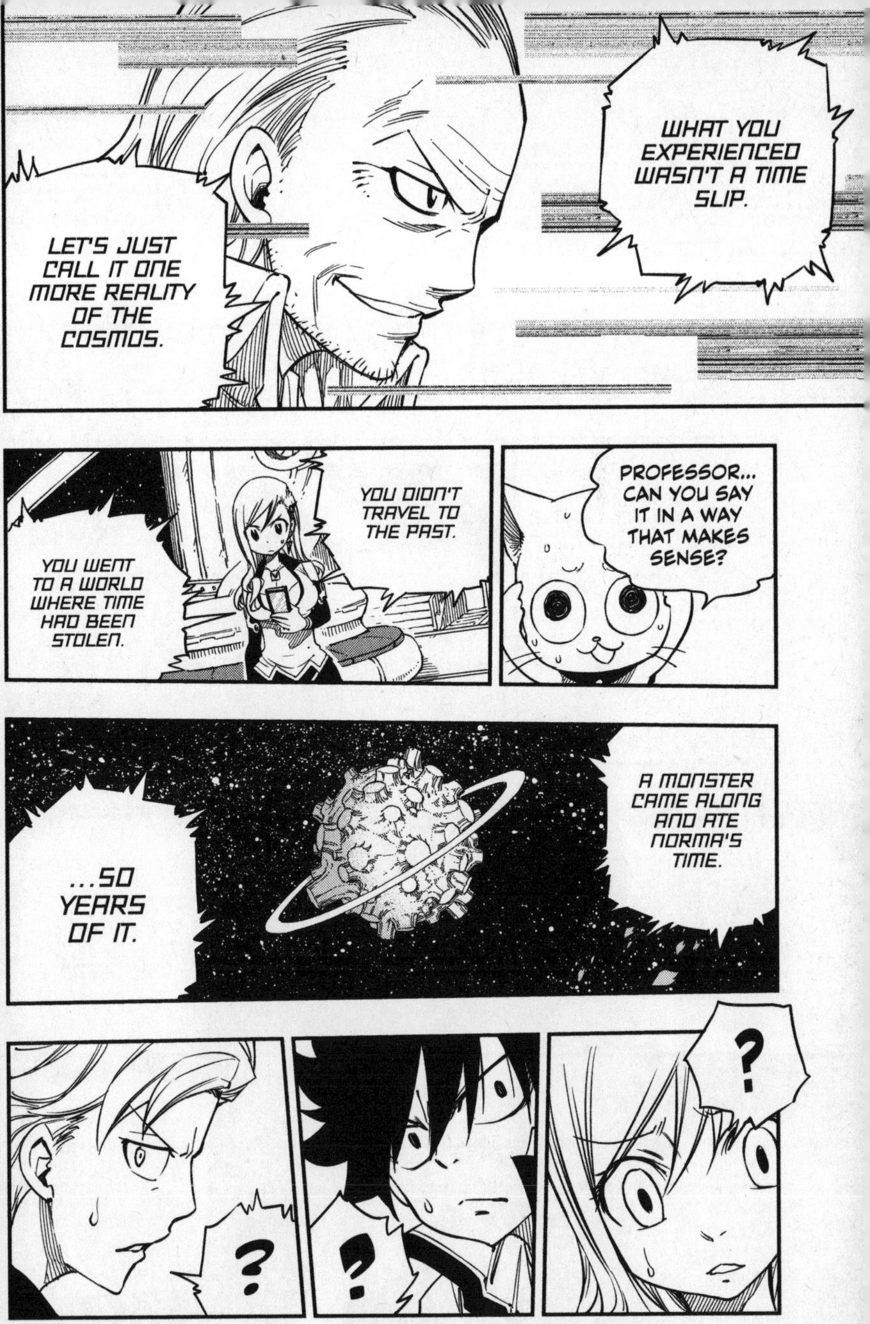
WHAT YOU EXPERIENCED WASN'T A TIME SLIP.
LET'S JUST CALL IT ONE MORE REALITY OF THE COSMOS.
PROFESSOR... CAN YOU SAY IT IN A WAY THAT MAKES SENSE?
YOU DIDN'T TRAVEL TO THE PAST.
YOU WENT TO A WORLD WHERE TIME HAD BEEN STOLEN.
A MONSTER CAME ALONG AND ATE NORMA'S TIME.
...50 YEARS OF IT.
?
?
?

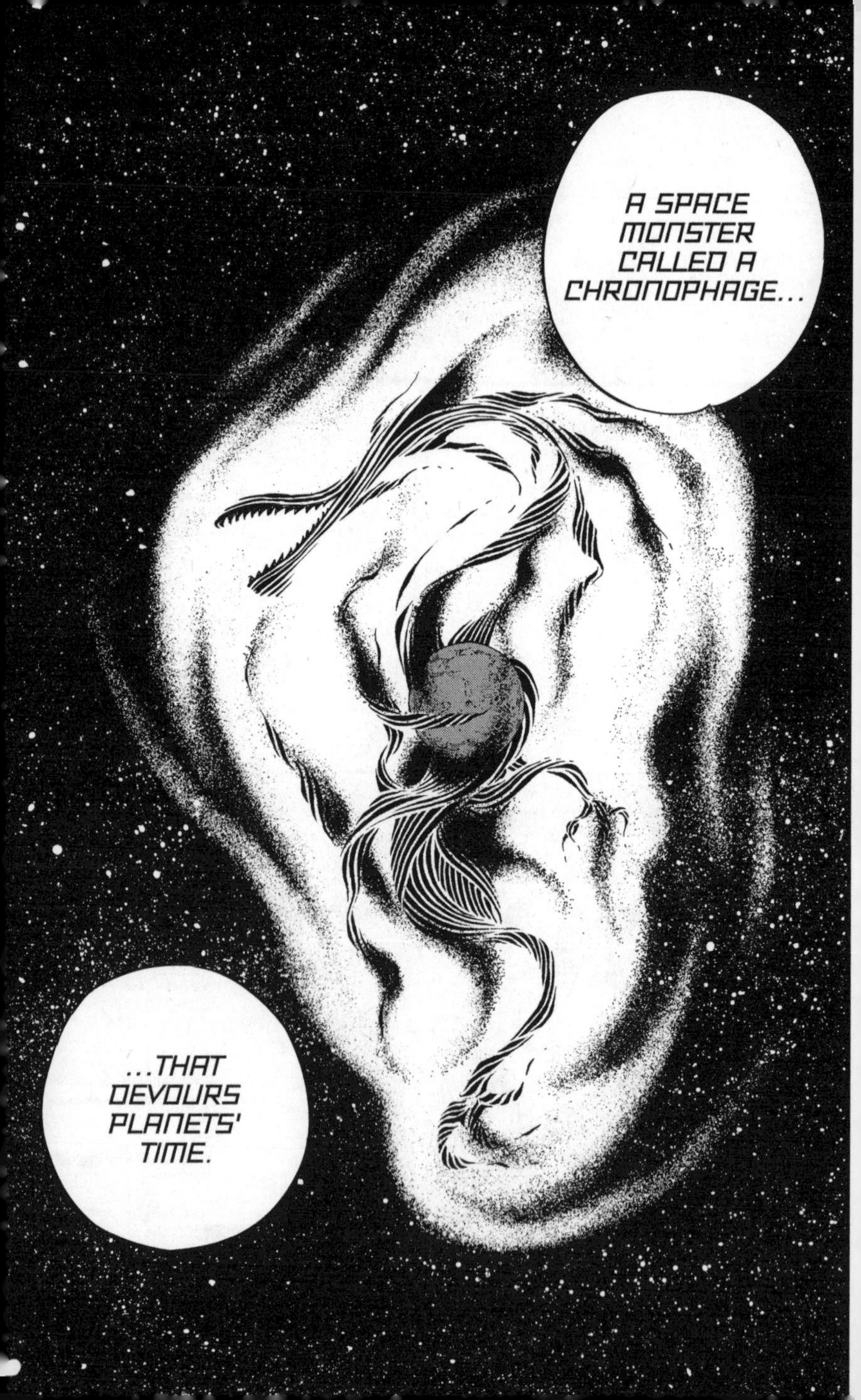
A SPACE MONSTER CALLED A CHRONOPHAGE...
...THAT DEVOURS PLANETS' TIME.

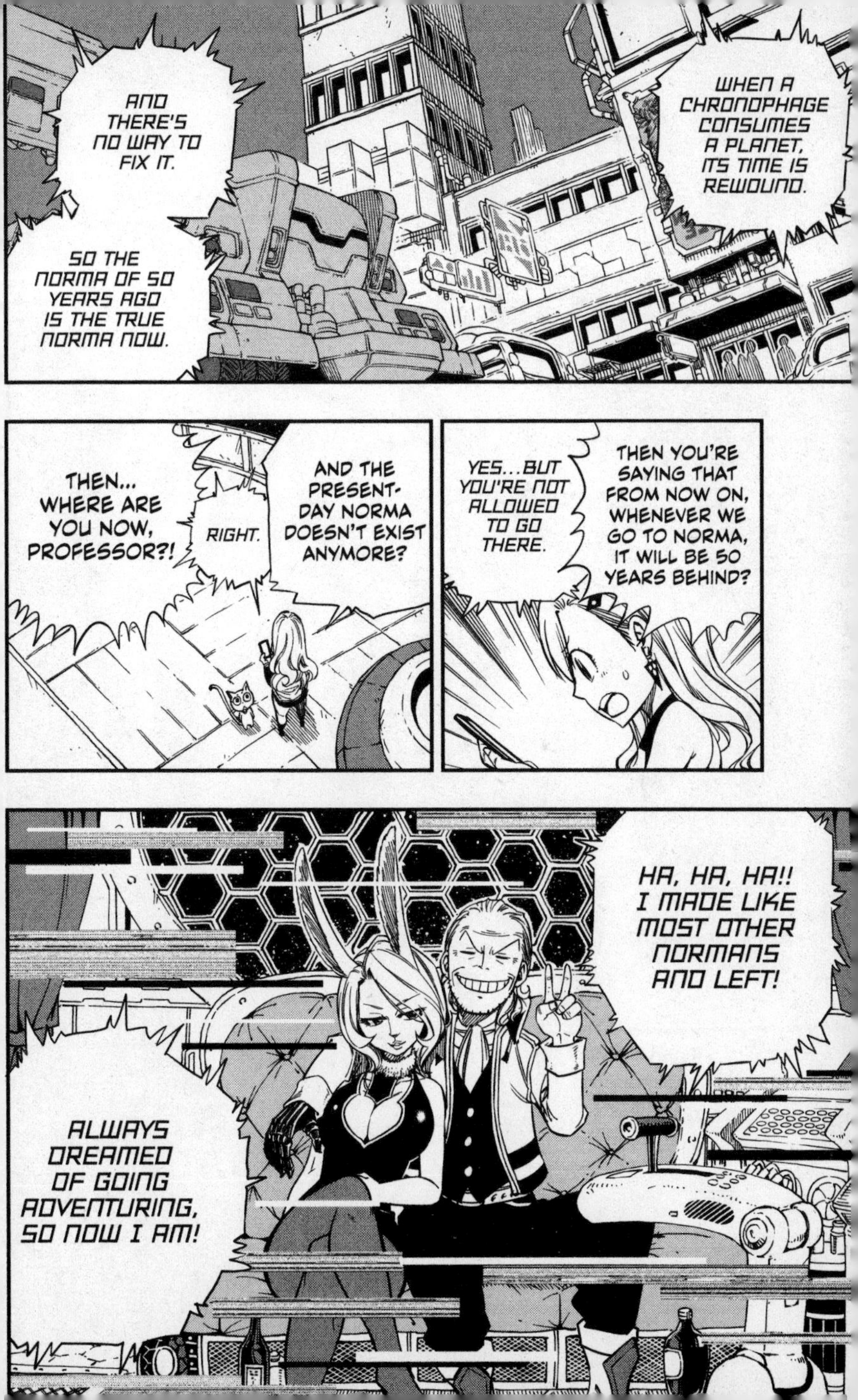
WHEN A CHRONOPHAGE CONSUMES A PLANET, ITS TIME IS REWOUND.
AND THERE'S NO WAY TO FIX IT.
SO THE NORMA OF 50 YEARS AGO IS THE TRUE NORMA NOW.
THEN YOU'RE SAYING THAT FROM NOW ON, WHENEVER WE GO TO NORMA, IT WILL BE 50 YEARS BEHIND?
YES...BUT YOU'RE NOT ALLOWED TO GO THERE.
AND THE PRESENT-DAY NORMA DOESN'T EXIST ANYMORE?
RIGHT.
THEN... WHERE ARE YOU NOW, PROFESSOR?!
HA, HA, HA!! I MADE LIKE MOST OTHER NORMANS AND LEFT!
ALWAYS DREAMED OF GOING ADVENTURING, SO NOW I AM!

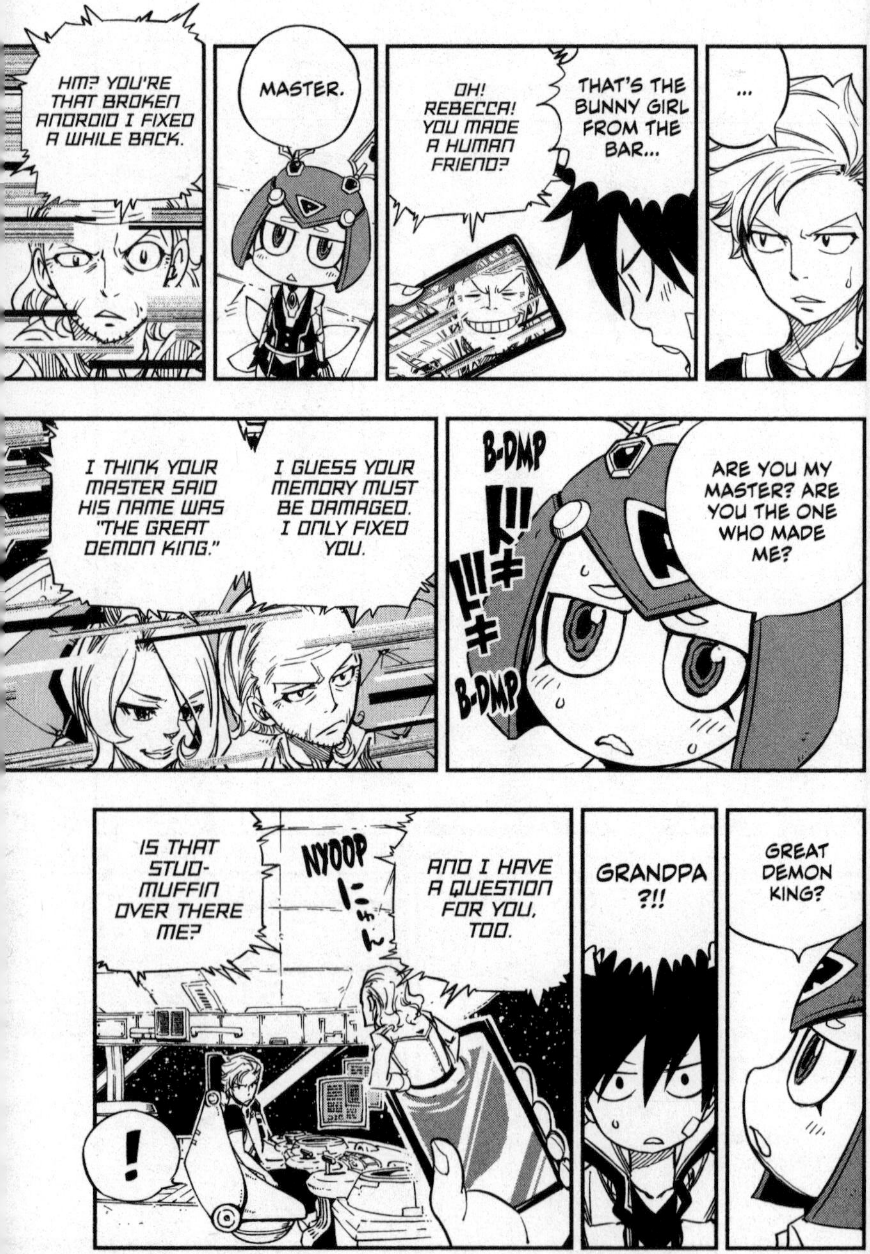
...
THAT'S THE BUNNY GIRL FROM THE BAR...
OH! REBECCA! YOU MADE A HUMAN FRIEND?
MASTER.
HM? YOU'RE THAT BROKEN ANDROID I FIXED A WHILE BACK.
ARE YOU MY MASTER? ARE YOU THE ONE WHO MADE ME?
B-DMP
ドキ
ドキ
B-DMP
I GUESS YOUR MEMORY MUST BE DAMAGED. I ONLY FIXED YOU.
I THINK YOUR MASTER SAID HIS NAME WAS "THE GREAT DEMON KING."
GREAT DEMON KING?
GRANDPA?!!
AND I HAVE A QUESTION FOR YOU, TOO.
NYOOP
にゅん
IS THAT STUD-MUFFIN OVER THERE ME?
!

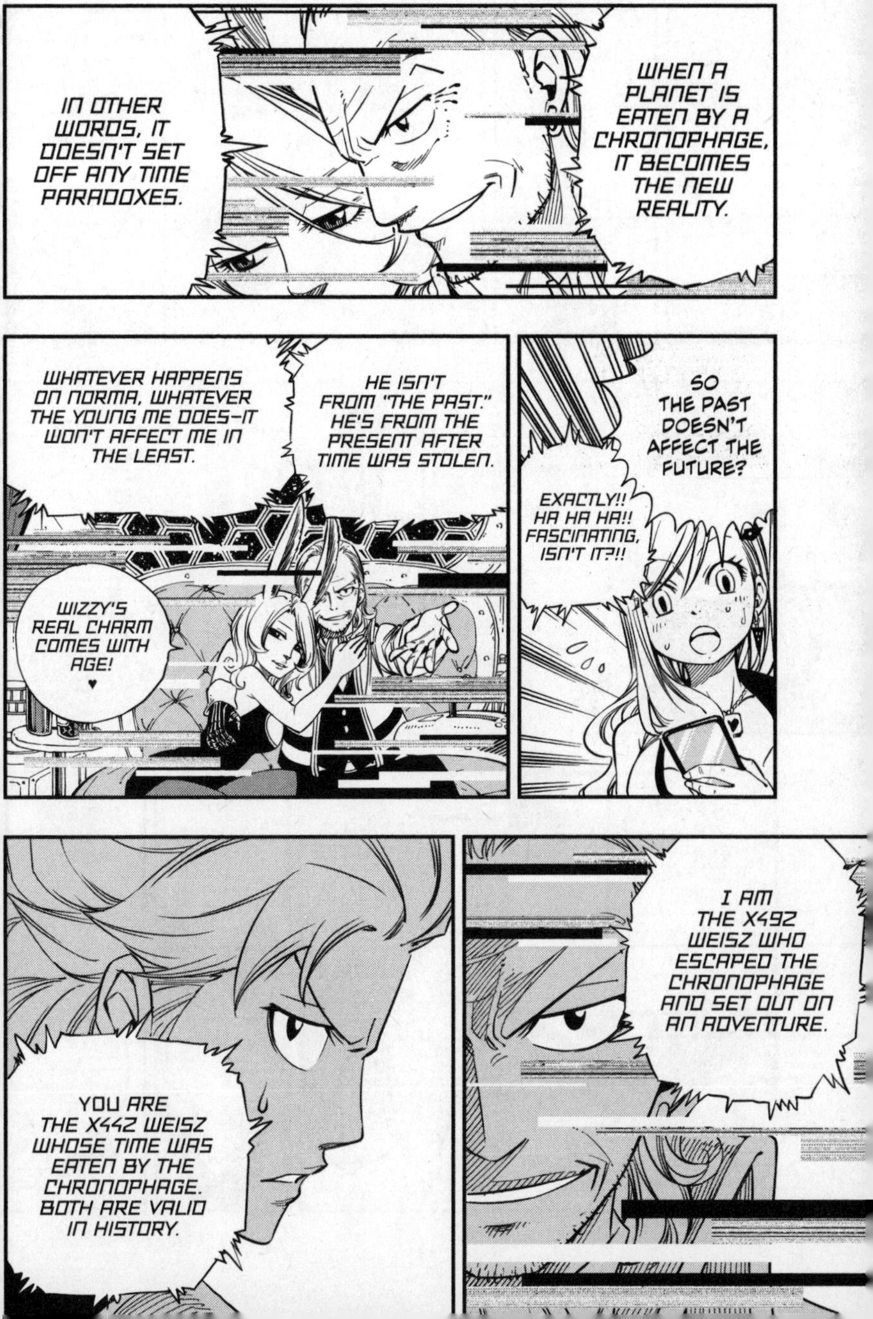
WHEN A PLANET IS EATEN BY A CHRONOPHAGE, IT BECOMES THE NEW REALITY.
IN OTHER WORDS, IT DOESN'T SET OFF ANY TIME PARADOXES.
SO THE PAST DOESN'T AFFECT THE FUTURE?
EXACTLY!! HA HA HA!! FASCINATING, ISN'T IT?!!
HE ISN'T FROM "THE PAST." HE'S FROM THE PRESENT AFTER TIME WAS STOLEN.
WHATEVER HAPPENS ON NORMA, WHATEVER THE YOUNG ME DOES—IT WON'T AFFECT ME IN THE LEAST.
WIZZY'S REAL CHARM COMES WITH AGE! ♥
I AM THE X492 WEISZ WHO ESCAPED THE CHRONOPHAGE AND SET OUT ON AN ADVENTURE.
YOU ARE THE X442 WEISZ WHOSE TIME WAS EATEN BY THE CHRONOPHAGE. BOTH ARE VALID IN HISTORY.

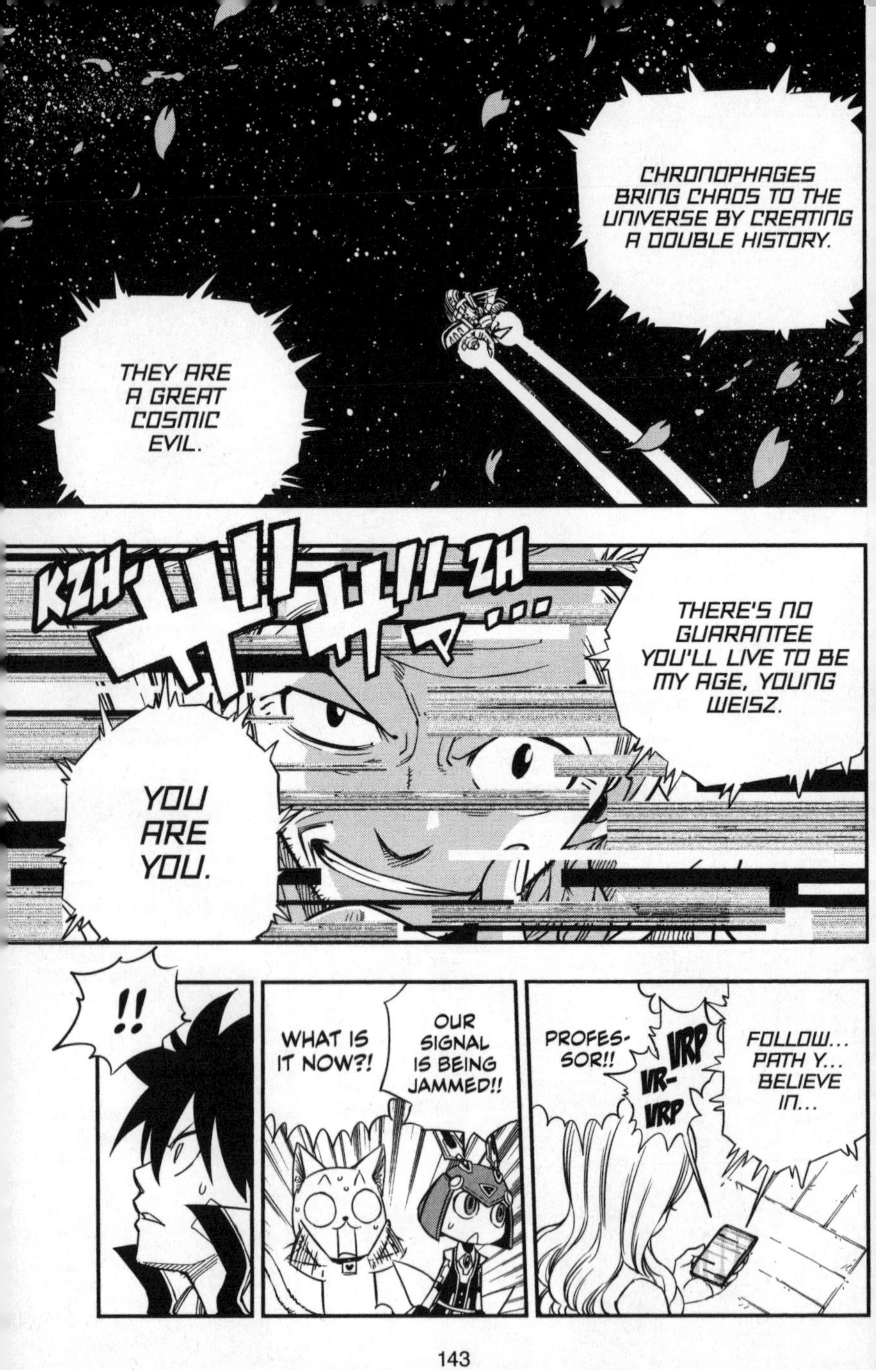
CHRONOPHAGES BRING CHAOS TO THE UNIVERSE BY CREATING A DOUBLE HISTORY.
THEY ARE A GREAT COSMIC EVIL.
THERE'S NO GUARANTEE YOU'LL LIVE TO BE MY AGE, YOUNG WEISZ.
KZH- ZH...
YOU ARE YOU.
FOLLOW... PATH Y... BELIEVE IN...
VRP
VR-VRP
PROFES-SOR!!
OUR SIGNAL IS BEING JAMMED!!
WHAT IS IT NOW?!
!!

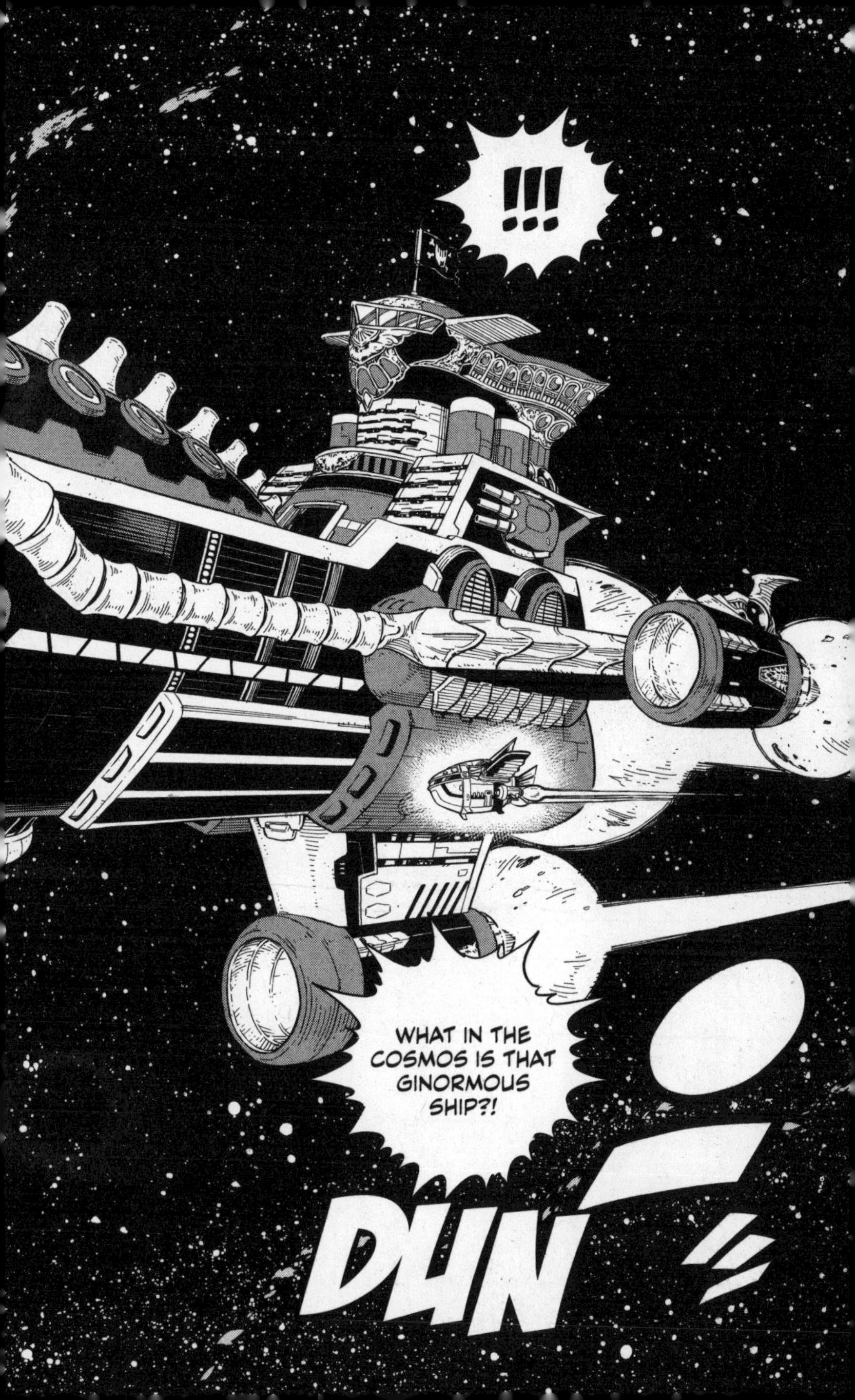
!!!
WHAT IN THE COSMOS IS THAT GINORMOUS SHIP?!
DUN

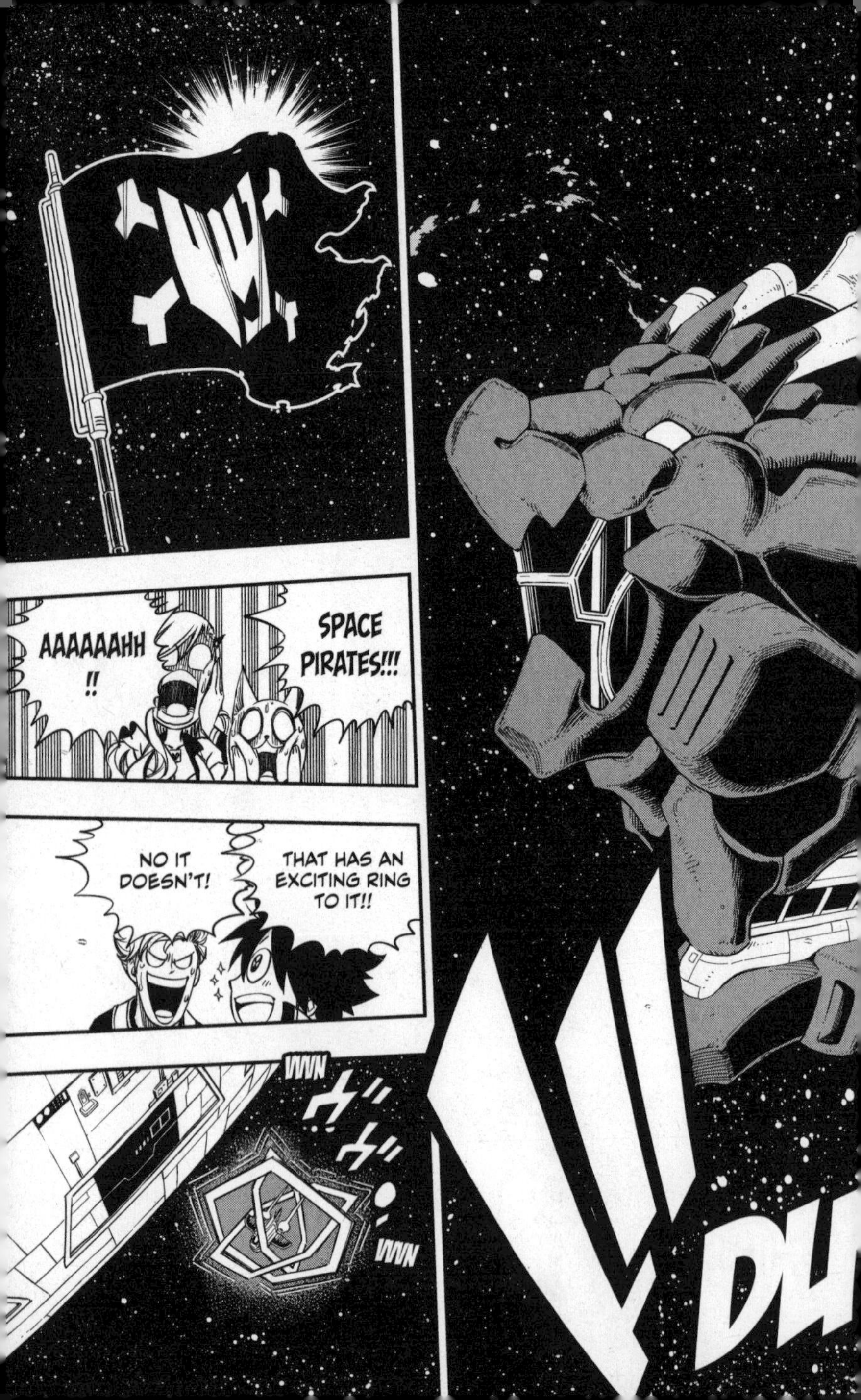
DH
SPACE PIRATES!!!
AAAAAAHH !!
THAT HAS AN EXCITING RING TO IT!!
NO IT DOESN'T!
VVVN
VVVN

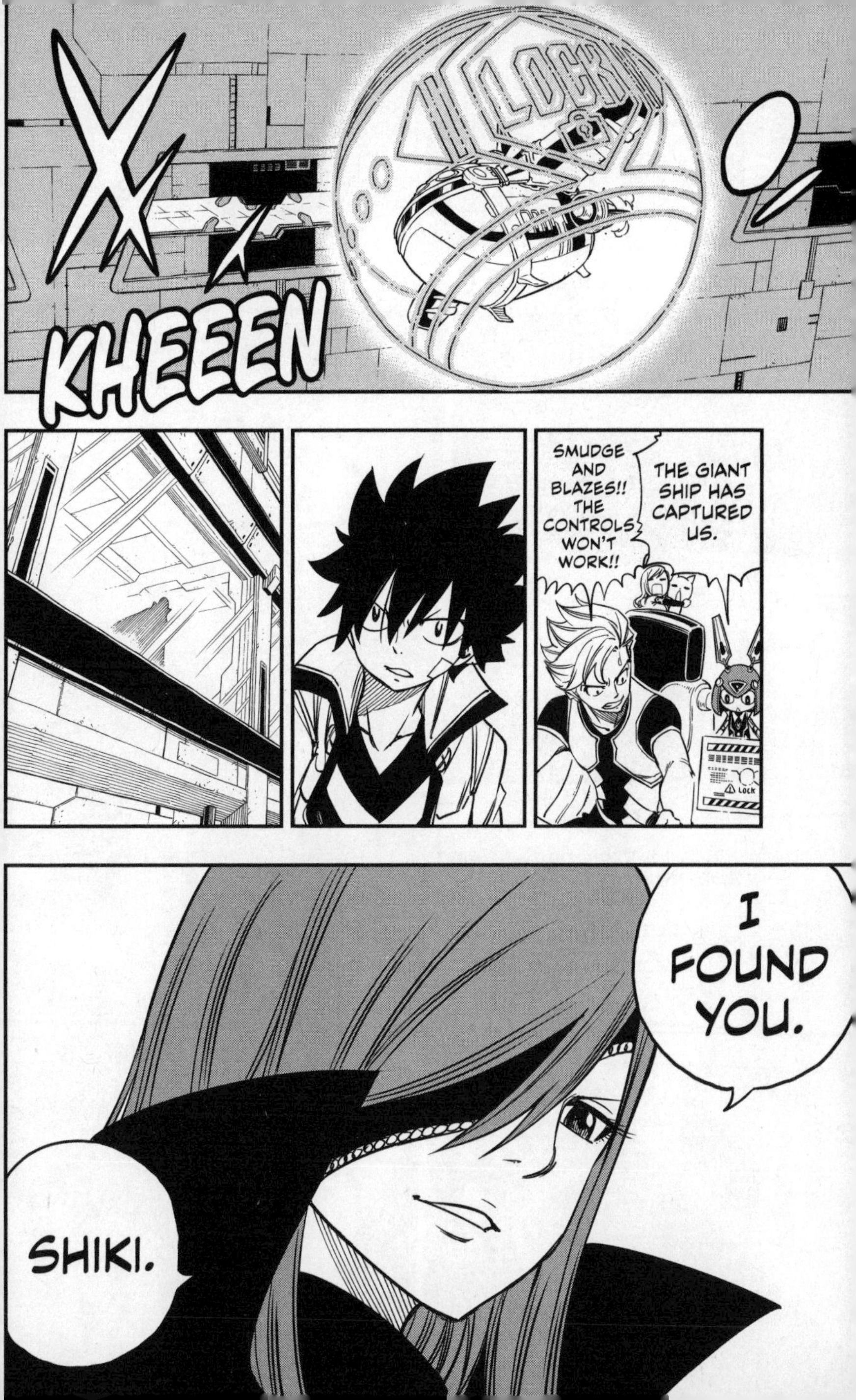
LOCK
KHEEEN
THE GIANT SHIP HAS CAPTURED US.
SMUDGE AND BLAZES!! THE CONTROLS WON'T WORK!!
LOCK
I FOUND YOU.
SHIKI.

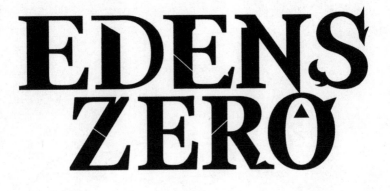

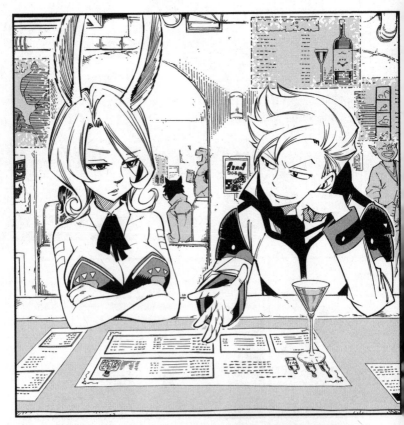

**CHAPTER 12: THE SKULL FAIRY**

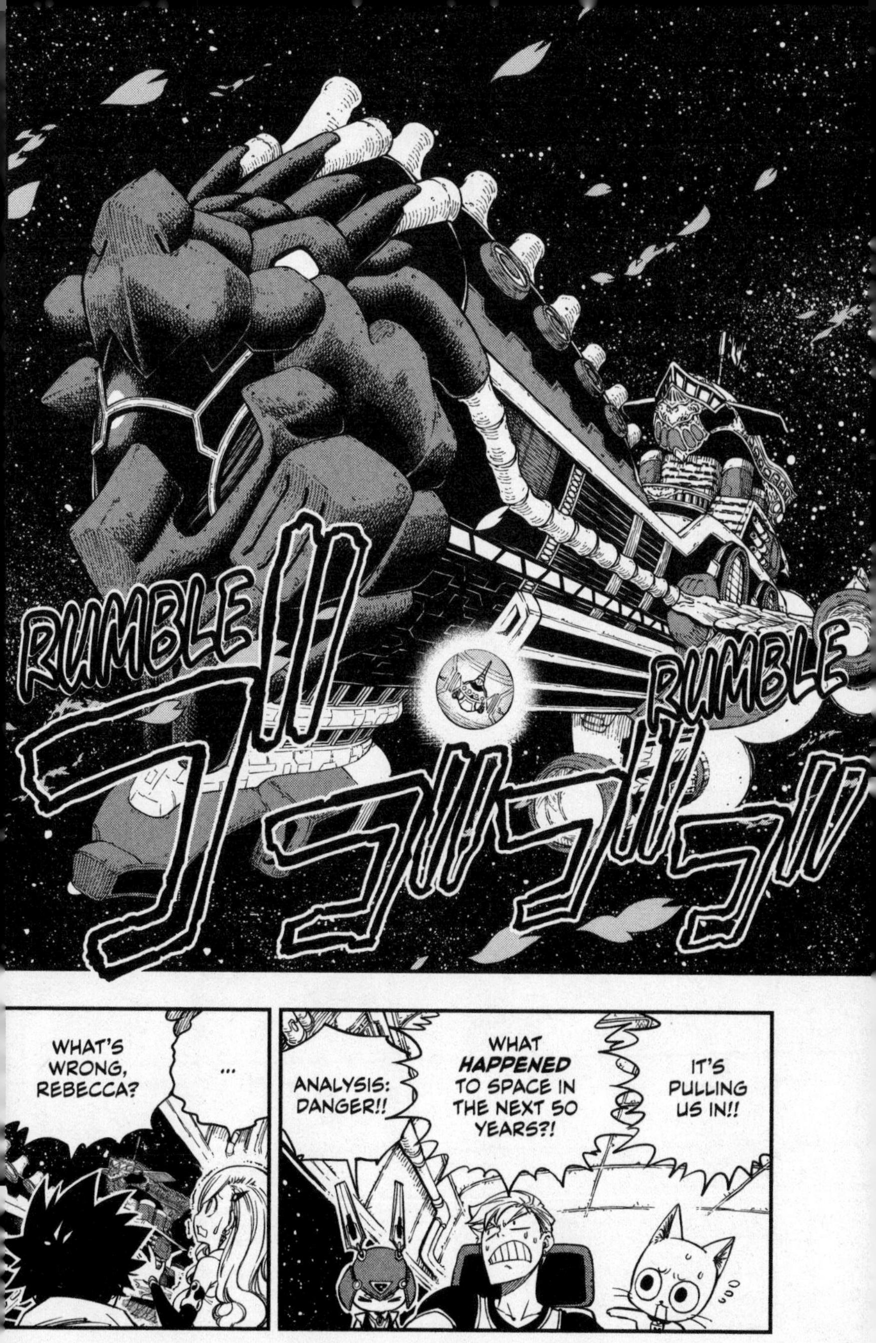
RUMBLE
RUMBLE
IT'S PULLING US IN!!
WHAT **HAPPENED** TO SPACE IN THE NEXT 50 YEARS?!
ANALYSIS: DANGER!!
...
WHAT'S WRONG, REBECCA?

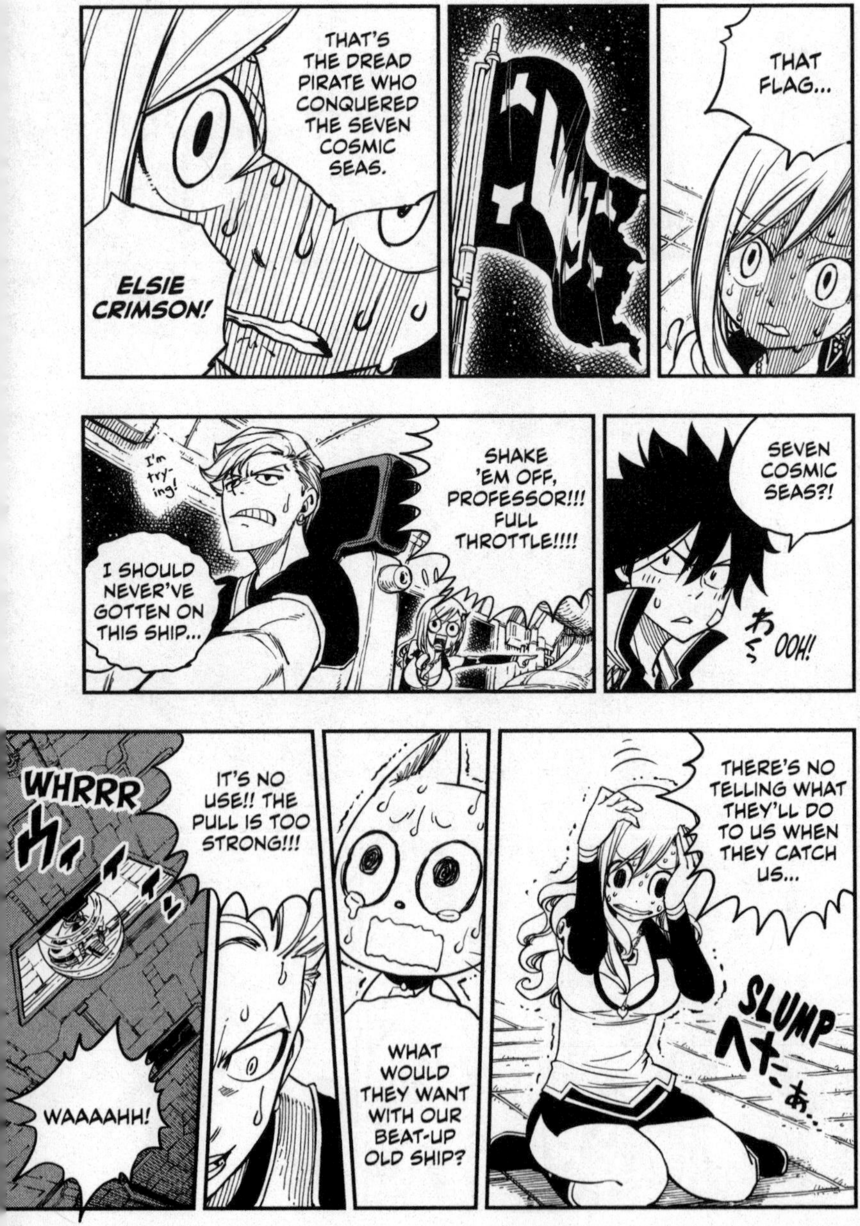
THAT FLAG...
THAT'S THE DREAD PIRATE WHO CONQUERED THE SEVEN COSMIC SEAS.
ELSIE CRIMSON!
SEVEN COSMIC SEAS?!
OOH!
SHAKE 'EM OFF, PROFESSOR!!! FULL THROTTLE!!!!
I'm try-ing!
I SHOULD NEVER'VE GOTTEN ON THIS SHIP...
THERE'S NO TELLING WHAT THEY'LL DO TO US WHEN THEY CATCH US...
SLUMP
WHAT WOULD THEY WANT WITH OUR BEAT-UP OLD SHIP?
IT'S NO USE!! THE PULL IS TOO STRONG!!!
WHRRR
WAAAAHH!

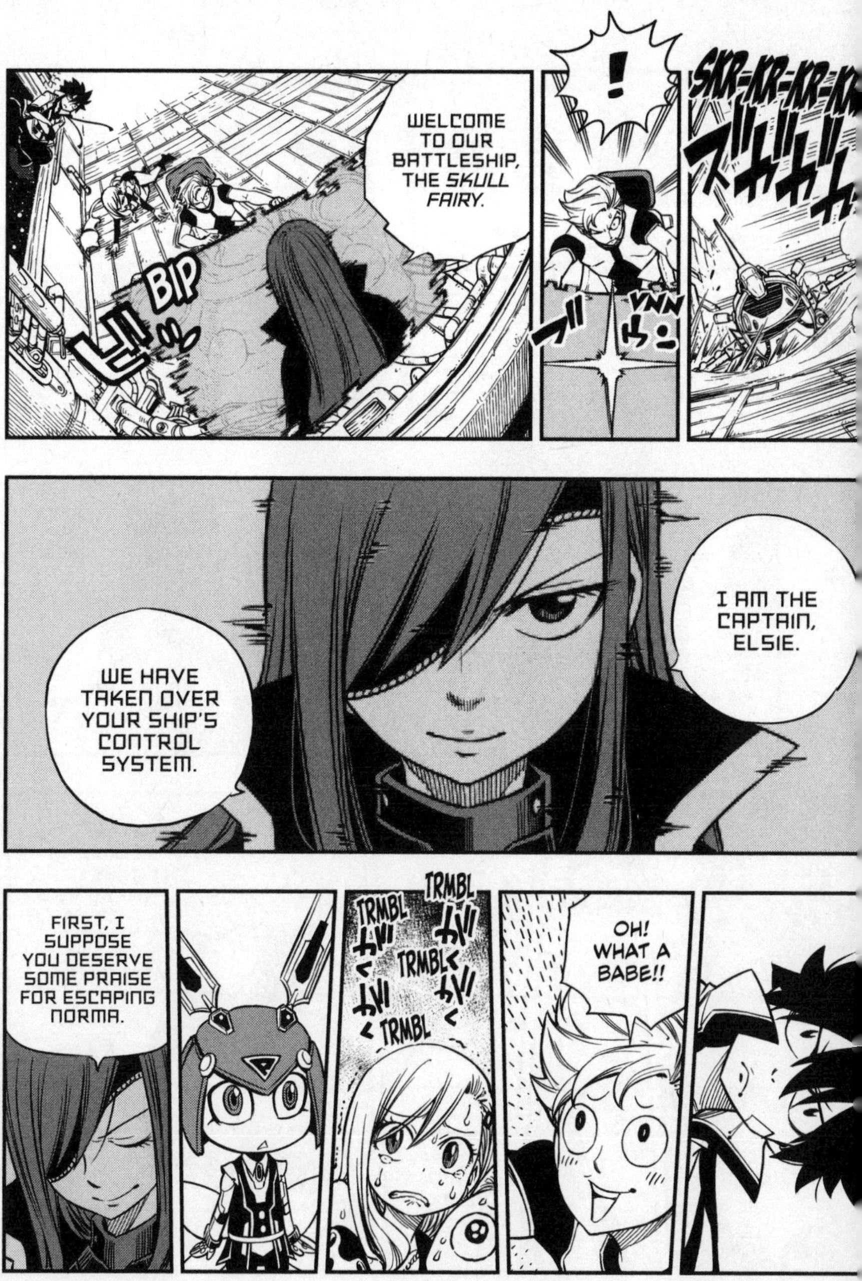
SKR-KR-KR-KR
!
VNN
WELCOME TO OUR BATTLESHIP, THE *SKULL FAIRY*.
BIP
I AM THE CAPTAIN, ELSIE.
WE HAVE TAKEN OVER YOUR SHIP'S CONTROL SYSTEM.
OH! WHAT A BABE!!
TRMBL
TRMBL
TRMBL
TRMBL
FIRST, I SUPPOSE YOU DESERVE SOME PRAISE FOR ESCAPING NORMA.

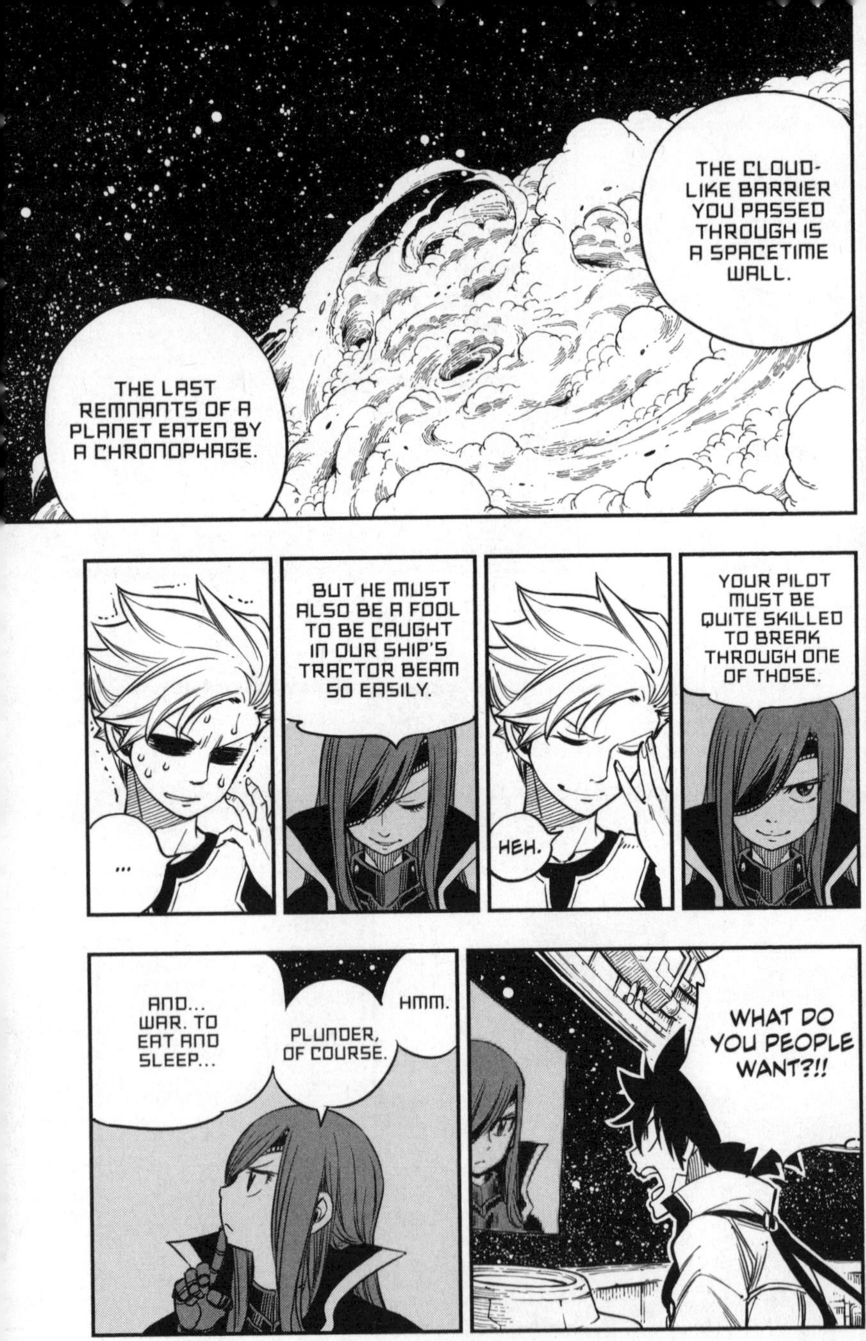
THE CLOUD-LIKE BARRIER YOU PASSED THROUGH IS A SPACETIME WALL.
THE LAST REMNANTS OF A PLANET EATEN BY A CHRONOPHAGE.
YOUR PILOT MUST BE QUITE SKILLED TO BREAK THROUGH ONE OF THOSE.
HEH.
BUT HE MUST ALSO BE A FOOL TO BE CAUGHT IN OUR SHIP'S TRACTOR BEAM SO EASILY.
...
WHAT DO YOU PEOPLE WANT?!!
HMM.
PLUNDER, OF COURSE.
AND... WAR. TO EAT AND SLEEP...

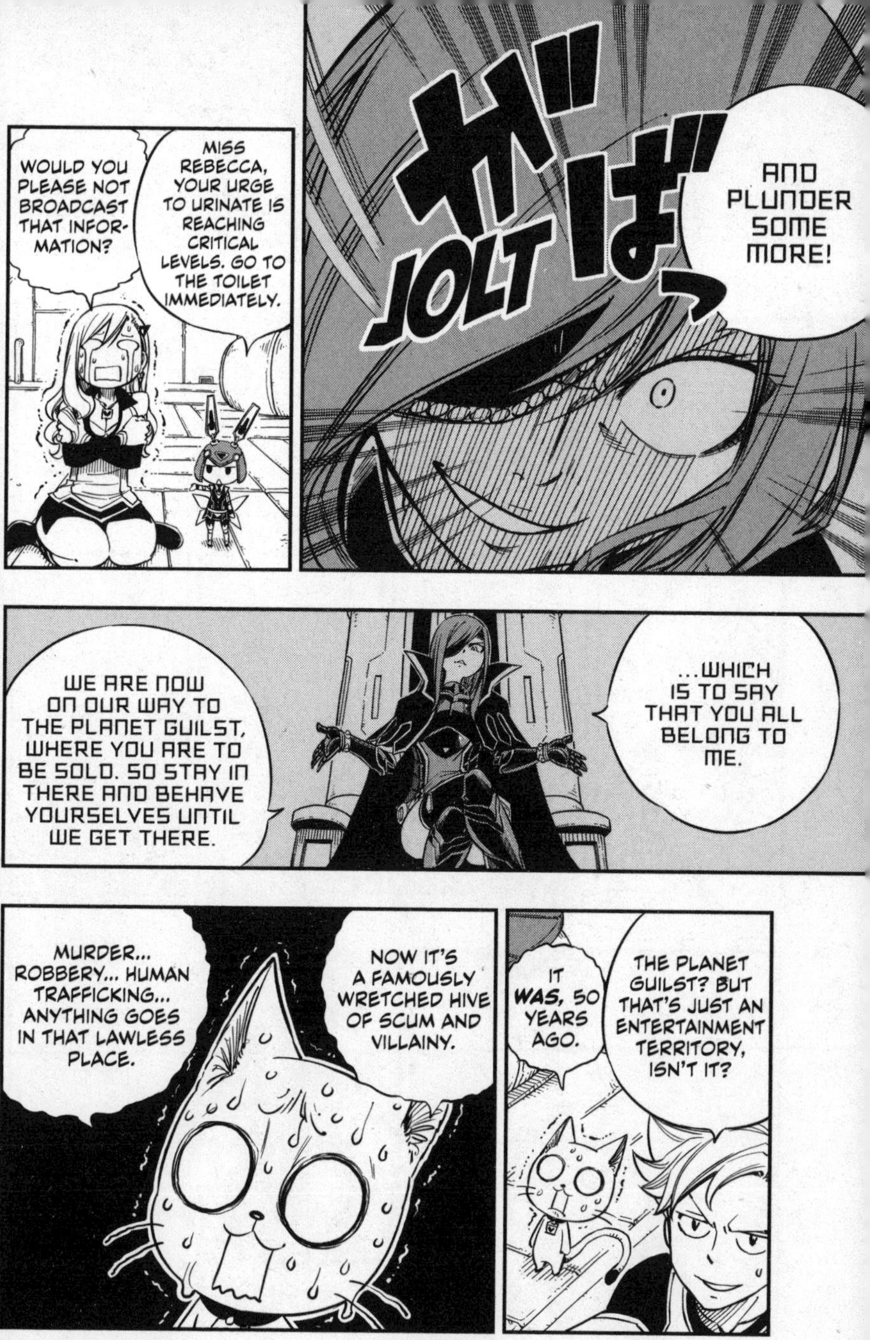
AND PLUNDER SOME MORE!
ガばっ
JOLT
MISS REBECCA, YOUR URGE TO URINATE IS REACHING CRITICAL LEVELS. GO TO THE TOILET IMMEDIATELY.
WOULD YOU PLEASE NOT BROADCAST THAT INFOR-MATION?
...WHICH IS TO SAY THAT YOU ALL BELONG TO ME.
WE ARE NOW ON OUR WAY TO THE PLANET GUILST, WHERE YOU ARE TO BE SOLD. SO STAY IN THERE AND BEHAVE YOURSELVES UNTIL WE GET THERE.
THE PLANET GUILST? BUT THAT'S JUST AN ENTERTAINMENT TERRITORY, ISN'T IT?
IT WAS, 50 YEARS AGO.
NOW IT'S A FAMOUSLY WRETCHED HIVE OF SCUM AND VILLAINY.
MURDER... ROBBERY... HUMAN TRAFFICKING... ANYTHING GOES IN THAT LAWLESS PLACE.

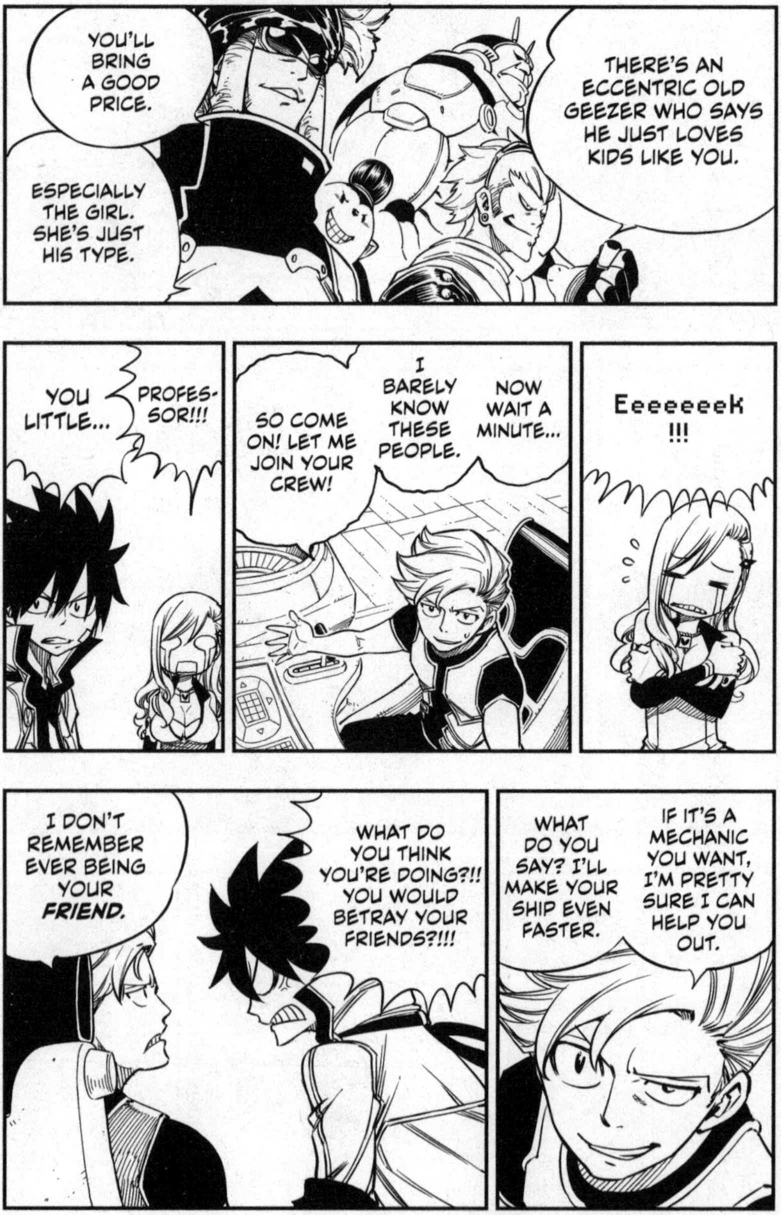
THERE'S AN ECCENTRIC OLD GEEZER WHO SAYS HE JUST LOVES KIDS LIKE YOU.
YOU'LL BRING A GOOD PRICE.
ESPECIALLY THE GIRL. SHE'S JUST HIS TYPE.
Eeeeeeek!!!
NOW WAIT A MINUTE...
I BARELY KNOW THESE PEOPLE.
SO COME ON! LET ME JOIN YOUR CREW!
PROFES-SOR!!!
YOU LITTLE...
IF IT'S A MECHANIC YOU WANT, I'M PRETTY SURE I CAN HELP YOU OUT.
WHAT DO YOU SAY? I'LL MAKE YOUR SHIP EVEN FASTER.
WHAT DO YOU THINK YOU'RE DOING?!! YOU WOULD BETRAY YOUR FRIENDS?!!!
I DON'T REMEMBER EVER BEING YOUR ***FRIEND.***

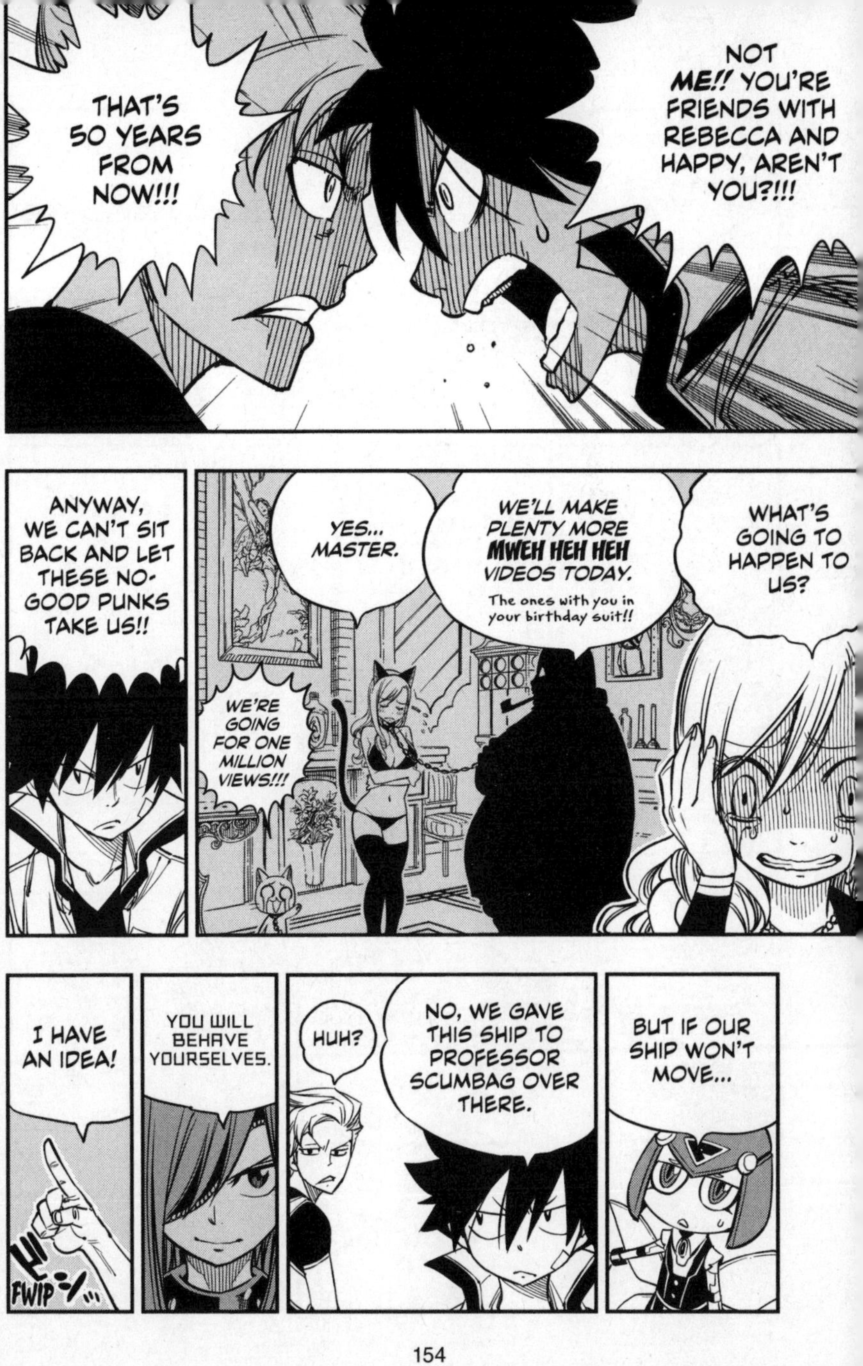
NOT ME!! YOU'RE FRIENDS WITH REBECCA AND HAPPY, AREN'T YOU?!!!
THAT'S 50 YEARS FROM NOW!!!
WHAT'S GOING TO HAPPEN TO US?
WE'LL MAKE PLENTY MORE MWEH HEH HEH VIDEOS TODAY.
The ones with you in your birthday suit!!
YES... MASTER.
WE'RE GOING FOR ONE MILLION VIEWS!!!
ANYWAY, WE CAN'T SIT BACK AND LET THESE NO-GOOD PUNKS TAKE US!!
BUT IF OUR SHIP WON'T MOVE...
NO, WE GAVE THIS SHIP TO PROFESSOR SCUMBAG OVER THERE.
HUH?
YOU WILL BEHAVE YOURSELVES.
I HAVE AN IDEA!
FWIP

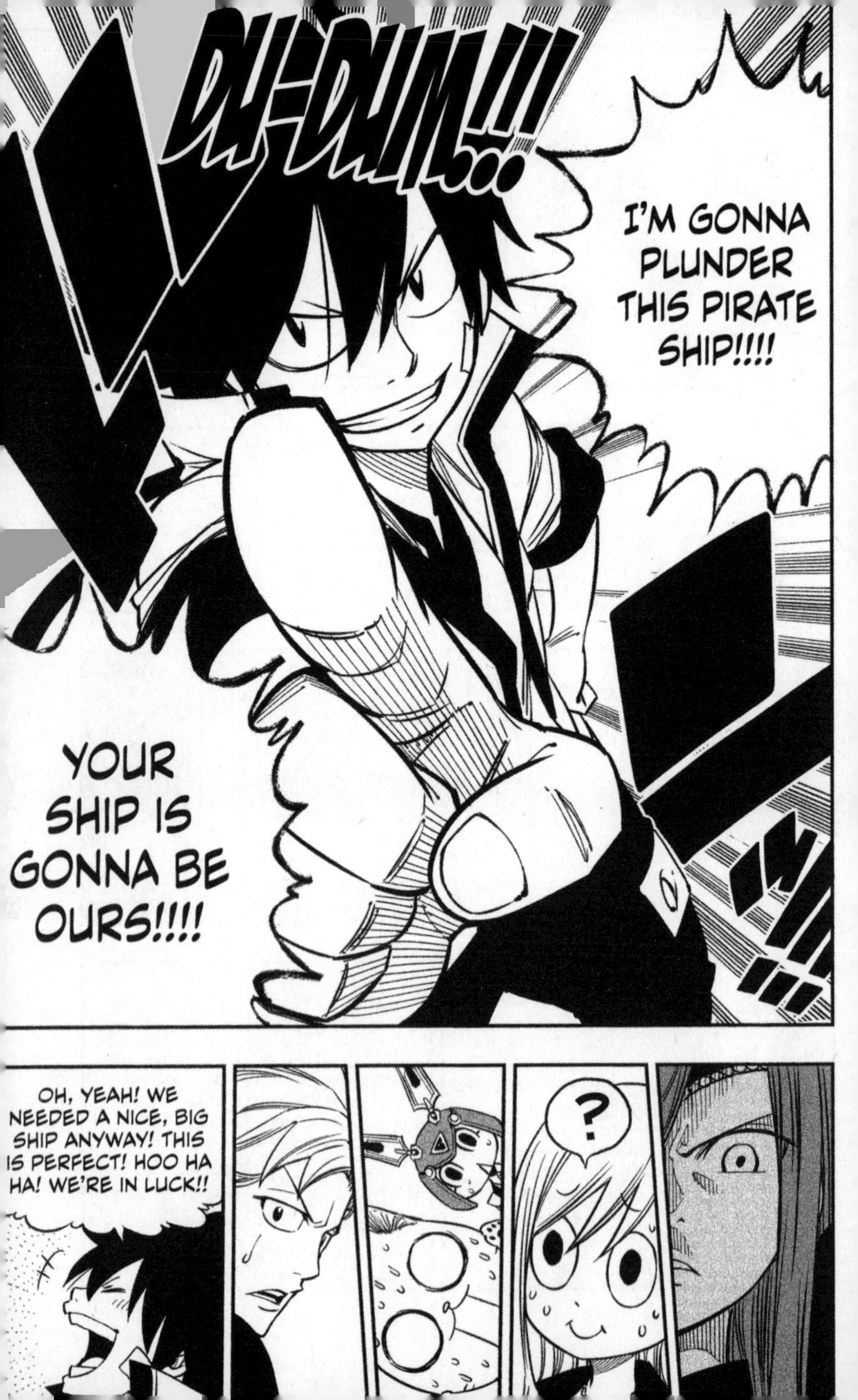
I'M GONNA PLUNDER THIS PIRATE SHIP!!!!
DU-DUM...!!
YOUR SHIP IS GONNA BE OURS!!!!
?
OH, YEAH! WE NEEDED A NICE, BIG SHIP ANYWAY! THIS IS PERFECT! HOO HA HA! WE'RE IN LUCK!!

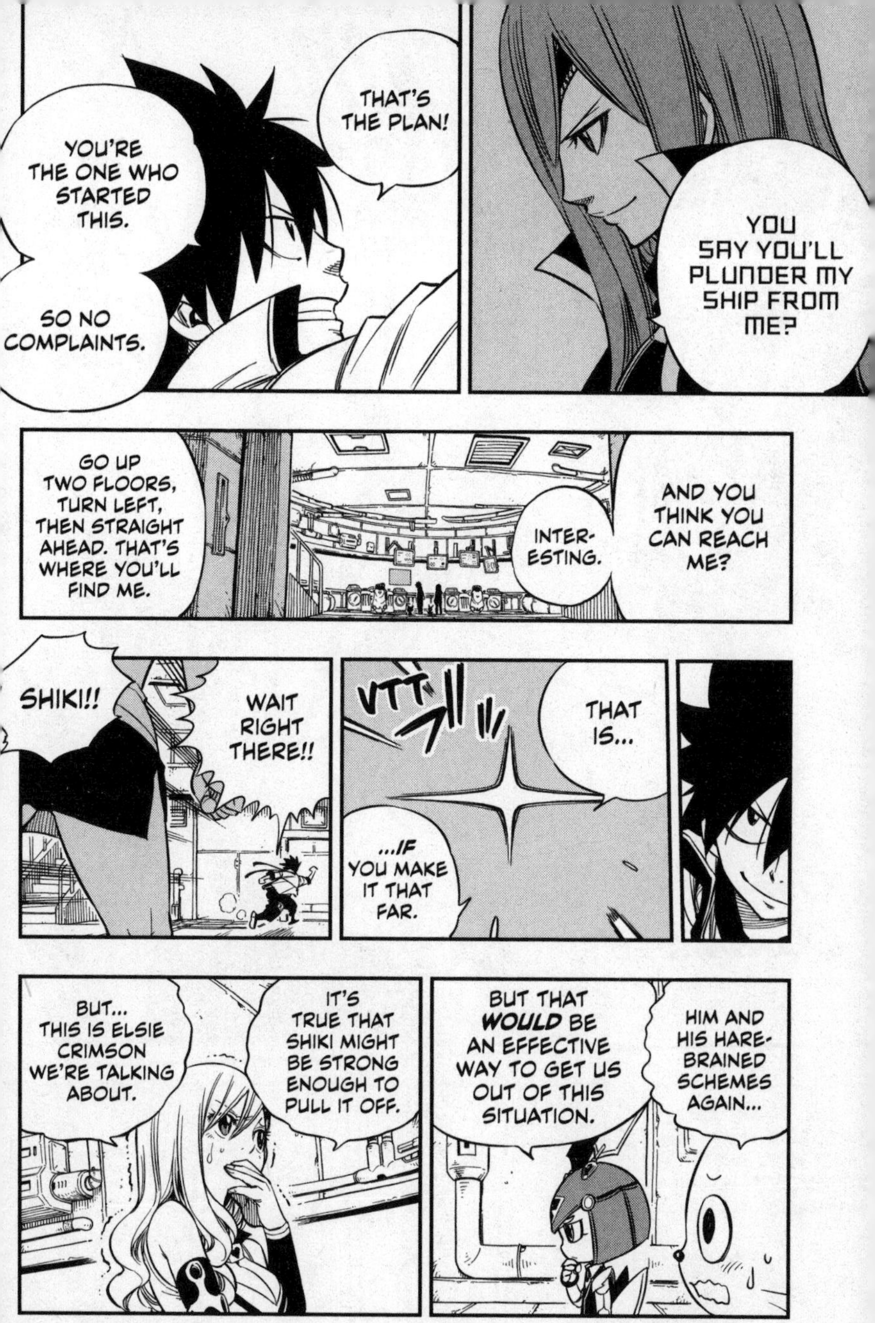
YOU SAY YOU'LL PLUNDER MY SHIP FROM ME?
THAT'S THE PLAN!
YOU'RE THE ONE WHO STARTED THIS.
SO NO COMPLAINTS.
AND YOU THINK YOU CAN REACH ME?
INTER-ESTING.
GO UP TWO FLOORS, TURN LEFT, THEN STRAIGHT AHEAD. THAT'S WHERE YOU'LL FIND ME.
THAT IS...
VTT
...IF YOU MAKE IT THAT FAR.
WAIT RIGHT THERE!!
SHIKI!!
HIM AND HIS HARE-BRAINED SCHEMES AGAIN...
BUT THAT *WOULD* BE AN EFFECTIVE WAY TO GET US OUT OF THIS SITUATION.
IT'S TRUE THAT SHIKI MIGHT BE STRONG ENOUGH TO PULL IT OFF.
BUT... THIS IS ELSIE CRIMSON WE'RE TALKING ABOUT.

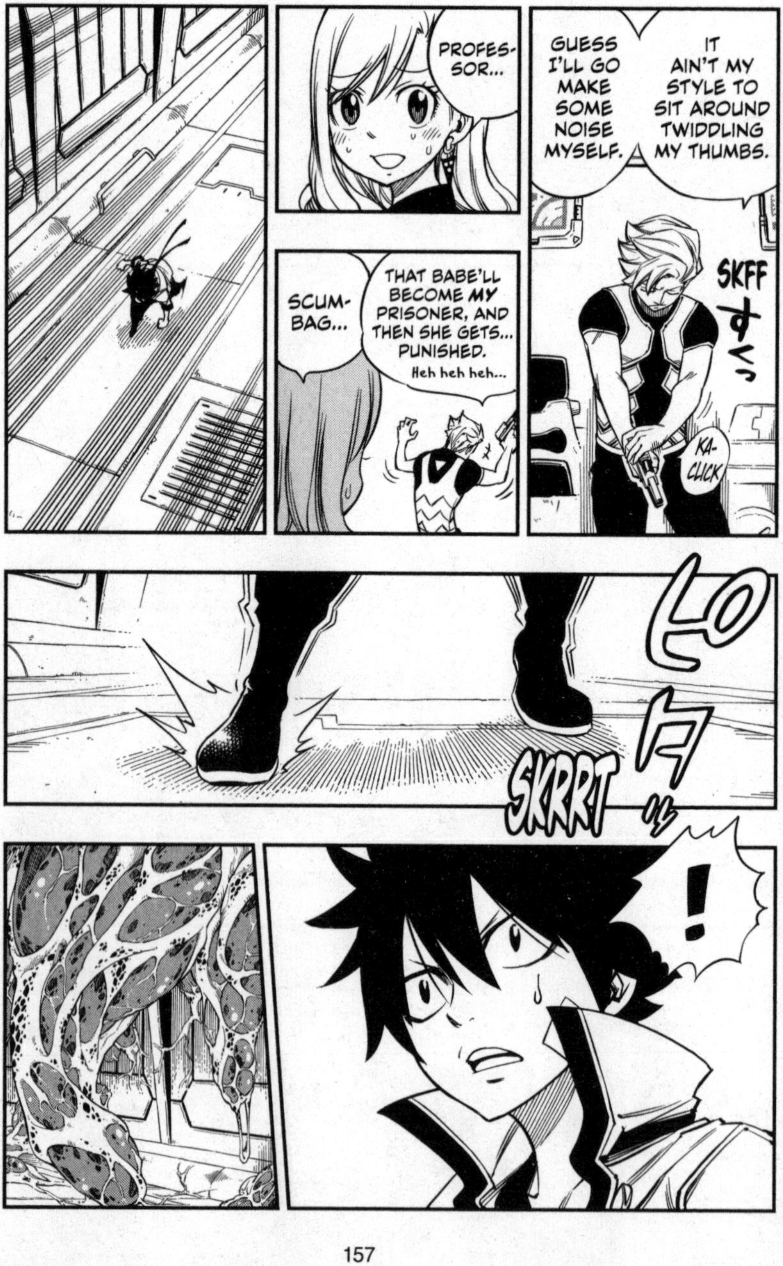
IT AIN'T MY STYLE TO SIT AROUND TWIDDLING MY THUMBS.
GUESS I'LL GO MAKE SOME NOISE MYSELF.
SKFF
すくっ
KA-CLICK
PROFES-SOR...
THAT BABE'LL BECOME *MY* PRISONER, AND THEN SHE GETS... PUNISHED.
Heh heh heh...
SCUM-BAG...
ピタッ
SKRRT
!

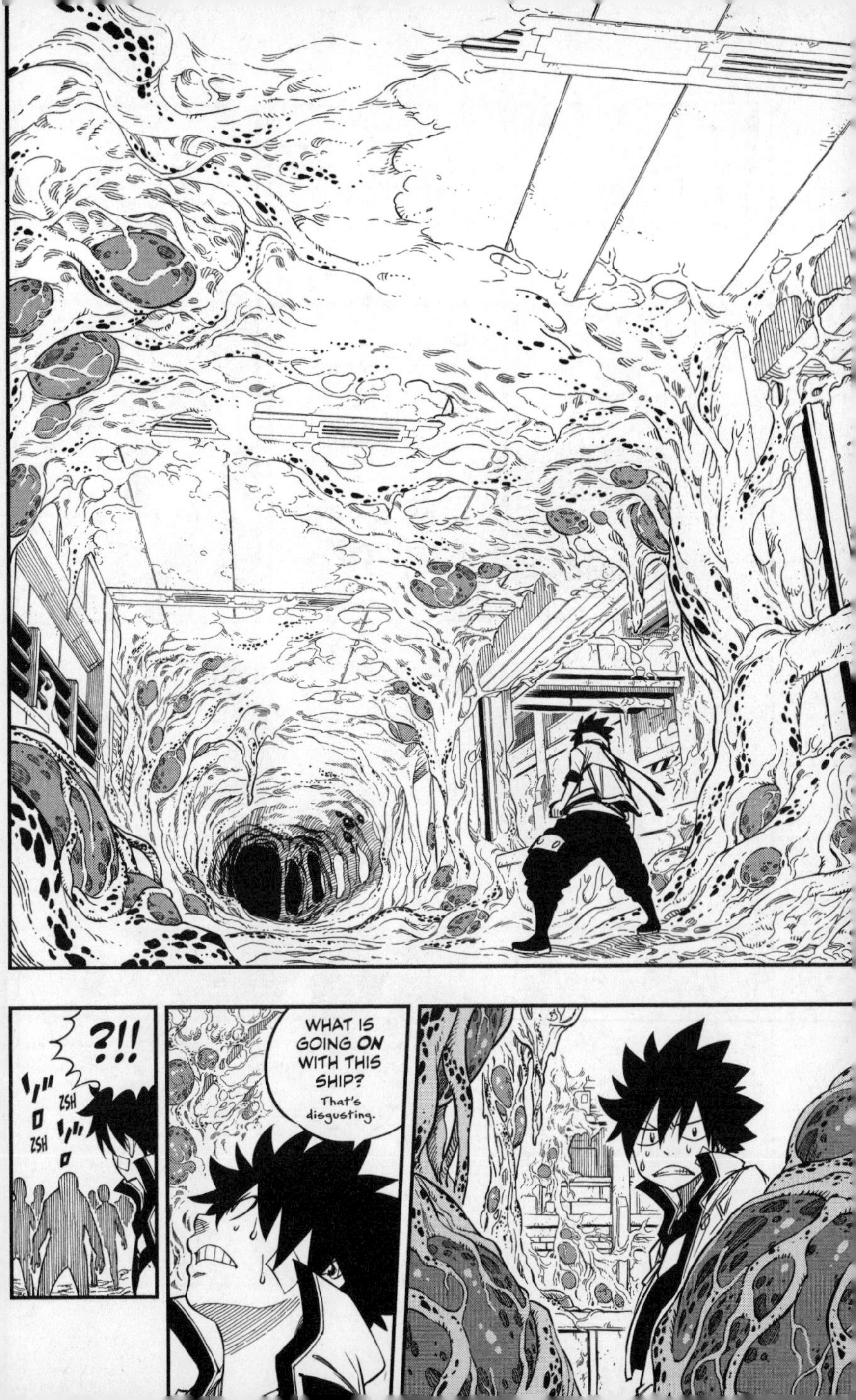
WHAT IS GOING ON WITH THIS SHIP?
That's disgusting.
?!!
ZSH
ZSH

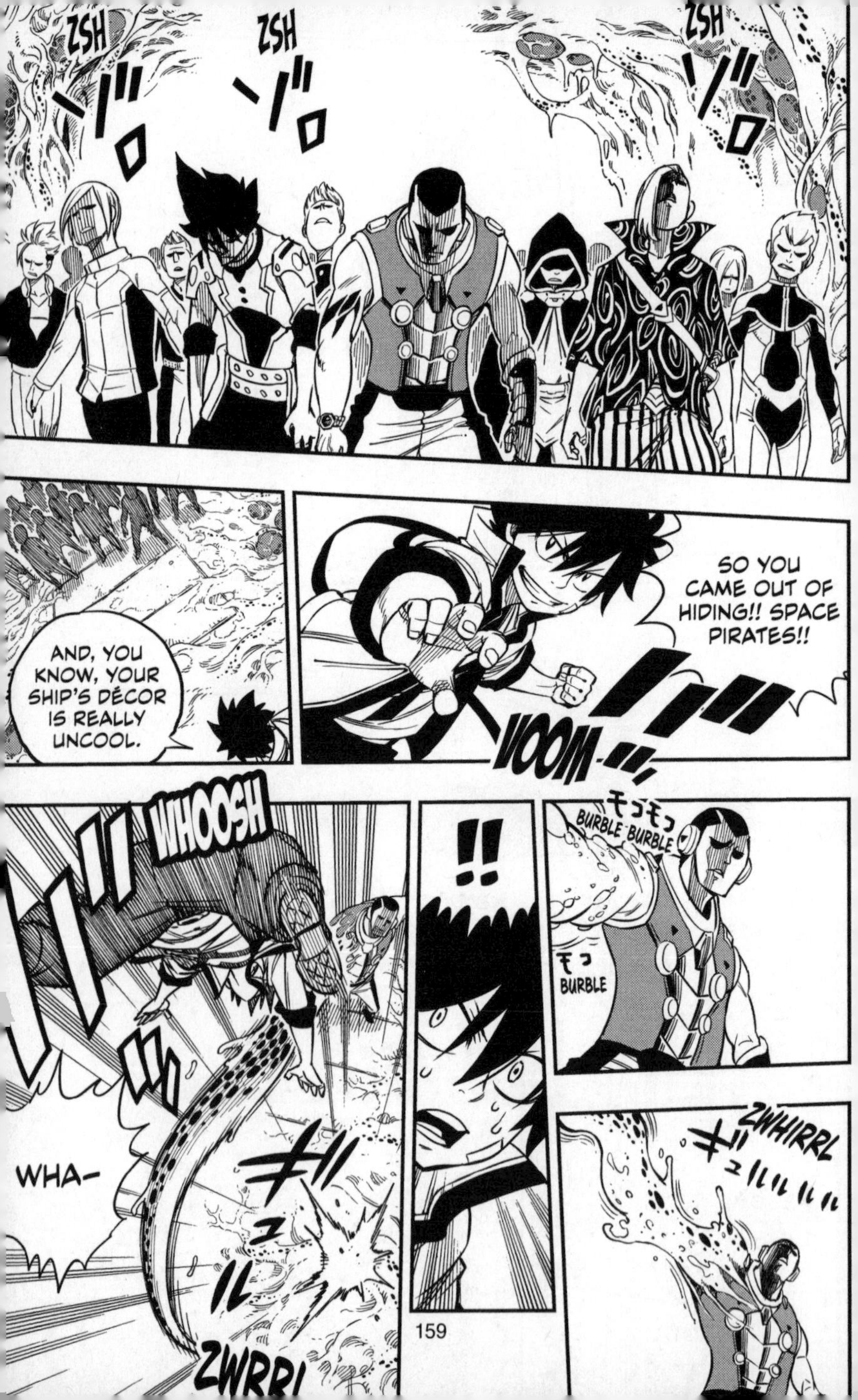

ZSH
ZSH
ZSH
SO YOU CAME OUT OF HIDING!! SPACE PIRATES!!
VOOM
AND, YOU KNOW, YOUR SHIP'S DÉCOR IS REALLY UNCOOL.
BURBLE BURBLE
BURBLE
ZWHIRRL
!!
WHOOSH
WHA-
ZWRRI

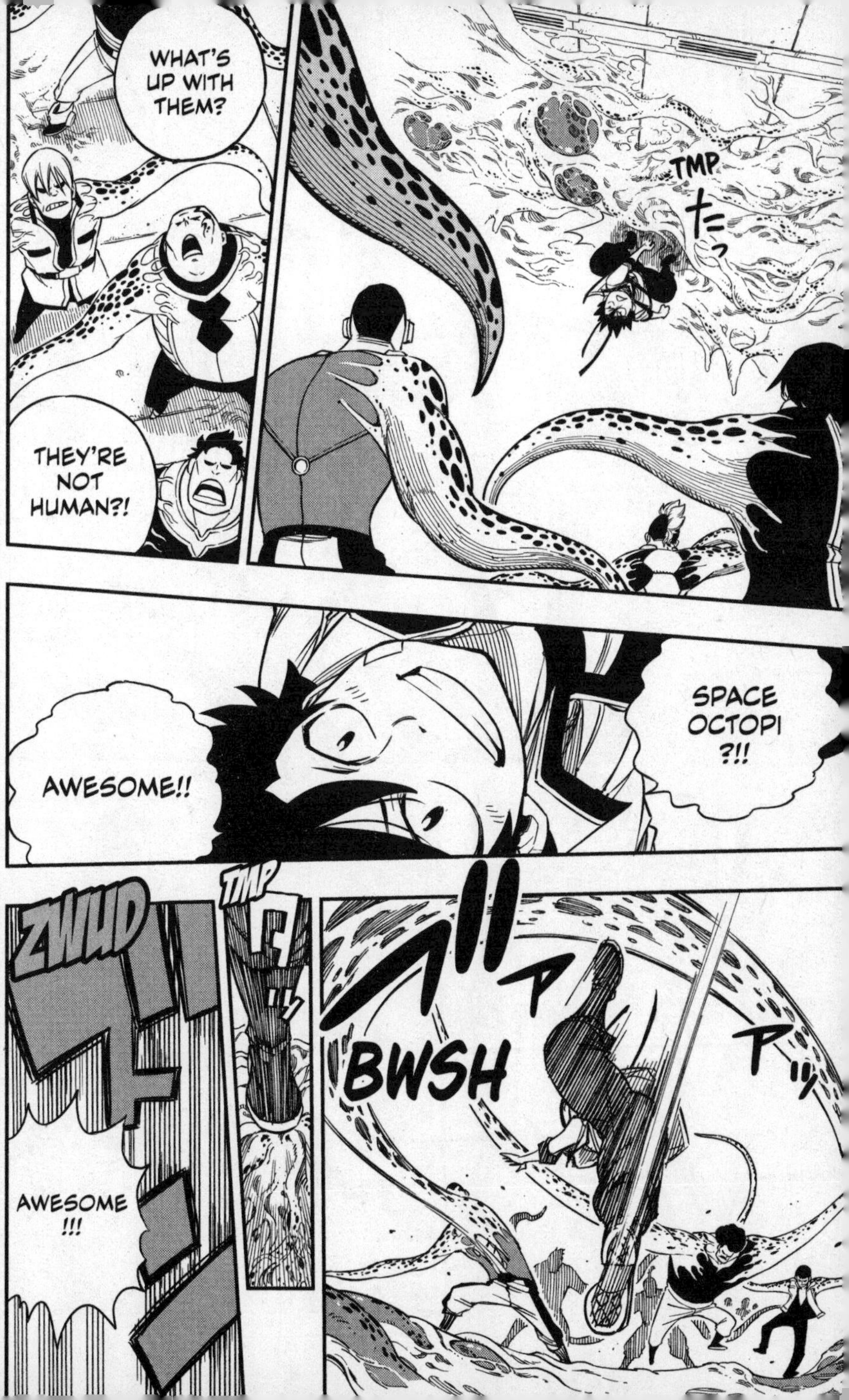
TMP
WHAT'S UP WITH THEM?
THEY'RE NOT HUMAN?!
SPACE OCTOPI ?!!
AWESOME!!
BWSH
TMP
ZWUD
AWESOME !!!

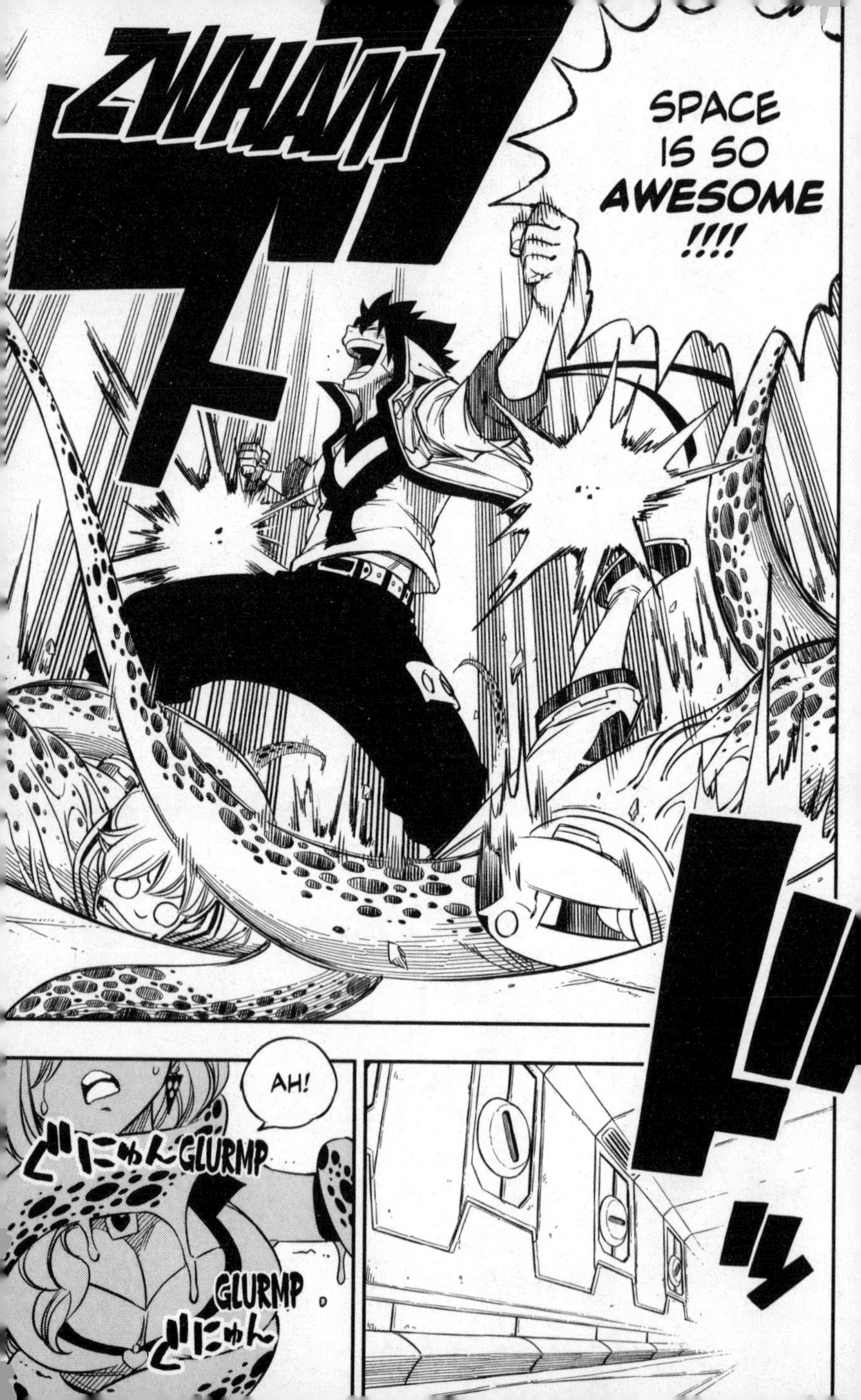
SPACE IS SO AWESOME!!!!
ZWHAM
AH!
ぐにゅん GLURMP
GLURMP ぐにゅん

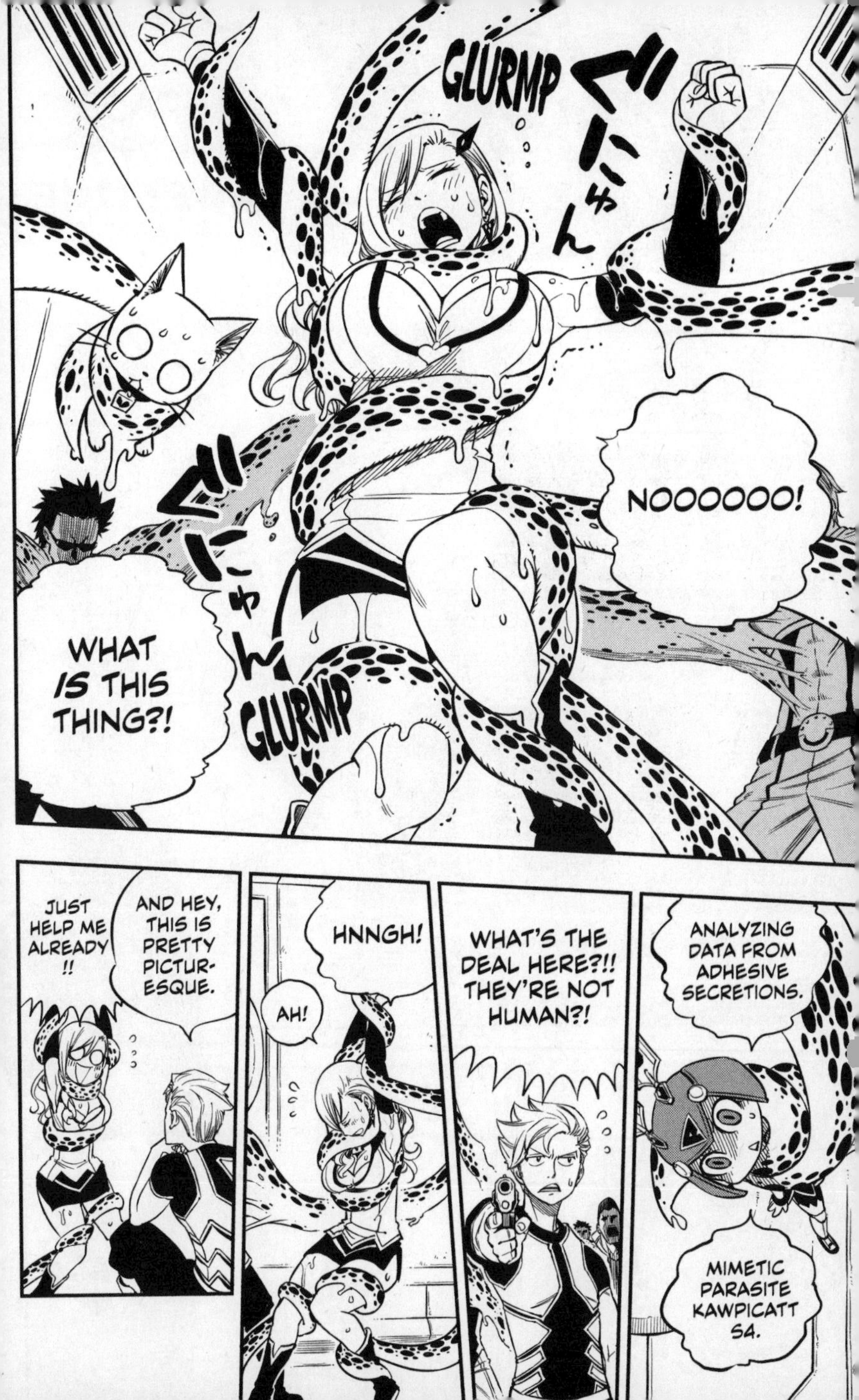
GLURMP
NOOOOOO!
WHAT *IS* THIS THING?!
GLURMP
ANALYZING DATA FROM ADHESIVE SECRETIONS.
MIMETIC PARASITE KAWPICATT S4.
WHAT'S THE DEAL HERE?!! THEY'RE NOT HUMAN?!
HNNGH!
AH!
AND HEY, THIS IS PRETTY PICTUR-ESQUE.
JUST HELP ME ALREADY !!

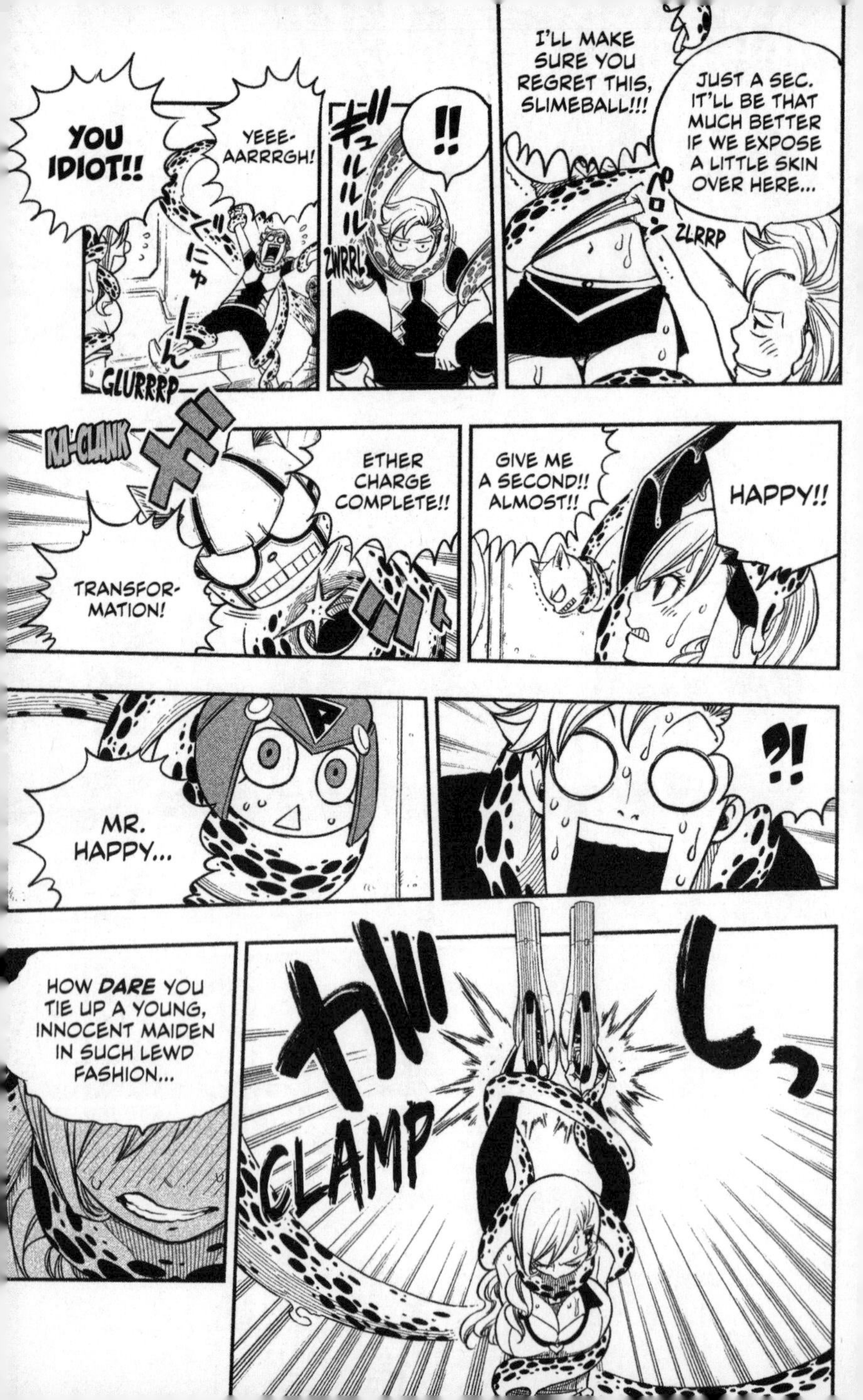
JUST A SEC. IT'LL BE THAT MUCH BETTER IF WE EXPOSE A LITTLE SKIN OVER HERE...
I'LL MAKE SURE YOU REGRET THIS, SLIMEBALL!!!
ZLRRP
!!
ZWRRL
YEEE-AARRRGH!
YOU IDIOT!!
GLURRRP
HAPPY!!
GIVE ME A SECOND!! ALMOST!!
ETHER CHARGE COMPLETE!!
KA-CLANK
TRANSFORMATION!
?!!
MR. HAPPY...
CLAMP
HOW *DARE* YOU TIE UP A YOUNG, INNOCENT MAIDEN IN SUCH LEWD FASHION...

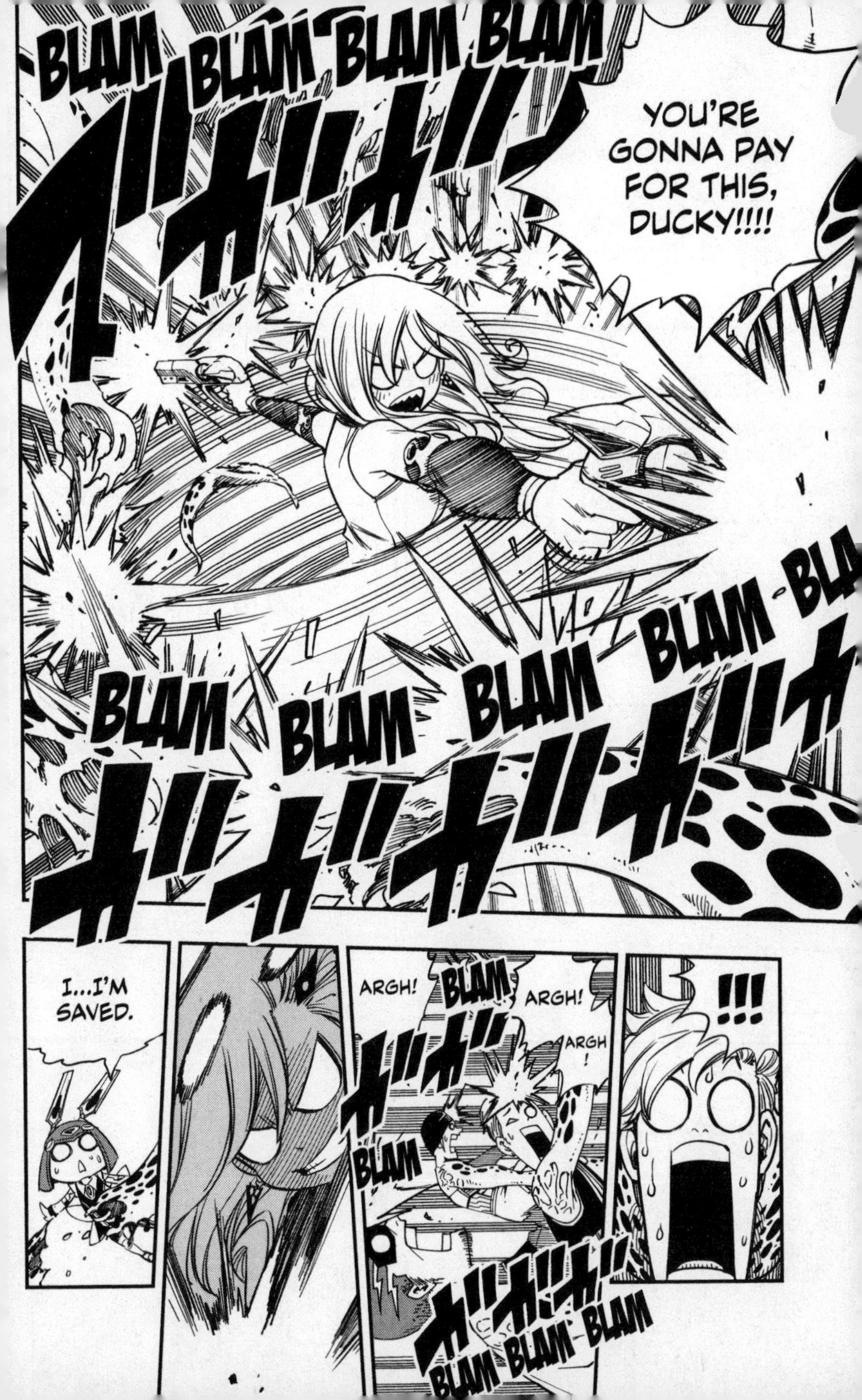
BLAM BLAM BLAM BLAM
YOU'RE GONNA PAY FOR THIS, DUCKY!!!!
BLAM BLAM BLAM BLAM BLA
!!!
BLAM
ARGH!
ARGH!
ARGH!
BLAM
BLAM BLAM BLAM
I...I'M SAVED.

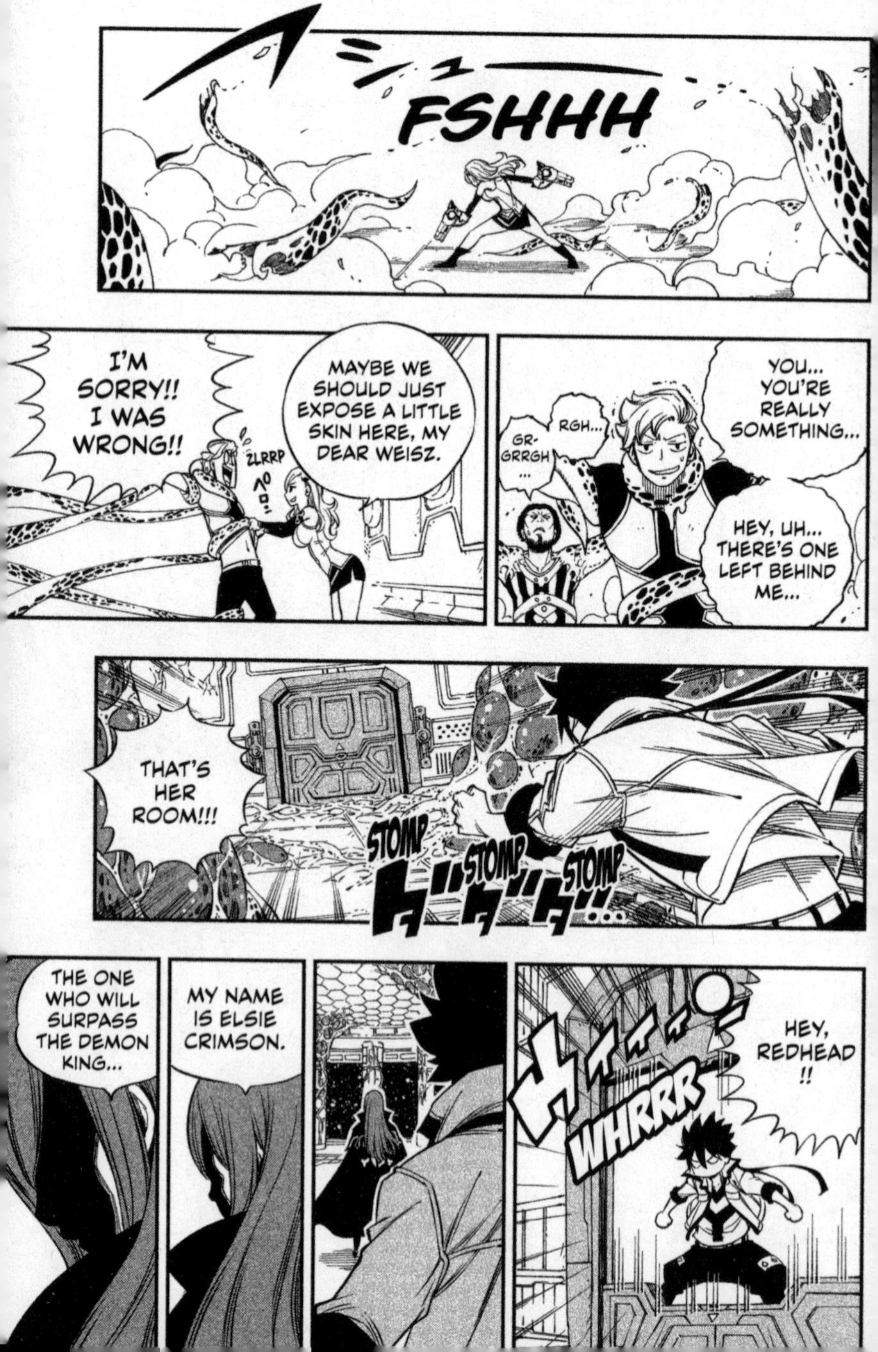
FSHHH
YOU... YOU'RE REALLY SOMETHING...
RGH...
GR- GRRGH ...
HEY, UH... THERE'S ONE LEFT BEHIND ME...
MAYBE WE SHOULD JUST EXPOSE A LITTLE SKIN HERE, MY DEAR WEISZ.
ZLRRP
I'M SORRY!! I WAS WRONG!!
THAT'S HER ROOM!!!
STOMP
STOMP
STOMP
HEY, REDHEAD !!
WHRRR
MY NAME IS ELSIE CRIMSON.
THE ONE WHO WILL SURPASS THE DEMON KING...

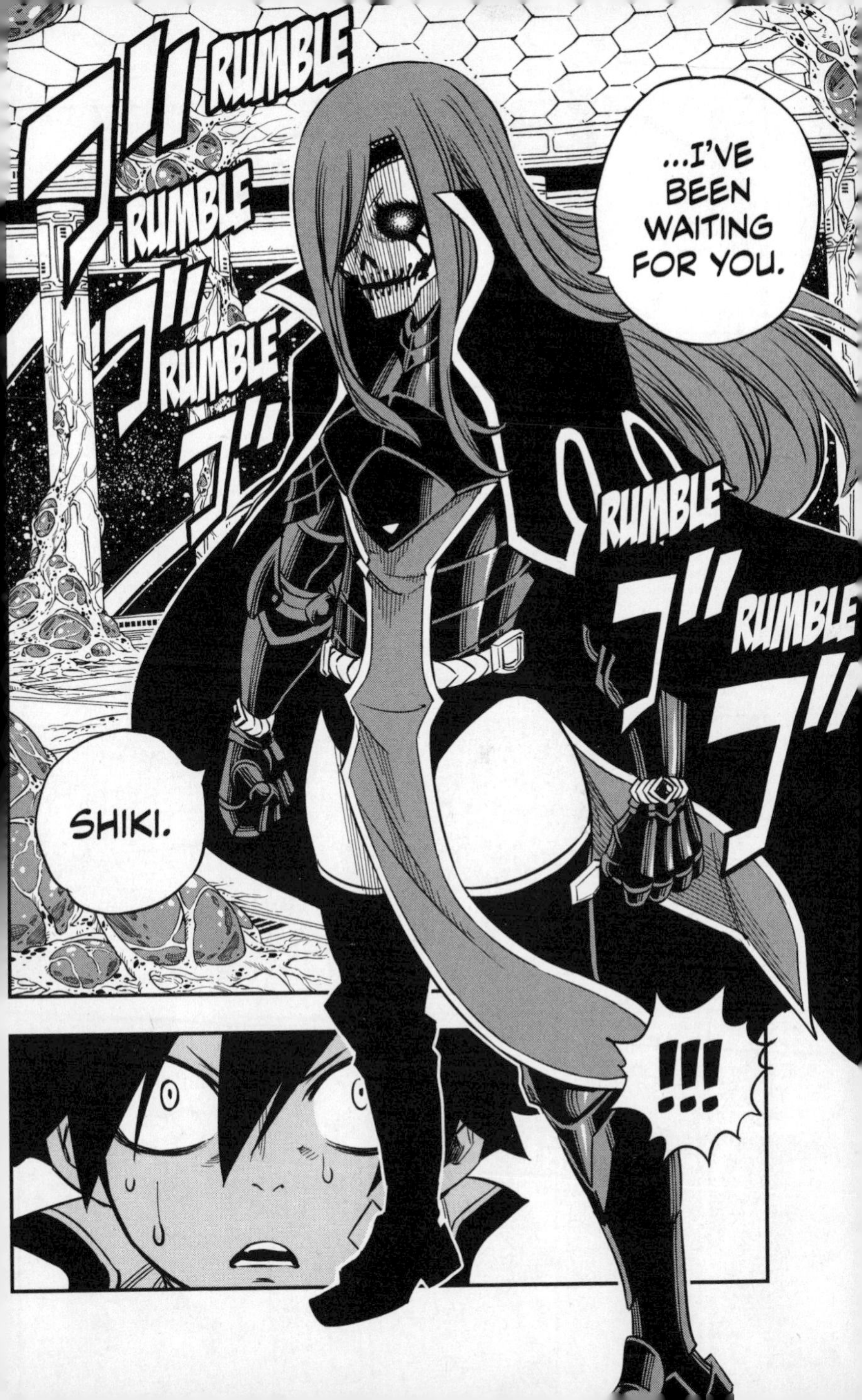
RUMBLE
RUMBLE
RUMBLE
...I'VE BEEN WAITING FOR YOU.
RUMBLE
RUMBLE
SHIKI.
!!!

# EDENS ZERO

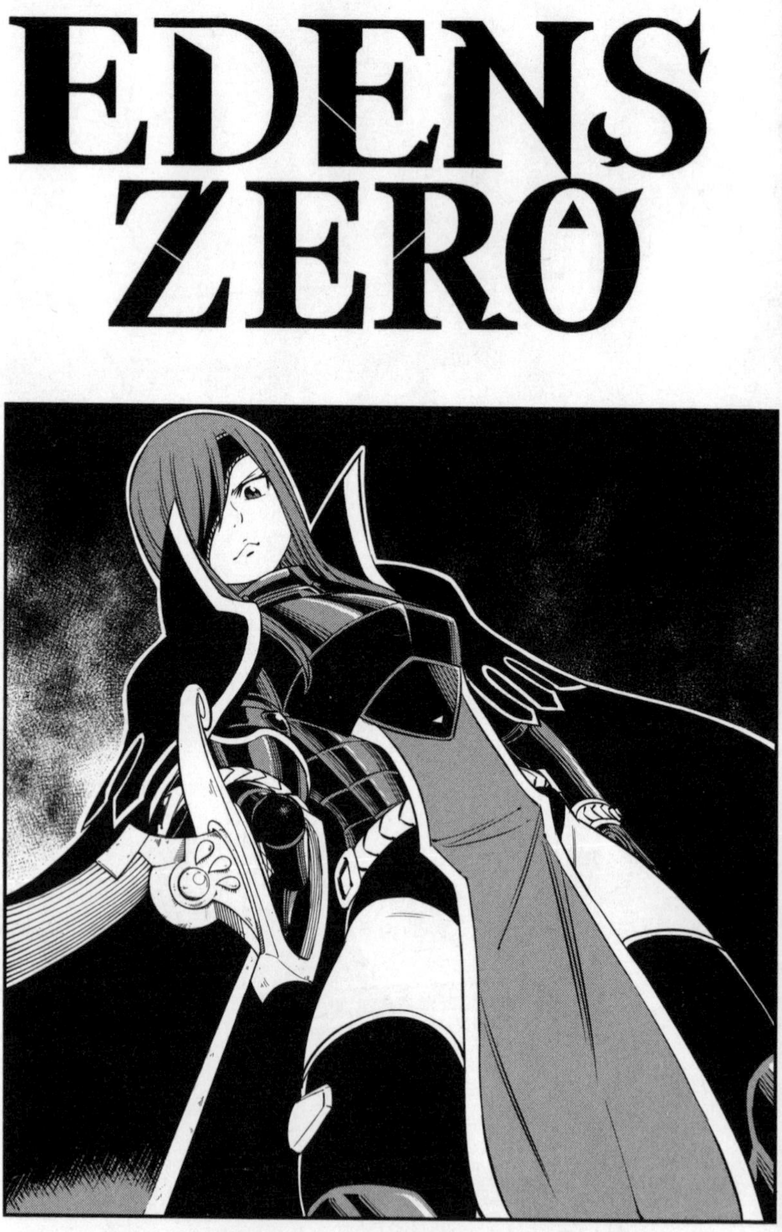

## CHAPTER 13: SHIKI VS. ELSIE

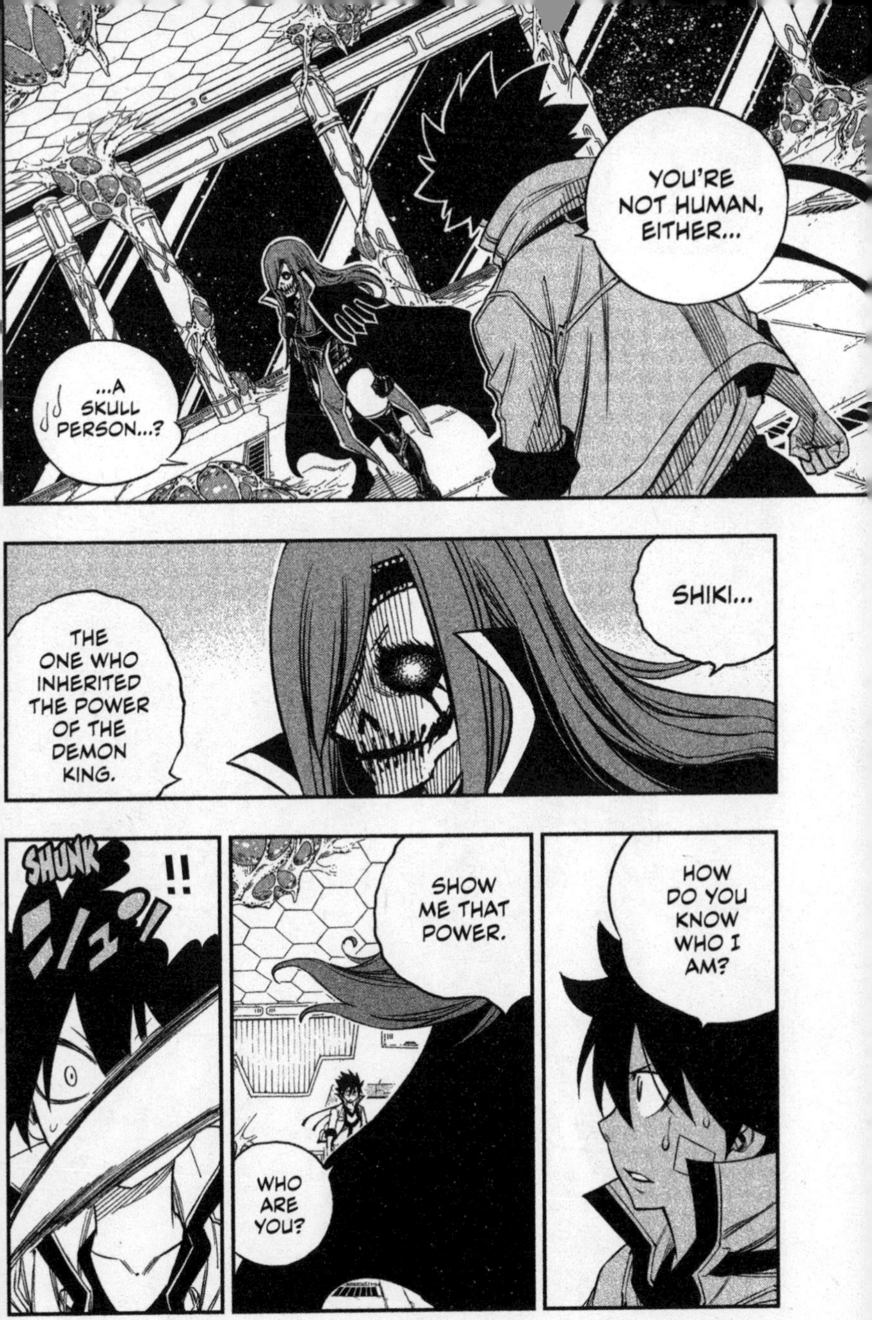
YOU'RE NOT HUMAN, EITHER...
...A SKULL PERSON...?
SHIKI...
THE ONE WHO INHERITED THE POWER OF THE DEMON KING.
HOW DO YOU KNOW WHO I AM?
SHOW ME THAT POWER.
WHO ARE YOU?
SHUNK
!!

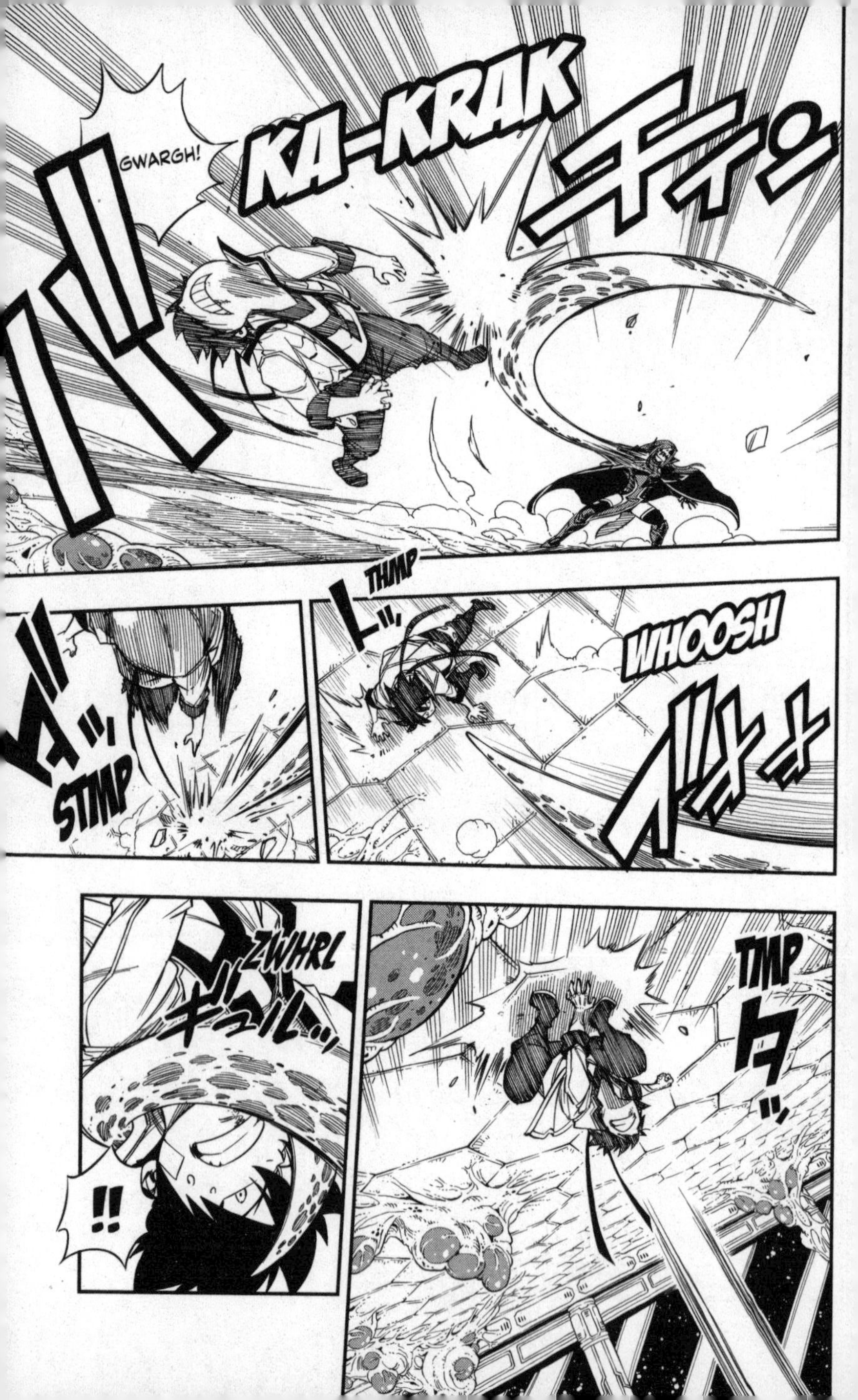
GWARGH!
KA-KRAK
WHOOSH
THMP
STMP
TMP
ZWHRL
!!

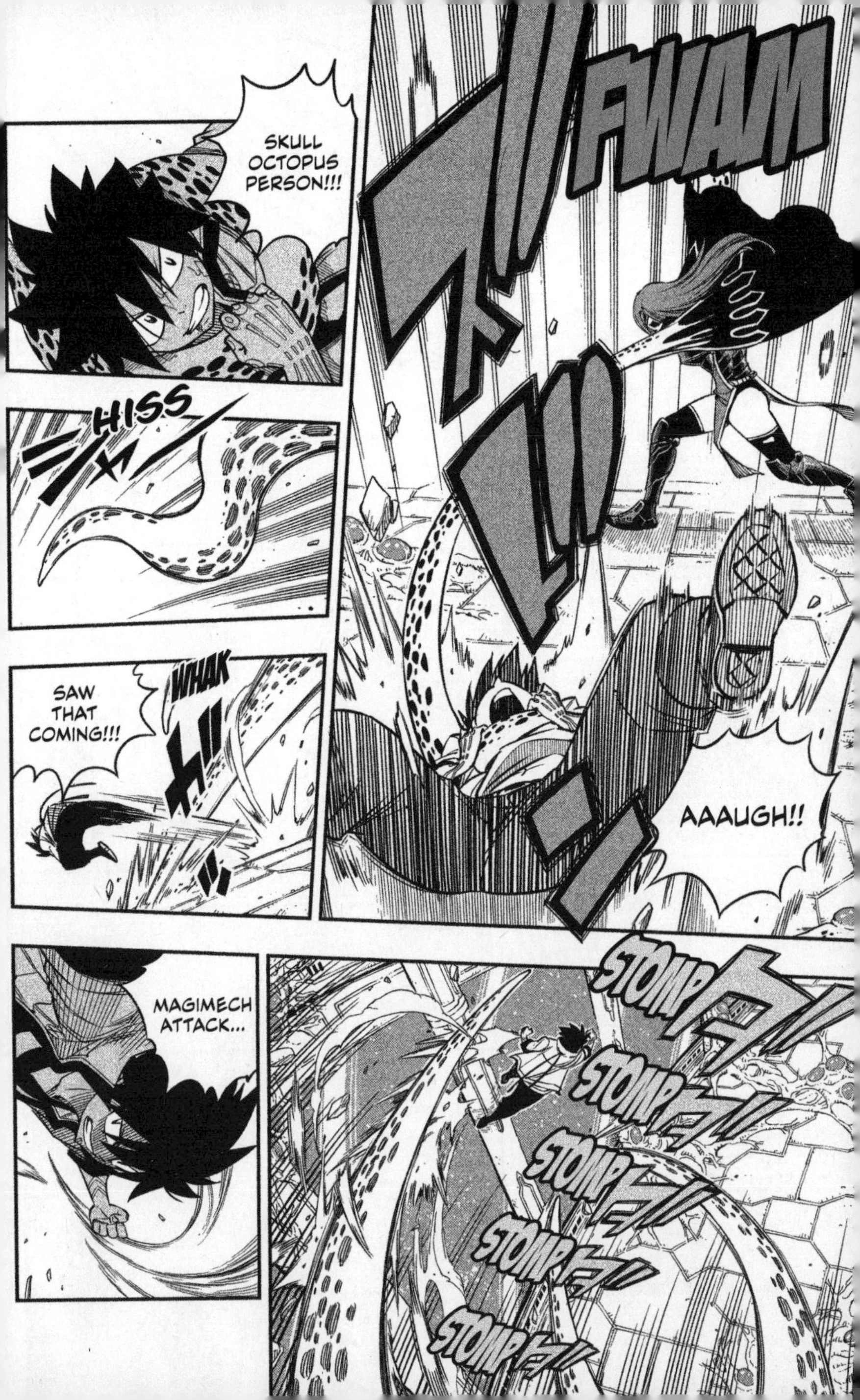
FWAM
AAAUGH!!
SKULL OCTOPUS PERSON!!!
HISS
SAW THAT COMING!!!
WHAK
STOMP
STOMP
STOMP
STOMP
STOMP
MAGIMECH ATTACK...

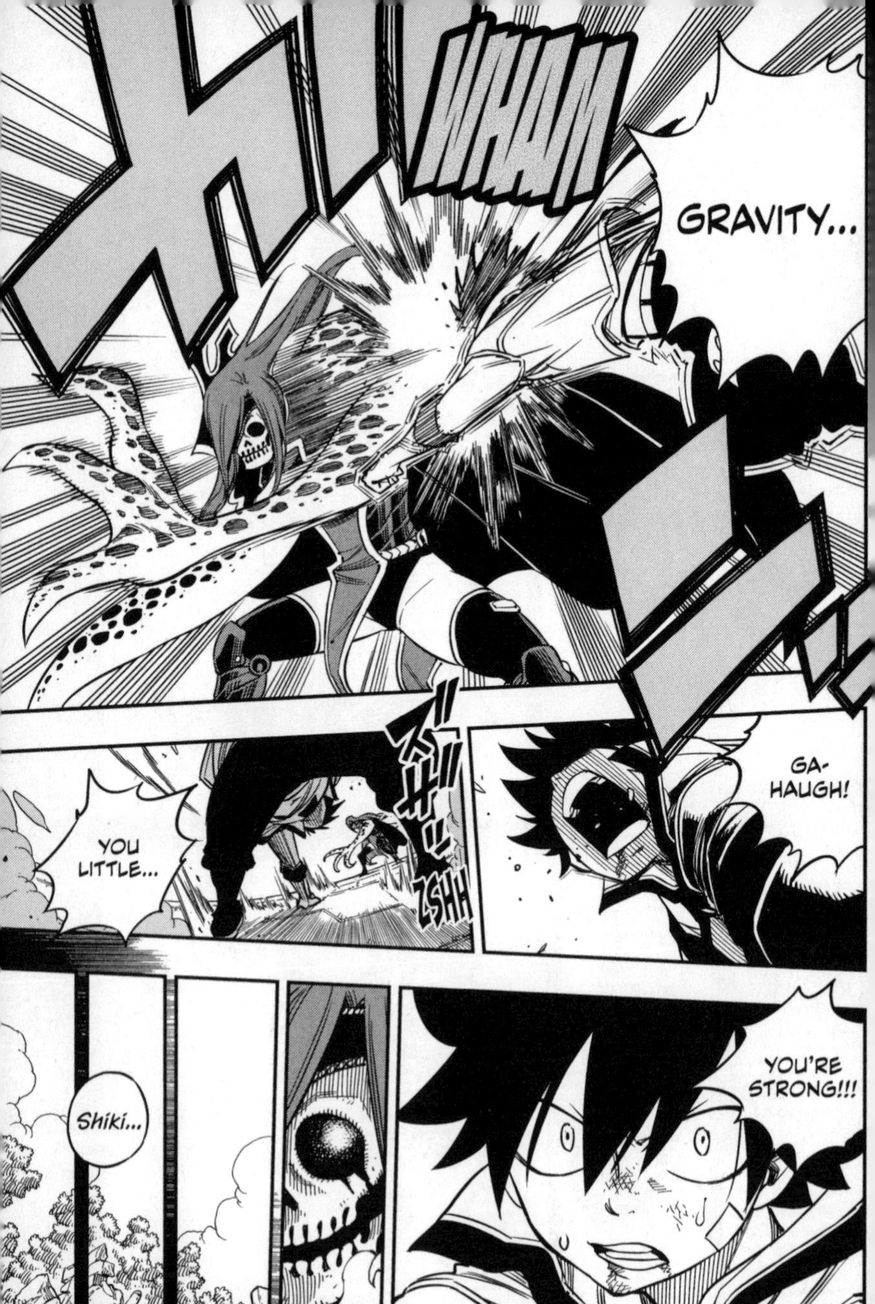
WHAM
GRAVITY...
GA-HAUGH!
ZSHH
YOU LITTLE...
YOU'RE STRONG!!!
Shiki...

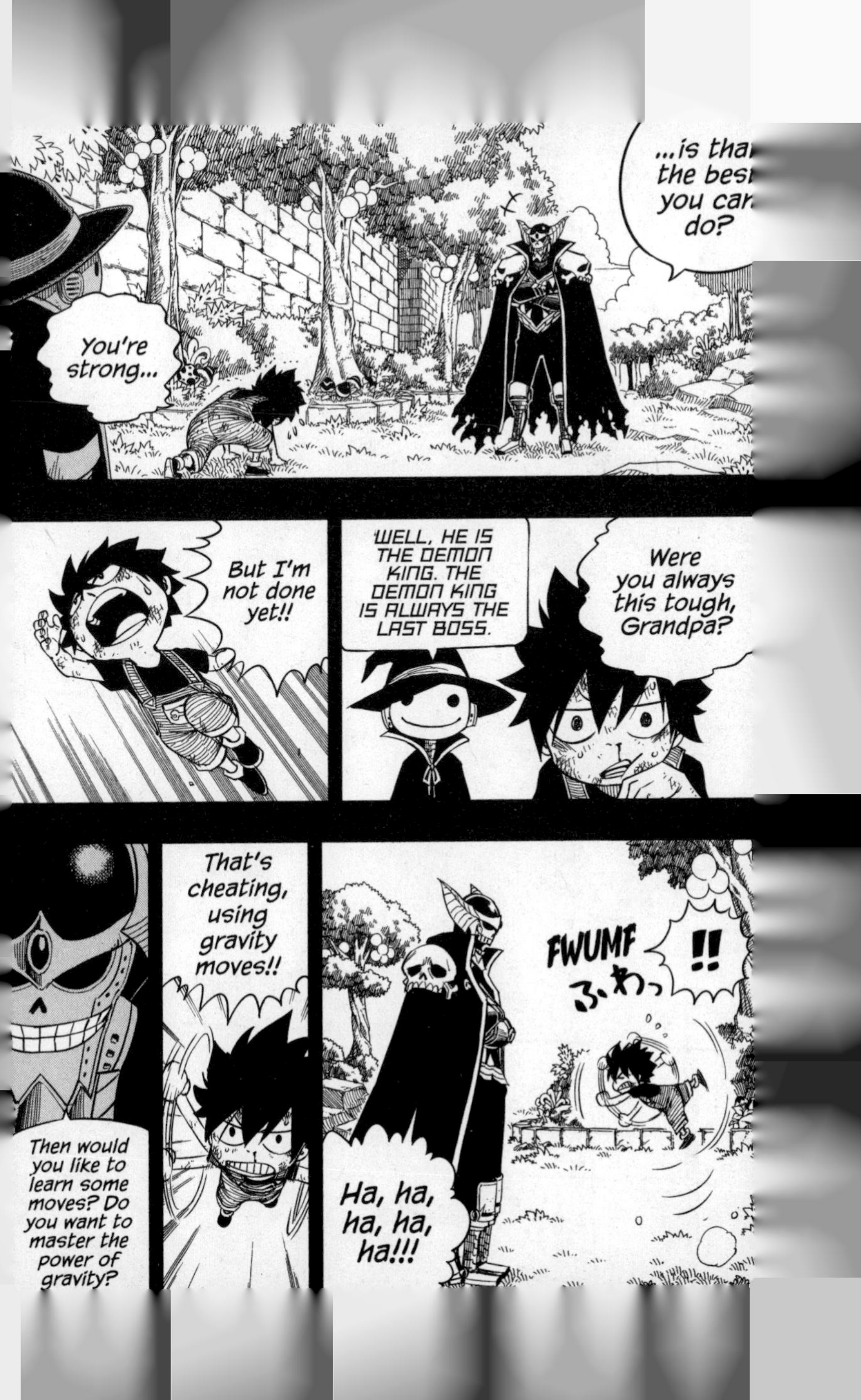
...is tha
the bes
you ca
do?
You're strong...
Were you always this tough, Grandpa?
WELL, HE IS THE DEMON KING. THE DEMON KING IS ALWAYS THE LAST BOSS.
But I'm not done yet!!
FWUMF
ふわっ
!!
Ha, ha, ha, ha, ha!!!
That's cheating, using gravity moves!!
Then would you like to learn some moves? Do you want to master the power of gravity?

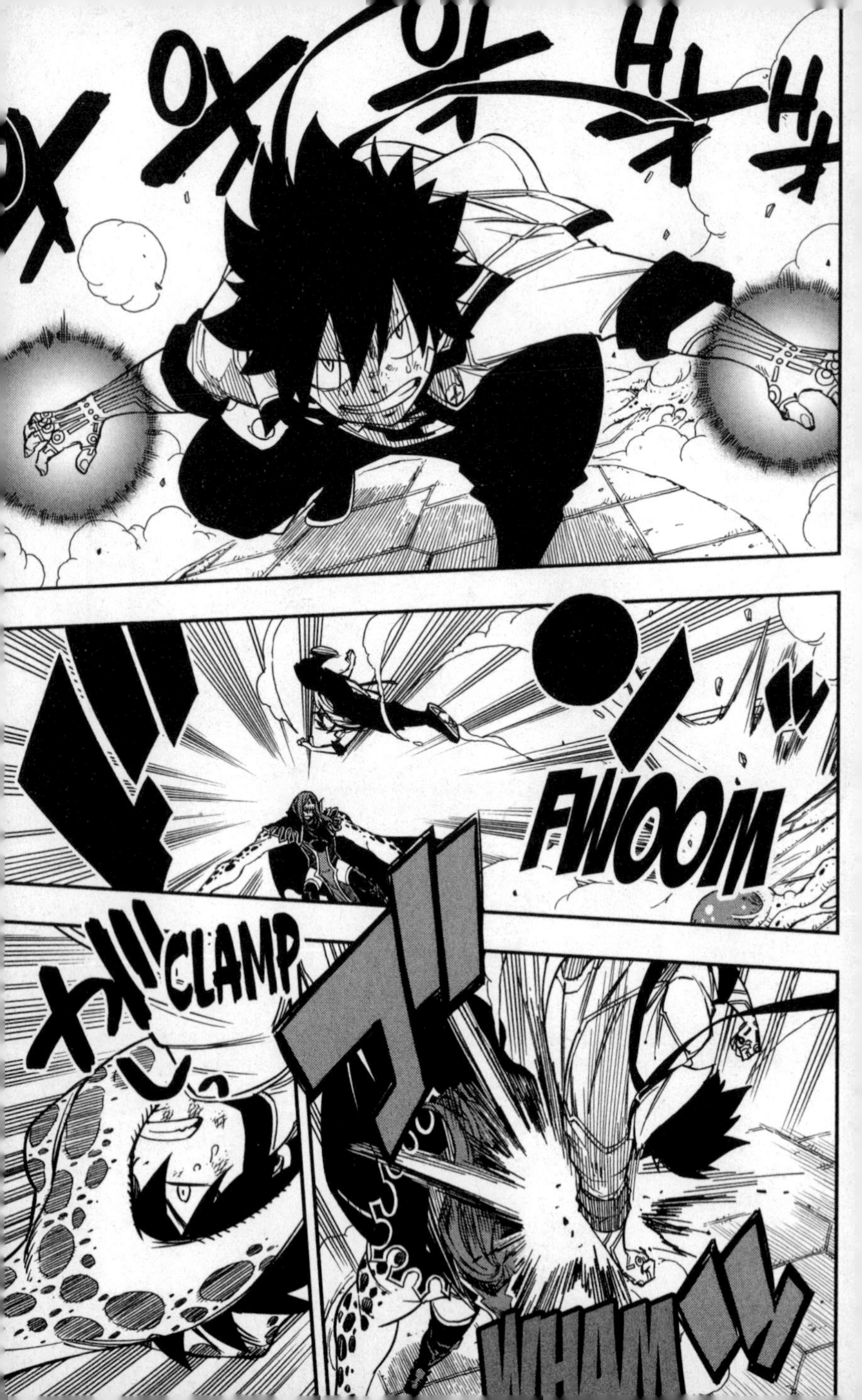
FWOOM
CLAMP
WHAM

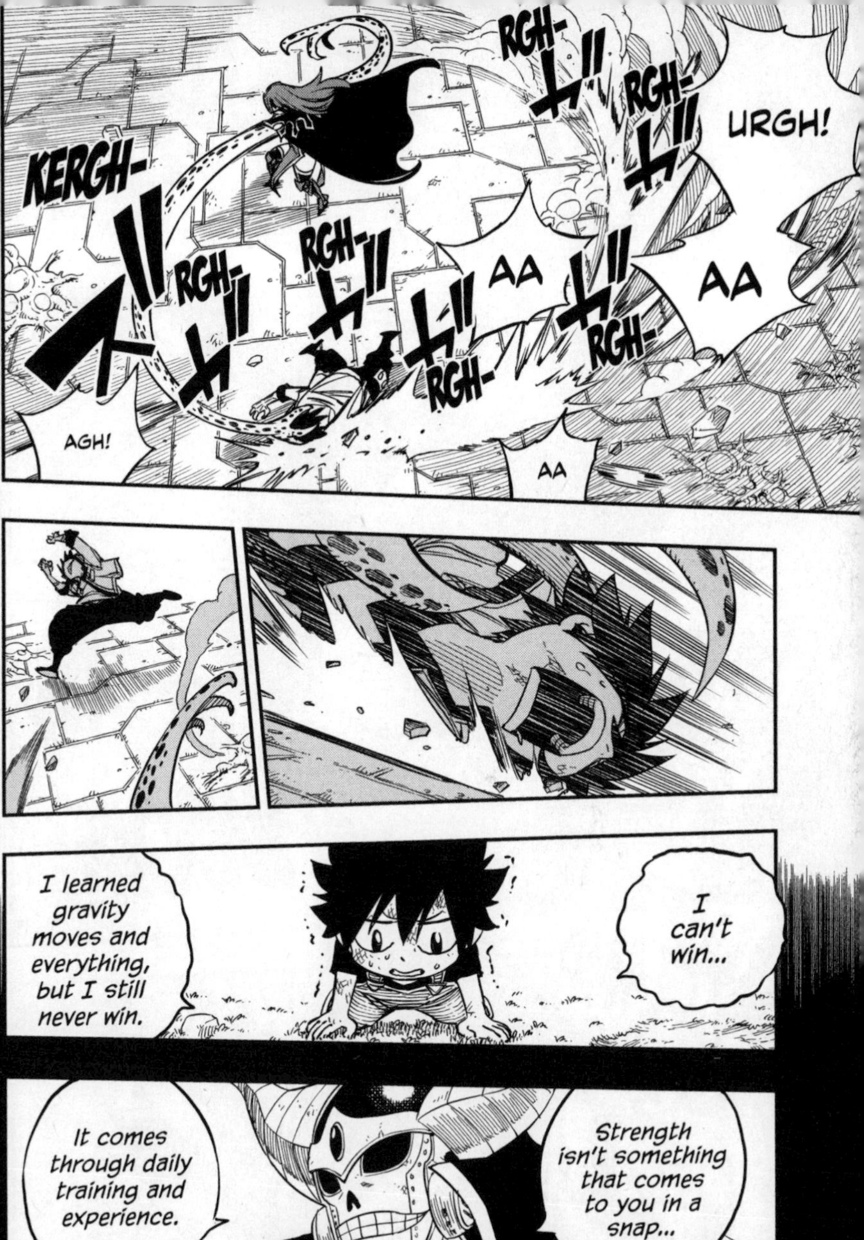
URGH!
RGH-
RGH-
AA
RGH-
AA
RGH-
RGH-
KERGH-
RGH-
AA
AGH!
I can't win...
I learned gravity moves and everything, but I still never win.
Strength isn't something that comes to you in a snap...
It comes through daily training and experience.

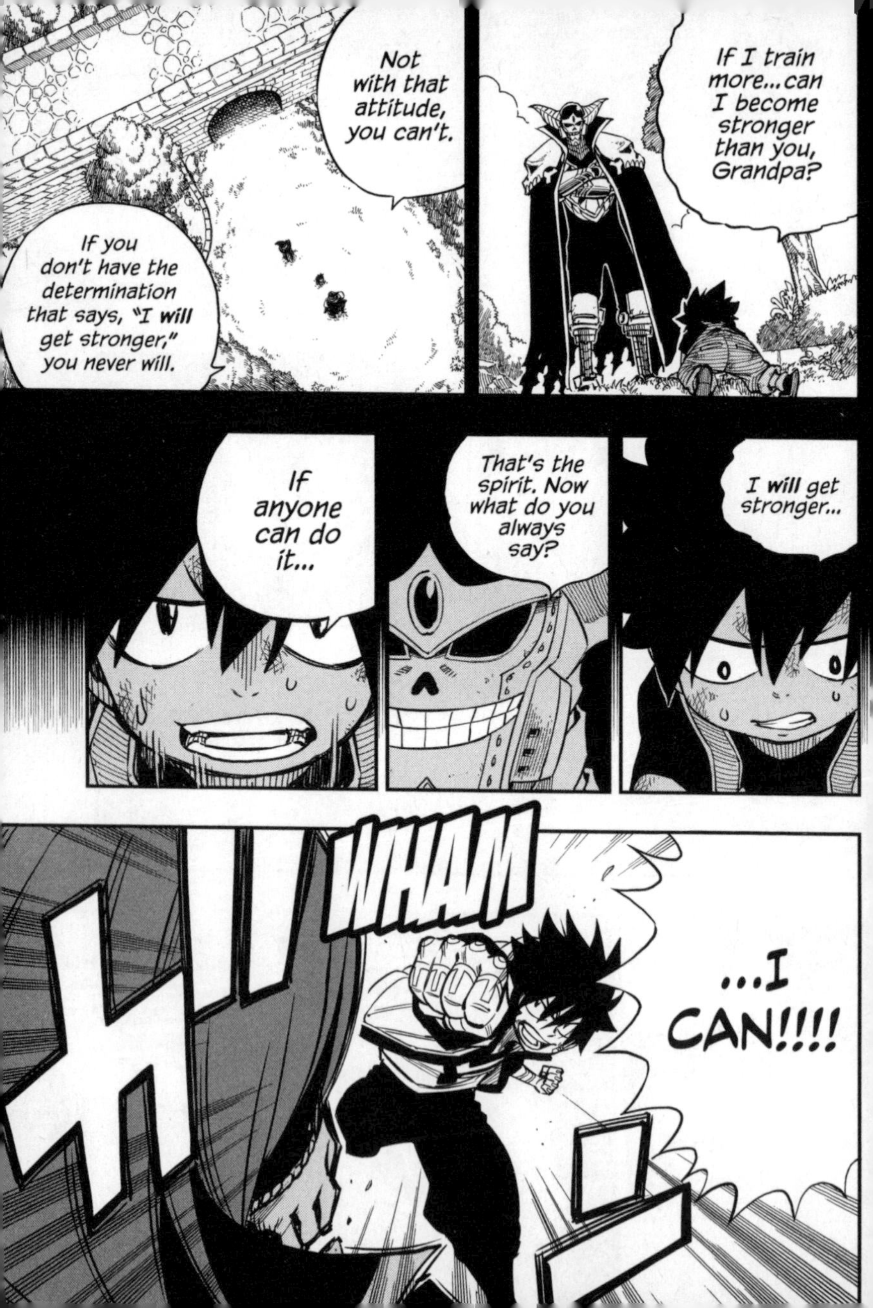
If I train more...can I become stronger than you, Grandpa?
Not with that attitude, you can't.
If you don't have the determination that says, "I will get stronger," you never will.
I will get stronger...
That's the spirit. Now what do you always say?
If anyone can do it...
WHAM
...I CAN!!!!

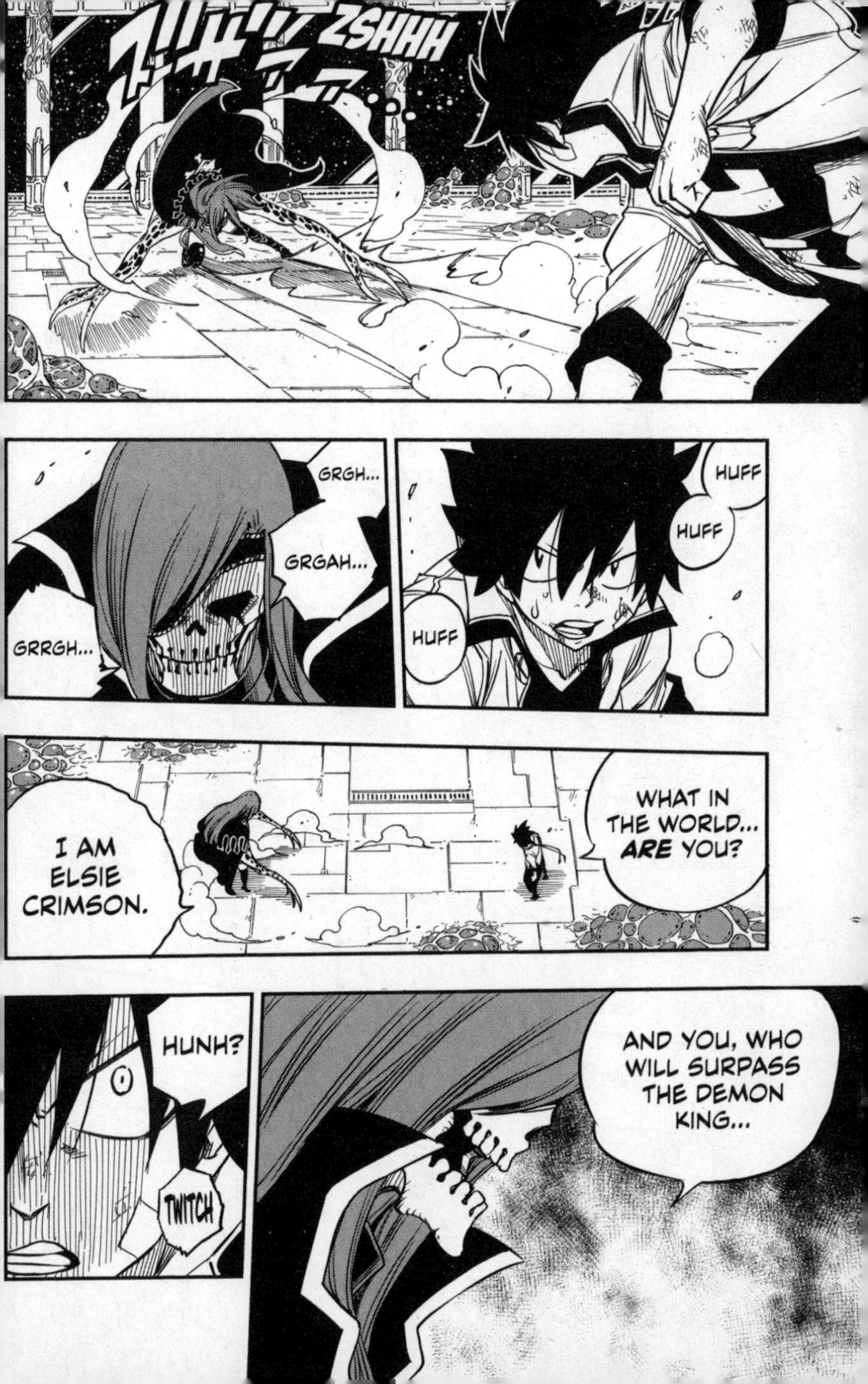
ZSHHH
HUFF
HUFF
HUFF
GRGH...
GRGAH...
GRRGH...
WHAT IN THE WORLD... **ARE** YOU?
I AM ELSIE CRIMSON.
AND YOU, WHO WILL SURPASS THE DEMON KING...
HUNH?
TWITCH

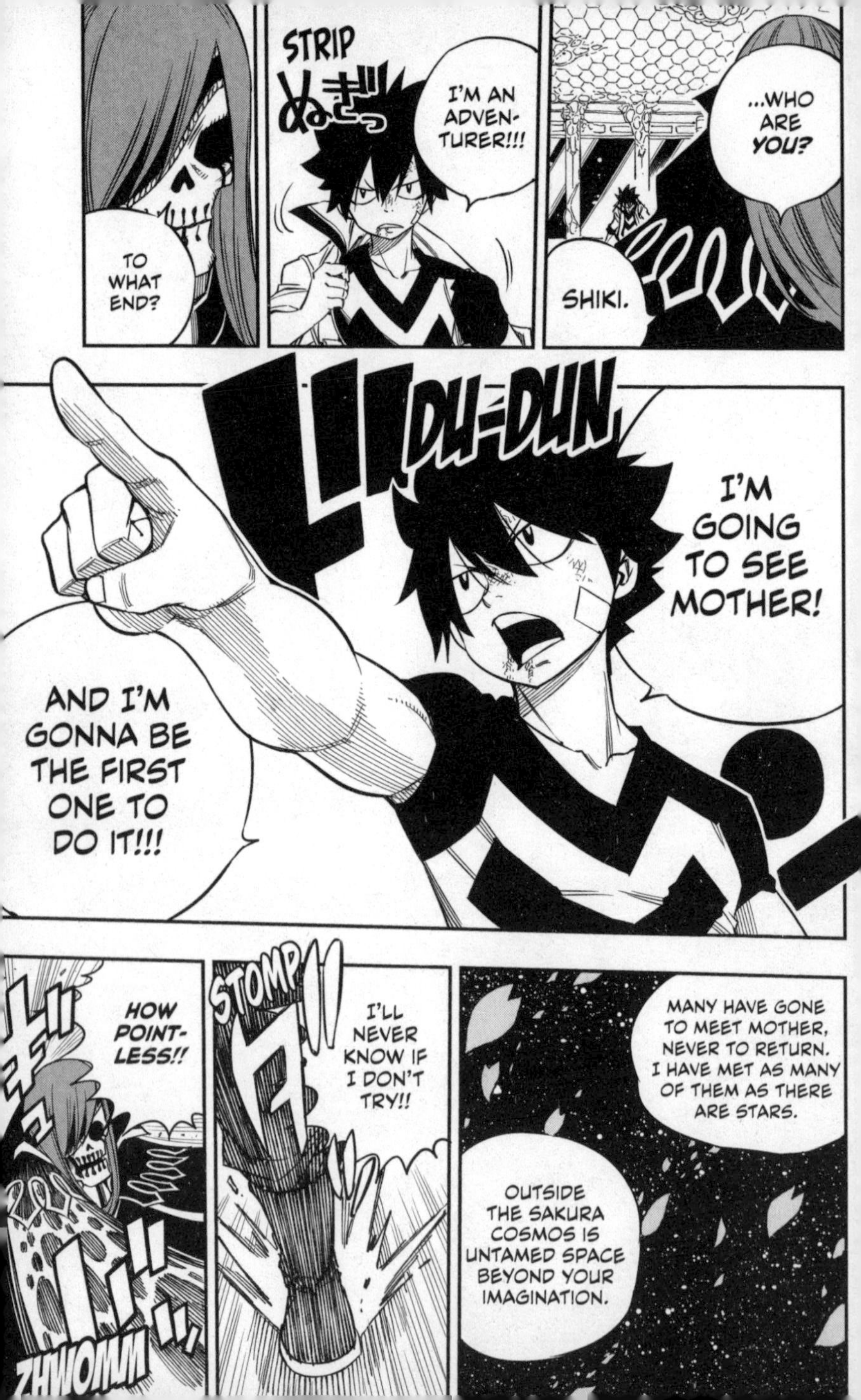
...WHO ARE YOU?
SHIKI.
STRIP ぬぎっ
I'M AN ADVENTURER!!!
TO WHAT END?
DU-DUN
I'M GOING TO SEE MOTHER!
AND I'M GONNA BE THE FIRST ONE TO DO IT!!!
MANY HAVE GONE TO MEET MOTHER, NEVER TO RETURN. I HAVE MET AS MANY OF THEM AS THERE ARE STARS.
OUTSIDE THE SAKURA COSMOS IS UNTAMED SPACE BEYOND YOUR IMAGINATION.
STOMP
I'LL NEVER KNOW IF I DON'T TRY!!
HOW POINTLESS!!
ZHWOMM

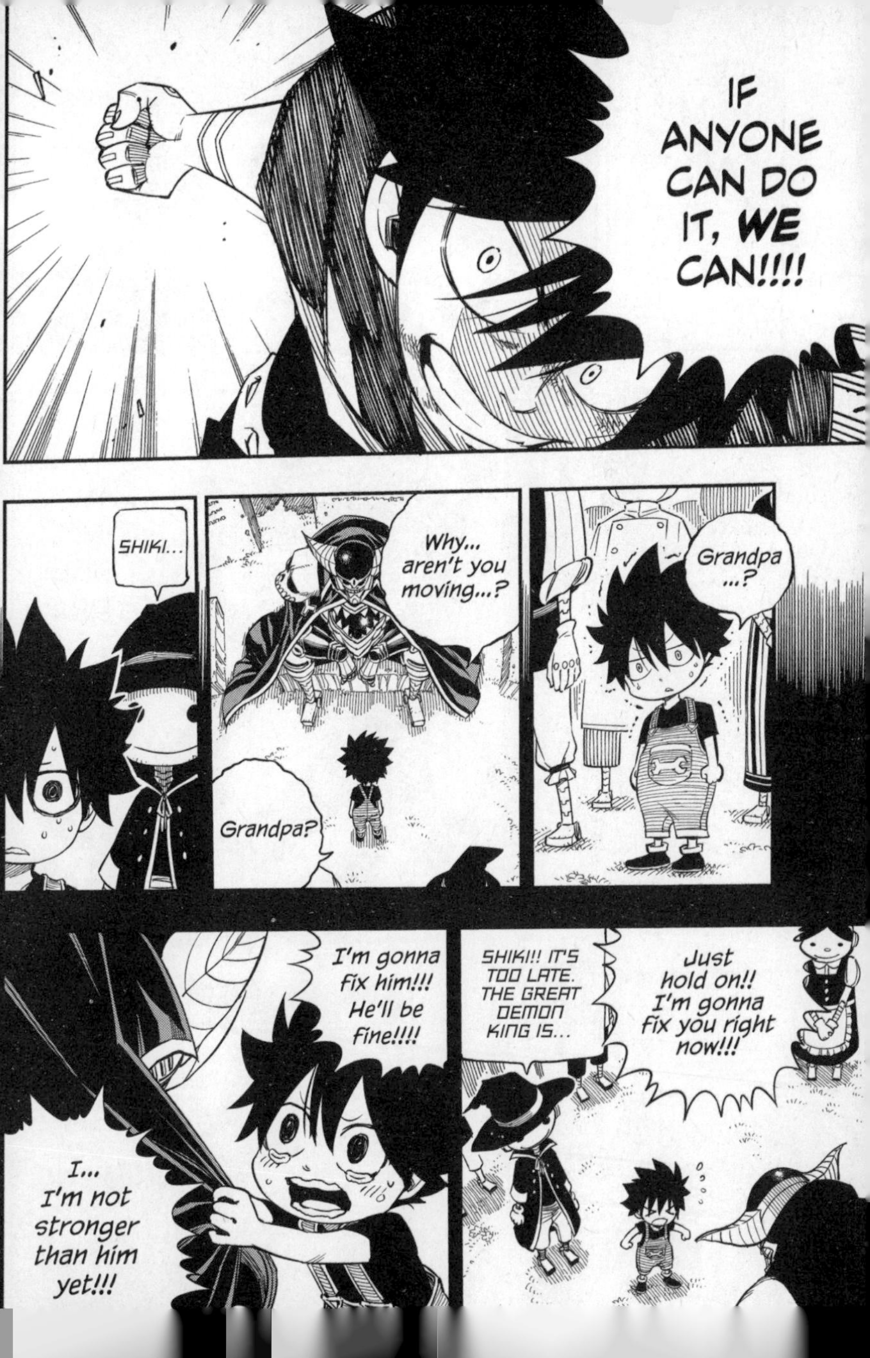
IF ANYONE CAN DO IT, **WE** CAN!!!!
Grandpa ...?
Why... aren't you moving...?
Grandpa?
SHIKI...
Just hold on!! I'm gonna fix you right now!!!
SHIKI!!! IT'S TOO LATE. THE GREAT DEMON KING IS...
I'm gonna fix him!!! He'll be fine!!!!
I... I'm not stronger than him yet!!!

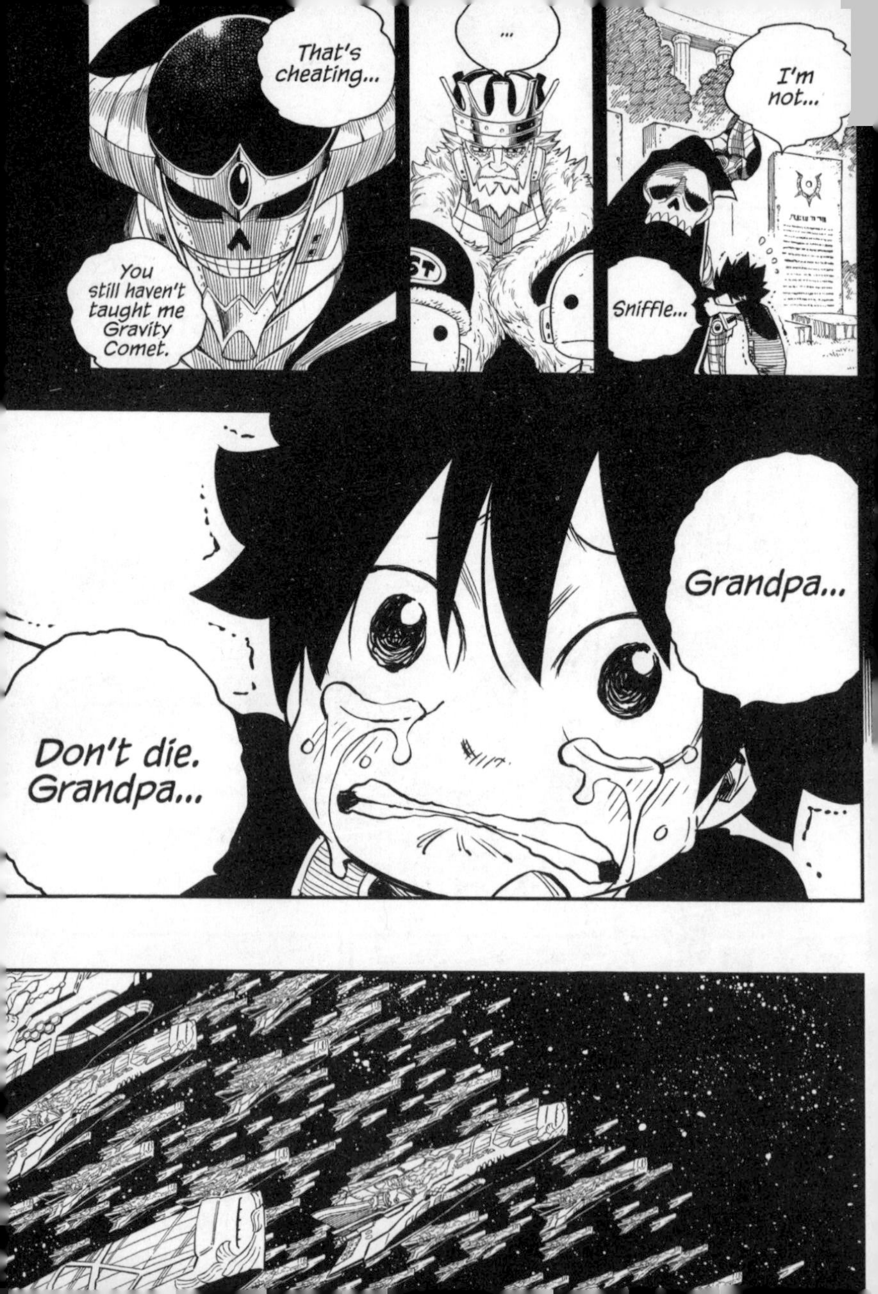
I'm not...
Sniffle...
...
That's cheating...
You still haven't taught me Gravity Comet.
Grandpa...
Don't die. Grandpa...

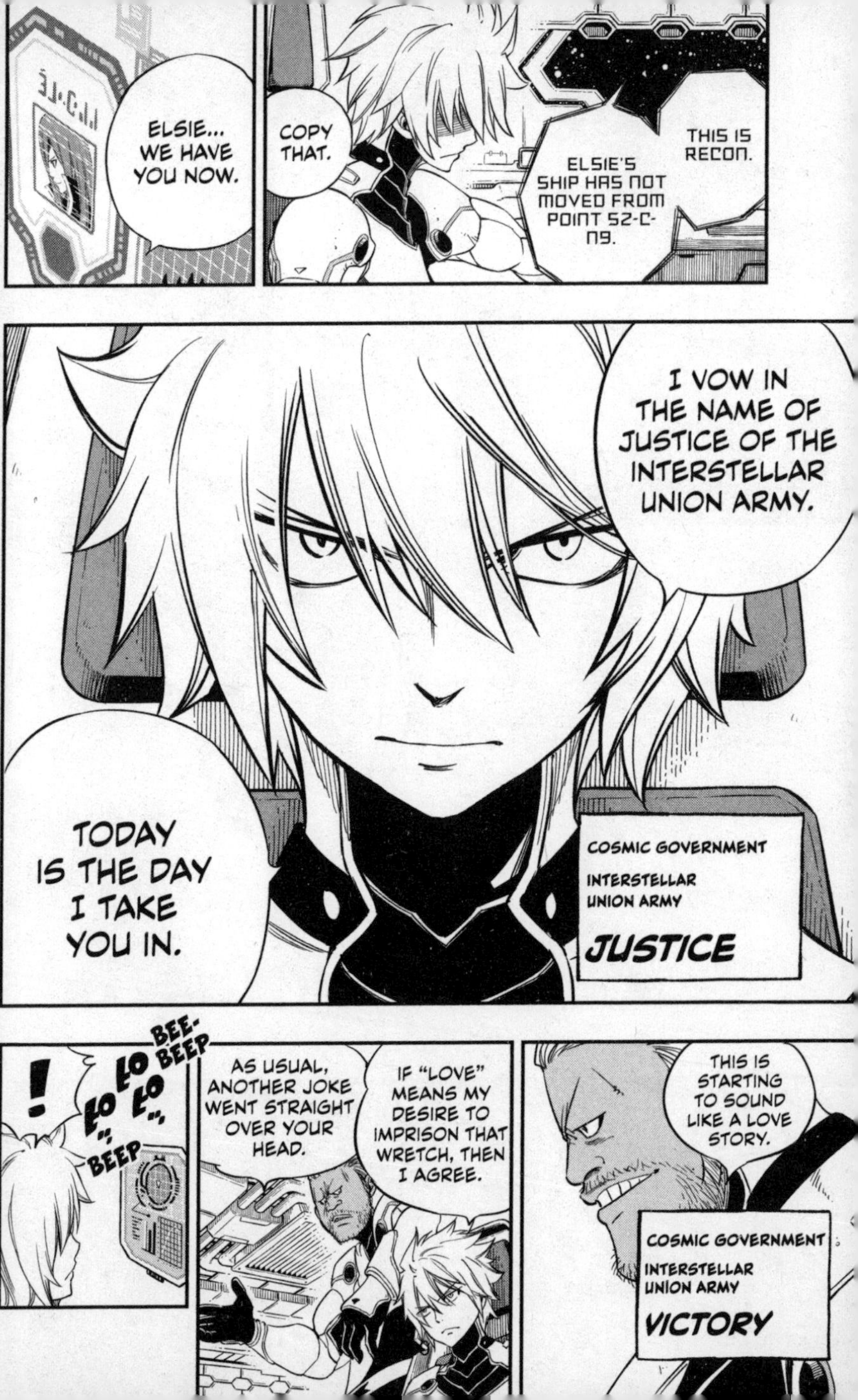
THIS IS RECON.
ELSIE'S SHIP HAS NOT MOVED FROM POINT 52-C-N9.
COPY THAT.
ELSIE... WE HAVE YOU NOW.
I VOW IN THE NAME OF JUSTICE OF THE INTERSTELLAR UNION ARMY.
COSMIC GOVERNMENT INTERSTELLAR UNION ARMY JUSTICE
TODAY IS THE DAY I TAKE YOU IN.
THIS IS STARTING TO SOUND LIKE A LOVE STORY.
COSMIC GOVERNMENT INTERSTELLAR UNION ARMY VICTORY
IF "LOVE" MEANS MY DESIRE TO IMPRISON THAT WRETCH, THEN I AGREE.
AS USUAL, ANOTHER JOKE WENT STRAIGHT OVER YOUR HEAD.
BEE-BEEP
BEEP
!

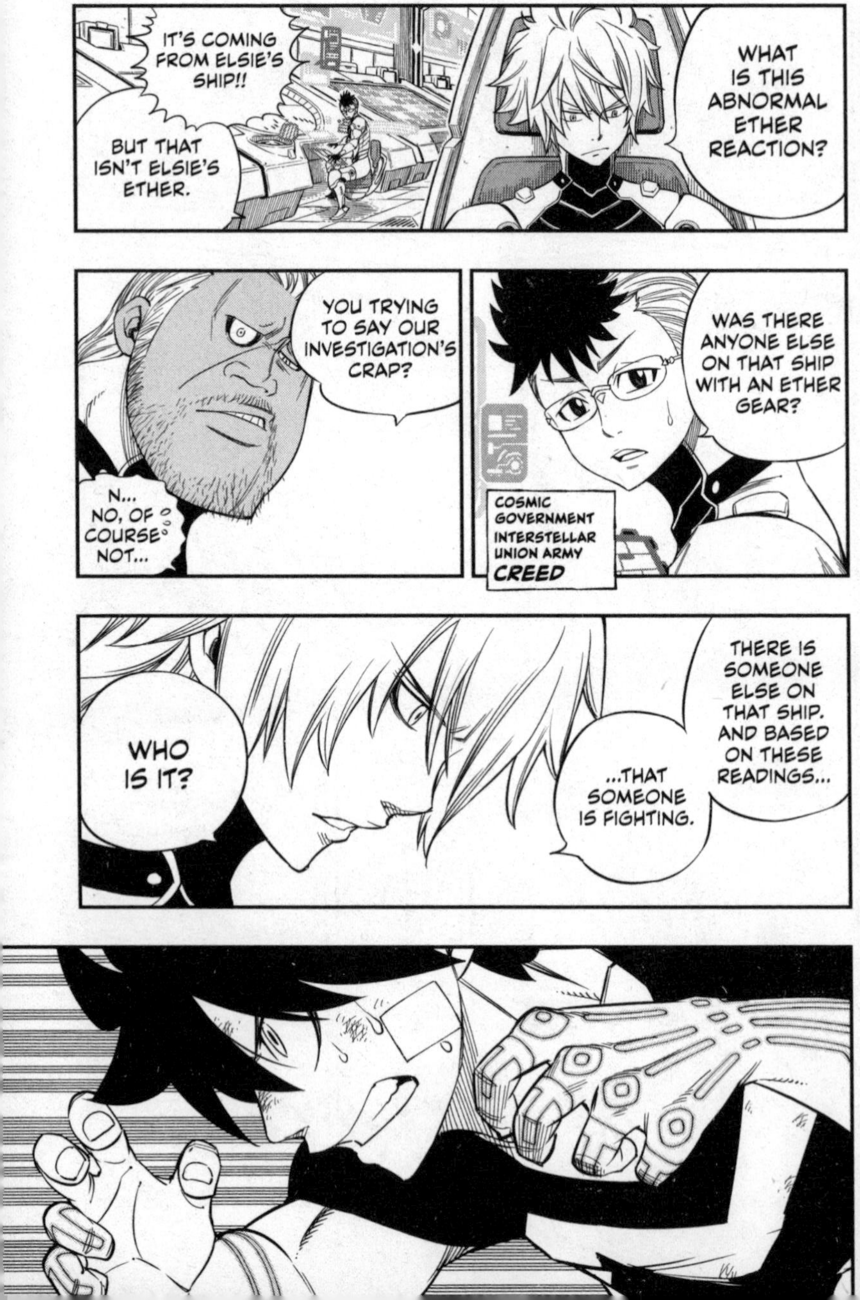
WHAT IS THIS ABNORMAL ETHER REACTION?
IT'S COMING FROM ELSIE'S SHIP!!
BUT THAT ISN'T ELSIE'S ETHER.
WAS THERE ANYONE ELSE ON THAT SHIP WITH AN ETHER GEAR?
COSMIC GOVERNMENT INTERSTELLAR UNION ARMY CREED
YOU TRYING TO SAY OUR INVESTIGATION'S CRAP?
N... NO, OF COURSE NOT...
THERE IS SOMEONE ELSE ON THAT SHIP. AND BASED ON THESE READINGS...
...THAT SOMEONE IS FIGHTING.
WHO IS IT?

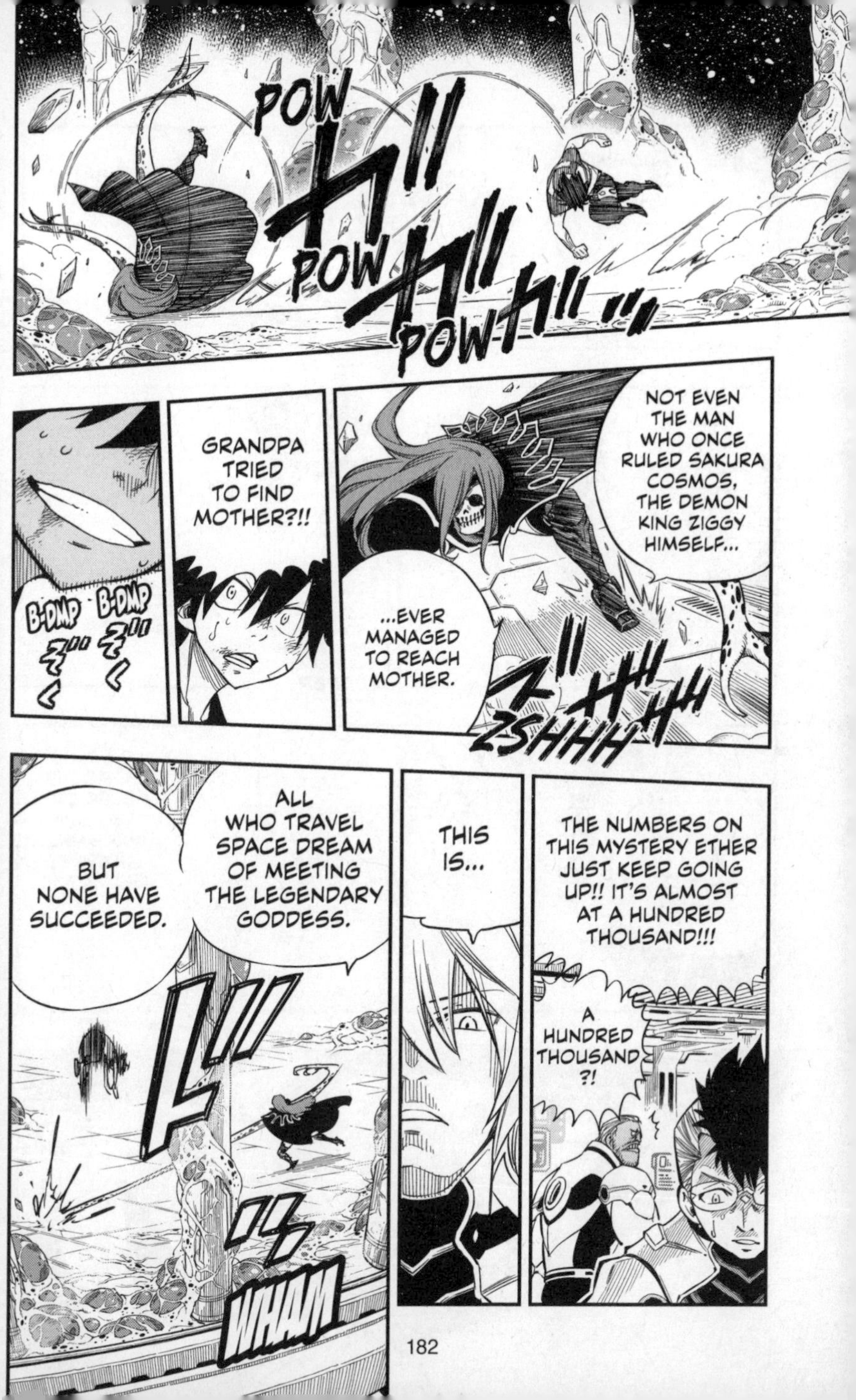
POW
POW
POW
NOT EVEN THE MAN WHO ONCE RULED SAKURA COSMOS, THE DEMON KING ZIGGY HIMSELF...
...EVER MANAGED TO REACH MOTHER.
ZSHHH
GRANDPA TRIED TO FIND MOTHER?!!
B-DMP B-DMP
THE NUMBERS ON THIS MYSTERY ETHER JUST KEEP GOING UP!! IT'S ALMOST AT A HUNDRED THOUSAND!!!
A HUNDRED THOUSAND?!
THIS IS...
ALL WHO TRAVEL SPACE DREAM OF MEETING THE LEGENDARY GODDESS.
BUT NONE HAVE SUCCEEDED.
WHAM

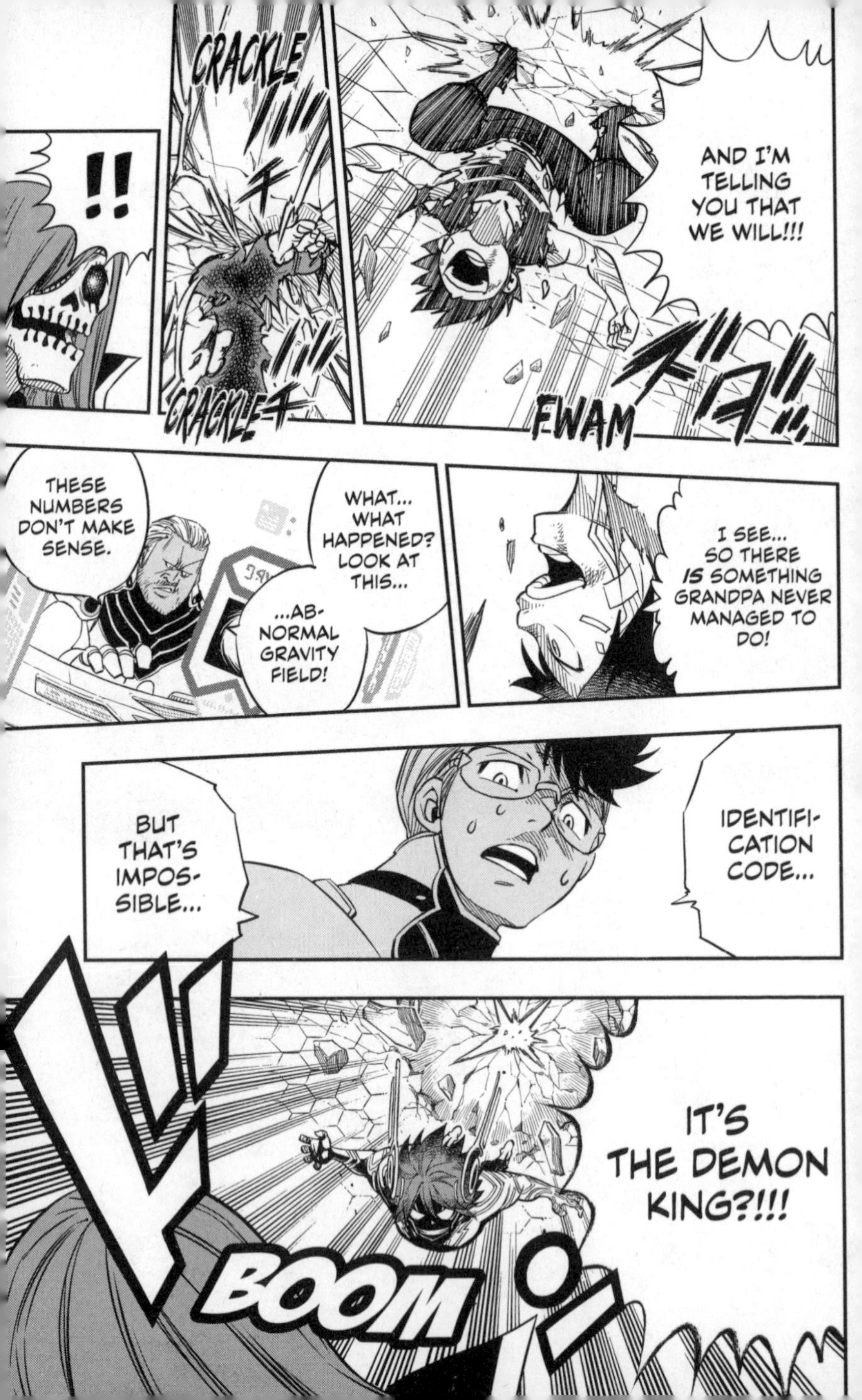
AND I'M TELLING YOU THAT WE WILL!!!
FWAM
CRACKLE
CRACKLE
!!
I SEE... SO THERE *IS* SOMETHING GRANDPA NEVER MANAGED TO DO!
WHAT... WHAT HAPPENED? LOOK AT THIS...
...AB-NORMAL GRAVITY FIELD!
THESE NUMBERS DON'T MAKE SENSE.
IDENTIFICATION CODE...
BUT THAT'S IMPOSSIBLE...
IT'S THE DEMON KING?!!!
BOOM

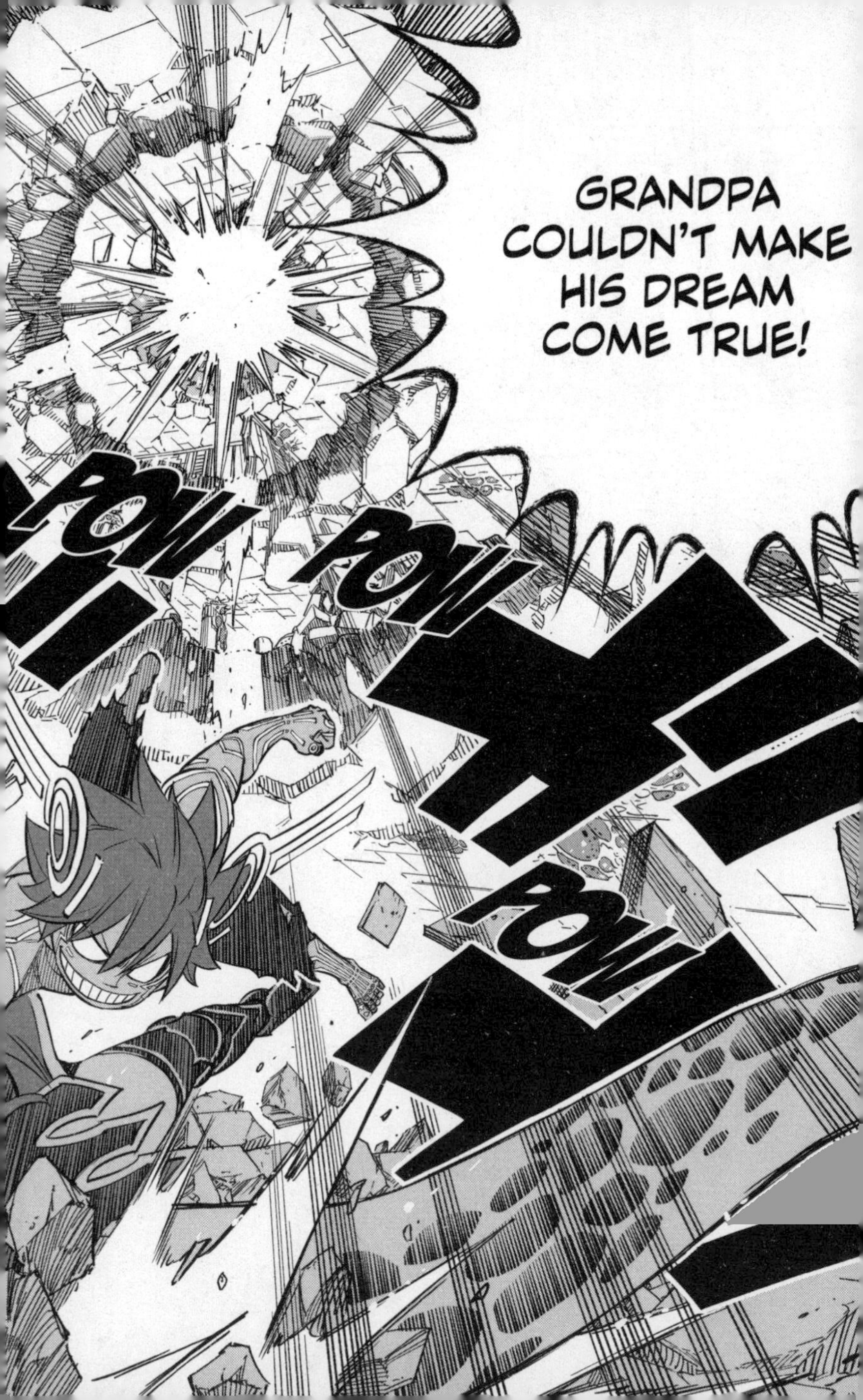
GRANDPA COULDN'T MAKE HIS DREAM COME TRUE!
POW
POW
POW

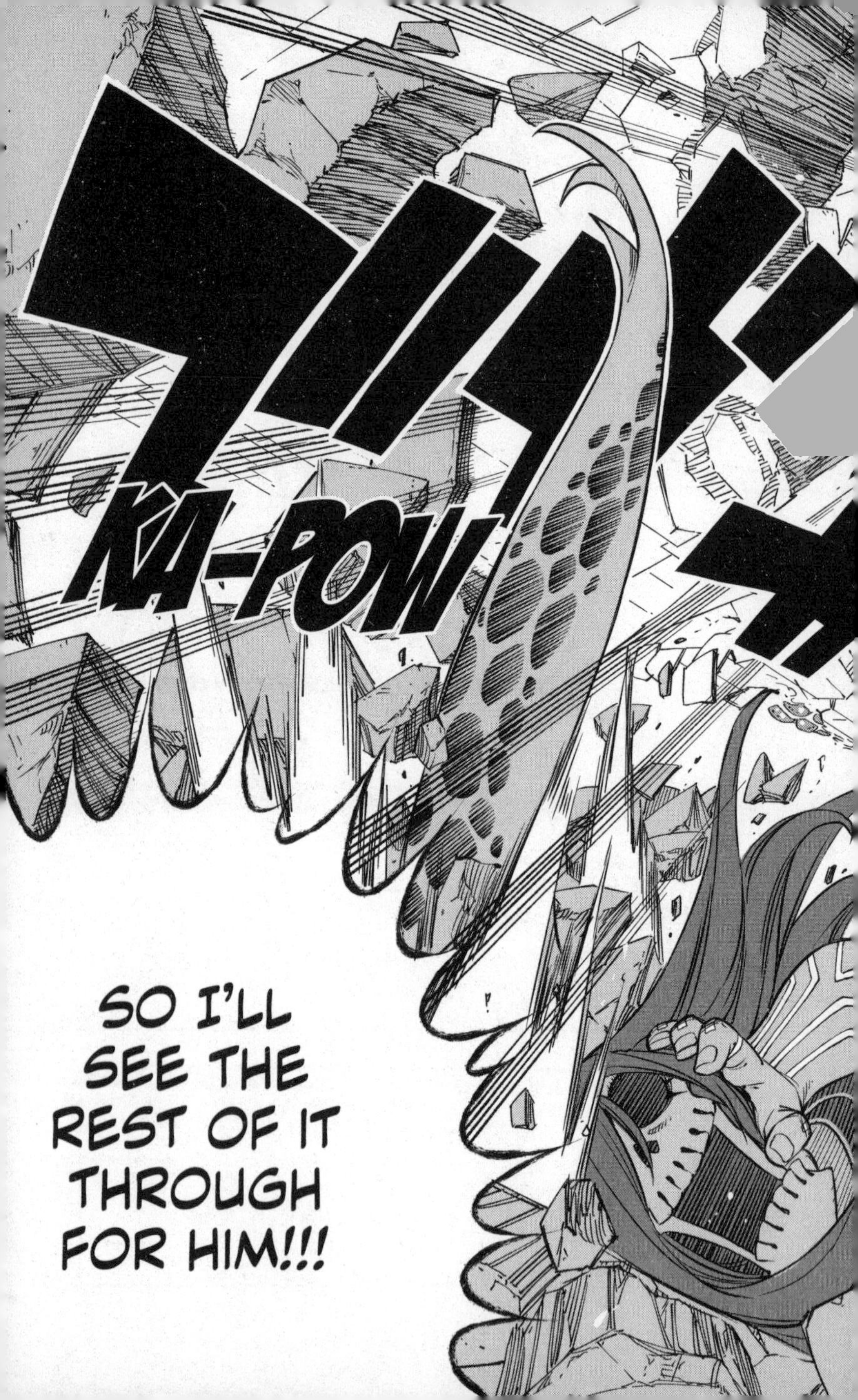
KA-POW
SO I'LL SEE THE REST OF IT THROUGH FOR HIM!!!

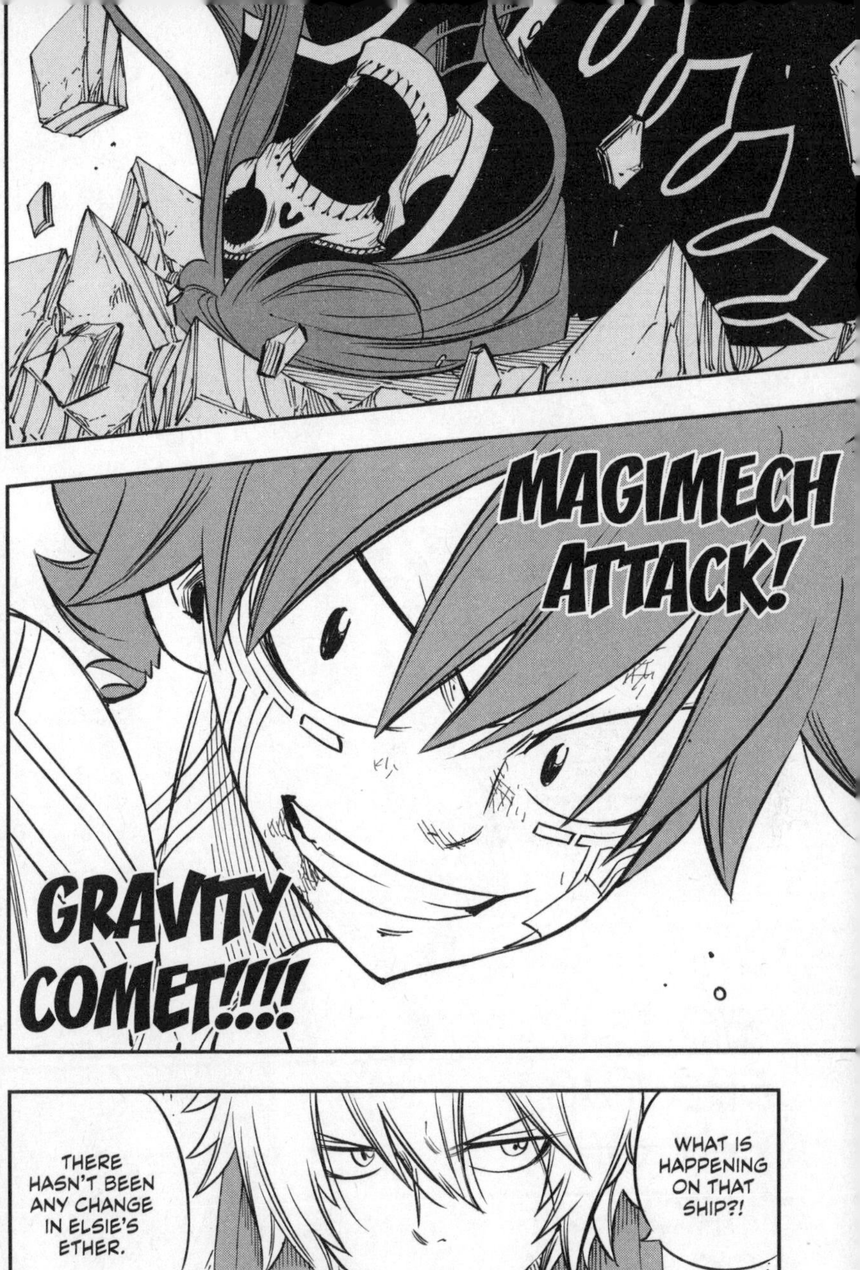
MAGIMECH ATTACK!
GRAVITY COMET!!!!
WHAT IS HAPPENING ON THAT SHIP?!
THERE HASN'T BEEN ANY CHANGE IN ELSIE'S ETHER.

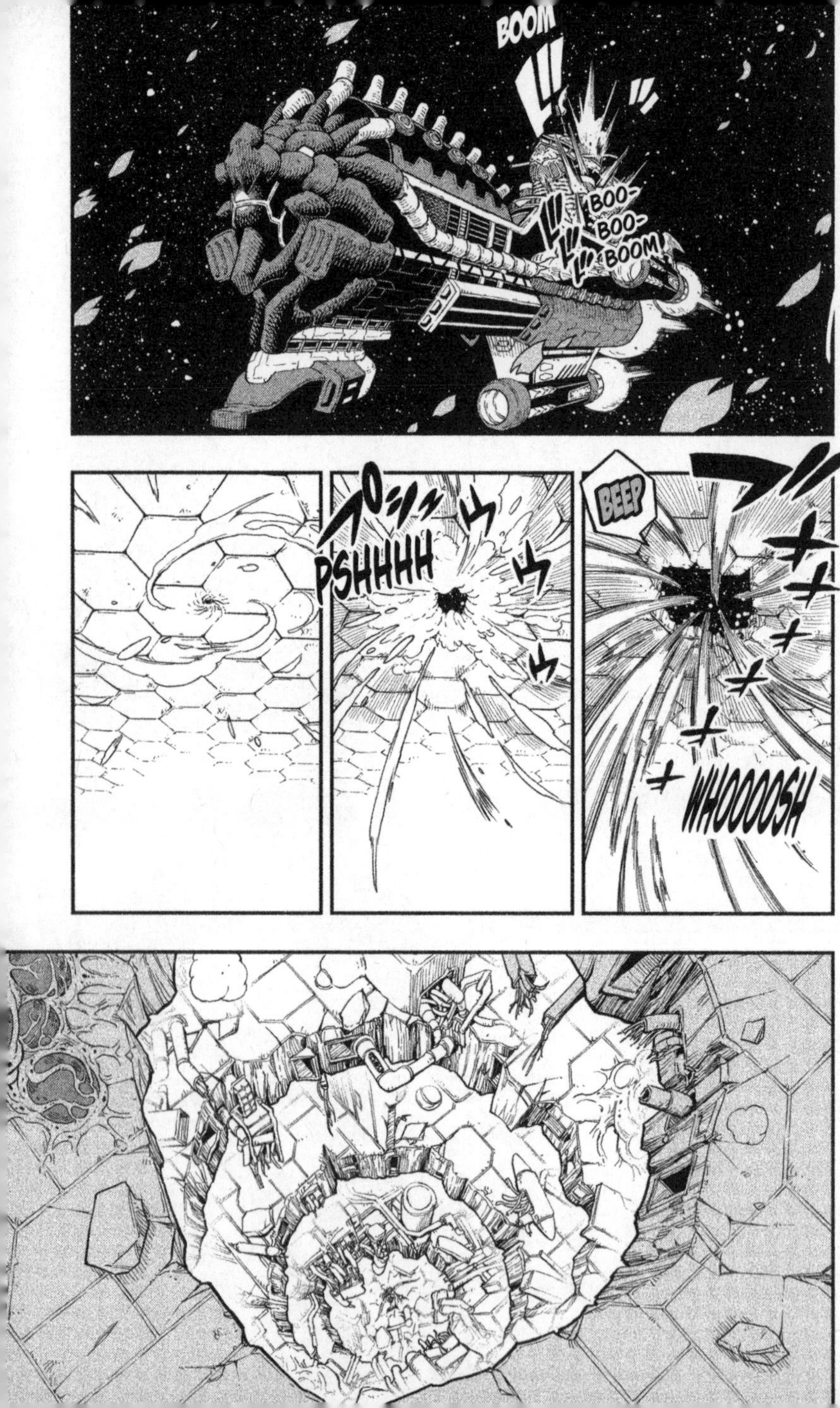
BOOM
BOO-
BOO-
BOOM
BEEP
WHOOOOSH
PSHHHH

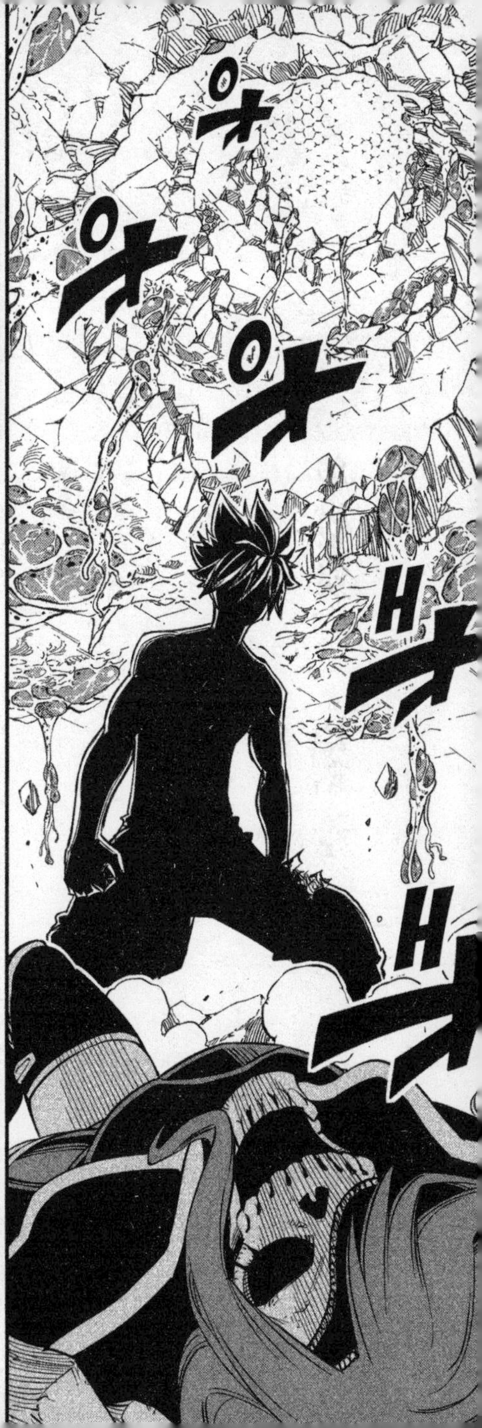
H
H
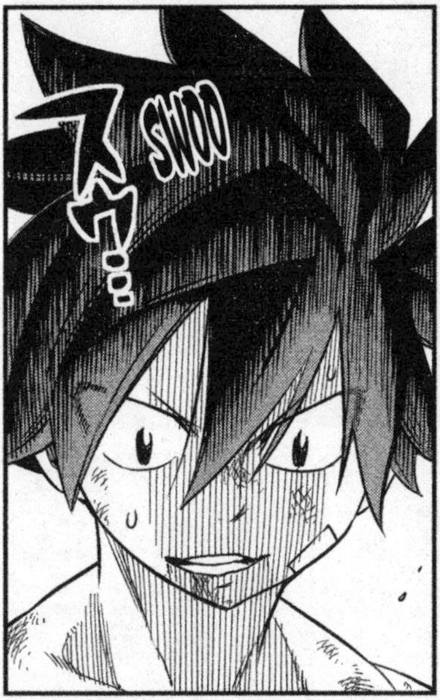
SWOO
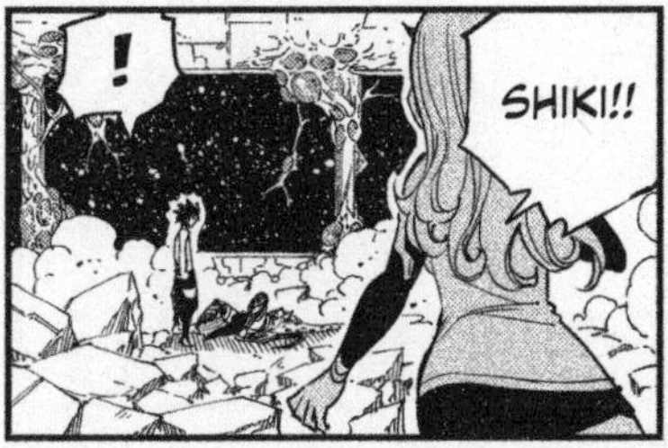
SHIKI!!
!
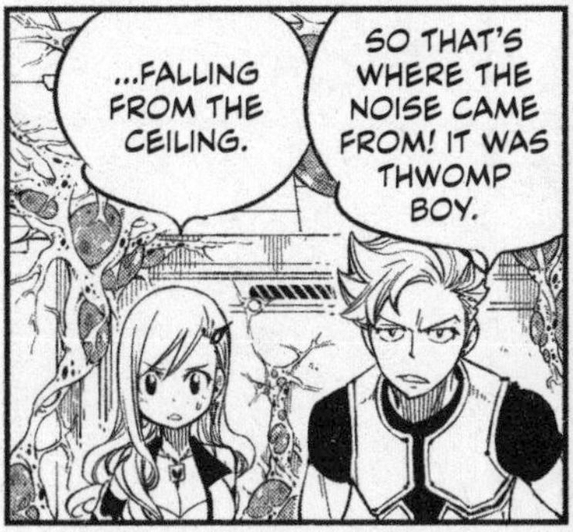
SO THAT'S WHERE THE NOISE CAME FROM! IT WAS THWOMP BOY.
...FALLING FROM THE CEILING.

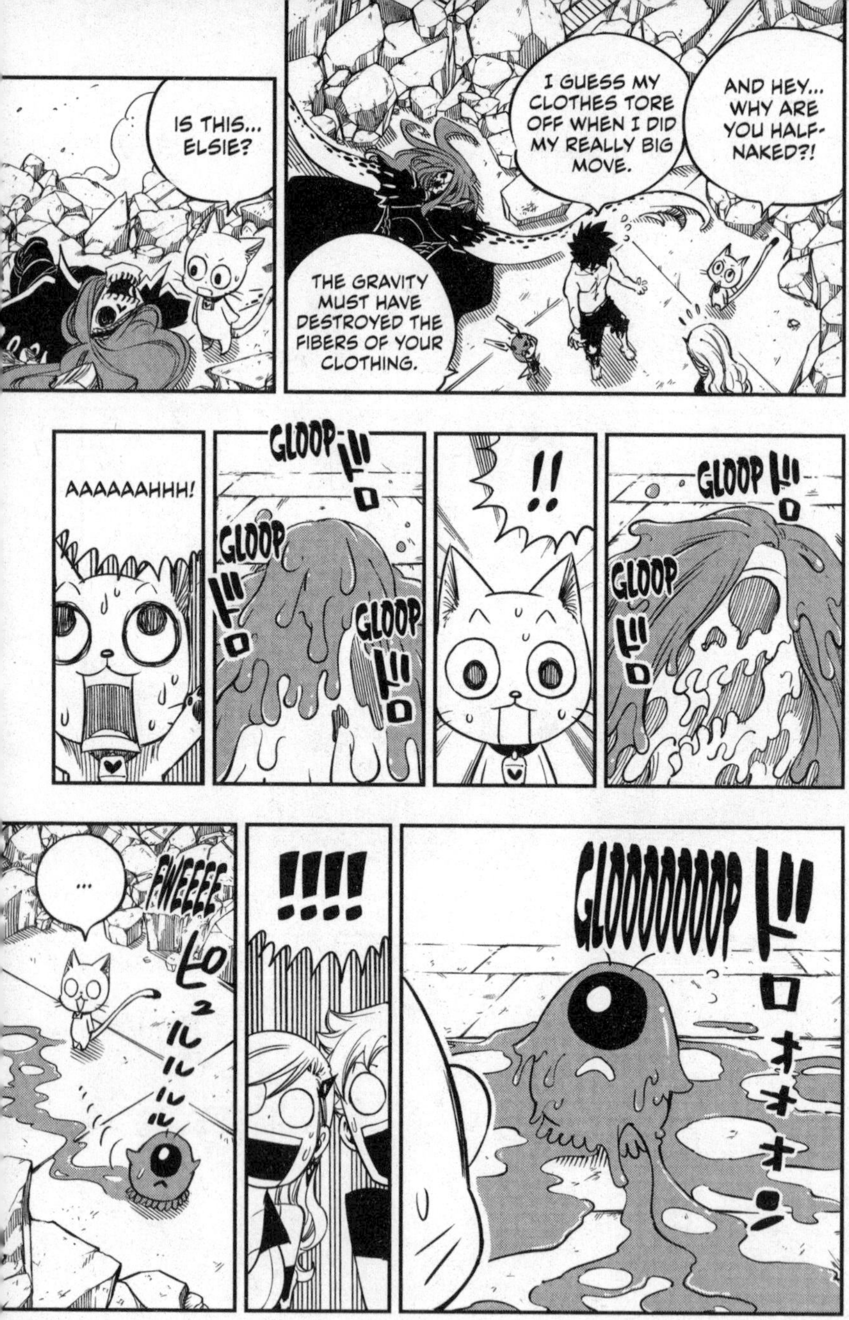
AND HEY... WHY ARE YOU HALF-NAKED?!
I GUESS MY CLOTHES TORE OFF WHEN I DID MY REALLY BIG MOVE.
THE GRAVITY MUST HAVE DESTROYED THE FIBERS OF YOUR CLOTHING.
IS THIS... ELSIE?
GLOOP ドロ
GLOOP ドロ
!!
GLOOP- ドロ
GLOOP ドロ
GLOOP ドロ
AAAAAAHHH!
GLOOOOOOOOP
!!!!
...
FWEEEE

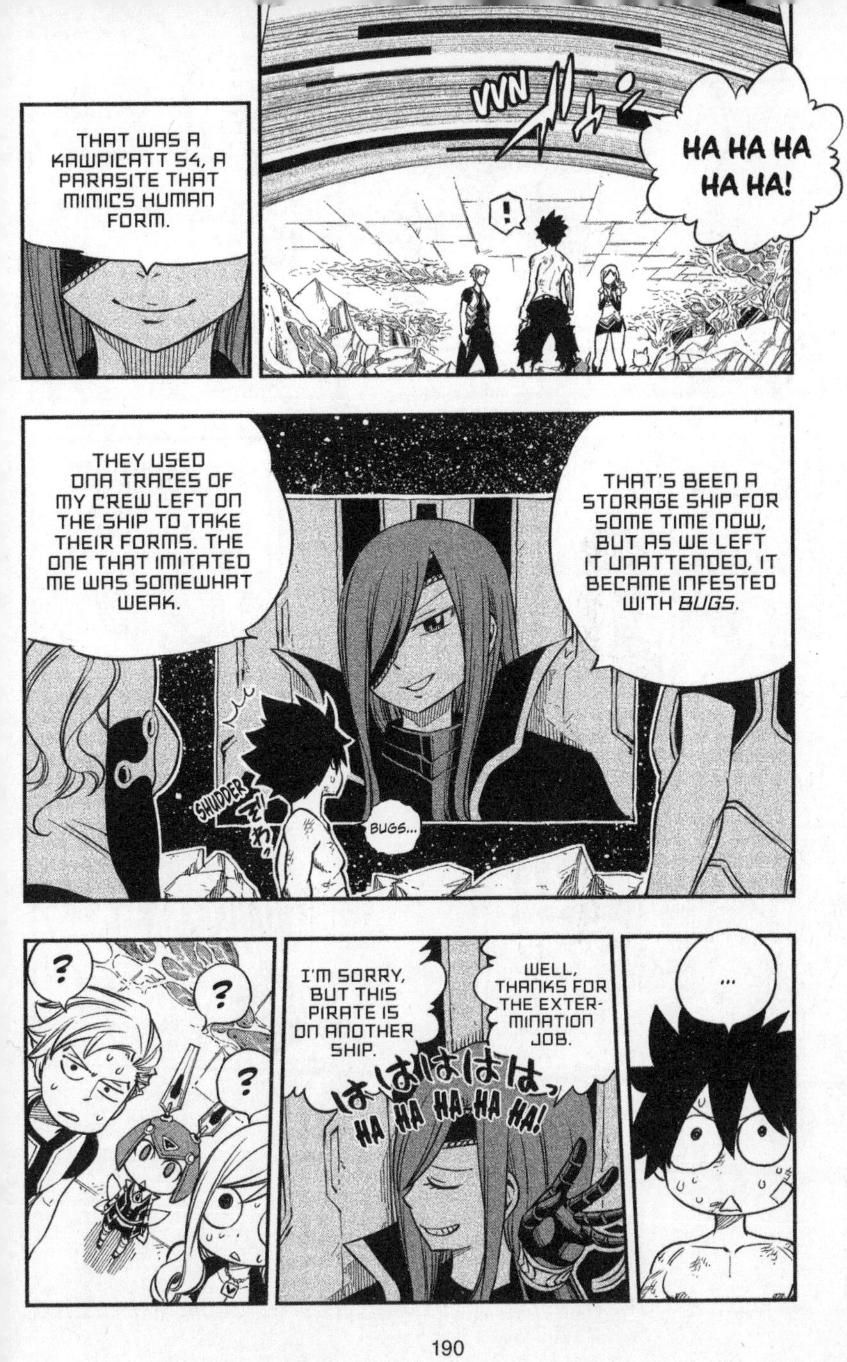
HA HA HA
HA HA!
VVN
!
THAT WAS A KAWPICATT 54, A PARASITE THAT MIMICS HUMAN FORM.
THAT'S BEEN A STORAGE SHIP FOR SOME TIME NOW, BUT AS WE LEFT IT UNATTENDED, IT BECAME INFESTED WITH *BUGS*.
THEY USED DNA TRACES OF MY CREW LEFT ON THE SHIP TO TAKE THEIR FORMS. THE ONE THAT IMITATED ME WAS SOMEWHAT WEAK.
BUGS...
SHUDDER
...
WELL, THANKS FOR THE EXTER-MINATION JOB.
I'M SORRY, BUT THIS PIRATE IS ON ANOTHER SHIP.
HA HA HA HA HA!
?
?
?

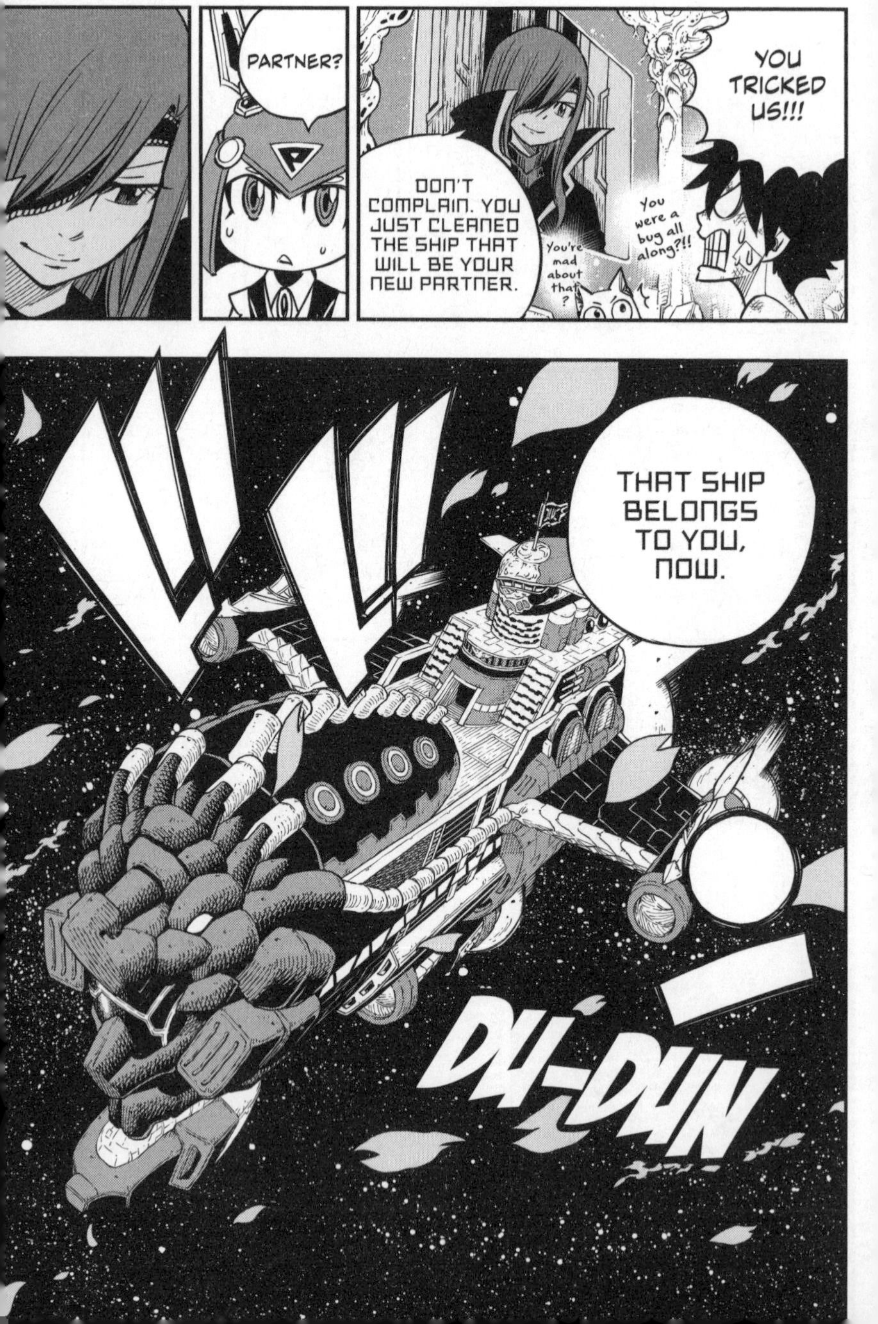
YOU TRICKED US!!!
You were a bug all along?!!
DON'T COMPLAIN. YOU JUST CLEANED THE SHIP THAT WILL BE YOUR NEW PARTNER.
You're mad about that?
PARTNER?
THAT SHIP BELONGS TO YOU, NOW.
DU-DUN

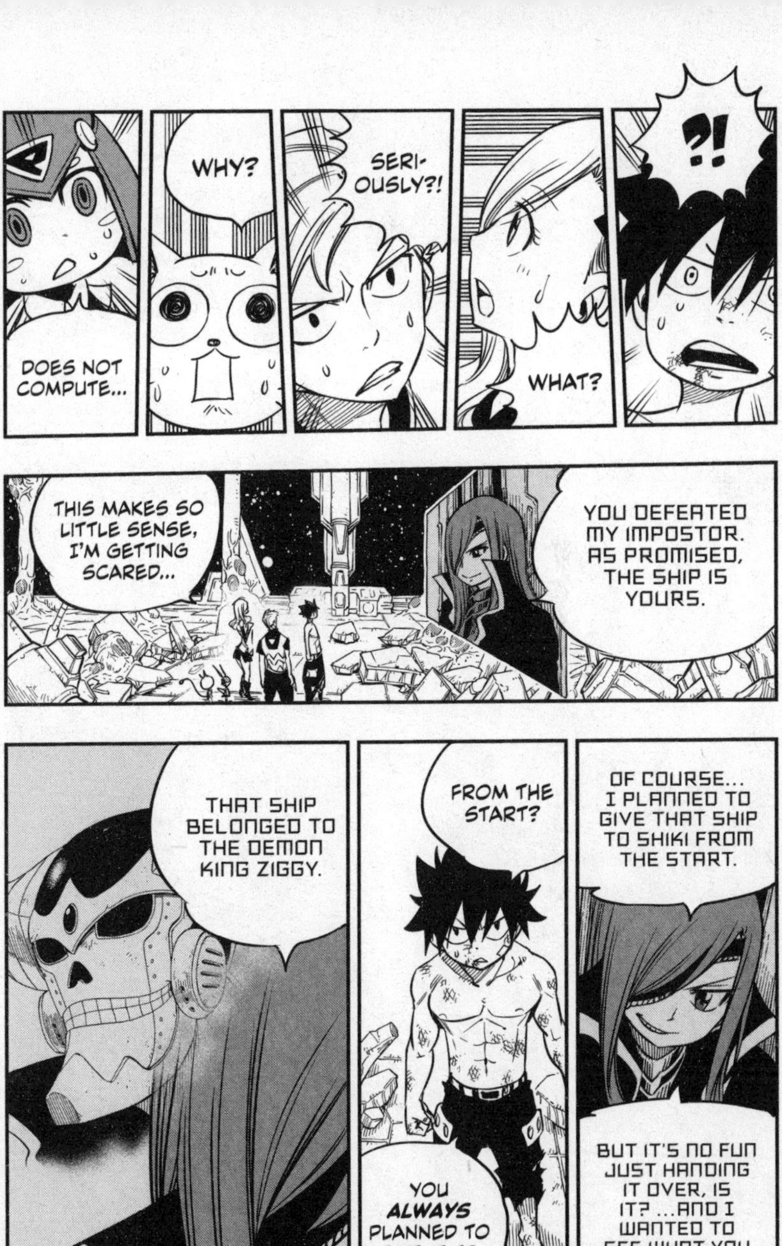
?!
WHAT?
SERI-
OUSLY?!
WHY?
DOES NOT COMPUTE...
YOU DEFEATED MY IMPOSTOR. AS PROMISED, THE SHIP IS YOURS.
THIS MAKES SO LITTLE SENSE, I'M GETTING SCARED...
OF COURSE... I PLANNED TO GIVE THAT SHIP TO SHIKI FROM THE START.
BUT IT'S NO FUN JUST HANDING IT OVER, IS IT? ...AND I WANTED TO SEE WHAT YOU COULD DO.
FROM THE START?
YOU **ALWAYS** PLANNED TO GIVE IT TO ME?
THAT SHIP BELONGED TO THE DEMON KING ZIGGY.

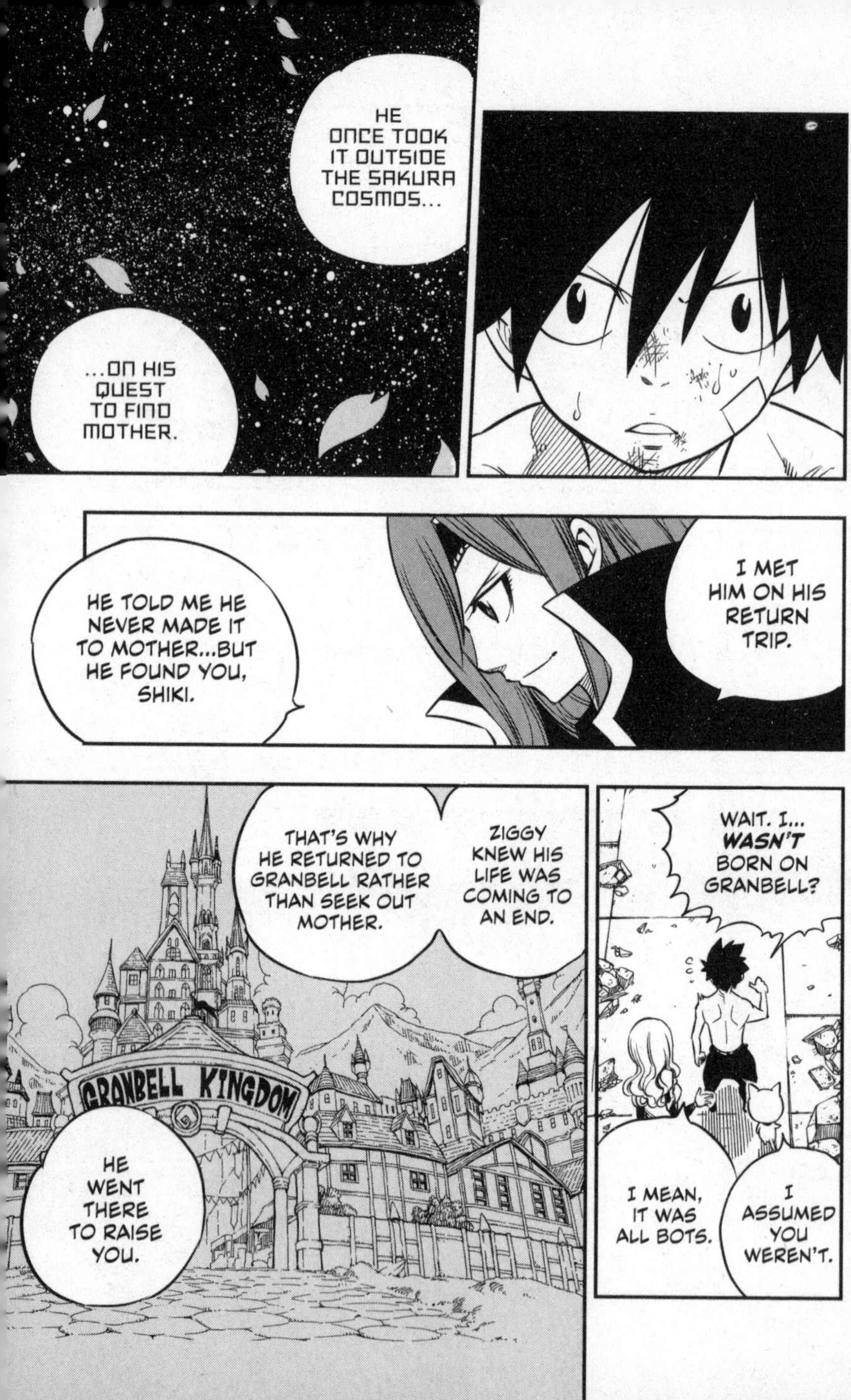
HE ONCE TOOK IT OUTSIDE THE SAKURA COSMOS...
...ON HIS QUEST TO FIND MOTHER.
I MET HIM ON HIS RETURN TRIP.
HE TOLD ME HE NEVER MADE IT TO MOTHER...BUT HE FOUND YOU, SHIKI.
WAIT. I... *WASN'T* BORN ON GRANBELL?
I ASSUMED YOU WEREN'T.
I MEAN, IT WAS ALL BOTS.
ZIGGY KNEW HIS LIFE WAS COMING TO AN END.
THAT'S WHY HE RETURNED TO GRANBELL RATHER THAN SEEK OUT MOTHER.
GRANBELL KINGDOM
HE WENT THERE TO RAISE YOU.

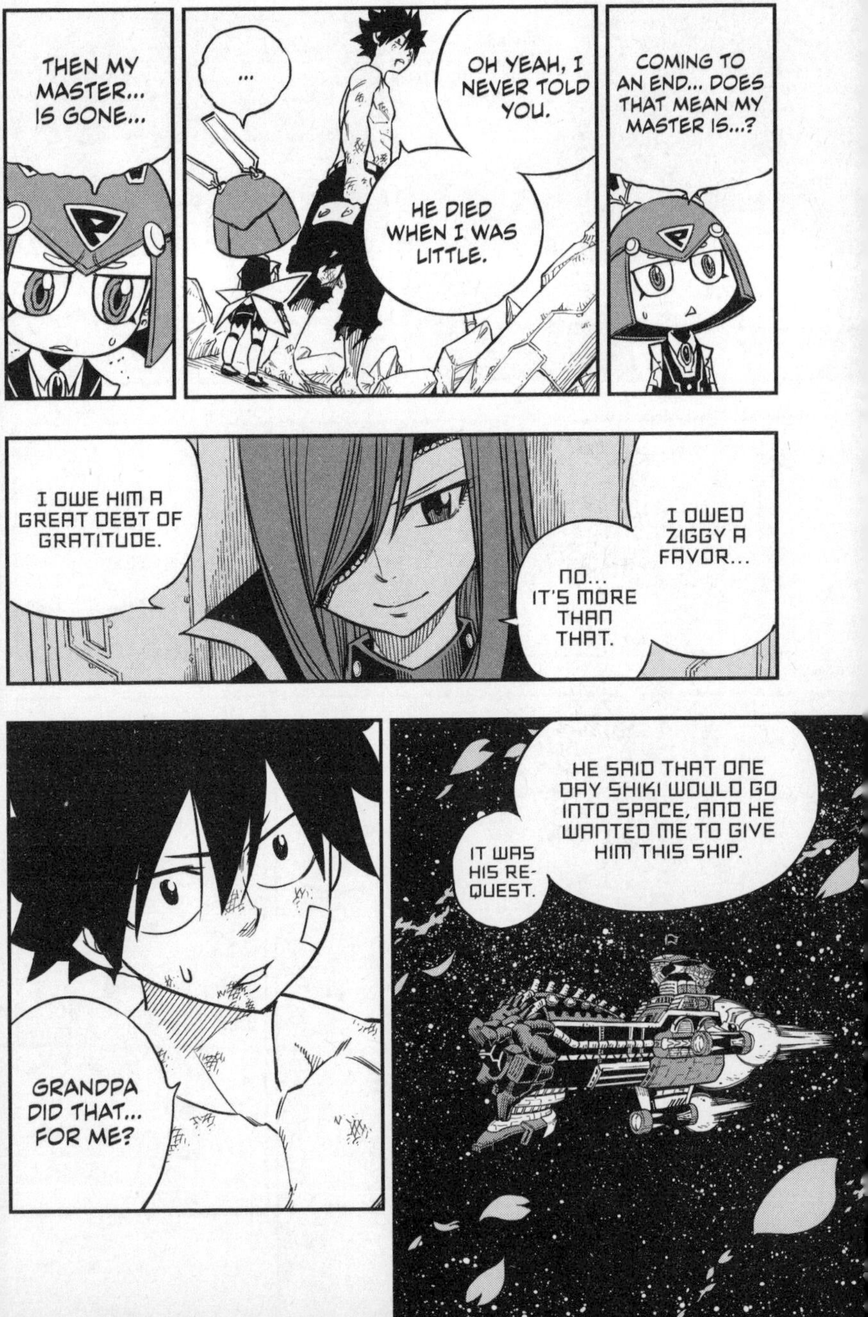
COMING TO AN END... DOES THAT MEAN MY MASTER IS...?
OH YEAH, I NEVER TOLD YOU.
HE DIED WHEN I WAS LITTLE.
...
THEN MY MASTER... IS GONE...
I OWED ZIGGY A FAVOR...
NO... IT'S MORE THAN THAT.
I OWE HIM A GREAT DEBT OF GRATITUDE.
HE SAID THAT ONE DAY SHIKI WOULD GO INTO SPACE, AND HE WANTED ME TO GIVE HIM THIS SHIP.
IT WAS HIS RE-QUEST.
GRANDPA DID THAT... FOR ME?

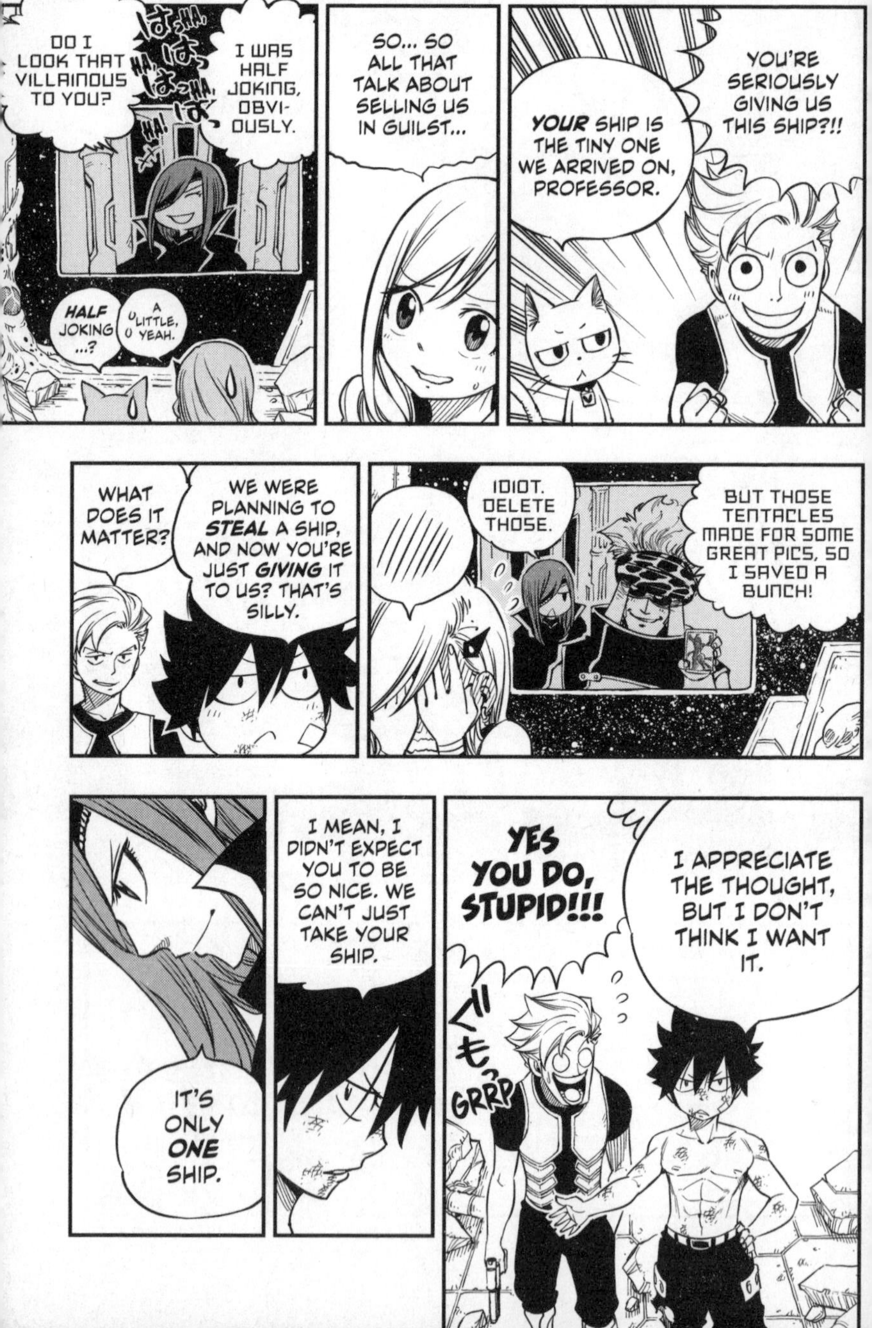
YOU'RE SERIOUSLY GIVING US THIS SHIP?!!
YOUR SHIP IS THE TINY ONE WE ARRIVED ON, PROFESSOR.
SO... SO ALL THAT TALK ABOUT SELLING US IN GUILST...
I WAS HALF JOKING, OBVIOUSLY.
HA, HA, HA, HA!
DO I LOOK THAT VILLAINOUS TO YOU?
HALF JOKING...?
A LITTLE, YEAH.
BUT THOSE TENTACLES MADE FOR SOME GREAT PICS, SO I SAVED A BUNCH!
IDIOT. DELETE THOSE.
WE WERE PLANNING TO STEAL A SHIP, AND NOW YOU'RE JUST GIVING IT TO US? THAT'S SILLY.
WHAT DOES IT MATTER?
I APPRECIATE THE THOUGHT, BUT I DON'T THINK I WANT IT.
YES YOU DO, STUPID!!!
GRRP
I MEAN, I DIDN'T EXPECT YOU TO BE SO NICE. WE CAN'T JUST TAKE YOUR SHIP.
IT'S ONLY ONE SHIP.

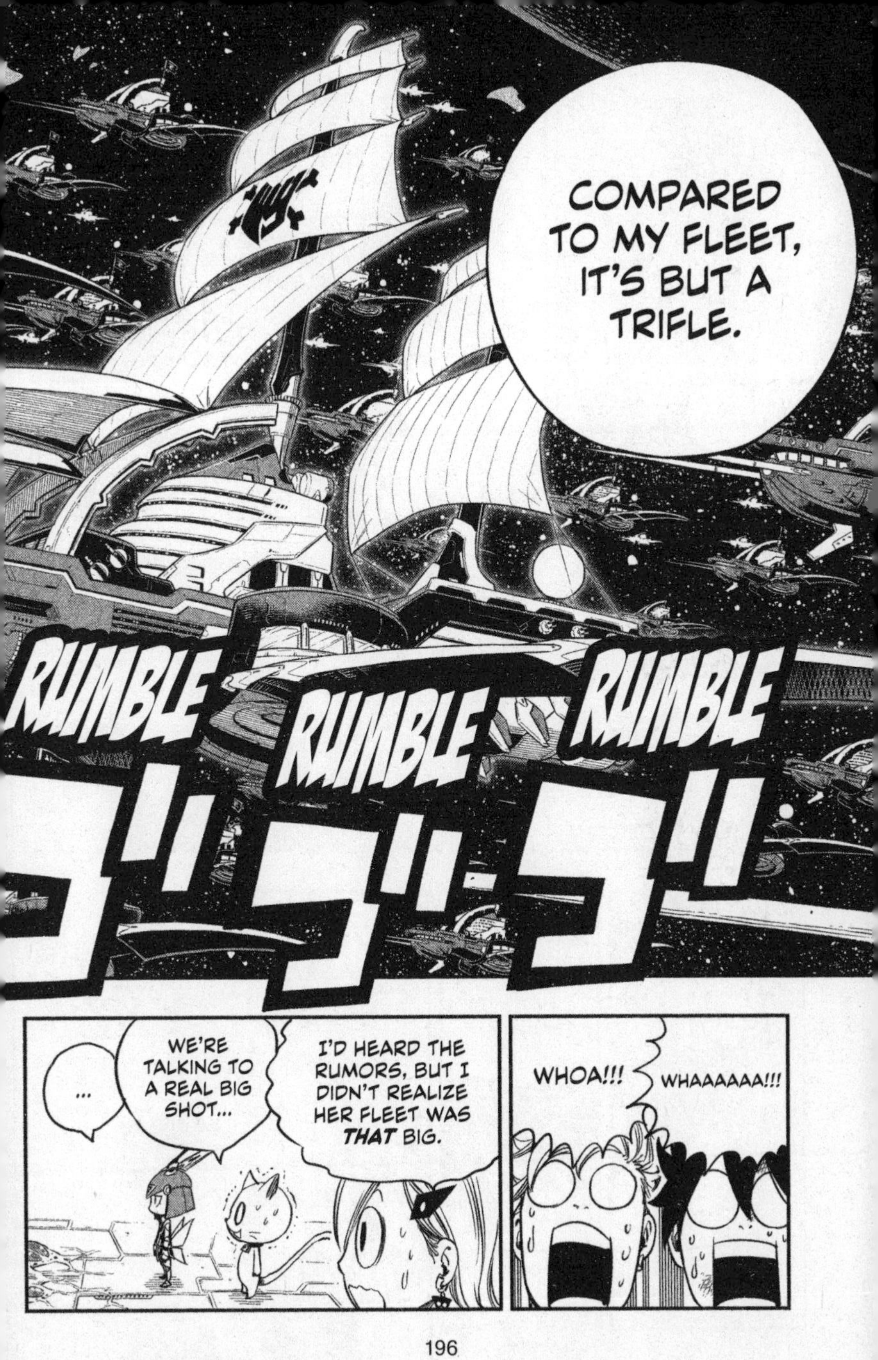
COMPARED TO MY FLEET, IT'S BUT A TRIFLE.
RUMBLE
RUMBLE
RUMBLE
WHAAAAAA!!!
WHOA!!!
I'D HEARD THE RUMORS, BUT I DIDN'T REALIZE HER FLEET WAS *THAT* BIG.
WE'RE TALKING TO A REAL BIG SHOT...
...

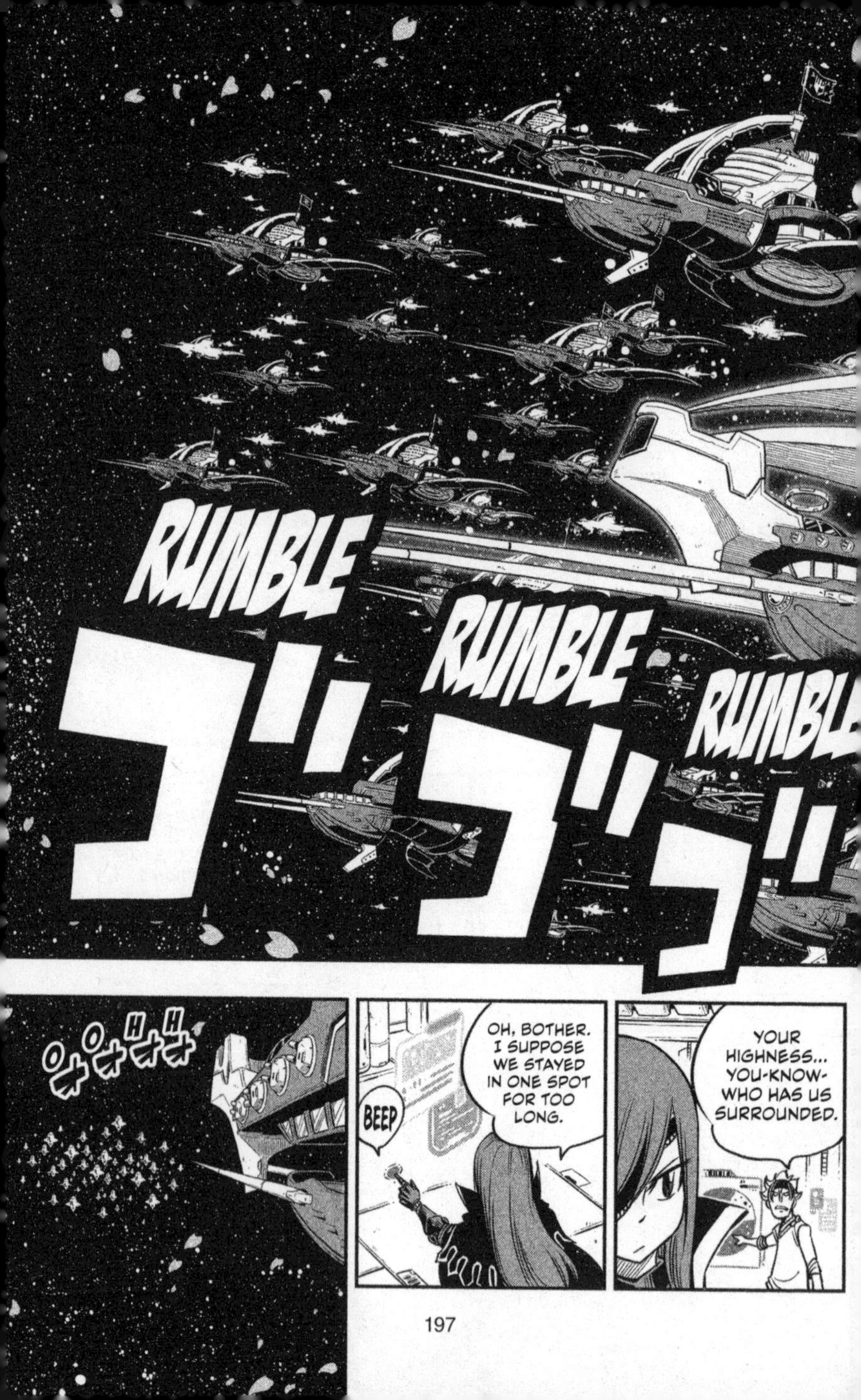
RUMBLE
RUMBLE
RUMBLE
YOUR HIGHNESS... YOU-KNOW-WHO HAS US SURROUNDED.
OH, BOTHER. I SUPPOSE WE STAYED IN ONE SPOT FOR TOO LONG.
BEEP

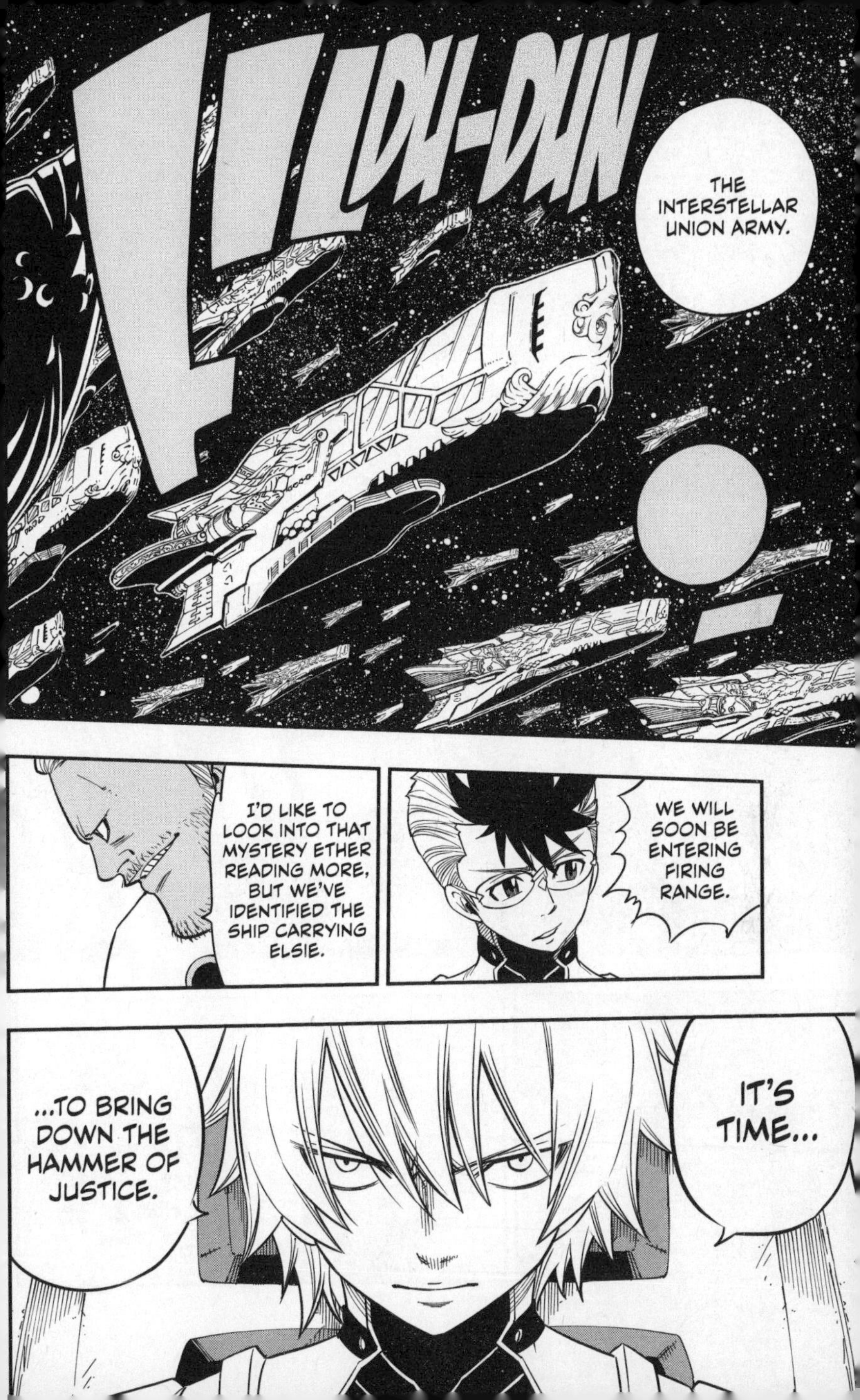
DOH-DUN
THE INTERSTELLAR UNION ARMY.
WE WILL SOON BE ENTERING FIRING RANGE.
I'D LIKE TO LOOK INTO THAT MYSTERY ETHER READING MORE, BUT WE'VE IDENTIFIED THE SHIP CARRYING ELSIE.
IT'S TIME...
...TO BRING DOWN THE HAMMER OF JUSTICE.

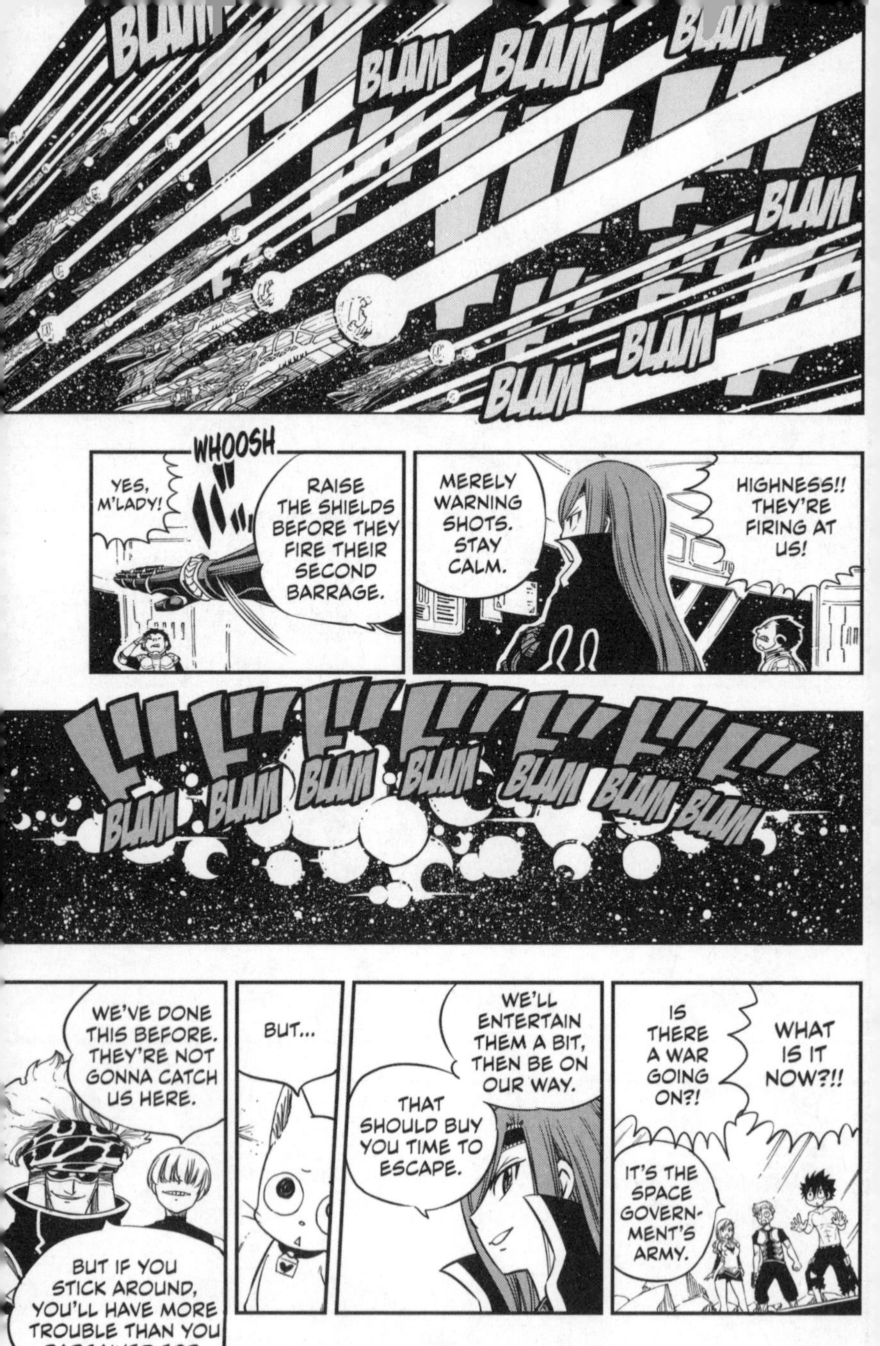
BLAM BLAM BLAM BLAM BLAM BLAM BLAM
HIGHNESS!! THEY'RE FIRING AT US!
MERELY WARNING SHOTS. STAY CALM.
WHOOSH
RAISE THE SHIELDS BEFORE THEY FIRE THEIR SECOND BARRAGE.
YES, M'LADY!
BLAM BLAM BLAM BLAM BLAM BLAM BLAM
WHAT IS IT NOW?!!
IS THERE A WAR GOING ON?!
IT'S THE SPACE GOVERNMENT'S ARMY.
WE'LL ENTERTAIN THEM A BIT, THEN BE ON OUR WAY.
THAT SHOULD BUY YOU TIME TO ESCAPE.
BUT...
WE'VE DONE THIS BEFORE. THEY'RE NOT GONNA CATCH US HERE.
BUT IF YOU STICK AROUND, YOU'LL HAVE MORE TROUBLE THAN YOU BARGAINED FOR.

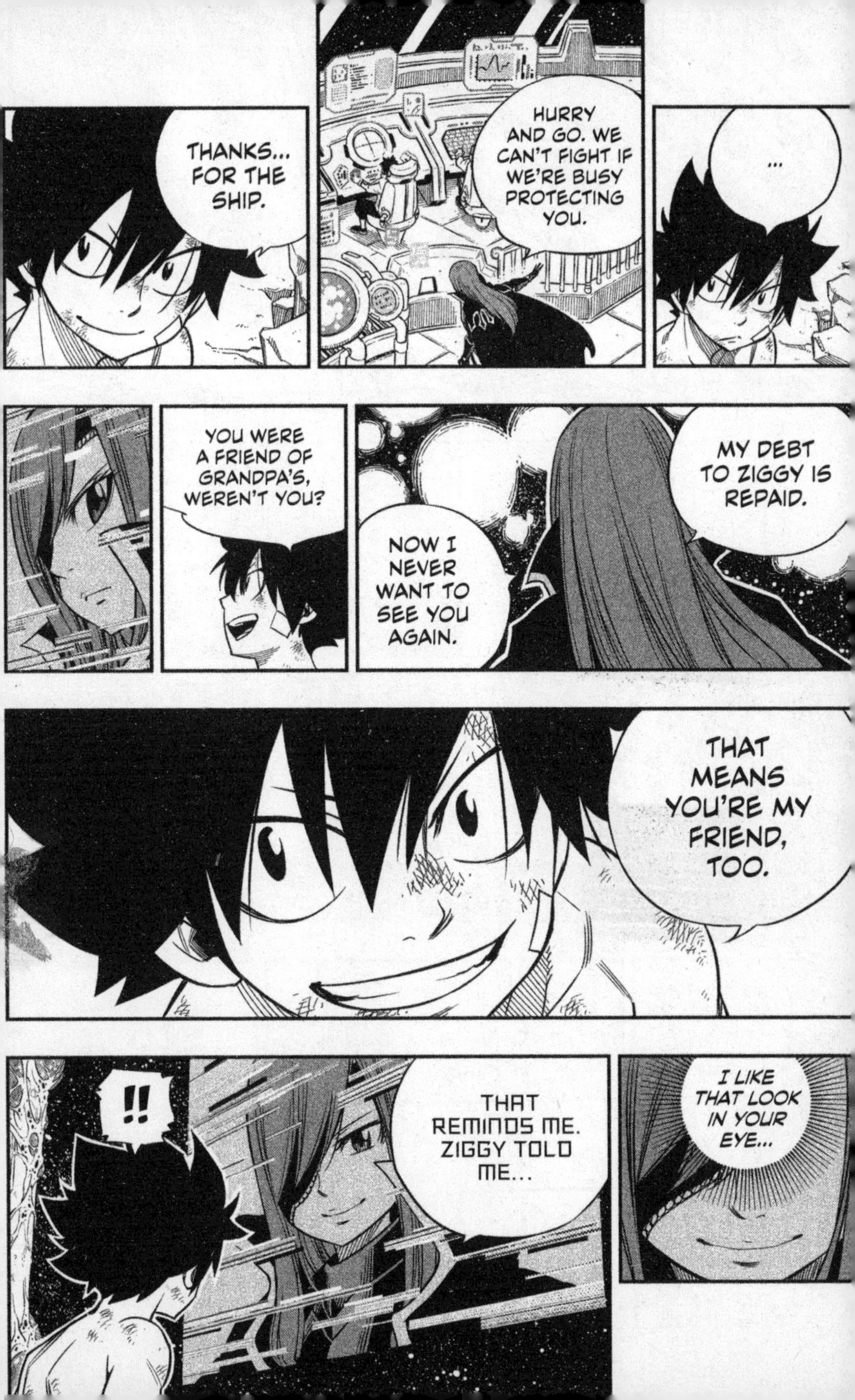
...
HURRY AND GO. WE CAN'T FIGHT IF WE'RE BUSY PROTECTING YOU.
THANKS... FOR THE SHIP.
MY DEBT TO ZIGGY IS REPAID.
NOW I NEVER WANT TO SEE YOU AGAIN.
YOU WERE A FRIEND OF GRANDPA'S, WEREN'T YOU?
THAT MEANS YOU'RE MY FRIEND, TOO.
I LIKE THAT LOOK IN YOUR EYE...
THAT REMINDS ME. ZIGGY TOLD ME...
!!

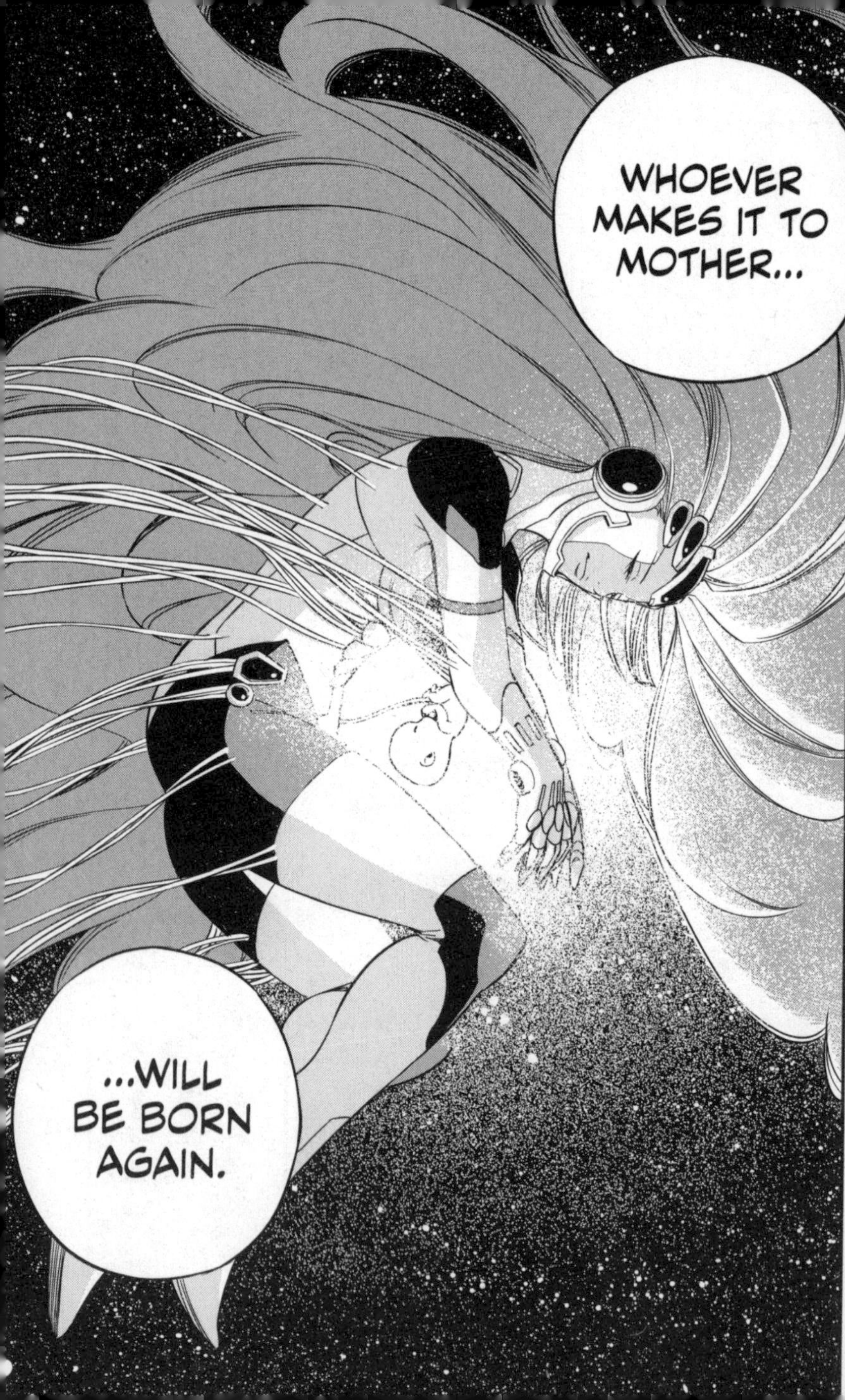
WHOEVER MAKES IT TO MOTHER...
...WILL BE BORN AGAIN.

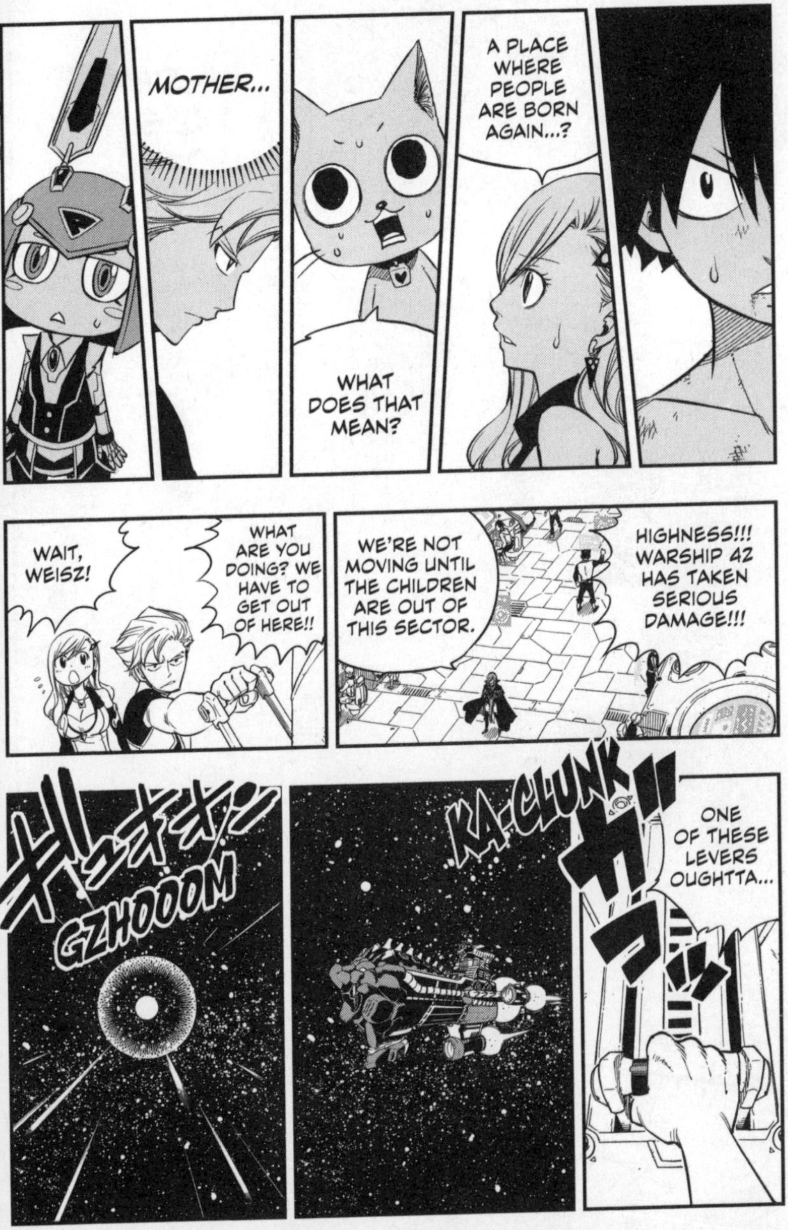

A PLACE WHERE PEOPLE ARE BORN AGAIN...?
WHAT DOES THAT MEAN?
MOTHER...
HIGHNESS!!! WARSHIP 42 HAS TAKEN SERIOUS DAMAGE!!!
WE'RE NOT MOVING UNTIL THE CHILDREN ARE OUT OF THIS SECTOR.
WHAT ARE YOU DOING? WE HAVE TO GET OUT OF HERE!!
WAIT, WEISZ!
ONE OF THESE LEVERS OUGHTTA...
KA-CLUNK
GZHOOOM

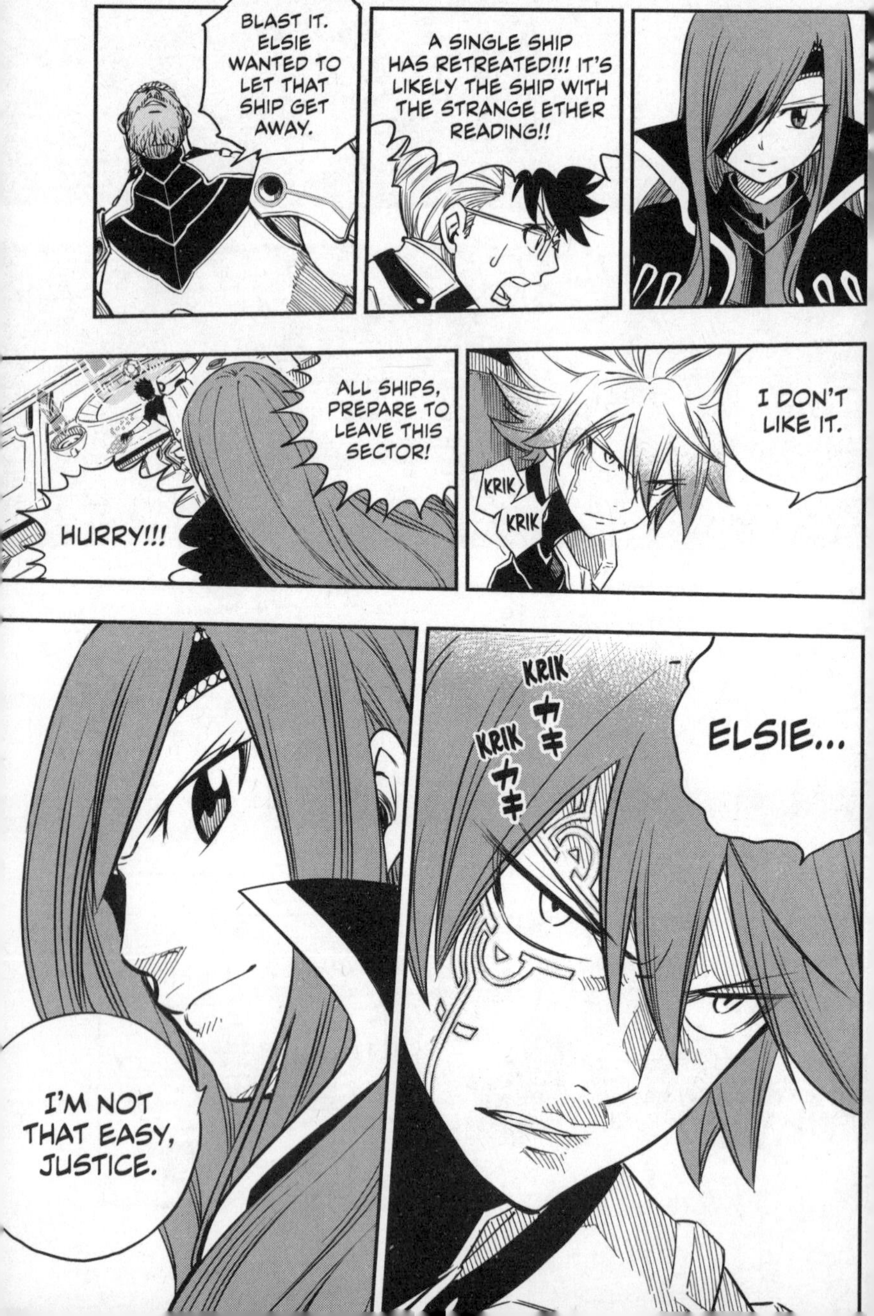
A SINGLE SHIP HAS RETREATED!!! IT'S LIKELY THE SHIP WITH THE STRANGE ETHER READING!!
BLAST IT. ELSIE WANTED TO LET THAT SHIP GET AWAY.
I DON'T LIKE IT.
KRIK
KRIK
ALL SHIPS, PREPARE TO LEAVE THIS SECTOR!
HURRY!!!
ELSIE...
KRIK
カキ
KRIK
カキ
I'M NOT THAT EASY, JUSTICE.

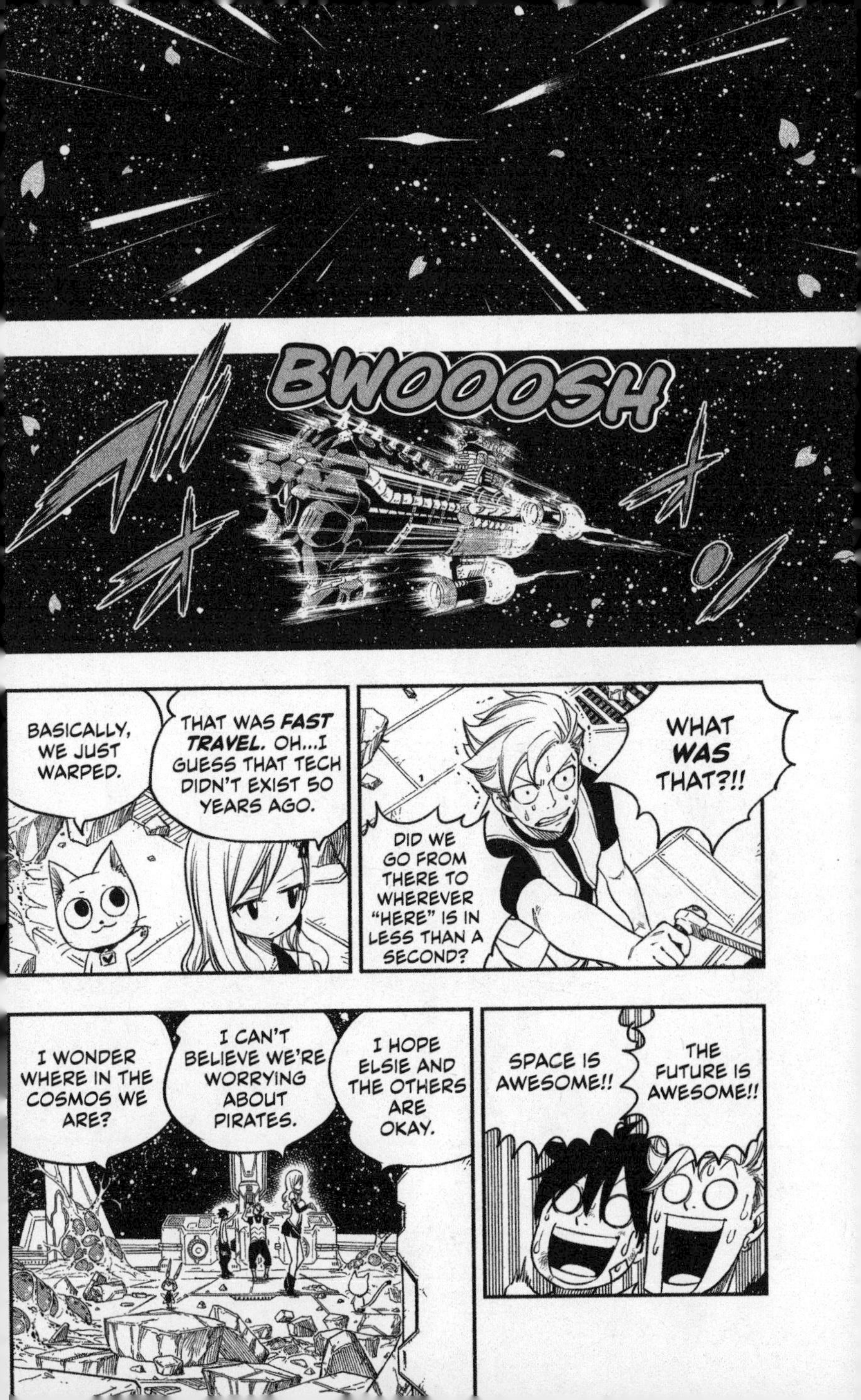
BWOOOSH
WHAT WAS THAT?!!
DID WE GO FROM THERE TO WHEREVER "HERE" IS IN LESS THAN A SECOND?
THAT WAS FAST TRAVEL. OH...I GUESS THAT TECH DIDN'T EXIST 50 YEARS AGO.
BASICALLY, WE JUST WARPED.
THE FUTURE IS AWESOME!!
SPACE IS AWESOME!!
I HOPE ELSIE AND THE OTHERS ARE OKAY.
I CAN'T BELIEVE WE'RE WORRYING ABOUT PIRATES.
I WONDER WHERE IN THE COSMOS WE ARE?

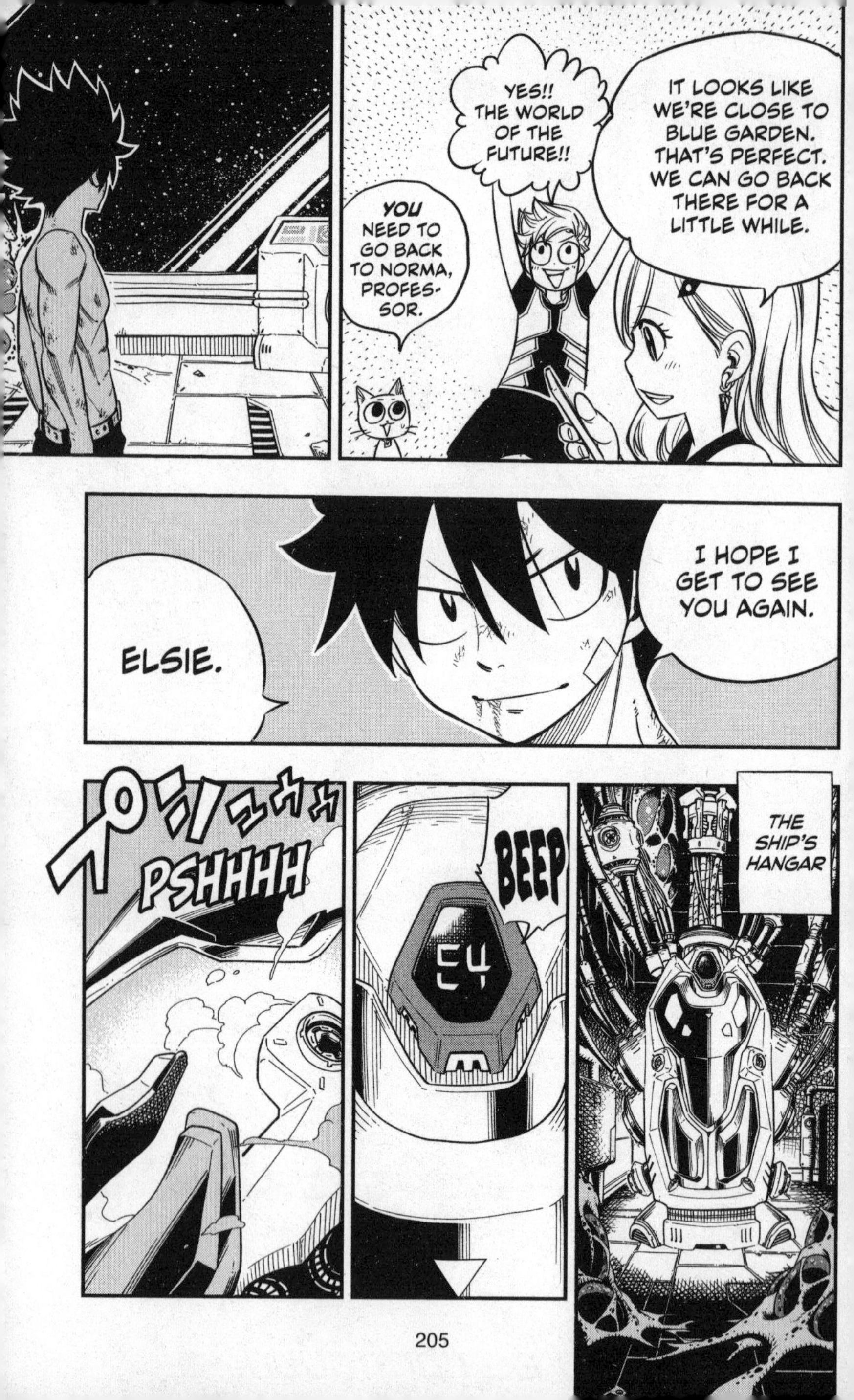
IT LOOKS LIKE WE'RE CLOSE TO BLUE GARDEN. THAT'S PERFECT. WE CAN GO BACK THERE FOR A LITTLE WHILE.
YES!! THE WORLD OF THE FUTURE!!
*YOU* NEED TO GO BACK TO NORMA, PROFESSOR.
I HOPE I GET TO SEE YOU AGAIN.
ELSIE.
THE SHIP'S HANGAR
BEEP
PSHHHH

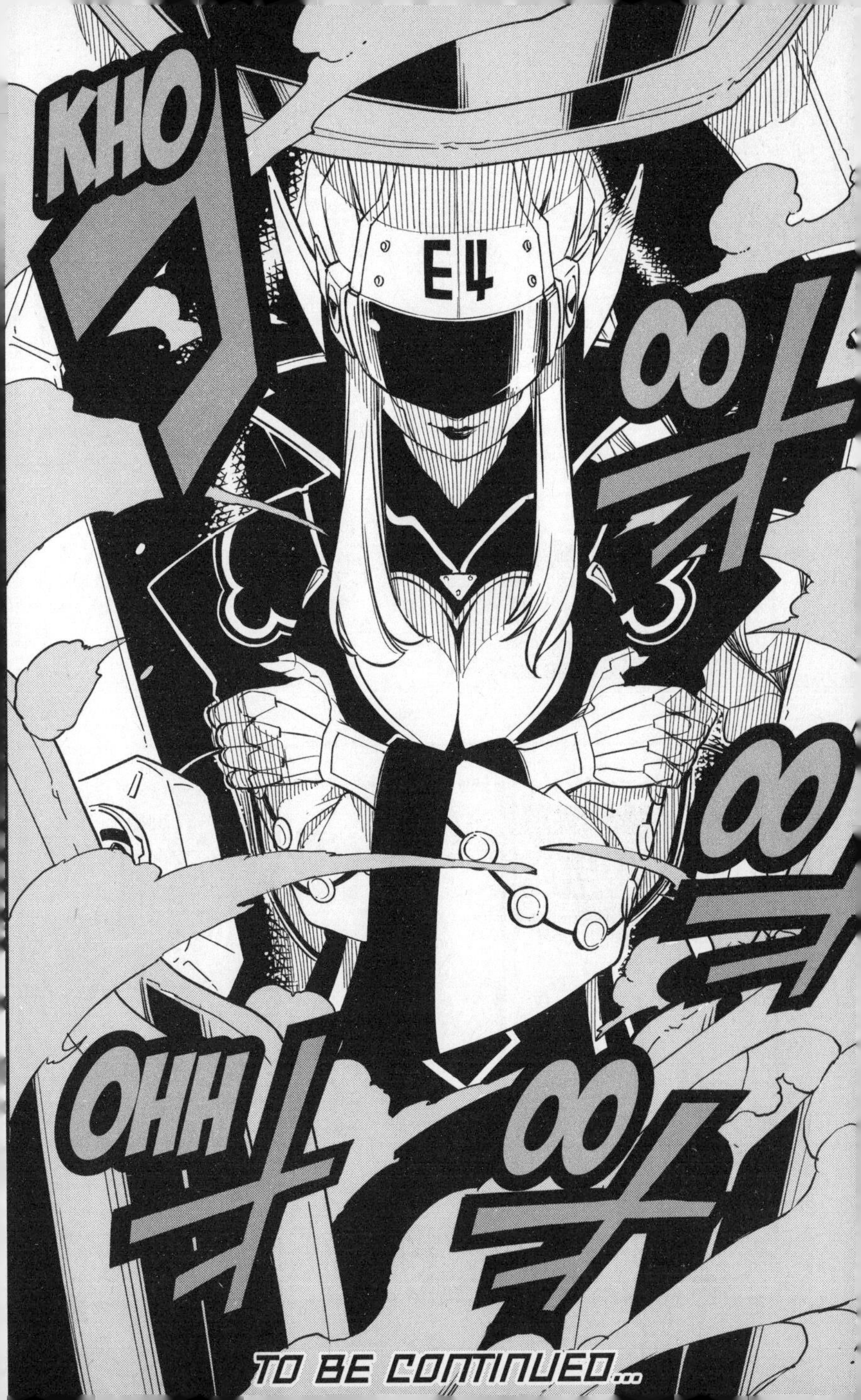
E4
KHO
OHH
TO BE CONTINUED...

# AFTERWORD

This volume gives us another really out-there story element, introducing the word "chronophage." It eats a planet and steals its time, so it *seems* like there's a time slip, but it doesn't create a time paradox, thus sealing away the most interesting part of all time travel stories to date. You might wonder why I would have done such a thing, but this story element is going to come into play later. I think.

And we add new members to the team, Weisz and Pino. Their roles are pretty clearly laid out, so it's fairly easy to get them to do what I want, and I made Weisz an interesting sort of character that hasn't shown up much in my previous works, the "one of the good guys, but still a scumbag" type. Pino is a character I originally thought up to put in Happy's position (the mascot). But as I got a little deeper into planning, it was getting complicated figuring out how to put Pino in the first chapter, so for that chapter, I had Happy stand in as the mascot.

Anyway, up until now, we've mostly been focusing on world-building episodes, but the story should really get moving in the next volume.

I hope you enjoy it.

D0664244

*EDENS ZERO* volume 2 is a work of fiction.
Names, characters, places, and incidents are the products of the author's imagination or are used fictitiously. Any resemblance to actual events, locales, or persons, living or dead, is entirely coincidental.

A Kodansha Comics Trade Paperback Original.



Published in the United States by Kodansha Comics,
an imprint of Kodansha USA Publishing, LLC, New York.

Publication rights for this English edition arranged through
Kodansha Ltd., Tokyo.

First published in Japan in 2018 by Kodansha Ltd., Tokyo.

ISBN 978-1-63236-757-0

Original cover design by
Atsushi Kudo, Erisa Maruyama (Gxcomplex).

Printed in Mexico.

www.kodanshacomics.com

9 8 7 6 5 4

Translation: Alethea and Athena Nibley
Lettering: AndWorld Design
Editing: Haruko Hashimoto
Kodansha Comics edition cover design by Phil Balsman